Cultural Studies and Language Learning

A Research Report

Multilingual Matters

Please contact us for the latest book information:
Multilingual Matters,
Bank House, 8a Hill Road,
Clevedon, Avon BS21 7HH,
England

MULTILINGUAL MATTERS 63
Series Editor: Derrick Sharp

((Cultural Studies and Language Learning))

A Research Report

Michael Byram,
Veronica Esarte-Sarries and
Susan Taylor

MULTILINGUAL MATTERS LTD
Clevedon • Philadelphia

Library of Congress Cataloging in Publication Data

Byram, Michael
Cultural Studies and Language Learning: A Research Report/Michael
Byram, Veronica Esarte-Sarries and Susan Taylor.
p. cm. (Multilingual Matters: 63)
Includes bibliographical references and index.
1. Language and languages — Study and teaching. 2. Language and culture —
Study and teaching. I. Esarte-Sarries, Veronica. II. Taylor, Susan. III Title. IV.
Series: Multilingual Matters (Series): 63.
P53.B937   1990
407   dc20

British Library Cataloguing in Publication Data

Byram, Michael
Cultural Studies and Language Learning: A Research Report (Multilingual
Matters: 63).
1. Foreign languages. Teaching.
I. Title. II. Esarte-Sarries, Veronica. III. Taylor, Susan.
418.007

ISBN 1–85359–089–4

Multilingual Matters Ltd

Bank House, 8a Hill Road,   &   1900 Frost Road, Suite 101
Clevedon, Avon BS21 7HH,   Bristol, PA 19007
England   USA

Copyright © 1991 M. Byram, V. Esarte-Sarries and S. Taylor.

Typeset by Proteus Micro-Applications, Worle.
Printed and bound in Great Britain by The Longdunn Press Ltd, Bristol.

Contents

Preface

The present volume is one of four books — all published by Multilingual Matters — which contribute independently to a general theme: the relationship between language and culture in foreign language teaching. *Cultural Studies in Foreign Language Education* (by Michael Byram) comprises a series of essays on the philosophy of language teaching and suggests some theoretical avenues for exploration in search of greater clarity on fundamental issues. It includes too a chapter which draws on the empirical research carried out at the University of Durham.

Mediating Languages and Cultures (edited by Dieter Buttjes and Michael Byram) is also related to the empirical research project in that it arose out of an international symposium held in Durham during the project. It seeks to provide a European context for language and culture teaching through analyses of developments in several European countries, theoretical articles, reports of empirical research, accounts of teacher training programmes, and discussions of the role of language and culture teaching in multicultural societies and across national frontiers.

Investigating Cultural Studies in Foreign Language Teaching (by Michael Byram and Veronica Esarte-Sarries) and *Cultural Studies and Language Learning* (by Michael Byram, Veronica Esarte-Sarries and Susan Taylor) both report the Durham Project at greater length. The former aims to bridge the gap between research and teaching, and between research and curriculum development which is in the hands of teachers. It provides the findings of the project in a quickly accessible form and describes a small-scale experiment in teacher-training and curriculum development arising from them. It is intended above all for teachers and hopes to draw them into reconsideration of the purposes and processes of foreign language teaching in general education. The latter, this present volume, gives a full scientific account of the study of 'the effect of language teaching on young people's perceptions of other cultures' to use the project's official Economic and Social Research Council title. The aim was to investigate the widely-held assumption that language teaching has

vii

positive effects on learners' attitudes towards and understanding of foreign peoples and cultures.

Durham,
April 1989

Acknowledgements

Our thanks are due to many people for their co-operation and help in the work described in this report, and they are mentioned in the companion volume *Investigating Cultural Studies in Foreign Language Teaching*. Here we would like to record above all our gratitude to Doreen Wilson, our project secretary, who sadly did not live to see the publication of the research in which she took a personal and lively interest beyond the duties of her post.

The research described in this book was funded by the Economic and Social Research Council under the title 'The Effect of Language Teaching on Young People's Perceptions of Other Cultures' (Reference No. C00232177) for three years from 1 April 1985.

The research was made possible by the co-operation of the education authorities and schools involved and by the agreement of parents, pupils and teachers who participated. Our thanks are none the less gratefully expressed despite the need for the recipients to remain anonymous.

A Social Science Research Fellowship awarded by the Nuffield Foundation in 1988–89 to one of the authors — Michael Byram — enabled us to complete this book and the companion volume more quickly. That same author would like to express thanks to the Provost and Fellows of King's College, Cambridge for their hospitality during part of the period of tenureship.

Introduction

Purposes and Contexts

This book is an account of a research project and its findings. It is part of our attempt to make the research accessible to as wide a public as possible, for without a wide readership, we believe, there is little point in doing research. The public we have in mind includes researchers, teachers and teacher trainers. In many cases two or even all three of these roles are united in the same person but often they are not, and this means we have to write for more than one kind of reader. In order to do so we have in fact written this and a companion volume. The relationship between the two will be explained below.

The object of our investigation is an aspect of foreign language teaching. We are concerned particularly with language teaching in secondary education, although the issue we address is significant in all kinds of language teaching throughout the world. That issue is variously called 'background or area studies' (in the English tradition) 'Landeskunde' (in Germany), 'teaching culture' (in North America) and 'civilisation' (in France). It will however become clear that we prefer the term 'cultural studies' and do not confine ourselves to the definitions and contents associated with the previous labels. Our interest embraces all that pupils learn or acquire in terms of knowledge, information, attitudes and perceptions with respect to one or more foreign countries and peoples whilst they are participating in language lessons.

The mode of our investigation is empirical, and is an attempt to describe and analyse both teaching processes and learning outcomes, and the relationship between experience inside and outside classrooms and schools. The operationalisation of the research resulted in the project being focused on the teaching of French in the first three years of secondary education in two comprehensive schools in the North East of England. In these schools, as in most others, the French language was taught with reference to France and the French way of life. Thus our investigation was concerned primarily but not exclusively with what pupils learned about the French way of life during lessons, and through other sources and influences inside and outside school.

The rationale for the research arises from a widely held assumption, among teachers and the general public, that language learning does and should include some, generally unspecified, cultural learning and hence results in some beneficial effect on learners' attitudes towards foreign people. The phrase 'broadening pupils' horizons' is often used in general discussion. In the following quotation a more technical phrase 'areas of experience' is used but it none the less refers to the same assumptions and encapsulates the belief that there are two principal dimensions to language teaching:

> Given that the distinctive contribution of foreign language to the curriculum lies above all in the linguistic and literary and in the human and social areas of experience, the broad areas of foreign language learning are clearly twofold.
> (HMI, 1987: 4)

The document from which this quotation is taken is part of a debate about the nature and aims of foreign language teaching which is another contributing factor to the rationale for this research. The debate is focused on the role of foreign language teaching in British schools in the second half of the twentieth century, and in particular on teaching in comprehensive schools where all pupils are expected to learn a foreign language. The debate is also fuelled by discussions and innovations in language teaching at the international level.

The rationale for the research can be summarised as follows. Language learning is considered to be an essential part of secondary education for all pupils. One of the principal justifications for this is the belief that language learning is a beneficial experience and influence on pupils' personal and social development, in preparing them for living in a society which has many ties with others and also itself comprises many individuals and groups from other societies. The belief is intuitive, with little rigorous evidence to support it. Furthermore any influence it may have on teaching methods is also intuitive and not necessarily well-founded. There is therefore a need to investigate the assumption and its consequences empirically in order first to verify this justification for language learning and second to provide a basis for reviewing the methods used.

The timing of the research also requires some explanation. Aside from

the various fortuitous circumstances which attend the genesis of a particular project in a particular place, the research originates in a specific
moment of change in language teaching. The change has been marked in
the British debate by the replacing of the label 'Modern Languages' by
'Foreign Languages' or, as a compromise, by 'Modern Foreign
Languages'. Behind the terminology lie a number of changes in the
purposes of language teaching, in the composition of the body of learners,
in teaching methods, and in analysis of languages for pedagogical
purposes.

Whereas the purposes of language teaching used to be to equip pupils
with the ability to read a foreign literature and to analyse and write in a
foreign language, the aims are now predominantly to provide them with
the competence to speak and otherwise communicate for 'practical'
purposes with native and non-native speakers of the language. Formerly
learners were those likely to continue their formal education beyond the
secondary level. Today they comprise all pupils in secondary education no
matter what career they aspire to. Teaching methods have also changed,
although in itself this is not new, for the history of language teaching has
been marked by the search after better methods. The most recent change is
characterised by an emphasis on teaching observable skills in language
performance rather than analytic understanding of linguistic phenomena.
Finally, perhaps the most significant change of all has been the introduction of the analysis of language in semantic and social as well as grammatical terms as the basis for determining the selection and order of presentation of language for pupils in the early stages of learning. These and
other changes are inter-related and are well documented in the literature
(e.g. Hawkins, 1987; Littlewood, 1981; Phillips, 1988). We propose here
simply to explain their significance for our research.

When pupils are to learn a foreign language for mainly verbal
communication for 'practical' purposes across national and cultural boundaries, teachers begin to re-assess the kind of non-linguistic knowledge
they introduce into their lessons. Rather than literary history or criticism,
they begin to consider what might be needed for successful interaction with
members of another society and culture. Second, the extension of teaching
to all pupils requires teachers to consider the interests of those who will not
continue language learning beyond secondary education. Finally, the
semantic and social analysis of language makes teachers more conscious of
the need to contextualise language by reference to its use in settings pupils
are most likely to meet. These various factors encourage teachers to
introduce into their lessons information about the way of life in a foreign

country — or, using the term in its social anthropological sense, the country's 'culture'.

This is then, in summary form, the configuration of factors in language teaching which forms the context for our research.

Empirical Research — and Development

The need for rigorous evidence of beneficial effects of language learning has not been well served. The issues are without doubt complex. Reviews and introductions (e.g. Buttjes, 1981; Byram, 1989; Zarate, 1986; Seelye, 1984) reveal a well established interest in cultural studies — especially in Germany and the United States — but little empirical research. From a social psychological perspective, Keller (in press) has attempted to measure the consequences of sojourns in the foreign country through pupil exchanges. There has also been recent work on the relationship between language learning and attitudes towards foreign peoples (Canavan et al., n.d.) whereas other previous work had focused on the relationship between attitudes and motivations (Gardner & Lambert, 1972) or on attitudes towards the language as a school subject (Burstall et al., 1974; APU, 1985; Buckby et al., 1981) or on attitudes towards foreign peoples but unrelated to language learning (Lambert & Klineberg, 1967) or on the effects of 'culture shock' during residence abroad, but again not specifically related to language learning (Furnham & Bochner, 1986; Kim, 1988).

The purpose of this research was however to study the relationships obtaining between learning a language as a school subject, perceptions of the associated culture (or cultures) and attitudes towards people of that culture. This required a new research design — to be described below — and careful limitations of the scope and ambitions envisaged. This book describes therefore an exploratory investigation in a case-study framework. Simple generalisation of the findings to other cases is not possible but the findings can none the less be of general interest to the three kinds of readership we have in mind. First we hope that the design and methods of research will be of interest to researchers irrespective of the subject, and that it may lead to replication and development. Second, we hope that teacher-trainers and others who influence teacher-training will find the subject and findings sufficiently significant to give them greater attention than they seem to do at present. Finally, we hope that teachers themselves will be encouraged to change and develop their practices in ways which might complement the work of researchers. It is because of this latter relationship of complementarity between researcher and teacher that a second book has been written as a companion to this.

The companion volume, *Investigating Cultural Studies in Foreign Language Teaching*, is designed to overcome a problem for teachers and at the same time to afford an opportunity for ourselves as researchers. The problem is that teachers are both the subjects, or informants, in research and also the people who are best placed to implement changes as a consequence of research. Yet because teachers are not usually trained to analyse research methods and findings, these are seldom taken into account in the informal curriculum development in which most teachers engage. The accompanying volume is therefore an attempt to make our research more accessible by describing the methods in a non-technical way and selecting findings for non-technical presentation. It is our hope that some readers of the companion volume will move on to this one and cross-references are supplied.

The opportunity for ourselves as researchers in the companion volume is to be able to expand the context of presentation. We introduce from the beginning a particular philosophy of language teaching and comment on the research findings in the light of that philosophy. Although we do not make the findings subservient to the philosophy, we believe that ultimately all empirical findings have to be interpreted from a specific viewpoint and we make ours explicit from the outset. In this present book the methodology and findings are allowed to speak for themselves and we introduce our own viewpoint only at the end. Secondly, we introduce into the companion volume material from another piece of work of a different and more tentative nature. In this volume we are concerned only with one specific research project. Finally we allow ourselves a more speculative stance in the companion volume.

Composition of this Book

The focus of our research is then on the relationships among pupils' attitudes, perceptions and possible sources of and influences on both, including notably foreign language teaching. The composition of the book reflects the different elements in the focus as well as the relationships among them. It also gives space to the exploratory nature of the research and the methodology involved.

The first chapter not only sets the scene and discusses the relationship of the research to developments in language teaching, it also introduces the methodology and gives an overview of the techniques employed and the kinds of data collected. Chapter 2 deals with the collection and analysis of pupils' perceptions of aspects of French culture. These are illustrated in depth by reference to specific topics and second by description of the perceptions of pupils grouped by school French class, in preparation for a later chapter. Chapter 3 moves on to attitudes. It describes the collection of data on pupils' attitudes towards, primarily, French people but also towards other peoples, and towards aspects of language learning *per se*. Chapters 4 and 5 deal with sources of and possible influences on perceptions and attitudes. In Chapter 4 the issues are discussed on the basis of data collected from pupils. In Chapter 5 the discussion is based on data from observations of the teaching process, including analysis of teaching material. Chapter 5 includes the characterisation of the teaching approach in four specific combinations of class and teacher, in terms of observable factors which appear to be related to the teaching of cultural information or knowledge. In Chapter 6 these characterisations are one element in developing descriptive modesl of four case-studies. Other elements include the analysis of pupils' perceptions and attitudes, grouped by class, and the sources and influences other than language teaching. Chapter 6 is thus an attempt to draw all the different aspects of the research together in order to describe the relationships which obtain among the different elements of the total phenomenon under investigation.

The final chapter re-introduces issues mentioned briefly in this introduction: the context of the research, the significance of a philosophy of language teaching and the relationship of research and curriculum development. Within the network of those issues and from an explicit viewpoint, the chapter draws some conclusions and looks forward to possible developments.

Finally, a remark about the length of the book and certain chapters in it. It is a characteristic of qualitative research—and especially case-study enquiries—that evidence cannot be summarised with the succinctness of statistical tables or diagrams. Some chapters thus contain many quotations from interviews, often of considerable length. Frequently, several quotations are used to illustrate one point partly because no single statement is representative and partly to indicate that the point at issue has a degree of generality within the study. At the same time, readers can form their own view of the evidence more easily if we offer a range of material, although we cannot make available every interview transcript for re-analysis in the way we can present all our statistical data. In principle however all our interview evidence is available and stored on computer at the University of Durham. Those who work in qualitative research will be familiar with this dilemma, and with the need to find the balance between presenting sufficient evidence and making the book of a readable length. It is for the reader to decide how successful we have been.

1 The Context of Research: Defining the Topic and Developing the Design

Introduction

By 'context' of this research we refer to factors in the topic to be investigated, factors in the planning of an appropriate approach to the topic and factors in the implementation. As many as possible of the latter should be anticipated and taken into consideration in the planning, and anticipation depends to a large extent on knowledge of the topic for investigation. Despite this inter-relationship we propose for clarity's sake to consider the context from two points of view: definition of the topic and development of research design.

The following account of the cultural studies dimension of language teaching which we shall discuss historically and comparatively as well as considering the contemporary situation, is not just a critical survey of appropriate literature which has in fact been done elsewhere (Byram, 1989). We shall continue the argument mentioned in our introductory chapter, that the research described here, like any other, arises from a specific contextual configuration of factors in the subject area, and has a particular purpose within that context. Our account of cultural studies is therefore an explicit indication of the general import of the research, irrespective of particular findings.

Similarly the planning of the research is influenced by contemporary developments in methodology and design. Qualitative methods in educational research have enjoyed higher esteem in recent years especially for classroom research (e.g. Burgess, 1985; Sherman & Webb, 1988) and case-study has also become common. Furthermore our work must also be seen within developing traditions of research into foreign language teaching (Allwright, 1988; Mitchell, 1988). We shall however pay less attention to

1

these issues as this is not a book on research methodology. We shall confine ourselves in the second part of this chapter to an explanation of the factors taken into consideration in the planning of the research and the methods by which some but not all problems were overcome.

'Culture' in Foreign Language Teaching: An Overview

It is not our intention to provide a thorough analysis of the position of cultural studies within foreign language teaching but to indicate the level of significance 'culture' is given in historical and contemporary perspectives. In essence we shall suggest that though considerable significance is attributed at different stages and to differing extents in various countries, the realisation of that significance in practice is less then satisfactory, especially in Britain.

Histories of language teaching already indicate this trend. Of four major works written in English, the two published by British writers (Howatt, 1984 and Hawkins, 1987) do not mention cultural studies explicitly. Neither mention 'culture' or related concepts in their index and neither address the debate on educational aims for language teaching which might have induced them to discuss the relationship of language and culture learning. Two North American authors reflect the greater awareness present in the language teaching debate in their countries. Kelly (1976: 315) argues that 'cultural awareness was critical to the (teaching) methods developed during the twentieth century' and that 'the cultural orientation of language teaching has always been one of its unstated aims' (1976: 378). He also points out, however, that 'cultural teaching has had varying fortunes in modern languages' (1976: 379). Stern, in his more systematic treatment (1983: chap. 12), traces the contribution of anthropology and sociology to thinking in the United States in particular but begins with the generalisation that 'language teaching theory today is in fact acquiring a sociolinguistic component but still lacks a well defined sociocultural emphasis' (1983: 246). He treats separately the tradition of *Kulturkunde* or *Landeskunde* in Germany for it has been and continues to be the country with the most lively and prolific debate (Buttjes, 1988 and Byram, 1989: 58–79). Elsewhere, however, Stern suggests that though the value of the teaching of culture has been widely recognised 'in practice it played a subordinate role'. It is also debatable whether the amount of discussion in Germany has produced a significant influence on practice, any more than has been the case in other countries: 'In practice most European countries do not teach about the foreign culture in any systematic fashion' (Halls, 1970, cited in Stern).

The reasons for the lack of serious theoretical or practical interest in teaching culture in Britain, reflected in the absence of interest in the issue in Howatt and Hawkins, are difficult to surmise and even more difficult to document. Stern quotes four successive versions of a 'Memorandum on the Teaching of Modern Languages' produced by a British teachers' association from 1929 to 1979 but culture is given little prominence. Despite appearances, the development of area studies in secondary schools — under titles such as European Studies or German Studies — remains a marginal concern, for two principal reasons. First such courses did not necessarily include language learning and were not always taught by linguists and, second, they were — and to some extent still are — taught to pupils of low achievement and were consequently and unfortunately accorded little status or theoretical interest. In short, the history and the historiography of cultural studies, especially in Britain, demonstrates at best lip-service and declarations of intent but no achievement of significant status within language teaching in schools.

The lack of substantial progress in cultural studies in the classroom is probably due to a number of factors; for example the emphasis in courses for future language teachers on the study of 'classical' literature, or the view that competence in a language is a matter of mastering grammar. Where teachers have in fact attempted to teach culture, it is the lack of definition of what is to be taught and the problem of what to select from the seemingly endless and complex phenomena of 'culture', which lead to dissatisfaction and a return to the priority of language teaching. In such circumstances it is evident that practice needs theoretical guidelines and although culture teaching theory is by no means as extensive and well developed as language teaching theory, there have been various approaches. Much of the work has concentrated on definition of concepts, discussion of aims and purposes and delimitation of fields of interest, including determining which disciplines might contribute to further clarification. There has been little empirical research, and in general theoretical work has addressed some issues and largely ignored others.

Four key areas can be identified. The first is the issue of the value of cultural studies within language teaching and the contribution it makes to learners' whole education. In many respects this is the best developed and largely taken for granted. Recent statements of the value of teaching culture can be found, for example, in Robinson (1985: 1–7) and Byram (1989: 39–57). General statements on the aims of foreign language teaching usually include references to developing learners' tolerance and under-standing of other peoples and cultures.

A second area involves the development of an adequate didactic for the teaching of culture and this too has occupied theorists for some time. It includes a number of issues: the need to identify an appropriate approach to cultural analysis for pedagogical purposes, the development of a theory of cultural learning in the circumstances of foreign language teaching, and the relationship of a curriculum of language and culture learning to general curriculum theory and development. The problem of cultural analysis has long occupied the energies of American theorists in particular because the question of what should be selected from a culture and in what order has appeared extremely difficult if not insoluble. Nostrand (1979) notably has proposed a model for cultural analysis but such analysis presupposes a particular view of teaching and learning, namely that they consist primarily of transmission of a body of knowledge. Models of learning which empha-sise acquisition of procedures and understanding of cultural phenomena could shift the emphasis and reduce some of the difficulties, although the question of what is an appropriate analytical approach is still relevant.

Learning theory for cultural studies is also still under-developed. Some contributions depend on work in social-psychology on the exper-ience by migrants or immigrants of 'culture shock' a phenomenon recently analysed at length by Furnham & Bochner (1986). Such work is surveyed by Acton & Walker de Felix (1986). Both cognitive and affective learning are involved in culture learning and further complicated by questions of motivation for learning a particular language and culture as a school subject, part of pupils' general — and compulsory — education. There is clearly much still to be done to develop an adequate theory of culture learning in the classroom.

The third issue within this second area of enquiry is the relationship of a language and cultural studies curriculum to the whole curriculum. This is generally neglected, although some authors stress connections with social studies (e.g. Nostrand, 1985; Lambert, 1974) or global education (Seelye, 1984: 216–43) or world studies (Starkey, in press). Often, however, the need to establish cultural studies within language teaching appears to dominate collections of articles (e.g. Raasch et al., 1983; Buttjes, 1981; Valdes, 1986). Links with other disciplines remain in terms of looking to anthropology and psychology and others as sources of ideas for cultural analysis or teaching techniques (e.g. Zarate, 1986 and 1988).

In principle the development of an adequate didactic should precede and determine the third area of enquiry, the methodology of cultural studies teaching. A methodology should ideally take into account learning theory and the decisions as to what is to be taught and how it relates to other areas of the curriculum. Practice cannot and has not however waited, and teaching techniques dependent as much on serendipity and intuition as on learning and curriculum theory have been developed to differing degrees in different countries. In the United States 'culture assimilators, capsules and clusters' are based on the notion of training learners in appropriate behaviour (Seelye, 1984). Insights from ethnography are fundamental to the work of Genevieve Zarate (1986). In other cases, social problems or themes and project work guide the proposals for classroom applications (cf. various contributions to Buttjes, 1981 or Raasch et al., 1983).

The fourth general area for theoretical work is that of assessment and evaluation. Testing learners' cultural skills or knowledge is treated in some American literature (e.g. Valette in Valdes 1986, and Seelye, 1984: 164–89) but has not much occupied writers in other countries. In Britain the current view appears to be that only 'practical communication' can be assessed and other aims are dependent on achieving success in mastering linguistic objectives (HM1, 1987: 57). The empirical evaluation of the cultural studies element in a foreign language course appears thus far to be entirely absent from the literature — a gap this present book will begin to fill.

Let us consider next the current situation. We already suggested above that from an historical perspective, language teaching in Britain has ignored cultural studies even more than in other countries. That this continues to be the case is evident from the absence of British publications amongst those cited in respect of theoretical work. Furthermore, documents from official sources — such as the one cited in the previous paragraph — do not encourage teachers to take cultural studies seriously. This is not to say that cultural studies is entirely absent — as the rest of this book will show — but it is often given a subordinate place, despite some pupils' active appreciation of its significance and interest. Here for example are two statements from secondary pupils interviewed during out study:

I: Do you do more language than about France?
P: We do about France and then it mingles with about France when we learn about the language, the vocabulary and that.
I: Which do you prefer?
P: . . . Learning about it better, 'cause I'd like to find more about the place rather than how to say 'where's the toilet?' and things like that. I'd rather learn about the place. (127/18)

I: Have you enjoyed your French so far?
P: Yes.
I: Equally all the way through?
P: Yes it's more this year 'cause it's not all — in the first two years it was all language but this year we're doing a bit, like, French, — the way of life in France.
I: And that's more enjoyable?
P: Yes. (103/44)
(References here and later are to the corpus of transcripts.)

Considered from a contemporary comparative perspective, the British lack of interest continues to contrast with other countries. Surveys of the situation in Scandinavia, the two Germanies and France provide evidence of some interest in cultural studies (Buttjes & Byram, in press) even if more would be desirable. In France a new research project studying pupils' images of other peoples has recently begun (Cain, 1988). In the world of English as a foreign language there are signs of a growing interest now that communicative language teaching has become widely accepted (Harrison, 1990). The publication of a new collection of American articles (Valdes, 1986) and a new edition of Seelye's work (1984) indicate a maintenance of interest in the United States, even though there are scarcely any new material or ideas involved.

The strongest presence of a socio-cultural element in British foreign language teaching has in fact been in higher education — particularly in the polytechnics — where 'area studies' has replaced the study of literature as the main focus of some undergraduate courses. This is now beginning to spread into schools at Sixth Form level, where examination boards are currently encouraging courses involving the study of social issues in the country whose language is being studied. This is nevertheless taking place without adequate theoretical underpinning or teacher-training despite the laudable attempts to provide help in finding teaching materials (e.g. Hare, 1987).

To conclude this sketch of the position of cultural studies in foreign language teaching, it is only necessary to say that the research to be described in this present book and its companion volume would no doubt be considered by many teachers and theorists to be in principle central to language teaching yet in practice subordinate to other pressing needs. Our position, however, is quite simply that language teaching does involve culture teaching whether teachers wish it or not. Culture teaching is a central if hidden strand of the foreign language curriculum, with consequences for pupils' learning which cannot be overlooked. It is therefore essential to investigate current practices — and simultaneously to push onward with theoretical work — in order to clarify and justify the teaching of foreign languages as part of general compulsory education.

Planning the Research Design

It is commonplace to suggest that social and educational research poses problems for any researcher who would like to isolate and investigate a specific issue, because specific issues are always 'contaminated' by other factors beyond the researcher's control. We should however be aware that this commonplace is a consequence of a specific way of perceiving reality as if it can be neatly cut into sections for examination. Another kind of social researcher, the novelist, does not conceive reality in this way and does not consider the 'contamination' a problem. It might be objected that novelists do not strive after observer-independent objectivity in their description of reality, that by contrast social researchers attempt to prove an account from which their own subjectivity is eliminated by conventions of validity, reliability and generalisability. Yet many novelists also strive after a 'realism' which will ensure the validity and generalisability of their work and the notion of 'reliability' among objective observers is dependent on similarity in their conceptualisation of reality.

We suggest therefore that a description of the 'problems' of research design, of the desire to eliminate or control 'contaminating' factors reveals a particular view of reality and the nature of research and research findings. What we shall propose here instead is an account of how our research design — to use a photographic analogy — composed a picture with deep focus. At the centre of the picture is the main issue of the effect of language teaching in attitudes and perceptions. Other elements of reality are also in focus — relationships between teachers and pupils, influences of parents and siblings, for example — and they are given as much attention as the central issue. We offer the whole picture and point out the nature of the composition, but we do not encourage the reader to mask off the parts of the picture which are not central. We do encourage the reader to remember that the picture was taken from a particular angle using a particular 'camera'. The angle is a function of a specific philosophy of language teaching and the choice of 'camera' is a consequence of a specific view of reality as a seamless whole.

At the centre of our picture then is the complex of ideas that foreign language teaching is significantly related to pupils 'insights' or 'perceptions' and 'tolerance' or 'attitudes' with respect to foreign cultures and peoples. The relationship is often assumed to be unidirectional and causal: language teaching causes pupils to have particular kinds of insights and attitudes. It is also assumed that the effects will be 'beneficial' or 'positive': that the perceptions will be true to reality and the attitudes be such that action in respect of foreign people based upon them will be amicable. It is conceivable however that the relationship among teaching, perceptions and attitudes are multidirectional. The number, and degree of truth, of perceptions may cause attitudes to be amicable. Amicable attitudes may affect teaching or the acquisition of insights or both — and so on. These potential complexities in the relationships are also part of our investigation even though they are not usually mentioned in the claims for language teaching.

There are other factors in the picture. Pupils learn a foreign language in schools over a number of years. This is of course not the only possible way of organising language learning and an intensive course covering the same ground in a matter of weeks would alter the maturity factor, i.e. the fact that pupils are still developing both psychologically and physically whilst they are learning the foreign language. Second, language teaching is merely one of the learning experiences through which pupils might be affected in respect of their perceptions and attitudes. It is both preceded and accompanied by other learning in school and other experiences outside school. Some of the more evident sources of learning can be mentioned here. The mass media, including television and children's magazines show aspects of life in the world beyond pupils' usual experience, including life in other countries. Parents and other adults narrate their own experiences and give their own opinions on life abroad. Geography as a school subject is not confined to study of the native country, even in the primary school phase. It is quite conceivable that such other factors have greater influence on pupils than language teaching. For example, the influence of a grandfather narrating his experience of travelling abroad as a soldier in wartime may be much more powerful and take place much earlier in a child's life than the language teacher's accounts of contemporary life in the same country. A camping trip organised by a primary school teacher with no professional training in planning the first experience of a foreign culture may be a lasting and dominant impression even after a second trip organised as part of a language course by a specialist teacher. It is important therefore that such factors be held in clear focus.

Returning to the factors at the centre of our picture, we should also be aware of the complexity of the three elements. In particular 'teaching' is itself a complex factor. We cannot consider the effects of 'teaching' as if it were a simple process. To do so might be adequate to verify the assumption that language teaching has some effect on perceptions and attitudes, but this would not give us any indication of how. The significance of the research would be reduced if it did not try to establish which aspects of the complex process of teaching were more directly linked to attitudes and perceptions than others. So the teaching process needs to be described in some detail. Perceptions and attitudes are equally complex phenomena requiring careful analysis.

In short, one approach to our research topic would attempt a design which isolated the postulated relationship between 'teaching' and 'perceptions' and 'attitudes' for verification. Other factors would be controlled, probably by statistical means, and causal relationships from teaching to perceptions and attitudes would be emphasised. The view taken here is that the verification of relationships is not sufficiently interesting in itself, even if it were possible to carry it out. What is also required is a full picture of the nature of the teaching process, the structure of perceptions, the relationships between or among other factors as well as teaching and so on. The probability that this view will not produce simple findings but a complex and even incomplete picture is not problematic if we accept that reality cannot be cut into neat sections for analysis.

Furthermore the anticipated advantages of simple results from isolation and verification procedures are probably more apparent than real. We have argued that this research takes place within a specific context of language teaching development. If it is to be given adequate recognition in that context it must not only present results but also descriptions of the whole reality from a new viewpoint. The descriptions may become more influential than the conclusions drawn from them, given the nature of the relationship between research and curriculum development. This consideration has, as pointed out in our introductory chapter, determined the way in which description and conclusions are presented here and in the companion volume.

We turn now to some of the practical problems which had to be anticipated in the research design. They include questions of sampling and generalisability, of access to pupils and teachers as informants, of choice of research methods. Generalisability from a statistical basis pre-supposes specific and clearly defined sampling procedures. This would have been possible if the research were concerned solely with verification of the assumption discussed above. Our interest in description and analysis of the teaching process militated against large-scale surveys of samples of pupils. Because the teaching process cannot at the moment be described in terms of universally accepted characteristics, it was not possible to survey a large sample of teachers and pupils with questions about teaching. A similar difficulty arises with respect to the characterisation of insights pupils may acquire. It was therefore necessary to introduce qualitative research methods which might result in the characterisations not yet available. Moreover given the complexity of factors other than teaching as potential influences, the use of qualitative methods was considered even more appropriate as a means of searching out and clarifying factors which are, in the first instance, intuitively significant. Qualitative methods are however too labour-intensive to allow large-scale sampling and consequently a case-study design was envisaged. On the other hand the value of quantitative methods was not overlooked and quantitative data and statistical analysis were also introduced within the case studies and will become evident below.

The operationalisation of the concepts under study will be dealt with in detail in subsequent chapters when research instruments and data collection are described. At this point we shall provide a brief inclusive account of the main concepts. Four general concepts needed to be made operational in such a way that they could be quantified, where appropriate, or analysed in qualitative terms. They are: perceptions, attitudes, teaching and extra-school experience. The first and third were dealt with primarily in qualitative terms and the second and fourth primarily quantitatively. None the less we did not accept either for the research as a whole or in operationalising the different concepts, the widespread tendency to separate qualitative and quantitative methods. We integrated the two wherever possible and appropriate, for example by using qualitative techniques to explore attitudes which were also measured by a quantitative test.

Perceptions of the foreign culture were operationalised as information about normal or typical behaviour and ideas of natives of the culture in question. Pupils were asked to produce such information in informal interviews.

Attitudes towards other peoples were operationalised in terms of levels of ethnocentricity with respect to 'the French'. A test was devised which combined measures of affective response towards groups of people and the notion of increasing social distance. Pupils were asked to take the test in their classes as a group. Attitudes were also explored with individual pupils in informal interviews where they were encouraged to articulate their attitudes in their own words.

The operationalisation of the concept of 'teaching' was carried out almost entirely through qualitative techniques using an ethnographic approach to characterising and categorising phenomena on the basis of long-term observation. This was supplemented by textual analysis of teaching materials and informal interviews with teachers.

Finally, factors in pupils' extra-school experience were elicited in written questionnaires and analysed in terms of social categories, of frequencies of certain kinds of experience or of access to certain kinds of person. Thus for example pupils were categorised in terms of socio-economic status, location of their homes, experience of visits to foreign countries and being related to people speaking languages other than English. Such categories could be quantified as potential sources of influence on pupils' attitudes, but the significance of some of these sources was also explored qualitatively in interviews. The operationalisation of concepts is summarised in Figure 1.1.

This combination of techniques was designed to be used in case-studies. It was decided that two secondary schools would be chosen. To select only one would severely limit any even informal generalisation as well as creating risks to the whole project if practical problems were to arise. More than two case-studies would have been impractical with respect to time and funds available. Similar considerations determined the choice of a study of two cohorts rather than a longitudinal study. Access to schools was then sought through formal and informal channels. Eventually two schools were chosen which were considered by the education adviser in the area and by the researchers themselves to be unexceptional for the area in terms of the kinds of pupil attending and the kind of language teaching practised. A further practical condition was that the teachers involved were prepared to accept close observation in their classrooms over a long period.

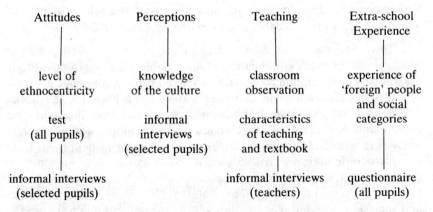

FIGURE 1.1 *Operationalisation of principal concepts*

These two schools provided then one cohort of pupils who had been learning French for three years. This particular group was chosen because at the time the minimal obligatory period of language learning in these schools, and most others regionally and nationally, was three years. It was then usual for more than 50% to opt not to continue language learning in the fourth year. The end of the third year was thus the latest point at which all the pupils could be investigated whilst still being taught, and this point represented the culmination of their learning experience and its effect on their perceptions and attitudes.

The second cohort was drawn from the eight primary schools which supplied the greatest numbers of new entrants to the two secondary schools. A similar number of approximately 200 pupils was sought who were in the final year of primary schooling and would therefore begin to learn a foreign language as they entered the two secondary schools in the following September. This cohort was comparable with the first in terms of social categories, experience of other countries and so on. In the primary schools, only the pupils were directly involved and teachers were simply asked to provide opportunity for the researchers to test and interview pupils in groups or singly.

In the secondary schools, teachers were asked to allow one researcher access to language lessons for observation over a long period. Access was agreed in advance although some classes were in the event not open to observation. In practice, too, it was not possible for the researcher to observe all the language lessons in two schools, which were some ten miles apart. These various factors eventually led to concentration on certain third year classes, involving many of the pupils in the older cohort. Observation took place over a period of eight months beginning in September and thus covering the major part of the school year. The general design of the research is represented in Figure 1.2.

This combination of data collection techniques required a similar combination of modes of analysis. Quantifiable data — from attitude measures and questionnaires — were analysed using a computer program of statistical techniques (in fact the 'Statistical Package for the Social Sciences' — SPSSx). Data from informal interviews were analysed by a combination of textual analysis 'by hand' and a computer program for text analysis (a modified version of the 'Report Generator'). Field notes from classroom observation were analysed by hand as were the French textbooks although some consideration was initially given to use of the 'Report Generator'. Some integration of the different techniques of data collection and analysis was undertaken as follows. Measures of attitudes were used to

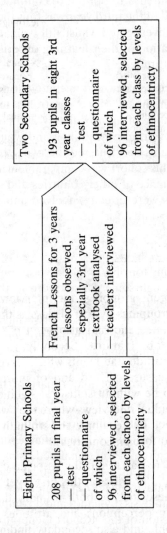

FIGURE 1.2 *General research design*

Eight Primary Schools

208 pupils in final year
— test
— questionnaire
of which
96 interviewed, selected
from each school by levels
of ethnocentricity

French Lessons for 3 years
— lessons observed,
especially 3rd year
— textbook analysed
— teachers interviewed

Two Secondary Schools

193 pupils in eight 3rd
year classes
— test
— questionnaire
of which
96 interviewed, selected
from each class by levels
of ethnocentricty

TABLE 1.1 *Levels of analysis*

A. *Independent analysis of each component*	B. *Construction of models*
Statistical Analysis (SPSSx) ethnocentricity test measures (dependent variable) and questionnaire measures (independent variables)	Four models of teaching and learning constructed around classroom observations of four teachers and classes, combining: — analysis of teaching and learning style — statistical and qualitative analysis of pupil attitudes — qualitative analysis of pupils' knowledge of the culture — statistical and qualitative analysis of sources of pupil attitudes and knowledge
Qualitative Analysis (Report Generator) informal interviews with selected pupils: — knowledge of the foreign culture — attitudes towards foreign people — sources of knowledge and attitudes — attitudes towards language learning	
Qualitative Analysis classroom observation: — years 1–3 — 4 case studies in year 3 textbook analysis informal interviews with teachers	

allocate pupils to different groupings for interviews. Further selections were made within the groupings by school class as this was shown to be of some statistical significance and had also been observed to be a major variable in classroom observations. Secondly, interviews with pupils included elicitation of attitude statements which served as validation of the quantitative attitude measures. Third and of more general significance factors which proved to be without statistical significance could none the less be explored in individual interviews where they were sometimes shown to be of great importance (for example the strength of influence of some parents or some visits to foreign countries).

Each aspect of the research and the associated analysis can thus be treated independently and provides at this first level some worthwhile and interesting findings. These include both primary data and findings, i.e. those throwing light on perceptions and attitudes with respect to the foreign culture and people and also secondary findings from data elicited incidentally particularly during interviews, e.g. primary pupils' expectation of language lessons.

At a second level the different aspects are brought together to create the complete picture. The purpose of this second level is to provide descriptive models of the relationships and effects among the various factors in the study. Four models are presented as a consequence of the eventual concentration in classroom observation on four classes. A summary of the kinds and level of analysis is provided in Table 1.1.

2 Pupils' Perceptions of Other Cultures

Operationalisation of 'Perceptions'

In order to establish pupils' 'perceptions' of foreign cultures — and in particular of French culture — it was necessary to decide what might count as indicators of their views and insight into the French way of life. This was to be done by getting them to talk about their views in semi-structured interviews. The interviews were, however, also used for other purposes: to validate the semantic differential tests of pupils' degree of ethnocentricity, to elicit their views and expectations of French teaching as they had experienced it or expected to experience it at secondary school, and to elicit their opinions on the sources of their knowledge of foreign cultures, in particular French culture.

For these purposes a list of areas or aspects of culture was drawn up, bearing in mind the kinds of information typically included in ethnographic accounts of specific cultures, as well as our own experience of language teaching. To this were added a number of questions on sources of information, attitudes towards foreign people, statements about pupils' own attachment to a particular nationality, experience of French lessons in school and experience of foreign travel. Since an interview covering all of those issues would have been too long for any individual interviewee, a core of important issues was determined, supplemented by a list of 'sub-issues'. In this context 'sub-issues' referred to aspects of culture which from personal teaching experience and observations in the schools were not expected to be much known to pupils. 'Sub-issues' does not signify that these are areas which were considered less important.

As a consequence of these deliberations, an interview schedule for secondary pupils was drawn up, piloted and modified. Since a number of people were to interview, the schedule suggested the kind of wording which it was hoped would be used, but in no way was this intended to be read to pupils (Appendix 1). In practice the interview transcripts show a wide range of approaches depending on the interviewee and the interviewer. In some cases the pupils were overawed or otherwise uncooperative and the interviewer reduced the amount of detailed questioning which would otherwise become staccato question and answer with most answers being 'I don't know'. In the vast majority of cases, pupils were co-operative and relaxed in interviews and the interviewer pursued particular lines of development as the occasion arose. In certain cases, individuals had unusual and interesting experience and views and were encouraged to speak freely without specific guidance from the interviewer's schedule. As a general strategy however, the interviewer was given a sheet of information about the interviewee with specific questions to pursue arising from the background questionnaires and with three or four sub-issues specified. In this way all the sub-issues were covered systematically at different times. The interviewer was then asked to write comments on the interview on the same sheet. The one important piece of information which was withheld from the interviewer was the ethnocentricity rating — 'high', 'medium' or 'low' — from the semantic differential test, described in Chapter 3. This was done in order not to prejudice the interviewer's perception of the interviewee.

The sample of secondary pupils for interview was made up of four pupils with each ethnocentricity rating from each of eight classes in the two schools, making a total of 96 interviewees. In addition it was decided to attempt to interview all the pupils from the four classes observed in depth. Although, due to school time-tabling factors, it was not possible to interview all members of these four classes, this none the less resulted in another 38 interviews. These were called the case-study interviews, and were dealt with separately in analysis. Interviews lasted between 20 minutes and 60 minutes with the majority being around 40 minutes.

Interviews with primary pupils followed the same general pattern. However, as anticipated and demonstrated in the secondary pupil interviews, there were many 'sub-issues' which were not generally known to pupils. In order to avoid fruitless question and answer which destroys a good informal interview relationship, it was decided to cut down questions on sub-issues to a minimum and only to pursue them with any individual pupil who might show evidence of being particularly well informed. Again several interviewers were involved, and interviewees were again selected to represent different degrees of ethnocentricity and the different feeder schools. A similar total was reached to provide a balance of primary and secondary pupils. Ninety-two pupils were interviewed.

The large number of interviews and the length of each interview provided a vast amount of material, certainly more than 2,000 pages of transcript. In order to cope with this amount of material, it was decided to use a computer program. This is a specially modified version of a text processing program, the Report Generator which will identify and collect sections of the whole text corpus according to keywords or identifiers attached to each section. In order to use the Report Generator the following steps were taken:

— transcription of audio-recordings onto microcomputer
— annotation of each interview using a list of keywords developed from the interview schedules and from a preliminary coding of a random selection of interviews; each interview is divided into sections of any size up to 50 lines and each section is given any number of keywords
— again on the microcomputer, the transcript is divided into sections and each section is annotated with numbers corresponding to the keywords, with indicators of the interviewees' sex, age, ethnocentricity rating, foreign travel experience and school class
— the data is then transferred to the mainframe computer and all the transcripts are connected as one file on which the Report Generator can operate
— selections from the corpus are made using combinations of keywords and other indicators such as gender, ethnocentricity rating, age. This then enables the listing, for example, of all statements by girls in secondary schools on their views of French food.
— the file created by this operation contains all the sections of text annotated with these indicators and is printed as a separate corpus for analysis and interpretation by the researcher.

Thus the Report Generator helps the researcher to handle the vast quantity of material, without taking the responsibility for analysis and interpretation out of his/her hands. There is a preliminary stage of interpretation in the annotation of transcripts according to the list of keywords and in the dividing of the text into sections. Since any number of keywords can be allocated to a section and since a complex statement about, for example, French food, the pupil's attitude to it and how representative a particular kind of food is, can be given several keywords simultaneously, the danger of over-simplification by keywording is mitigated. Similarly, since the sections can be of any length — and 50 lines was determined after a preliminary analysis as being the limit beyond which we did not need to go — a complex statement can be analysed whatever its length and given as much context from the transcript as required.

None the less it has to be recognised that the use of this system is not atheoretical. When a particular combination of keywords is used to select material from the whole corpus, a particular sub-corpus is created. In the first instance the whole corpus was, in fact, stored as two files on the computer, one for secondary and one for primary interviews. This was done partly for practical reasons — the two files combined would have taken an immense amount of computer space and the computer would have been slow to search the combined file — and partly for the theoretical reason that the project is above all concerned with comparisons between younger and older pupils. When selections are made from these two files, further sub-corpora are created and when the sub-corpus text is read as a whole it creates a particular impression in the reader's mind which he/she then seeks to analyse and explain. Were a different combination used, it is quite possible that a different analysis would emerge from what is, in essence, a different creation of a sub-corpus. This may be more evident in some cases than others. For example, the 'topic approach' (see below) selects, say, all utterances about the dress and appearance of French people irrespective of speakers' characteristics and in an arbitrary order. On the other hand the 'input approach' selects secondary pupils' utterances about what they learn from teachers or textbooks but groups them according to the class to which they belong. This creates eight sub-corpora or 'texts' which are read independently and then compared. This particular selection was made because the statistical analysis and the classroom observation had both indicated that school class is a significant factor. Since gender is also significantly related to attitudes it would also be interesting to analyse boys' and girls' accounts of teachers and textbooks. Another possibility would be to select utterances according to ethnocentricity rating, to see if any patterns of responses to teacher and textbook arise from the three categories to which pupils were allocated. The decision to create corpora according to school class first is an illustration of the interaction between the different techniques in the project.

Selection of Approaches to Interview Analysis

Given the large amount of material available — even without the extra case-study interviews — many possibilities for analysis were available, e.g. each of the main issues or sub-issues guiding the interviews could be analysed thematically. In the decision about which approaches should be taken the following points were taken into account:

(a) One primary aim was to compare secondary pupils' perceptions with what they had been observed to be taught in class, in order to gain insight into the nature of the contribution of teaching to pupils' images and perceptions. In theory, the whole group of secondary pupils should be compared with the whole group of primary pupils in the expectation that the fact of having been taught French would make a significant difference to perceptions. However, since the statistical analysis had already shown that Age (which reflects primary v. secondary) does not have a simple relationship to attitudes but is in a complex relationship with school class and gender (see Chapter 3), it was decided that perceptions too should be analysed in a more differentiated way.

(b) Another purpose for interview analysis was the validation of the tests of ethnocentricity or attitudes towards French and other people. Questions to this end had been included in the interview schedules and this approach will be covered in Chapter 3.

(c) As a consequence of the identification of different teaching styles and observations of four classes in depth (see Chapter 5), it was considered worthwhile to take particular note of the perceptions of pupils from these classes, treated as separate groups or class case studies.

(d) Some pupils had also been asked to talk specifically about teachers' ways of teaching cultural studies, again as a consequence of the observed significance of different teaching styles. This approach will be dealt with in Chapter 4.

(e) Since pupils had been rated as having high, medium or low degrees of ethnocentricity, it is also possible to compare perceptions across these groups for particular themes on the hypothesis that attitudes and perceptions are related. Similarly since gender correlates significantly with attitudes (see Chapter 3), it is also worthwhile exploring if and how perceptions differ significantly between boys and girls.

(f) Since statistical analysis indicates some association between pupils' membership of a specific school class and degree of ethnocentricity and that gender in particular is perhaps a factor interacting with the school class factor, it is worth considering the range of perceptions within each class. In the first instance this is based on the 12 interviews carried out in each class, but is then enriched in the four observed classes by interviews with almost all the pupils.

(g) In the course of interviewing more than 200 pupils, some individuals stand out as being particularly interesting. There are various kinds of reasons, for example unusual experience of foreign travel, particularly articulate and explicit views, interesting sources of information and influences, extremes of attitudes or just nice people to talk to. It is in some cases worth examining transcripts holistically.

As a consequence of these various factors, four broad 'approaches' were identified and used as guidelines for determining which sub-corpora should be extracted from the whole.

The 'topic' approach

Four topics were selected for analysis. Two main topics were chosen partly because they were known to be frequently mentioned in class, partly because pupils had generally been well informed about them in interview and partly because they are particularly visible but also fundamental aspects of any culture. These two topics are 'Food' and 'Dress and Appearance'. Two sub-topics were chosen: 'Geography of France' and 'Religion in France/Growing up in France'. The latter was known to be little discussed in class and generally little known by pupils. Yet it might be particularly interesting to investigate the images held by those pupils who did have some knowledge, precisely because it must be knowledge gleaned outside class. 'Geography of France' was chosen because it is dealt with incidentally in lessons but seldom given explicit attention.

The information and images from these four topics could then be compared to our knowledge of what pupils had been taught as a result of classroom observation and textbook analysis. This would be one aspect of the investigation of the particular effects of language teaching and other sources of knowledge.

The 'input' approach

Since particular teaching styles were considered significant as a consequence of classroom observation and because statistical analysis had indicated an unexpected decrease in positive attitude scores associated with exposure to France, French people and relations of other linguistic backgrounds (see Chapter 3), it was decided to investigate these aspects of 'input', i.e. sources of perceptions and attitudes. This means first considering what secondary pupils say about teachers and textbooks as sources of information. For primary pupils, statements about sources outside school were considered. Second it was decided to investigate the relationship of experience or lack of experience of France to one main topic, 'Dress and Appearance', since visits to France were hypothesised to be significant potential sources of knowledge.

The 'attitudes' approach

The third approach involved the analysis of pupils' attitudes to foreign people and places and to learning languages. It had two aspects. First, by analysing statements of attitudes it would be possible to validate the categorisation of pupils into degrees of ethnocentricity on the basis of the semantic differential test. Anomalies could be examined in depth to see if individuals gave any indication of reasons for the anomaly; for example disparity between semantic differential score on the French, Germans or Americans and actual statements about these peoples, and their perceptions of them.

The second dimension is the opportunity to look for attitude statements bearing on pupils' potential or actual motivation to learn a foreign language. The relationship between attitudes to and perceptions of foreign people, and attitudes to language learning is potentially interesting. Moreover the significance of experience of foreign countries, and particularly France, might be taken into consideration in this complex relationship.

Ultimately the effects of language teaching — and other sources of perceptions of France and French people — on pupils' perceptions and attitudes might throw some light on motivation and attainment in language learning, although statistically achievement in French was not significantly related to semantic differential score (see Chapter 3). The 'attitudes' approach will be treated in Chapter 3.

The 'case-study' approach

In view of our intention to link the analysis of pupils' perceptions (and attitudes) with the observation of their experience of French lessons, it was necessary to analyse the 'combined' knowledge of a class on the full range of issues raised in interview. This would then provide a basis for the attempt to integrate the different parts of the research, as described in Chapter 6.

Perceptions of Life in France: Two Illustrations

The material available would allow a wide range of topics to be analysed at length but for reasons of space only the four topics mentioned above are presented here or in the companion volume. The first major topic for analysis in this volume is that of 'physical appearance and dress'.

Although the textbook used in the two schools does not draw explicit attention to the way people dress and their physical appearance — and consequently teachers do not seem to introduce the topic — this was considered an important aspect of the culture and included as a main issue in the interviews, i.e. it was discussed with all the pupils interviewed. The approach was justified in that it became evident that pupils had quite definite and sometimes complex views and seemed to find it easy to talk about. Furthermore it is evident both from interviews and from analysis of the textbook (see Chapter 5) that the lack of explicit reference does not mean that pupils do not acquire impressions of dress and appearance from French lessons as well as from their own visits and other outside sources. Our other major topic, 'food' and everything connected with cuisine, is by contrast frequently introduced into lessons by textbook and teachers, and pupils again tended to find this an easy topic to discuss, as will be evident from the account in the companion volume.

Questions used to approach the issue of appearance and dress were of the following kind:

'If you saw a group of boys and girls/adults in your town would you notice they were French without hearing them speak? How?'

In some cases interviewers prefaced this area of discussion by stating 'I'd like to talk now about how people dress in France and what they look like,' thus indicating the general types of visual percepts of which the participants might make use. In some cases selections of photographs were used. These consisted of both black and white and colour photographs of French and English individuals and family groups, with two additions per set of photographs of other European nationals such as the Italians or the Swiss. The aim of using the photographs was not to assess how accurate pupils were in picking out the French but to find out which kinds of visual cue were considered most salient by them when asked to identify nationality from physical appearance. Another approach used was to ask pupils whether it was possible to describe a 'typical' French person (man, woman or one of the interviewee's own age group). The aim was not to elicit stereotypes but rather to allow the interviewee to summarise his or her views of any identifiable physical characteristics. Indeed in many cases this question served to provide an opportunity for the refutation of the kinds of stereotypes provided by sources such as the media, though as will be seen below this varied somewhat as a function of age and experience.

As the interviews were flexible in nature and not heavily structured, each interviewer was free to use whichever approach appeared suitable; the contents of the responses were, however, similar. Whilst the kinds of visual indicators of nationality can be grouped for summarising purposes under the two main headings of dress and physical appearance, interviewees clearly would make use of both kinds of indicator in any one response. Thus some of the examples given below will make reference to both dress and physical appearance, as separation and splitting of responses might otherwise disrupt the continuity of the more extended passages.

For both main headings, of dress and physical appearance, ways of perceiving the French could be divided into two rather obvious global categories — those indicating perception of the French as similar, and those seeing them as different in one or more respects. This was an issue upon which most pupils, including the younger age group, were able to comment in some form; types of 'don't know' response were rare. It is possible that too heavy a reliance on the 'just the same' type of response could suggest a lack of reflection upon this issue or some form of quick closure strategy. However it is also possible that this type of response may be indicative more of a dearth of experience, perceptual acuity, or even, conversely, a quasi-moral stance, particularly amongst the older age group, who might not wish to be seen to regard other nationalities as different in any way.

Dress

For this issue the analysis is not structured around the dimension of age, school class or any of the other factors. For each example membership of the relevant groups are given and analysis of any group differences are presented at the end of each section. (E = 'ethnocentric rating'; N = 'non-ethnocentric rating'; M = 'medium ethnocentricity rating'; for details see Chapter 3).

It might be assumed by the adult reader that in asking pupils for their views of French dress, spontaneous comments upon French fashion, in the sense of the *haute couture* fashion industry, would be elicited. This was not found to occur in any but a small number of responses, and so pupils were asked as a separate sub-issue if they had heard about French fashion. The answers being in the main negative not much material was gathered upon this. Thus the kind of dress under present consideration is everyday dress of all age groups, which does of course include perception of contemporary, what might be termed 'street' rather than designer-house fashion.

Teenage fashion was of course of particular interest to some groups of interviewees. It should be noted therefore that a temporal element would modify perceptions of these artefacts of French culture even more than that of others. Further, lapses of time between meeting French people and being asked to comment upon their dress could arguably modify comparisons to an even greater extent. Thus, for instance, French teenage fashion might have been recalled from the summer previous to the time of interviewing the secondary school sample (June and July 1986) or from even further back. Whilst those particularly interested in clothes might recall the style of dress accurately, for others the comparisons made might be less accurate.

For those with no first-hand experience of French people reliance upon information from other sources, such as the textbook and the television, could further modify accuracy. Clearly language textbooks cannot update their photographs of ephemera such as teenage fashion every year; still less could schools afford to invest every year in any such texts. However, in the absence of being able to do this it is presumably incumbent upon the teacher to provide material to counteract impressions which may be harmful. Whilst dress and physical appearance might be thought to be superficial aspects of people or peoples it will be seen below that some strong evaluations were based upon little contemporary information. Similarly the stereotypes provided by television presented even more 'dated' views. As has been mentioned above in other sections several television serials were being transmitted at the time of interviewing, which were quoted as sources of information. In some cases these were made explicit, in how many cases they had had a subliminal influence is of course unknown. (To give but one example which puzzled at least one interviewer for a while, a number of pupils spoke of French women as wearing 'flowery dresses'; as this is an attribute often applied to English rather than French dresses the provenance of this is only apparent if one watches TV offerings such as ' 'Allo, 'Allo'. Though pupils, including the junior interviewees, were aware usually that this series was set in the time of the Second World War, they did not necessarily modify their responses in the light of this knowledge.)

Dress perceived as similar

As was stated above one simple form of distinction of responses could be made into those where the French were perceived as similar or 'just the same' in dress, and into those where at least some form of differentiation was apparent, even if, for example, for only one age group, or for one detail, all others being regarded as similar to English dress. For some pupils an evaluative component was apparent in their responses, though not in the majority (of over three quarters of the cases). In approximately three quarters of the cases differences in dress were perceived (the responses termed evaluative with their explicit or implicit comparisons being included in this proportion). However, in a quarter of the cases no differences in dress were articulated, i.e. pupils concluded that the French were, in dress, 'just the same' with no details of apparel or of subgroups volunteered.

The responses, therefore, of those finding no differences in dress whilst numerous were not extensive. Both pupils with experience of France and without experience were found to give this type of response, though this was possibly modified to some extent by gender. The role of experience, gender, class groups and ethnocentricity is discussed below, after a presentation of the main types of response.

A secondary school boy (rated in the 'ethnocentric' group) reflected upon the image of French dress provided by the textbook and his experience gained from both family and school visits to France. Upon being asked whether his textbook provided information upon another issue (French views of the English) he replied:

P: Well the only thing we have got is they know they are a lot better dressers than us. Well they think they are definitely a lot better dressers than us but apart from that I can't think of anything.
I: Well you mention the way people dress. If there were a group of people here in town would you be able to pick out the French from them without hearing them speak?
P: From pictures in class and what we have been doing about clothes, they are not that much different at all but they think they are better dressers. That is what it says in the textbook but there was no evidence of that in France. Apart from a lot more clothes shops around the main city area. (310/19,20)

Statements of similarity were less frequent among the younger age group than among the older age group. However one can detect in some cases the emergence of the use of information about one's own culture to make sense of another. For instance it is possible that in the following rather hesitant example the junior school girl of no experience of France (medium ethnocentric group) is attempting to express, inter alia, that diversity is a feature of both cultures:

I: And what about the way people are, the way people look, the way they dress in France?

P: . . . Really just the same . . . er . . . they have all the fashions like we do, modern fashions . . . er . . . on the telly when I saw the students they wore about the same as what we do, modern things, that's the young people and the old people I think they'll just wear the same as what the older people here do . . . er . . . the English are rather smart. I think they would be . . . er . . . they will have people like we have, scruffy or something like that.

I: Do you think you could — if there was a group of French people in town here, do you think, without hearing them speak, do you think you could pick them out as French?

P: Er . . . I don't think so, I cannot tell them from how they look or anything, they'll just look the same. (515/13,14)

One of the reasons for there being a greater number of responses characterised as different amongst the younger age group is possibly because of the greater reliance upon sterotyped images in the absence of experience. However, refutation of the stereotype and conclusions of similarity were becoming apparent:

Well I think they look very similar to us but then again I don't think they're people who wear berets and strings of onions round their necks, but I don't think they wear suits, just casual people, who like to wear and dress how they please, yes. (566/14)

A refutation of another image, the 'smart' Frenchwoman, was also apparent from time to time, in the next example with an added reflection upon the importance of the context. Following a prompt from the interviewer upon whether French women are more smartly dressed than English women a secondary school girl, with no experience of France (non-ethnocentric group), concluded:

Not really . . . all people are different though when they go out . . . some might be. (296/4)

A typical example of how experience of France may not result in greater perception of detail, even when confronted with photographs is as follows:

I: What about how French people look and dress, how do they look and dress?

P: Just like, just the same as us like what we wear.

I: OK. So if there was a group of French people walking round Hillside you wouldn't be able to tell they were French just by looking at them?

P: No. Just the same as us.

I: OK. If I were to show you these pictures you couldn't say which people
are French and which people are English?
P: No.
I: You think they all look about the same?
P: . . . Yes they all look the same. (408/19,21)

Dress perceived as different

When differences of dress were mentioned most responses were not in
the form of clear evaluations, either positive or negative, but rather non-
evaluative factual statements. Of the responses in which some kind of
evaluation appeared to be present, approximately 11% were positive and
about 10% negative. Whilst in many cases these statements were intermin-
gled with other non-evaluative statements about other items of dress, three
(all secondary school girls) were classified as 'mixed' evaluative responses,
in that they were clearly in favour of some aspects of French dress whilst
reacting against others. For the majority, for whom dress may not have
been a salient issue, differences either of detail or in general were given
with no obvious evaluations.

There was a tendency for some pupils to notice differences in the dress
of, for instance, one age group but not in that of another. Amongst the
secondary school age group differences in the dress of their contemporaries
were noted more readily than in that of older age groups. The types of
details of dress perceived as different varied widely, as will be illustrated
shortly. In passing it might be noted that amongst French dress details not
ever mentioned by any of those interviewed was the meaning of 'bleu de
travail'; neither experience of France nor the textbook appeared to prompt
recollection of this detail of French life which, if minor, is at least not
infrequent. Neither did the occasional prompt to this effect produce any
result.

The kinds of details perceived as different in French dress included, in
order of descending frequency, different items of dress (such as the beret)
styles of dress, colours, and, occasionally, the use of particular materials.
Those making evaluative judgements frequently noted and appraised the
same types of details of dress, others also included comments upon
whether the clothes were 'fashionable' and 'smart' or 'scruffy', terms which
can probably be regarded as evaluative amongst these age groups. It was
found, not surprisingly, that secondary school girls made the greatest
number of evaluative comments, followed as a group by primary school
girls, secondary school boys, and finally, with only one such comment,
primary school boys.

Different items of dress

Under this heading are included references to what came to be regarded as a stereotyped response: the image of the Frenchman dressed in a beret, wearing a striped jumper or tee-shirt, sometimes carrying a string of onions (or even garlic) round his neck, sometimes provided with a bicycle. The stereotype was made use of more frequently by the primary age group than by the secondary school pupils. However, it was not concluded that this was the dress of all Frenchmen, though the origin and purpose of the assemblage varied considerably. The source was often obvious:

I: Is there anything else that would be different apart from the food do you think?
P: I think the way they dress. I see the French in blue and white shirts, riding bicycles with garlic around their neck.
I: How have you got that picture do you think?
P: I have seen them on TV before.
I: What was it on can you remember?
P: It was . . . I think it was in a 'Carry on Laughing' film.
I: Yes. Because one or two people say they have seen an advertisement recently like that. I am trying to find out which advertisement it is because I don't know it. So it was in the 'Carry on Laughing'?
P: Yes.
I: Was that a man or a woman?
P: It was a man.
I: Was he old or young?
P: Fairly young.
I: Do you think they dress like that all over?
P: I'm not sure, I don't know. They might do and they might not. (347/6)
(Junior boy with no experience of France, E group.)

One boy attempted to locate the provenance of the costume:

I: You were talking about Australian clothes being a bit different do you think any French clothes would look any different?
P: Well I've heard they, like, wear stripy shirts and like berets on their head.
I: Do you think they wear those in all parts of France or do just some people wear them?
P: Just some people wear them.
I: Have you any idea where they wear them or who wears them?
P: Um . . . somewhere near the south because it'd be sunny and they'd like

be wearing, like, the berets and the short-sleeved tee-shirts. (471/23)
(Junior school boy, no experience of France, N group.)
(It will be noted from this and many other quotations that children in this
area of England use the word 'like' as a hesitation expression.)

Other reasons were advanced for the wearing of striped clothes in
response to other issues:

I think they would be paid less because most of us have better clothes
than them. Because they have like striped shorts or something all the
time on the telly. (341/11) (Junior boy with no experience of France, E
group.)

For some the image of stripes tended to wander:

. . . they wear berets and like they wear stripy trousers and things like
that and the ladies when they're dancing they wear like hats with
wiggly flowers on or something . . . (492/14) (Junior girl, with
experience of France, N group.)

The wearing of berets was not viewed by all as a solely adult male
preserve. One junior school girl (with experience of France, group N)
made a rare reference to fashion in the wider sense also:

P: Well I'd notice them and, like, they seem to wear different clothes to
us, like they wear, nearly all the time they wear different fashions to us
and they nearly always wear berets and they — don't really know how
I'd pick them out but I think I'd know them.
I: You think the fashion is different?
P: Yes.
I: Can you say how?
P: Well they always picked out new clothes and I watch fashion shows and
most of the fashions come from France, a lot of famous fashions, they
nearly always wear them there that's why you can nearly always pick
them out 'cause they always wear berets over there even the boys. (565/
21)

Of the 16 responses made referring to the stereotype, with little
accompanying refutation or qualification, 13 came from the junior school
pupils; the remaining three were provided by secondary school boys. One
boy with both family and school visit experience of France (E group) chose
it as an example of a different characteristic of France:

P: It's all, like, the same streets and all that . . . they nearly dress the same.

I: Nearly dress the same?
P: There's a few differences.
I: What differences are there?
P: . . . They all wore stripy vests when we were there.
I: Did they?
P: Yes, there were a few like that. (217/8)

Other items of dress emphasised as different or worn more frequently than in England included references to regional costumes:

P: . . . like, we think the fashion is better in France but there was some funny clothes.
I: Tell me a bit more.
P: Just funny clothes, like gaudy colours and things. Things like that, we saw a couple of fairs where they were all dressed up in Breton costume.

Another difference thought possibly to be regional was noticed by a secondary school boy with much experience of France (E group). Referring to adults, he said:

Well I think when they are dressed up smart they're dressed the same I think, but they seem to wear a lot of flat caps I saw in the place where I was at but I'm not sure again whether that's typical of France or just the region.

Some without experience of France made use of seeing French people in England:

I know once we were in town and there was some English people with some French people and you could tell they were French because of the way they were speaking and they were dressed differently, you know, scarves round their necks and things like that and boots, so they do dress slightly differently but not all that differently I wouldn't think, I don't think I would be able to pick them out if I just saw them. (326/21)

Opinions regarding details such as whether French teenagers wore trousers more or less frequently varied considerably, as did the emphasis on casual clothes as opposed to the more tailored image. Having heard of French fashion one junior school boy with experience of France (N group) elaborated:

P: In Paris they would be all posh clothes whereas in most parts of France if they were wearing shorts they would wear shorts with palm trees on them, things like that. They might wear trousers that only come down to their knees and things like that.

I: What about the children? Is that what they wear?

P: No the children just wear normal clothes like adults would wear in this country. (373/19)

Another junior boy, who had no experience of France (E group) had seen a television programme of a fashion show shortly before the interview:

I: What's your impression of French people then?

P: Funny . . . they wear, like, different clothes to us, things like that.

I: What's different about their clothes?

P: The way they dress. A lot of them wear suits — the men, and the women wear fancy dresses and things like that. (452/15)

Some children were thought also to be smartly dressed:

I: What about children how do you think they dress?

P: . . . Like they used to do a long time ago here, like, short trousers and a cap and a tie.

I: How do you know these things about . . .

P: I've just seen them on French programmes and imagined them. (531/15) (Junior boy, no experience of France, N group.)

The wearing of shorts produced feeling of antipathy in at least one junior girl with no experience of France (E group):

P: No, I just think that sort of thing, I might say something to them that I don't really like France and that.

I: Why don't you like the French people very much?

P: The way they dress and the way they are, I just don't really like them.

I: How do French people dress then?

P: Well in short trousers.

I: Is this the men or the women or the children?

P: The men and, like, jumpers. The women just, like, skirts and tee-shirts and jumpers sort of thing. That's the way I think of them.

I: Is that very different to how we would dress over here?

P: No, not really. Maybe the men in short trousers. (378/10)

A girl in the same school class (M group) used her knowledge of French costume to provide a reason for choosing France as a country to live in:

I: Why would you like to live there?

P: It is a nice place and I enjoy speaking French and in each village there would be an old lady in Victorian costume — in national costume and it is nice because you can go up to them and they are very kind and have a conversation with them. (379/4)

She elaborated later:

P: It's quite a long black dress, white like scarf on their head. White jacket and mainly a black shirt or something and for the men it is 'flarey' trousers and mainly the same. (379/17)

Perhaps inevitably for the younger age group, both with and without experience of France, it is possible that information about various different countries became confused:

P: If you go into any of the old villages there is lots of old men and they are separated with the women. The women stand with black veils on and the men hardly see them. The men all of them wear like suits and they have berets and they look really weatherbeaten. The kids are really different.

I: Yes. What are they like?

P: Well the kids are just like us but they have different habits. They look like us — like, the Japanese look different — but they look like us they have the same colour skin so they are just really the same except the accents and different habits.

I: What sort of habits would you say are different?

P: Well I couldn't really say, I can't think of many. They don't wear berets. It seems most of the men what are about forty or fifty start wearing berets but all of them have like blood red on the cheeks and nearly everyone has a walking stick they are so old. (340/10) (Junior boy with experience of France and Spain, M group.)

For two junior girls with no experience of France, French clothes are possibly equated with anything thought to be foreign:

P: Er . . . just like them, you know them things, them thin things that you just wrap round like you — go — . . . er . . . like . . . Indian people wear but not a sari or anything like that, I can't really get it all out . . . er . . . . (522/9) (N group)

P: They don't make them, they don't sew them they just wrap cloth round them.

I: Sorry?
P: They just wrap cloth round them.
I: Yes?
P: They don't sew their clothes.
I: No. How have you heard about that?
P: Well, I've seen some people, I don't know if they're French or not.
I: What did they look like?
P: Well, they had like Chinese eyes and that, don't know what else. (458/ 19) (E group)

The absence of experience did not however impede another girl in this age group (E group) from producing a more extensive and reflective response:

P: They could wear different things for different jobs, like we do. They could wear tight black trousers and stripy blue and white top for the onions and everything and on the ice-cream van — well I don't know really but you could just put a jumper and pair of trousers on and then have the pinny for . . .
I: So you think people dress differently for the different jobs they do?
P: Yes, I think so.
I: So the onion seller would have to wear stripy jumper and ice-cream man is just going to have ordinary jumper. What else is going to be different about the way they dress?
P: Well it is a different country, it is colder here and warmer there and then in the winter they might have to wear more things than us because it is colder and it is hotter in the summer, you see. That's what I think. (454/19)

Styles

The observation that clothes vary according to climate is apparent already in the above example. This kind of observation featured frequently in the next most numerous grouping of responses, termed 'styles'. These responses emphasised less exotic types of differences than, for example, regional costumes, but concentrated more upon matters such as thickness, length and general shape of the clothes.

The junior pupils' responses made several references to the effect of climate upon clothing worn:

Well their dress isn't all that much different to England but I think they are less dressy than us because it is cold down here. (409/29)

(Primary boy, no experience of France except passing through Parisian airports, N group.)

In answer to the question regarding whether he would recognise French people in his town he elaborated:

You would probably see the French and German not as fully dressed as the English. We live in a colder country than France and Germany because they are lower down so you could probably tell by the dressing. An Englishman would be all — you could tell he was English. Dressed properly with pullovers and that on while French you would probably see in a tee-shirt or something. (409/29)

The experience of friends and relations was frequently a source of information for this as for other issues:

P: I don't know like, they could just wear, like, a shirt and a top like a dress or something . . . like, they could just dress like us or they could like dress in like long dresses like.

I: How long, right down to the floor or just . . .

P: Like just down to there, in between the knee and the ankle.

I: What makes you say that? Have you seen any pictures?

P: I don't know like but my cousin brought like these dresses back for my Mum and like they were all long and like they were like just long and then there was some with like sort of beads fastened on to them.

I: So did she like them, were they nice?

P: They were alright but not my type. (484/11) (Junior girl, no experience of France, N group.)

The image of the French as well-dressed was apparent amongst some of the junior girls and influenced responses upon other issues:

I: Do you think they are well paid or not well paid?

P: Most of them are rich. French people are rich.

I: What makes you say that?

P: Because they all seem to be well-dressed on photos and that. (Junior girl, no experience of France, E group.)

Having stated further that their trousers and skirts were different she elaborated upon the latter:

Well theirs could be like flouncy, ours are quite tight.

Whilst this might appear to be merely the product of an imagination activated by being interviewed, and using information from her own experience to make sense of a social world with which she was not very familiar, this contrast in the shape of clothes was one frequently echoed by older pupils. An oft-used epithet was 'baggy'. Clearly, shape is similar to colour in being an attribute of popular fashion subject to frequent change, though the transient nature of style was not mentioned by interviewees. Four secondary school boys picked 'bagginess' out as a defining characteristic:

I: What about the people. I mean if you saw a group of people, let's say round here, on the street and without hearing them speak would you be able to pick out the French?
P: Yes, straight away from their clothes and that.
I: What's different about their clothes?
P: Like they're baggier . . .
I: Are you thinking of the young people then?
P: Young and old. (161/15) (School visit to France, M group.)

Similarly another boy with school visit experience of France only (E group), notes this attribute *inter alia*, but makes a distinction between age groups:

I: If you were to see a group of people in town here, would you be able to pick out the French from them, without hearing them speak I mean?
P: Probably yes because the way they dress. You can tell. Like the French have the same type of trainers on and baggy tops and things round their neck and everything. That's how you mostly find out.
I: You are thinking of young people now?
P: Yes.
I: What about older people, adults, what do they dress like?
P: Normally. Couldn't really pick them out.
I: So young people you would think of as dressing differently in a different style?
P: Yes. (135/18)

Television is again a source:

I: What about people from different bits of France do you think they dress differently at all, from different parts of France? Or look different?
P Yes.
I: Yes, whereabouts do you think?

P: Boulogne.
I: Yes, what do they look like there?
P: . . . Like all baggy clothes, unfashionable like.
I: Old-fashioned clothes. Yes, did somebody tell you that or is that from pictures you've seen?
P: I've seen it on telly before. (288/17) (Secondary school boy, M group.)

Girls tended to be more emphatic in their appraisal of style and added another dimension to the analysis of shape, that of 'flared-ness'. In the following two examples other aspects of dress and various evaluations are also included, to preserve the continuity of the exchange:

P: Well, they were old-fashioned 'cause they wore what, like, had just gone out in England. It must have come in when it went out in England.
I: So what sort of things were they wearing when you were in France?
P: . . . Flares and that, different colours.
I: These looked a bit dated did they? What about the colours that they were wearing?
P: Dull, like dull, like scruffy, I thought they were like scruffy.
I: What was that, people of all age groups or just . . .
P: The majority of people I saw, like, they were scruffy and that. (298/22) (Secondary girl, school visit to France, E group.)

Age was seen as an important factor for one secondary school girl (E group, no experience of France), who had strong opinions, both positive and negative, about dress and physical appearance. Throughout the interview the theme of money was reiterated:

P: Well the way they dress and everything you just think straightaway I bet they've got stacks of money.
I: Yes? Is that the people that you've met who came over here (reference to school exchange)?
P: Yes. (156/19)

Later she made distinctions between age-groups:

. . . and (I) like the early twenties to the late twenties but as soon as they get past 35 they start going down and wearing flares and flower power and all that stuff . . .
. . . what I like about the clothes is I like the way they have trousers to here and then the nice coloured socks (indicating current teenage mid-calf length). (156/24)

Colours

An emphasis on different colours from those popular in current English fashion produced the next substantial group of responses. Again the majority of responses were non-evaluative (though inevitably those remarks with clear appraisals tended to be more noteworthy). Some distinction, parallel to that made for style, could be drawn between the responses of the two age groups, the junior children being more concerned with the colours of clothes of older age groups, whereas the principal interest of the secondary school pupils was with their contemporaries' clothes.

One junior boy with no experience of France (N group) made an unusual but plausible connection between climate and dress. In response to one of the photographs, of a family on a beach he stated:

. . . in England they wouldn't dress like that. Because of their bathing suits they are more coloured than in England.

Further, when asked if he could recognise French people in England he rationalised:

P: No because they might wear dark clothes in England when they come over because it would be dull and if they wore bright clothes they might think they looked daft.
I: They might think they looked daft over here in bright clothes?
P: Yes.
I: Why is that?
P: Because most people over here, when it is bright, they wear bright clothes but when it is dull they wear dull clothes.
I: You mean in weather like this when it is misty and dirty they would wear dull clothes?
P: Like, if it was sunny you would wear something fancy. (543/21)

For another junior, a girl with no experience of France, E group, another factor influenced colour. Referring initially to the men she reasoned:

P: All in black. Like the rich ones would dress all in black and the not as rich would dress in brown. Like all in brown.
I: What about the women, how would they dress?
P: Like gold necklaces and everything. That's what they remind me of. Like the women remind me of short hair in a bob. Children remind me of long hair. Like French children.

I: And the way they dress?

P: I like the way children dress.

I: How is that?

P: Like . . . it reminds me of the dresses that come down and come over like that. That's what it reminds me of. I like them dresses. Like what they used to wear.

I: So ballooning out dresses. (453/11)

This particular interviewee might be described as one of those thought to use 'playful images' by Piaget (1975) and Furth (1980). Having first stated that she had never heard of French fashion she then continued on to another line of thought which is given here, though tangential, to indicate a distinct, though rare, style of interaction when being interviewed:

It really reminds me of them being really nice and smart and posh. I would like it if I lived there. I can't imagine what it would look like outside though. I wouldn't imagine it was trees and bushes and things. Not really. I would just imagine it like . . . grass that is really overgrown like all over. That's what it reminds me of — that's all. Like for the town it would be really big thingy with a giant grandfather clock. As big as the skyscrapers that you can get. (453/11)

A secondary school boy with no experience of France (N group) did not perceive differences in teenage fashion but in adult styles:

. . . you tend to be able to pick out like continental people, like French people, by the way they dress because those are more colourful and sort of more dressy than we are. I don't know — the women have a scent about them like perfume and everything that you can pick out. (104/17)

Another noted the influence of French teenage fashion upon English clothes:

P: When they come over you sometimes see them in X (local town) they always seem to have packs on their backs or something like that. Their clothes are sometimes a bit different, a bit brighter sometimes and now we sort of get French clothes coming over to England more. I think they wear them a lot in France and they wear them a lot in England so you can't really tell now as much.

I: But the fashion that influences us is brighter you say?

P: Well on them sometimes it's brighter they seem to wear a lot more summer wear it seems, they must have good weather or something in

France. (244/18) (experience of France, E group.)

For some the colours worn were unthinkable:

P: But I noticed that some people dressed different, in different places.
I: And what was different about those people then exactly?
P: Well just the colours that they wear — that we wouldn't dream of. Something like gold, well some people wear gold I mean not like them. I think I've seen a woman in a shop wearing a gold suit, I don't mean gold I mean gold . . . (283/22) (school visit to France, N group.)

One boy with school visit experience of France, to Boulogne only, (M group) concluded that old people were not well-looked after in France; this was on the basis of their clothes:

They were dark, yes, mainly dark clothes. (196/20)

It is possible that he had equated certain widows' or elderly countrywomen's clothes with want rather than with custom.

Opinions regarding colours thought to be unusual were polarised, into the either unusually bright or conversely the dull:

I: What sort of colours do you think are popular in France?
P: . . . White.
I: What about the boys do you think they wear the same sort of clothes as English boys?
P: No.
I: What's different?
P: Well English boys wear like bright colours and theirs were wearing like black and grey.
I: Was that last year?
P: Yes. (234/17) (Secondary girl, school visit experience, M group.)

But:

P: They just wear weird clothes and that, I think, to England.
I: What, they wear different sorts of clothes?
P: Yes.
I: What sort of clothes do you think they wear?
P: Ones that I don't like.
I: How do you mean? What sort of colours — or styles?

P: Mainly colours. They wear bright gaudy colours and that. (146/23) (Secondary girl, no experience of France, M group.)

The fashionable and the unfashionable

Included above amongst the non-evaluative comments have been some evaluations of aspects of dress. In this and the next section on dress all comments appear to make some kind of evaluation, whether positive or negative. Though they are often more forcefully expressed than those of interviewees not passing judgement, it has to be borne in mind that comments designated were in the minority (approximately 21% in roughly equal proportions of positive to negative). Of the 22 comments, using the fashionable–unfashionable type constructs (including 'ahead-of-us', 'behind-us'), 14 were made by secondary school girls, nine being positive comments and five negative comments. (As explained, any one interviewee might make more than one kind of comment, be positive about some aspects, negative about others, and merely record yet others non-evaluatively; thus statistics relate to parts of responses, being separate thought-units, rather than to individuals.)

Representative of the positive evaluations were the following comments:

I: If you saw a group of people in town would you be able to pick out the French?

P: Yes, because they're dead fashionable and nicely dressed and clean and tidy and they wear nice fashionable clothes and they've got a lot of style.

I: How does it compare with ours?

P: Like Vogue and that, 'cause a lot of English people don't buy so many stylish clothes like the French 'cause most of them can't afford — I suppose that in France like there's lots of snazzy dressers.

I: Yes. Did you notice that when you saw French people here?

P: Yes, there's a lot of smart people.

I: Have you seen the exchange people here?

P: Yes.

I: How did they compare with — how did they dress compared with the way that . . .

P: They dress like — really loud and we dress like — if we went away we'd just wear jeans or a skirt or a smart skirt, we'd never wear bright clothes and that.

I: So they're brighter and more fashionable?
P: Yes. (140/20)

and:

P: I think they are ahead of us because when I was in France they were saying that the clothes they were wearing were just starting to come in in England. (Secondary boy, family and school experience, M group.)

Conversely the older Frenchwoman is not always seen as fashionable:

P: Well I think they are a bit more daring with some of the clothes and we wouldn't know where to find them in our shop windows. Their clothes seem to be really bright, where in England it's not like calmed down, greens and reds.
I: Yes, what about the styles, I mean the shapes of the clothes, are they any different?
P: I thought some of them looked to me old fashioned . . .
I: Yes . . .
P: . . . But if that's the style I mean I suppose middle-aged women don't, like, want to keep in the fashion.
I: No. What about the men do you think they dress differently?
P: No.
I: You couldn't really tell a French man from an English man?
P: No. (183/22) (Secondary girl, school visit experience of France, N group.)

The response of one girl suggested a burgeoning sense of the relativity of fashion, though she was not very explicit:

P: They don't seem in fashion but they will be in their way, but they don't dress the same as if they've anything on.
I: Yes . . .
P: . . . 'cause I saw one when I was on a bus, I saw a group of boys and girls just playing on their bikes and that, they didn't seem — like they had baggy trousers on — maybe it was their fashion but . . . (295/20) (Secondary girl, had travelled through France, M group.)

Less generous was:

I: What about the people and the way they dress?
P: Dead old-fashioned.

I: Sorry.

P: Very old-fashioned, they still wear flares, most of them wear flares and dead big collars and that and the kids wear jeans and jumpers.

I: What about the adults what do they wear?

P: Well, just jumpers and skirts I never saw anyone in anything like different, just like skirts and jumpers and trousers and things like that, there's no punks or anything over there, can't say anything like that, they don't like say have styles of their own over there, like we have punk and mods and things like that, they just all dress the same.

I: And the older people, the people as old as me, what about them?

P: Just jumpers and trousers and suits and things like that. (227/25) (Secondary girl, school visit experience, E group.)

The 'smart' and the 'scruffy'

Two epithets used quite frequently by interviewees are arguably evaluative. These were 'smart' and 'scruffy' which, whilst sometimes associated with the fashionable/unfashionable construct, could be considered an independent dimension. Being 'tidy' or its opposite is considered under the same heading.

The role of the textbook is apparent in the following example:

From what I have seen most of them look pretty smart. Even if they have got a tee-shirt on — when you see them in textbooks they haven't got any stains down the front. They are always dead clean. I don't know whether that is just because they are out of textbooks and they got people to pose or whether it is true or not. (132/14) (Secondary boy, no experience of France, M group.)

Even before starting French at secondary school, some pupils have this image:

P: Most of them are rich. French people are rich.

I: What makes you say that?

P: Because they all seem to be well dressed on photos and that. (552/13) (Junior girl, no experience of France, E group.)

and:

P: I haven't seen anybody but I think they dress like . . . they are smart and they like to dress in a suit all the time. (424/15) (Junior girl, no experience of France, M group.)

In the above three examples the interviewees did not look at the photographs sometimes used. It was noted that sometimes individuals in suits were picked out as being French on the basis of their wearing suits (in fact both individuals, a young woman and an elderly man were English).

The comments regarding 'smartness' came from secondary school boys and primary school girls. Secondary school girls did not appear to subscribe to this view:

I: What was different about their clothes?
P: Like they weren't tidy. (262/5) (No experience of France, M group.)

A primary girl with experience of France concluded that clothes in France were 'old-fashioned' and had observed, *inter alia*, farmers in the South of France wearing:

Like all tatty trousers and shirts (M group.)

The absence of experience for another junior girl (M group), did not prevent her having the following view of France:

I: Yes. What would you think it was like to be a French person, living in France?
P: . . . I think some of them would be poor, not as well off as the English are.
I: Yes. Why, how would you know they were poor?
P: Probably 'cause the way they dressed and where they lived.
I: So what would their houses be like?
P: They wouldn't be like ours, they wouldn't be big they would be like little cottages.
I: Yes. And how would they dress if they were poor?
P: Could have like trousers with holes in and shirts with holes in. (483/5)

This image of France recurred from time to time in discussion of other issues, such as housing, particularly amongst the junior age group.

Views of French dress generally indicate that many differences in style and detail are perceived, but it is clear that opinions are diverse, and frequently make distinctions amongst age groups. The same age groups of interviewees are capable of holding polarised views about the general image of the French dresser: either fashionable or unfashionable, smart, (the 'chic' image, though this term was never used) or rather untidy. From the above examples of those with no experience of France other sources were apparent, in the case of pupils at one secondary school (Newfarm) a source of information was French pupils on exchange visits in previous years.

The breakdown of types of responses, by groups such as age, gender, experience of France, ethnocentric group, and school class for secondary pupils, is given below.

Role of experience, age and gender

It was decided to investigate whether experience of going to France, age group and gender made any difference to perceptions of French dress. Whilst this is perhaps not a particularly important issue, it serves as a comparison for pupil perceptions of physical differences analysed below. For this purpose broad categories were created of those with experience of France (school and family holiday experience) and those with no experience. Two broad categories, of those perceiving the French as 'different' in some aspects of dress, and those seeing them as 'similar' have been used. For this purpose the 'different' category includes both the non-evaluative comments and the evaluative comments, insofar as they imply differentiation. The totals for each age and gender group are given below in Table 2.1.

Whilst it has been observed that the proportion of those seeing the French as different in some aspect of dress is much greater than those seeing them as similar, having no experience of France appears to make more difference to the perceptions of the two primary groups than to the secondary ones. However, of those with experience, secondary school boys had the highest proportion of those seeing the French as different. As has been shown above in quotations, the kinds of differences perceived were

TABLE 2.1 *Perception of French dress by age and gender group*

Seeing French dress as:	No experience of France		Some experience	
	Different	*Similar*	*Different*	*Similar*
Secondary boys	11	6	18	4
Secondary girls	14	7	15	5
Primary boys	21	3	6	6
Primary girls	24	6	8	1
Totals	70	22	47	16

diverse, sometimes positive, sometimes negative. It is possible however that future research might wish to focus more rigorously on selected aspects of perceptions, and see if age, gender and experience do confirm some of the above trends.

The role of experience is likely to play an ambivalent role when combined with exposure to French teaching. In that case some secondary school pupils have received, according to their teachers (see Chapter 5) various inputs designed to stress similarities amongst nationalities, rather than differences, and to reduce stereotypes (of, for example, the popular image of the French onion-seller). Several teachers saw their role as partly to reduce putative perceptions of differences, so those pupils who see the French as 'similar' may not be lacking experience or perceptual acuity.

Physical appearance

Analysis of the 137 responses concerning the physical appearance of the French indicates similar trends to those for dress. The majority of the sample (approximately 69%) saw the French as looking different in at least some small physical detail, though, as was the case for dress, pupils frequently differentiated between age-group and between the sexes. A few evaluative comments were made also, but those were smaller in number than for dress (approximately 7%). However it was noticeable that of this small minority eight of the ten evaluative comments were made by girls (six secondary and two primary pupils).

Comments upon physical appearance were generally less extensive than those upon dress. As matters such as hair styles were included under this heading it was found that constructs similar to those describing dress were sometimes used. There was evidence also of some physical adjuncts of the dress stereotype; the Frenchman sporting the beret, stripy jumper and onions was sometimes thought to have a dark moustache and/or dark hair.

Comments that the French look 'just the same' as the English, therefore made up just under one third of the responses for this sub-issue. It was not the case that pupils who saw the French as similar in dress also saw them as similar in physical appearance; all possible combinations of choices were represented (similar in both, different in both, similar in dress but not in physical appearance and vice versa).

Where differences were perceived these were again diverse and sometimes contradictory, though there was possibly greater agreement, of a somewhat stereotyped nature, than regarding dress. The kinds of differences perceived by the pupils included, in descending order of frequency, facial features, skin colour and sun-tan, facial expression (as distinct from features) hair cuts, behaviour and movement, hair colour, and occasionally, height and make-up.

Physical appearance perceived as similar

Where pupils were not, or did not feel able to comment upon any physical differences, responses tended to be succinct. The following secondary school pupil had noted that clothes were baggier but about physical appearance concluded:

No, just look the same as us, same as in our street (School visit experience, M group.)

Probings to see if there were any perceptions of regional physical variations did not elicit any differences beyond an increase in sun-tan in regions thought to be warmer (usually, but not invariably thought to be the South). No responses suggested any acquaintance with the historical distribution of different groups of peoples; the stereotypes elicited of the dark haired, slightly darker skinned Frenchman might be thought to derive from a somewhat Latinised image. It was not apparent that pupils had any knowledge of any of the other early inhabitants of France. (Concomitantly when discussing the sub-issue of language, there was no evidence that pupils were aware of recent movements to preserve minority languages and identities.)

Physical appearance perceived as different

Where pupils perceived the physical appearance of at least some age groups or either of the sexes as different, more than one defining characteristic was often noted, and occasionally evaluations were made of them. The face was most frequently mentioned (a total of 40 times) as the feature most recognisably different. All features such as the lips, eyes, eyebrows, mouth and nose were referred to, plus the stereotype of the moustache.

Research into the related field of development of racial awareness (e.g. Katz, 1983) has argued that children do not make use solely of characteristics such as skin colour in deciding upon the race of others, but other characteristics, such as facial features and hair, are also used as indicators. Whilst racial awareness is thought to develop early in the pre-school years, differentiation of people in terms of other groupings such as religion and nationality takes much longer to develop. It is possible that at certain stages, for instance in the junior school years, children may be more interested in establishing differences amongst peoples rather than similarities (this point will be discussed further below).

The face and facial features

The face as a whole, or individual facial features, were given as defining characteristics of the French by all age groups. Of the total 42 occasions upon which it or they were given, the largest group (of 16) came from primary school boys, followed with 13 instances by secondary school girls. However, it is possible that somewhat different emphases by interviewers could have slightly modified these results, in that some interviewers made greater use of the sets of photographs, thus encouraging the pupils to attempt to articulate and refine vaguely perceived differences. Whilst further focused research would be needed to establish more precisely any extent of differences in perception attributable to factors such as age, gender experience and school class, the types of features mentioned spontaneously did not differ qualitatively from those elicited by the photographs. Though pupils often made references not merely to one characteristic but to others also, such as hair colour, skin colour and so forth, for present purposes analysis will follow the same format as that for dress, presenting findings mainly under the above-mentioned headings.

The physical counterpart of the stereotyped dress image was often given at least in part, by those with no experience of France:

I: What do you imagine French people looking like?
P: Carrying onions about.
I: Go on.
P: Long moustaches. Don't know anything else.
I: Nothing else. Do you think everybody looks like that in France?
P: No not everybody.
I: What makes you mention that then?
P: Seen pictures of people on bikes with onions.
I: Where have you seen those pictures do you know?
P: On the tele. (509/11) (Junior school boy, E group.)

Another junior boy (E group) who had passed through a French airport recalled only French policemen:

Some of them had weird moustaches there. That was all I really noticed. (550/13)

Other pupils included the moustache with other details. After looking at the photographs another primary boy of no experience responded:

I: So you think if there was a group of French people walking around Hillside you would be able to tell they were French without hearing them talk?

P: Probably.

I: What sort of things would you look for, what sort of clues would you look for?

P: I'd look for their hair styles and the way their eyes formed.

I: The way their eyes formed, can you describe in a little bit more detail what you look for in their eyes?

P: If it was a man, his eyes are always open.

I: Wide open?

P: Yes. And if it — I don't know — if it's an English man his eyes are like half shut, not wide.

I: Oh, that's interesting. Anything else you'd look for?

P: No. French people usually have moustaches and if they have one it usually comes down to about here.

I: Like a droopy moustache?

P: Yes, and that's all really. (511/13) (N group.)

Eyes were frequently chosen as a defining feature, but perceptions of them were polarised into the wide and the narrow (sometimes with accompanying delineation of expression). One secondary boy included eyes amongst most of the other features. From the photographs he selected:

The lips again, the mouth and the eyes look always half shut. (248/23)

Some pupils selected the same types of features but found it hard to define what appeared different to them. One secondary boy with school visit experience only (N group) selected two photographs but the reasons for his choice were terse:

. . . I don't know just instinct really . . . just slim . . . eyebrows. The eyes — dark. (225/21)

Some pupils had relations who were wholly or partly French and were able to use this information:

P: And you can tell by the face 'cause some of them are dark skinned and you can tell by their eyes and things . . . I don't know, they're darker — most of them all have brown eyes . . . er . . .

I: Have you noticed that from pictures or from films?

P: From pictures and my cousin and my auntie have as well. (Junior girl, no experience of France, N group.)

Facial expressions

Facial expressions were sometimes mentioned and though they do not form the next most frequent category of indicators the examples are given here, as they are related to the facial features mentioned. Perhaps because they represent a more dynamic interpretation of the question of how French people 'look' evaluations were sometimes made. One of the more vehement or defensive responses came from a junior school girl with no direct experience of France (a member of the N group and not therefore classified as ethnocentric from her semantic differential score):

P: They look, some of them they seem to look suspicious like, they seem to be talking nice to you but like as if they have the evil eye.
I: Yes, is that from people you've seen or something your sister's said or . . ?
P: Yes, Joanne she was saying like when they went in this restaurant once they were talking nice and they seem to have that awful eye, a little suspicious as if to say what do you want, or something like that.
I: Have you heard that from several people or just one?
P: Well, I've heard it from my Dad . . .
I: Yes . . .
P: . . . and my Nana, 'cause her husband, he's been there before, that's probably it.
I: Yes. What did your Dad say about French people?
P: Well, like he says that they are good to you and they're not — there's some are friendly but some could be like hard with you and they're awful shouting and that.
I: And has he been to France to work or on holiday?
P: Like he went to work, goes with the work, they went to do some houses I think, can't remember and they went there and he was like — he stopped for the weekend I think and he says they went to a nightclub, that's how they found out about people, 'cause they couldn't see them during the day with them being . . . (559/8)

Sometimes aspects of English life, such as unemployment, might even inform pupils' choices:

I: What about a group of adults, would you be able to tell if they were French?
P: Sometimes, yes.
I: What sort of things would help you?
P: How they look and that, their expressions.

I: That's interesting, what sort of expressions do you think they would have?

P: Just be happier.

I: Do you think they would look happier. Why do you think they would look happier than English people?

P: Because they have jobs and that.

I: On the whole you think they would look happier. Do English people look miserable?

P: No, it's just French people like laugh a lot and that.

I: How do you know about that?

P: Just my Grandma has been. (166/17,18) (Secondary boy, no experience of France, M group)

As for many opinions regarding the French it was possible to find the opposite view expressed for example:

P: I don't know 'cause they, I don't know they just don't look very happy, they just look French.

I: Yes. Do you think generally they don't look very happy?

P: . . . No. I mean compared to the girl and there and there, they look happy and that. They just look, I don't know they just look, not English.

I: No. Do you think that you get the impression that French people smiled less when you were there, you were saying that they don't look happy.

P: No, not really they didn't like seem to have a good laugh and that, just like English people do and that. (298/21) (Secondary girl, school visit experience, E group)

Of the 14 who mentioned 'facial expression' all but two were girls, the number of the junior girls so contributing, equalling that of the secondary girls, though they could not all define what it was they found different. Person-perception and social-cognitive research has indicated, though not usually from a cross-cultural perspective, that children develop from giving largely physical characteristics when asked to describe others, to giving more psychological characteristics, particularly after the age of eleven. Whilst it is not clear that either sex is more likely to do this it is possible that at certain ages one group may have a more vested interest in making sense of others. The following is fortunately not a representative example but is included to illustrate a type of view which teachers should perhaps be aware may be held by some of their secondary school pupils. Sun-tans and other features were all mentioned and some approved, but most arresting was an illustration of her interpretation of French girls' expressions, in response to another issue:

I: What do you think they think of English people?

P: I don't think they're all that keen on them.

I: No?

P: 'Cause like the lasses I know they're dead bitchy with us, like English people.

I: Why do you think that is?

P: Well, they're always lashing dirty looks and everything. I hate people like giving me the run around.

I: I wondered if you'd ever heard some French people think that the English are unfriendly. You may think that they give you looks but sometimes they think that English people do that.

P: Yes, because I know a lot of English people don't like French people so we give them like dirty looks. I know whenever a French person like, when the French exchange was here, I always give the French 'meanies' — apart from the boys of course.

I: I see so it's the girls that get the 'meanies' is it? So if somebody said to you or some French person said 'I think the English are really unfriendly' what would you say to that?

P: If the French . . .?

I: If a French person said to you I think the English are really unfriendly what would you say?

P: I'd say that at least we don't go around like giving the looks that you give us so we just like do it in retaliation.

I: So what would you feel, would you be annoyed if they said that or would you . . .?

P: Yes, I would, I'd be mad because they've got no right to say things like that because I mean they're always, it's the only thing they do, they come in and think — when we had a French exchange they think oh, we'll treat this school as ours now, now we're here.

I: What about the difference between the girls and boys, do you think the boys do that as well?

P: No. I think the boys are a lot friendlier. (156/19) (No experience of France, E group)

Skin colour and sun-tan

The next most frequently cited defining characteristic was skin colour, usually thought to be sun-tanned. There were 20 instances of this (three secondary boys, three secondary girls, seven junior boys and seven junior girls). This choice possibly indicates a tendency to make use of information available to them from other sources. A common piece of knowledge or recorded fact was that the climate in France tends to be warmer, though knowledge of regional variations was not always accurate. There was not a great diversity in this group of responses and so only one typical example is given here (with additional thoughts upon their colour):

P: They are a bit different but they dress the same.
I: How do they look different?
P: Because I think the fact that they have more sun and they are a bit browner makes them look different.
I: Just browner? Is there anything else that makes them look different?
P: Their hair makes them look different because most people have black hair in France. (373/15) (Junior boy, family holiday experience of France, N group)

Hair colour and hair-styles

Examples above have made reference to hair colour. The majority of pupils saw French hair as dark or black. One observant junior boy (M group) who recalled much of his family holiday experience to France was unusual in noticing French children:

P: . . . the children just wear what they want and most of them are fair-haired. They look like they have had — what is the word? Like speckled.
I: Streaks?
P: Yes. (340/10)

References to hair-styles or cuts were more common than to actual hair colour (14 to 7). Again it was the girls, both secondary and primary, who noted this detail. The predominant opinion was that the French tended to have longer hair than the English, and judged by contemporary English fashion this appeared to make those concerned view French fashion as dated or even 'hippy', and was seen as a concomitant of the flared trousers, which caused dismay amongst some. A picture usually selected from the set of photographs was of a teenage girl with shoulder length hair. This choice was rationalised typically thus:

Their hair because they are always sort of scruffy. (Secondary girl, no experience of France, M group.)

She had noticed a few similar pictures in her textbook, as had others. Another girl already quoted for her vehement but ambivalent views elaborated thus upon Frenchwomen:

P: I don't like the way they have their hair because they nearly all of them look like hippies the way they have their hair.
I: Yes, how do you mean?
P: Like it's always long and they don't have any slides in or anything, they haven't got a fringe it's just all hanging down over the face. (156/27)

Behaviour

The last group of responses referred to what might be termed behaviour; some comments upon French character were included in these responses and are indicative of the interviewees' attitudes towards French people (an issue which is detailed below in Chapter 3. Some of the responses suggest that pupils have been exposed to stereotyped images of French behaviour, though it is also clear that there is quite a diversity of opinions:

I: Would you think of French people having a different physical appearance and way of acting from us?
P: They have a different way of acting like, they show their feelings more but I don't know about physical appearance . . . (101/26) (Secondary boy, no experience of France, E group.)

Another secondary boy of school visit experience (M group) thought that the French 'talk loudly and shout a lot', and that this would be an aid in identification. Yet another secondary boy who had not been to France (E group) had seen some French teenagers at his local sports centre. He concluded he could pick them out because they 'played a different style'. This he defined as 'Like, trying to show off I think.' It appeared to the interviewer that this particular respondent was extremely nervous as well as very small for his age and prone to a debilitating skin condition; thus it is not inconceivable that his views of the French and others were somewhat defensive

Again the opposite response was apparent:

I think it is just that they are very friendly. (120/16) (Secondary girl, no experience of France, N group.)

A junior boy added another dimension:

> Yes, I think they're more friendly, they want to help you all the time but they can't help you 'cause they're so keen to help you they forget what they're doing and . . . (367/23) (Family holiday experience, N group)

An unusual comment was made by one junior girl (with no experience of France, M group):

> Because sometimes they walk different to us. Sometimes move a bit more and look a lot more athletic and things. (353/15)

Several interviewees answered the question regarding recognition of groups of French in their 'home town' literally, and responded in terms of group behaviour. Though this might be a rather simplistic interpretation, embedded in these answers are some indications of attitudes towards the French. For example:

P: . . . if they came over here they'd probably look the same as us.
I: Have you seen any of the French visitors at this school?
P: Yes.
I: What was your impression there?
P: . . . I think they seem to talk more than we do, they seem to — like we're more silent than them I think. (154/10) (Secondary girl, no experience of France, E group.)

Another secondary girl (with no experience of France, M group) expressed a view which indicated also some of the feelings about her own environment:

I: Say there was a group of adults not ones your age, would you know if they were French without hearing them speak?
P: . . . I think the way they looked at all the things like the way they walked and acted towards things. Like I think they would be like quiet and that and not talk.
I: You think they would be quieter than English people?
P: Yes with being over England.
I: What about if they were in France?
P: I think they could have a good time really.
I: Would they walk differently — you said about the walking?
P: They would be walking like poshly over here but over there I think it depends who they were really.
I: So when you say they were walking poshly over here, how do you mean?
P: Well like looking about and looking down on everybody and that, snobbish.

I: What, when they come over to Britain? Why do you think they do that when they come to Britain?

P: Well because of all rubbish and they must think everybody is the same putting rubbish down and is not bothered and tidy, giving an impression we're untidy.

I: Oh I see they would think it was a bit messy?

P: Probably think the people were the same. (236/17)

Relationship of experience and gender to perceptions of physical appearance

Analysis of the types of responses made according to age, gender and experience groups is given below in Table 2.2. For this purpose the broad categories used are the same as those used for perceptions of dress above.

From Table 2.2 it appears that having some experience of France reduces the number of those seeing the French as different. More of the primary sample saw the French as different in some respect. It is possible that a greater reliance on stereotypes contributed to this finding. Reduction of interview data to rigorously controlled categories of response was not an initial aim of the project and so further statistical analysis of these differences has not been carried out. Future analysis and research could focus upon the effect of age, gender and experience upon perception as reported in interview data.

TABLE 2.2 *Perception of French physical appearance analysed by age, gender and experience of France*

	No experience of France See French physical appearance as		Some/much experience of France See French physical appearance as	
	Different	*Similar*	*Different*	*Similar*
Secondary boys	7	8	12	8
Secondary girls	17	4	8	7
Primary boys	19	3	8	6
Primary girls	18	5	5	2
Totals	61	20	33	23

A comparison with Table 2.1 'Perception of French dress' above shows that similar relationships obtain, in that the largest group of those who see the French as 'different' are those with no experience of France. For dress, the number of those in the primary groups is greater even than for physical appearance.

'Typical' French people and regional differences

As an adjunct to the main questions upon pupils' perceptions of French dress and physical appearance, pupils were asked if they thought it was possible to describe a 'typical' French person and whether they knew of any regional differences amongst people. Though in the main parts of the discussions about dress and physical appearance pupils were encouraged to focus upon details which they might use to differentiate French people from themselves, it was not assumed that they regarded all these details as evident nationally, though some perhaps did.

'Typical' French people

In being asked about the 'typical French', pupils were therefore being required to decide whether it was possible to generalise unequivocally about a people. It was found that the secondary pupils were less likely to think that it was possible to describe a 'typical' French person than were the primary pupils, and so rejected the possibility. Some pupils' responses suggest attempts at a more complex analysis. Whilst thinking that it was not possible to describe a typical French man or woman or teenager they had noticed some detail which appeared typically French about some groups. Yet others did not reject the possibility of describing the 'typical' French and gave an illustration, either of a stereotyped description or of a more idiosyncratic nature. The percentages of each age and gender group responding in these ways are given below in Table 2.3.

An example of the type of response rejecting the stereotyped image of the French came from this secondary school boy:

P: . . . there's no such thing as a typical Frenchman or woman.
I: But in the way they dress perhaps?
P: The way that they're portrayed say like onion sellers and that but it's not like that. (101/25)

Another secondary boy recollected having anticipated onion sellers on visiting France:

I thought there'd be like people riding bikes with onions and that but it was all different, like, just like over here . . . but they talk different and that . . . (161/13)

TABLE 2.3 *'Typical' French responses analysed by age and gender group*

	Not possible	Not possible but noted some differentiating detail	Typical French description given
Secondary boys	17	3	9
Secondary girls	10	6	11
Primary boys	9	4	14
Primary girls	8	2	14
Totals	44	15	48

More succinctly, but typically, a secondary girl responded to the question:

I: Is it possible to describe a typical French woman or man?
P: Not really because some wear flowery clothes and some wear stripes or patterns on. I couldn't really describe them because they are all different. (175/31)

Partial refutations of the stereotyped view were as follows from a junior boy:

Yes . . . most people say they wear berets and go around — most of them do wear berets but people think they go round in striped tee-shirts selling onions but they don't really do that and they wear normal clothes but they always wear a beret, always do, you can always tell a Frenchman. The French boys and girls they're no different to me, they're just exactly the same. (367/23)

Others suggested they were similar to English people but stressed a characteristic which appeared to typify them:

P: I suppose they (are) sort of funny people. They are always happy.
I: Oh funny in that way?
P: Yes.
I: Do they look — does their general appearance differ from ours?

P: Not really. Apart from the fashion.
I: I mean their physical appearance.
P: Oh — no.
I: So you pick them out mainly from the question of clothing?
P: Yes.
I: General happiness as it were?
P: Yes. They have always got a smile on their faces. You can see that.
(133/19)

Where pupils thought it possible to describe a typical French person some tended to produce stereotyped images and others what appeared to be idiosyncratic ones whose sources were not explicit. In the following example a secondary school girl had no difficulty describing French men but was more hesitant regarding women and teenagers:

I: Do you think it's possible to describe a typical Frenchman?
P: Yes, riding a bike with a black and white stripy tee-shirt with a string of onions round his neck.
I: What about a typical French teenager?
P: . . . No.
I: What about the typical woman then. If there's a typical Frenchman with his onions and his stripy ganzy what about a French woman?
P: . . . Fat with long curly hair, a hat on and a flowery dress. (325/17)

Whilst the former image was known to be one common in the media, in programmes and advertisements, the source of the latter was possibly a recent television programme. This image is the opposite of that suggested by some secondary school pupils:

. . . The men are pretty similar to what ours are, just suits and that, but the women are — they seem more dressy and their clothes sort of go together more in contour maybe — again the perfume. (104/18)

and further, from another boy:

She would be quite slim, most of them are. I've never seen a fat woman in France. (248/25)

About French men he concluded:

. . . they don't go bald as much and they've got like different mouths like they are more rounded and they have bigger noses and the eyes are more distinctive.

A more unusual image of the Frenchman came from another secondary school boy:

> Sometimes like . . . poses and different things like that — dark glasses and white jackets. (246/20)

A rather 'tailored' image made its appearance from time to time:

> The men have like suits on and the women have like . . . three piece suits on and they're all like modern. (208/20)

The responses of many of the primary age group were in the form of the stereotyped image:

I: Is it possible to describe a typical French person, what they look like?
P: I could imagine somebody going round on a bike dressed in trousers up to the knee and stripy tee-shirt with a string of onions round his neck. Selling onions.
I: Where do you get that picture from?
P: Well I have seen it in a book somewhere, I can't remember which book it was but I have seen it in a book. (461/19)

The images of onion and sometimes garlic featured frequently in the responses of the junior sample, not only when asked about the issues of food and physical appearance, but their incidence even coloured some children's views of whether they wished to visit France. Those who had been to France often informed their classmates and friends of various incidents. The following from a junior girl might be said to be a stereotype-confirming recollection:

I: And you said about wearing berets and selling onions, that's what everybody thinks isn't it?
P: 'Cause you like see them.
I: You see them, you saw them doing that?
P: Yes, French onions.
I: So you noticed that particularly did you?
P: Mostly they sell garlic on the market, oh we saw this lady on the ferry and she made herself a salad 'cause she had the things in a bag so she made herself a salad and it was a French person, she was going back on the ferry. (492/23)

For most the typical French person was described in terms of their dress but physical appearance and behaviour were occasionally included:

> He would be — most of them are pretty thin and if you look at his face, small eyes and they just walk about leisurely with — promenade you know, go into restaurants. (361/17) (Primary boy)

Generally it was not thought that it was possible to describe a 'typical' French teenager or child. This could perhaps be a reflection of a greater reliance upon stereotyped images of age groups other than the interviewees' own. As was noted in the sections on dress above the secondary school pupils, girls in particular, were interested in teenage fashion and noted many details of it. This could perhaps have led to a greater amount of differentiation with subsequent realisation that one could not generalise about the group. Stereotypes can only function effectively in the absence of discrimination and it was noticeable that the older age group made less use of stereotyped images than did the younger age group. Some research (e.g. Lambert & Klineberg, 1967) has suggested that as children pass through secondary school years they learn to use their own culture's stereotypes about other cultures. However, it would appear that with respect to the French, about whom the secondary school sample had received three years teaching, the older pupils produced fewer stereotyped images than did the younger pupils. Whether this is a function of education alone it is not possible to say, but one might conclude optimistically that it has some ameliorating function in that, as was seen above, some secondary pupils were keen to refute the stereotyped image. Against the idea that young people are socialised into their culture's images of others, must also be set the conclusions regarding increased capacities for differentiation (Harvey, Hunt & Schroder, 1961). Thus for some of the secondary school pupils an optimum time for receiving information about other peoples would have been reached. It was clear from interviews with some of the class teachers that they saw it as part of their role to reduce stereotyped and antagonistic views of the French (Chapter 5).

In short whilst certain images had a powerful hold amongst the primary sample, they were being eroded amongst the older sample.

Regional differences

Very little information upon regional differences amongst people was apparent. As noted above no knowledge of the history of the different regions was forthcoming, and responses upon regional differences were largely negative, stating that there were none. Those which made reference to physical differences did so in terms of skin colour relating to variations in climate, (as detailed in the sections above on physical appearance). The few differences in dress noted concentrated also upon climate variations. There was one recollection of what were probably regional costumes seen at a fair.

One secondary school girl could be seen to be making use of her knowledge of her own culture to decide upon others:

I: Do you think they might look any different?

P: Maybe like in Scotland, right up in the very highlands of Scotland I suppose the older generation could maybe dress quite different from what we do. Maybe in Paris the elderly might dress a bit different. (183/79)

Three secondary pupils saw differences in terms of Parisian versus other regions' styles, for example:

In Paris they would be — I think they would be more, more fashionable than the little villages by themselves. I think they won't be so — they wouldn't have so good clothes. (131/20)

Information upon regional variation followed therefore the same lines of thought as those detailed in the dress and physical appearance sections. It appeared that as in consideration of other issues such as housing and geography, little information upon the diversity of France had been either transmitted or recalled from lessons. Items mentioned, such as regional costumes, were the product of chance encounters on holiday, and references to skin colour variation were probably the result of reasoning from knowledge of the climate, rather than as a function of teaching.

Religion and 'Growing up' in France

The topics of 'Religion' and 'Growing up' were discussed with a sub-sample of the total of interviewees. 'Religion', it was already known, is not an issue introduced in any direct or explicit way into the textbook. Yet it can be reasoned that knowledge of any society must include some familiarity with religious institutions and beliefs. The notion of 'growing up' was intended as a means of investigating pupils' perceptions of the life cycle and its link with social institutions, again because it was considered that this is a fundamental aspect of any society. The sub-sample was chosen to represent the different school classes and the three levels of ethnocentricity within each class. The distinction between primary and secondary pupils allows us to consider how and to what extent the teaching of French increases and refines what pupils know. We shall consider each topic and age group separately.

'Religion'

Primary pupils

The 'ethnocentric' group had little or no knowledge of religion in

France. Of the 17 pupils questioned, 9 said they did not know anything, 6 offered answers which indicated little knowledge or a reasoning that it would be 'the same' as in England, and 2 had some definite view or information. Those in the second group can be represented by the following quotations:

P: Don't think they prefer Roman Catholics I think they'll just be — they might go to the churches in towns but I don't think they'll go very much.
I: What makes you think that?
P: . . . I don't know.
I: It's just the impression you have?
P: Yes. (491/16)

P: The religion . . . I should think that they were, yes, they would just be probably the same as us, except that there might be a few more pagans. No, I think they'd be more like us, yes. (361/24)

The two who were more expansive differ radically in the basis of their accounts. The first had been to France with his family and extrapolates from what he had noticed while there:

I: What about churches and religion in France, what have you heard about that?
P: I think they're more religious than us.
I: What makes you say that?
P: I don't know, there's lots of churches, lots of them.
I: What kind . . .
P: On Sunday when they're at the beach no-one comes to the beach like on Sunday.
I: So do you think of the French as being religious, very religious?
P: Yes.
I: What religion are they?
P: I don't know (548/18)

He does not need to use his imagination as the second does. This account merits quotation at length as an indication of the willingness of some pupils to co-operate and the need for the interviewer to clarify the basis of understanding in the interview:

I: What have you heard about the Church and religion?
P: I don't know anything about . . . Probably less churches than we have. I

don't think they believe in it as much as us, but I think they have churches.

I: Why do you think they don't believe as much as us?

P: Because they probably believe in a God that France, someone from France, a God that died about hundred years ago or something. They might have a statue or something in the town about him.

I: So they might believe in a different God?

P: Yes.

I: Where does the God come from that we believe in?

P: Er . . . I don't know he's not . . .

I: So you think that each country might have a different person or a different God to worship?

P: I think all England will have like God and France will have this French person that died about a hundred years ago. I think they sort of have different Gods or something.

I: When did our God die about? A long time ago?

P: Yes.

I: How long ago do you think that would be?

P: Two thousand years ago.

I: Longer ago than the French God was it?

P: Probably. Probably just a man that died but he was in the town or something.

I: Has anyone ever told you anything about this?

P: No, just guessing.

I: Have you ever thought about it before or is that the first time you have thought about it today?

P: Yes, the first time. (341/24)

The 'non-ethnocentric' group asked about religion were 22 pupils and fell into three similar groups but in different proportions to the 'ethnocentric' group: 10 in the first, 5 in the second, and 7 in the third. The answers of those in the second group were similar to the corresponding answers of 'ethnocentric' pupils; for example:

I: What have you heard about the churches and religion in France?

P: Well, I haven't but I suppose they could be a bit the same as ours. It could be the same religion or a different religion sort of thing if you want to go that far.

I: So do you think there is just the one religion in France?

P: Well I don't know really. In different parts they might have different religions you don't know. (454/26)

or:

I: No? OK. What about the churches and the religion in France do you know anything about that?
P: No . . . I know they're mostly Catholics. (511/18)

A visit to France does not necessarily clarify views:

I: What have you heard about religion and churches in France?
P: . . . That they are nearly just the same as ours really.
I: What religion are people in France?
P: I don't know.
I: Did you see any churches when you were there?
P: No. (427/30)

This contrasts with a pupil who had something quite definite to say because he had noticed and even visited churches on his visit:

I: What about things like churches and religion, what have you heard about churches and religion in France?
P: . . . They're very, some of them are a different religion and some of them aren't in the religion or some of them are in this religion and it gets complicated. They've got churches everywhere and cathedrals everywhere and when they're very interested in that sort of stuff.
I: What religion are they?
P: I don't know.
I: But you've seen churches you say.
P: Yes.
I: And visited churches.
P: Once when you could go and have a look round. (367/28)

Although the accounts of religion in France from those who do offer positive answers are not as extreme and imagination-driven as the last quotation in the ethnocentric group, there are none the less some striking accounts:

I: Tell me a bit more about the religion then.
P: Well they could have like, they might love someone else and in England they might love God and another bomb underneath his car or in his exhaust and probably blow up.
I: You said a different religion to us, what religion are they then?
P: They're French religion and we're British religion, they speak different and we speak different.

I: And we are — what are we?
P: Church of England things like that do you mean?
I: Yes. What are the French then?
P: I don't know really. (561/20)

The association of different language and different religion could account for the unexpected opinions from these non-ethnocentric pupils. The relationship is made quite clear by the same pupil earlier in the interview:

I: Yes. So you — so let's imagine you were talking to a friend of yours here in the class who's not been abroad, and you're describing what it is, what a foreigner is, what would you say then?
P: I'd say that a foreigner was somebody who talks different and comes from a different religion. (561/7)

In the medium group, 21 pupils were asked what they knew about religion and churches in France and 19 of them said they knew nothing. A few were asked if they thought there would be many differences but in such cases, as elsewhere, their response was to say 'the same'.

Of the three pupils in this group who had been to France, one had not seen any churches, one did not remember seeing any — 'I don't think they're that common' (410/28) — and only one had observed the buildings themselves:

I: Well we've talked about schools, we've talked about houses, what about things like — what do you know about religion and churches in France, what have you heard about that?
P: . . . Not really much, no.
I: Did you notice any churches when you were there?
P: No, I don't think so, like we were spending our time on the beaches and that.
I: Yes.
P: We did notice quite a few very tall churches and they were really pretty decorated and they're more decorated on the inside than the English churches. They have beautiful organs and we do have beautiful ones but I think these ones are more spectacular than ours.
I: What religion do you think they are?
P: I think they just believe in God just the same as us.
I: Yes, we're Church of England and so on aren't we, I mean in that way?
P: Yes.

I: Are they also Church of England?
P: Pardon?
I: Are they also Church of England?
P: No, I don't think so.
I: But you don't know?
P: No. (565/23)

One other pupil, when pressed with the question 'What religion are people in France?' first hesitated and then assimilated to British culture; '. . . I think they would be Church of England'.

The general lack of knowledge may arise from a lack of interest and experience of religion in pupils' own lives. One pupil spontaneously supplied the information that she is a church-goer but answered the same question about the religion of French people quite categorically:

I: The other thing I haven't asked you about is things like religion and churches. What have you heard about religion and churches in France?
P: Not much. I go to church in England but I haven't been to a church in a foreign country or heard anything about them.
I: What religion do you think they are in France?
P: I don't know. I haven't any idea. (424/27)

Secondary pupils

Secondary pupils in the ethnocentric group remain largely ignorant of religion in France and in this respect do not differ from the corresponding primary pupils. Nine pupils were asked what they knew of religion in France and only one could give any definite account which was accurate. Four had nothing to say and the four others were at best vague in their information. They were asked what they thought was the 'dominant' or 'majority' religion in France. The hesitation in the following examples may reflect both a lack of knowledge of France and a general lack of interest in religion:

I: What is the majority religion in France do you know?
P: . . . Christian.
I: What kind of Christian. Protestant, Catholic?
P: Don't know. (163/30)

I: What's the dominant religion in France?
P: . . . Catholic, I think. (290/24)

In one case the conversation between pupil and interviewer takes an interesting turn. The pupil seems to be taking the conversation at a tangent to the issue of religion in France and talks about matters which may have been discussed in R.E. lessons (see below, where a pupil specifically mentions R.E.), or in History which she mentions:

I: Now I wondered if you could tell me what you think it's like to grow up in France, what sort of things do you think a child might have to do when it's growing up? Do you think there are any religious festivals to do with growing up in France?

P: No, I don't think there is . . . like if they choose to do religion they have a choice, but the country has all different religions and they don't all have religious festivals to do with growing up.

I: No. Sorry, you mean that in the country it's got several religions and you could choose — have I got it right?

P: Yes, so some have festivals and some don't.

I: Yes. Have you ever heard anything about the main religions or the main churches?

P: No.

I: You mentioned about the Indians and their religion. What do you think of French religion?

P: Probably just the same as England but they have like — they don't have Church of England.

I: No?

P: They probably have Christianity unless it didn't spread over there.

I: Well I wondered if you'd ever heard about it spreading over there?

P: No, we had a bit in history. Like when people had to flee and they fled to different countries.

I: Where do you think Christianity has fled to? I mean spread to, sorry . . . No, I mean which countries do you think in Europe have Christian churches?

P: Probably America and France and Germany.

I: What about places like Italy and Holland?

P: They seem to have one main . . . religion. They might have small people who believe in Christianity.

I: So what do you think their religion is?

P: . . . Don't know.

I: What about Holland?

P: . . . The same as other countries, 'cause they're small so they don't really have a main religion, like just, like small ones.

I: Sorry, I don't quite understand, when you say small ones which . . .

P: Small groups that like believe in different . . .

I: Oh, I see so there might be lots of different small churches and not one main one, you mean?
P: Yes.
I: I get it. (121S/26)

With another pupil the interviewer appears to have wanted to establish how much the pupil knew about religion in England — aware perhaps of the problem of general disinterest — before asking about France. The interviewer may have been alerted to the issue by the pupil's implication that her knowledge is entirely dependent on R.E. lessons:

I: So you mentioned religion a bit. Say you had to tell someone what you think a normal sort of life for a French girl would be like what would it be like, what happens when they're young, do you think they have any religious festivals to do with growing up?
P: No, well the only religious festival I know is like Hindus and Jews because we do about that in R.E.
I: What do you think they do in the rest of Europe, what religion do they have?
P: Birthdays and Christmas and New Year — that's the only ones I can think of — like Easter.
I: So what, what religion is it in England?
P: . . . Pardon?
I: What religion do you think it is in England?
P: What do you mean?
I: Well what church is it?
P: Methodist.
I: Yes, so what do you think they have in France?
P: I don't know. (156/30)

At an earlier stage in the interview this pupil had begun to associate French attitudes to food with being religious, although the idiosyncracy of her views is something she readily admits:

I: No. What do you think French people think about their food, you said that they had more sort of meat and things, do you think they think differently about their food to English people?
P: Yes, because I tend to think that a lot of the French people are like religious type of people. I don't know why, I've just got this thing about religious people at the moment.
I: Yes, go on.
P: Not religious myself though.

I: No, tell us what you think. The French are religious you mean?
P: Yes.
I: What sort of?
P: Like 'cause they're always having like meat and like when you hear of Jesus here when he had his like Passover or something they had wine and all that stuff and that's another thing they're always drinking wine.
I: Yes, so they drink it because of it's significance with religion?
P: Yes. (156/17)

The only pupil in this ethnocentric group with any substantial knowledge relied on specific knowledge from the teacher and on a school visit to France:

P: They go to church on a night before like Christmas.
I: What on Christmas Eve?
P: Yes, we did it in school in second year.
I: Oh, did you, who was that with?
P: Mrs —
I: Can you remember what religion — what church they are?
P: Like some people when we went to X (a small town in France) were Catholics and they had to go to church when they were over there. So you know there is a Catholic church.
I: Are there any other churches?
P: I don't know. They don't do R.E. at school. I don't know why they don't because it is compulsory over here. They can do it. Some schools do it but everybody does it but there's nobody doesn't like do it but other schools don't do it at all.
I: Well it does vary from country to country and there are reasons but you know there are some Catholic churches. Do you think there are any other like we have Protestant or equivalent?
P: There was plenty of churches around like but don't know what they were. (301/15)

The proportion of divisions within the group of non-ethnocentric pupils with respect to knowledge of religion are very similar to those in the ethnocentric group. Thirteen pupils were asked (compared to 9 in the ethnocentric group) of which 6 (4) knew nothing, 5 (4) had some rather vague notions and 2 (1) had definite and reasonably accurate information.

Of the two with definite knowledge, only one explains the source:

I: If you were to imagine growing up in France, right from being a baby, in this country the first thing that happens is you get christened and so on, would you imagine that as being different, to grow up in France?

P: No, I wouldn't think so. I would think they are more religious than us.

I: They are more religious?

P: There are not many British people that religious, not in England anyway.

I: When you say they are more religious, what do you mean?

P: They seem to attend church more often than British people do and they have a lot of old churches in towns from the past that they still use to bring the community together for religious purposes.

I: Which particular religion, can you think of any one as being dominant?

P: I think Catholic.

I: Have you seen pictures of French churches and so on?

P: I have seen in R.E. a programme on a Centre run by these brothers, like a sort of monastery thing, where everybody from Europe can go and stay a couple of weeks and work and pray and everything. It was in a town in southern France. I've forgotten the name.

I: So you saw something there of the religious life. To go back to the growing up business, do you think of people going to church a lot as they grow up?

P: Yes, I think so. (104/30)

The second pupil has heard of the tradition of celebrating one's nameday:

I: Right, right, now I'm going to ask you a little bit about growing up in France. If you can imagine a child growing up from birth to your age — you're 14 now are you, yes? OK. What would it be like, would it be very similar to the way we grow up?

P: Yes.

I: What happens, what kind of church do they go to for instance?

P: I think it would be a Catholic church.

I: Would you be christened at birth?

P: I think so.

I: OK. Do they have any religious festivals to do with growing up in France?

P: Well they have two birthdays, you're called after a saint and you have your birthday when you were born and their birthdays, the saints. (273/33)

Otherwise pupils said they did not know anything because it had not been 'done' in lessons, saying typically 'we haven't got up to that yet' (137/20) and in the following quotation the pupil indicates that he does not expect to acquire knowledge from any other source:

I: What about religion and going to church and so on?
P: Same as England. I think most of them are Christians. There might be a few Catholics. Well they are all Christian like. I don't know. We have done nothing about, like, religion.
I: Without doing it have you seen anything about it elsewhere?
P: No, not really. (133/25)

The fact that very little account is given of religion in French lessons is particularly clear from the next quotation. This pupil is surely not the only one to have heard of and perhaps seen Notre Dame Cathedral as a Paris monument, and in many lessons in which pupils learn to give and understand directions 'l'église' is a frequently used vocabulary item. Yet in both cases it is probably rarely that the teacher explains the cultural meaning of 'Notre Dame' or 'l'église', and 'the church in it' as this pupil says:

I: Well one of the things I have almost forgotten is the question of the church and so on. Do you know anything about religion in France? What kind of church they have and so on?
P: Catholic I think.
I: Just Catholic?
P: I think so, I think that is the only one I have heard of.
I: Have you seen any pictures of famous churches at all?
P: No, not in France.
I: No. Notre Dame?
P: Oh, I have heard of it. I don't think we did anything about the church in it though. (313/40)

The medium group is again similar to previous groups. Eight pupils had no knowledge, 3 had some vague notion and 3 had something definite to say. Their responses are also similar in content. The only pupil whose response adds to the general picture indicates that he deduces his information from the media:

P: I think it would be most — I don't think there's like many church-goers in France as there are in this country — well certainly not all Christian church-goers anyway. I don't think — I think we're much the same — same sort of ages where you go to school and go to the next highest stage of school.
I: Yes, yes. What do you know more precisely about religion in France?
P: I think it's mostly Roman Catholic, I think. I don't know, I think so

from what I've like heard. Like the Pope I think he's — he goes to — I've seen when he's been to France — there's always been a lot of people there so I think it's mainly Roman Catholic, I think.
I: Yes. And the number of people going to church, do you think it's what, terribly high?
P: No, I don't think they're very big church-goers. (103/32)

A second pupil also refers to information on R.E. teaching in French schools. Both remembered this as information from their teachers, although they were in different classes:

I: Do you think they have any religious festivals to do with growing up?
P: No. Don't have R.E. I don't think.
I: No. Do you think they have any churches to go to?
P: . . . I think they will have but not many go.
I: No. Do you know what sort of church it is?
P: . . . More like a Sunday School thing.
I: You have no idea that there are several different churches for different religions. I just wondered if you had ever heard what the main church is in France. Like in England you can have Methodist, Church of England, Catholic, I wondered if you had ever heard which church is most common in France?
P: No, I don't think so.
I: You are quite right about them not having R.E. at school so have you been told about that as well?
P: Miss X told us.
I: Was that this year?
P: Yes.
I: So she was telling you a bit about the schools then was she? Did she tell you why they don't have it?
P: I think — she did but I think it was because you are not made to believe anything . . . or not made to . . . some people don't believe in God but you learn about God and if you don't believe in it it is just pointless. I think in late years in France you are allowed to take it if you want. (295/25)

It is probable that the topic was, however, not religion as such but life in schools.

Table 2.4 summarises the responses from primary and secondary pupils and indicates two principal conclusions. First, the level of ethnocentricity has no significant bearing on the degree of knowledge within the group. With the exception of a group of 7 non-ethnocentric primary pupils who had definite notions, the tendency in each group is for a large proportion of vague or non-existent information to outweigh the few who have some clear ideas. Second, there is no significant difference between primary and secondary pupils. Although two pupils recalled — without mentioning the difference between state and 'école libre' — they had been told that R.E. is not taught in schools, it is clear that French teaching over 3 years does not include an account of religious life in France. This is in a sense not surprising since as we said earlier there is no significant mention in the textbook and as we shall see in Chapter 5, teachers are guided by the textbook.

On the other hand, pupils in secondary school show no signs of the wilder assumptions that the French are 'mostly Jews' (492/16) or have their own God, evident in some of the primary pupils. This may of course be due to greater general maturity or a more realistic view of France in other respects influencing assumptions about that which has not been expressly taught. In the final analysis these two factors cannot be totally separated.

'Growing up'

The decision to ask pupils about 'growing up' in France was based on the notion that an anthropological analysis of French culture would take as

TABLE 2.4 *Knowledge of 'religion' by age and ethnocentricity group*

	None	Knowledge Vague	Definite
Primary:			
E group	9	6	2
M group	19	1	1
N group	10	5	7
Secondary:			
E group	4	4	1
M group	8	3	3
N group	6	5	2

one dimension the life-cycle of the individual, including initiation into different stages of life and into religious and other institutions.

There was a major difficulty in formulating questions which would tap this dimension since it was assumed — rightly, it seems from the observations in Chapter 5 — that this kind of presentation of French life would not figure in lessons or in the textbook. The question was all the more difficult to ask of primary pupils for whom neither knowledge of France in general nor this format of presentation of the life-cycle were available in school. It was felt, nonetheless, necessary to establish a basis for comparison between primary and secondary in this aspect of culture as in others.

In practice the formulation of the question seemed to leave interviewers uneasy, and primary pupils found it difficult:

I: So do you think it would be very different to grow up in France than it would be to grow up in this country?
P: Yes.
I: What would it be like to grow up in France? How would it be different?
P: . . . You've been used to England for so long and you just came to a different new country and you're not very keen on it.
I: Let's imagine that you were born in France, if you were born in France and not here in this country and you'd been brought up in France and your family and your friends are in France, do you think it would be very different?
P: Yes, it would be very different then if you were born in France.
I: What would it be like?
P: . . .
I: It's a bit hard is it?
P: . . . (476/20)

Pupils' answers included the assimilation of saying it would be 'the same'. A very small number appeared to see the point and attempt to use their imagination to answer and, perhaps, please the interviewer:

I: So on the whole do you think it would be very different to grow up in France than it would be to grow up in this country?
P: It might be — they'll maybe do different things to us like.
I: Like what, can you think what?
P: Like they could . . . their parents might be like different to what ours — they could be different and could like let the children go in different ways to us and they could like just let them grow up like, they could treat them different.

I: Why do you think they might treat their children differently?
P: I don't know, they could learn their children different things and it would be like make them like different to us like to grow up.
I: Can you think of an example at all of what might be different?
P: Er . . . they could like learn them to do things like what we like could know about but couldn't do like.
I: What sort of things?
P: I don't know, you sometimes see girls with French plaits in and er . . . like they could like just learn the children different things in schools they could learn different things and like grow up in a different way.
I: So do you think if you'd grown up in France and not in this country you might have been a different person?
P: Yes, could be a different personality and . . . (484/25)

Another kind of response was to concentrate on different environmental factors: the schools, the language, the clothes, the buildings would be different, for example:

I: Imagine that you were born in France, do you think it would be very different to be born and brought up in France?
P: Yes.
I: You think it would be. How would it be different?
P: . . . Don't know.
I: Do you think you would be a different person if you'd been born and brought up in France?
P: Yes.
I: In what sort of way do you think you might be different?
P: . . . Because I would speak different and I might dress different and different television programmes, that's all. (362/22)

One pupil — in the ethnocentric group — spontaneously gave evidence of an ability to decentre at the same time as assuming that the experience would be in essence the same:

I: Do you think it would be different if you were a French child instead of an English child, do you think you would be very different?
P: No, not really. I might think England was a strange country and that, I don't really know, maybe different, yes. (378/14)

Another put what may be the same point in a different formulation, that one would be 'used to it':

I: And growing up in France how would that be, what would it be like to grow up in France?

P: It would be easy 'cause they'd just get used to it like we do.

I: Would they have the same kind of things like getting baptised and getting married and all that sort of thing?

P: Ah, they'd get married and get baptised but I don't think they'd have everything that we grew up like.

I: What would be the difference then?

P: I don't think they'd have the same toys and like when we're born like, do you think that over there everybody would crowd round like they do here?

I: Perhaps.

P: And the baby gets lots of presents here, I don't know whether it does over there. (564/17)

Here it is also possible to see the interviewer linking the question with the framework of the life-style and, on this rare occasion, obtaining a response which can be interpreted within that framework. Given the lack of knowledge of religious festivals in France — and elsewhere, perhaps — it is not surprising that very few pupils could respond to this kind of question. It may be that they would not be able to understand the same kind of question in relation to their own lives.

It is however quite clear from the vast majority of the primary pupils that they have no substantial certain knowledge about the life-cycle as it might affect people up to, say, the age of twenty. It can be argued therefore that any perception of this kind found among secondary pupils could be largely if not exclusively attributed to French lessons.

It may be useful to state briefly at this point what kind of knowledge might be framed in the structure of socialisation of French children and young adults. The life-cycle can be seen as a number of events, usually of a religious and educational nature: *baptême, école maternelle, école primaire, première communion, entrée au collège, brevet d'études, entrée au lycée, baccalauréat ou CAP, service militaire, entrée a l'université ou profession, fiançailles, mariage* . . . The order of events may vary slightly and *service militaire* need not affect all — particularly women but also some men. To know the development of childhood, adolescence and adulthood in France — at a time when they are in the middle of a similar cycle themselves — pupils could be expected to know of these stages and of their significance. It can be said unequivocally before more detailed analysis that there are no substantial signs of this kind of framework — or indeed of much of the content — in the knowledge of secondary pupils. A most striking example is that only two of them appeared to know that their male contempories in France would have to face the probability of being drafted for *service militaire*.

Given that secondary pupils have both a greater maturity and more exposure to information about France, it seemed reasonable to ask them how they perceived the process of growing up in France and whether they thought they might prefer it to growing up in England. The fact that a few pupils clearly found the issue comprehensible and interesting suggests that the questions were potentially valuable. Only a few answers of any substance were obtained however. The overwhelming majority were extremely non-committal in their responses, saying either that they did not know because it had not been covered in lessons or that they assumed there are no significant differences.

In essence two issues were of concern to pupils: relationships in the family and opportunities for work. Relationships in the family in France were said by one pupil to be 'close' and she explains why she thinks so:

I: I was going to ask you a little bit about one or two other things like what you think it is like to grow up in France. I wondered what you thought it would be like to grow up as a French girl in France. What do you think it would be like?

P: Well I suppose it would be about the same as here. The family would be very close, you could always turn to the family if you had problems.

I: When you say they are closer, how do you mean?

P: Like when they have like a meal, the family is all together and I should think the brothers and sisters and Mum and Dad and I should think the Aunties are all together as well.

I: When did you say they would get together?

P: Like at mealtimes.

I: Oh, they all eat together usually?

P: Yes at the main meal.

I: Do you think they do that more than English people?

P: Yes because everytime they get the main meal of the day they will all like sit round the table but over here I don't think people are bothered about that.

I: Several people have said that they thought French people eat together more. Have you heard much about that, has your teacher said anything about that or in the books?

P: Yes, she said when they had the main meal they all sit round the table and like talk and that and it can last a few hours like a long time and like here everybody like rushes the food down to see the television or go out. Like over there they are close. (236/19)

Others considered relationships more in terms of parents being 'strict'. The origins of this impression are both in the textbook and in personal experience:

I: So growing up in France compared with here is a bit better is it?
P: Yes, I think so, yes.
I: How do you imagine French parents being — what French parents are like?
P: I think they're a bit stricter with their children. They have to come in a lot earlier than we do . . .
I: And what's given you that impression?
P: . . . I don't know really but I just think they'd be a lot stricter 'cause of the textbook. I've read things about what they have to do — like we read a passage once about a girl she had to be in for half past nine I think it was.
I: You read it?
P: Yes. (167/37)

In a second case the interviewer attempted to establish on what basis the pupil thought French parents were strict:

I: Do you think there are any things about family like that would be different? Do you think that children and teenagers have a different kind of family life to English ones or not?
P: I don't think they would go out as much and go to discos as much and enjoy themselves as much.
I: You think it's a bit stricter?
P: Yes.
I: Is that an impression you got from French people over there or any you've met here?
P: From over there.
I: What sort of time do you think they might have to be in?
P: About 8 o'clock or something like that.
I: What sort of time do you and your friends have to be in around here?
P: About 10.
I: Yes, is that at the weekend or week as well?
P: About half past ten at the weekend and about half nine to ten o'clock during the week. (298/9)

A third pupil sees the issue in more relativist terms and it is unfortunate that in this case the interviewer did not pursue the question of sources of impressions:

I: Yes. On the whole do you think, how have you visualised people of your age in France, what's it like to be growing up in France, would that be the same as here? What are parents like, French parents say?

P: I think it would be very different — very strict . . . well it's just that, see, I don't know but it's what I've been learning in different places — the way they're brought up they're brought up that way, the way we're brought we — see, it's the difference, they might think oh, smoking at their age — at my age — is nothing where for us it is — it's just the way they're brought up. (283/36)

One exception to this view was evident in one girl who contrasts what she had seen in the French metropolis with life in her own small town, to the detriment of the latter:

I: What do you think it is like growing up in France? Say you had to describe a child growing up from birth, say a French girl, what do you think their life is like?

P: Seem to be more grown-up than English are.

I: Yes, that's interesting. How do you mean?

P: They act more grown-up.

I: Is that both the boys and the girls?

P: Yes.

I: Is that ones you have met or ones who have been over here? Why do you think they are more grown-up?

P: Ones I saw in Paris.

I: What sort of things can they do that you can't do in England at your age? Is there anything — do you think they can go out more or go out less?

P: More.

I: You think they are allowed to go out? What can they go out to do you think? Clubs, discos, pubs. Have they got pubs to go to?

P: I think they have. More discos.

I: Is that all over or just in the towns?

P: All over I think. (295/23)

In this case, the interviewer seems to have felt the need to help the pupil articulate her point. A few seconds later she is more explicit about the basis of her comparison:

I: Do you think it is better to grow up in France or England?

P: . . . France I think.

I: Yes — why would you say that?

P: . . . More problems in England . . . doesn't seem to be any like drugs or anything like that in France. Things like that. They don't seem to drink as much . . . all of them are friendly more.

I: What to each other?

P: Mm.

I: Do you think people in England aren't very friendly or what?

P: No but I mean if you go to a disco and look at a girl then you get kicked in. That's what usually happens around our disco.

I: Who kicks them in?

P: Like you look at them and you say what are you looking at and there is trouble always.

I: Is there one near here that you can go to?

P: There used to be but this lad kicked the Manager in and they won't have them no more. Just the one down at St. Paul's. (295/23)

The contrast between the social environment of the pupils and that portrayed in textbooks or glimpsed during brief visits to France is an issue which is discussed in terms of textbook realism in Chapter 5. It is an issue which is not often discussed in the literature on language teaching but of which teachers in depressed areas are aware as will be evident from interviews with teachers in Chapter 5. In the questions on life-cycle, two pupils mentioned the associated issue of youth unemployment, particularly harsh in their areas, for example:

I: In general, it's a very general question but do you think as somebody growing up you would prefer to do so in this country or in France?

P: . . . I don't think I'd be bothered which really. I don't think there's much difference really.

I: Right. You wouldn't see there being much . . .

P: I might prefer it in France 'cause I don't think there's as much unemployment as there is in this country. When you leave school there's not much chance of you going straight into a job in this country where in France it might be a bit better chance.

I: That's something which when you leave school at 16 or so do you mean or what?

P: It depends if you — I think either case — I suppose if you stay on and get qualifications you might have a better chance but you can't go straight into a job.

I: So you see that as probably being a bit better in France?

P: Yes, I think so, yes. (103/34)

The paucity of responses on this theme of the life-cycle can perhaps be largely attributed to lack of exposure to this kind of information in the classroom. Other sources of knowledge, such as the media, are unlikely to be explicitly concerned with the life-cycle. Two pupils mentioned the point, with opposing opinions as to what might be desirable:

P: . . . We haven't done much about that really.
I: You haven't done that?
P: We usually talk about children about 14 or 15, sort of our age.
I: Yes.
P: We don't talk about babies or things like that.
I: Would that be interesting to you or are you more interested in people your age?
P: No, I'm more interested in people of our age, the things they do, things they like.
I: And older ones — people up to age 20 say?
P: . . . No, we don't do anthing about 20 we do about 15 or 16, we do about school children, secondary school children mostly and we do about the parents sometimes.
I: About them being stricter?
P: Yes.
I: What else?
P: . . . Nothing else really. (167/38)

The second is more detailed in his answer and also agrees with the interviewer's suggestion about the need to extend the range of interest:

I: You enjoy that, yes. What's your impression of the way people grow up in France? I mean, is that . . .?
P: Well I don't think that's quite as good as over here because we've been learning about French school recently and they're allowed to smoke in the playgrounds in some schools and all this smoking's nothing it's not that much different but I'd rather grow up over here.
I: Would you see them being — there being — this type of thing of being christened and going on to school at five and then on to secondary school and so on, how do you see sort of the life story of a young French person?
P: I'd say the school routine of growing up as being about the same but the discipline I don't know if that's as much, I'm not sure when they leave school what . . .
(inaudible question)
P: What age?

I: Well what age for a start, yes.

P: Well we haven't done about this at school yet, we've just done about the school life, concentrating on children our own age, so I don't know what happens when they leave school.

I: Right. What about — concentrating on your age not on younger children.

P: Well as you come up through the school we've done about whatever age but nothing about junior school or anything like this, you know, just starting senior school.

I: Would that interest you to do a bit more about that kind of thing, and say about what happens to people after school and so on?

P: Yes, I'd like to know like. If the junior school's the same then what happens after, yes that would be good. (310/34)

In short, this topic was little known to pupils even after three years in secondary school. As with 'religion', the lack of explicit attention to the topic in lessons associated with the lack of knowledge, irrespective of pupils' level of ethnocentricity or the kinds of experience they might have had outside school. This provides some support for a hypothesis that in some topics the effect — or lack of effect — of French teaching is crucial.

Class Case Studies

Anyone who listens to teachers talking about their pupils quickly notices that, in fact, they tend to talk about their classes, i.e. they talk about pupils in terms of the groupings they belong to for teaching and learning purposes. Individual pupils will be mentioned because of their high ability in a subject or because of their particularly poor behaviour in class or because of an unusual characteristic of some other kind. Individual characters are not forgotten, but classes are also perceived as having a group character. Pupils themselves, who often belong to different group-ings for different subjects, are also aware of the character of the class and its relationship with a teacher — and the effect on their own learning.

It was this kind of observation which led to the decision to concentrate on four specific combinations of class and teacher in the investigation of the teaching process, described in Chapter 5. Individual teachers had been observed with different classes — of varying age and achievement level — and it was evident that the teaching 'style', as far as cultural information and knowledge were concerned, was a function of the particular, unique combination of a specific group of pupils with a specific teacher. This observation was confirmed by teachers themselves as reflecting their own feelings about classes and the way they taught them.

It will also be pointed out in Chapter 3 that statistical analysis indicated a significant association between pupils' attitudes towards French people and their membership of a particular teaching group. Of course this variable is not a simple one; it probably reflects other significant variables such as gender and pupils' experience of other countries. It is, however, a further indication of the validity of observations in the classroom and analysis of teachers' and pupils' talk about their teaching and learning. In short a class of pupils learns as a class and has a shared awareness of teacher and subject, and a shared store of knowledge of the subject as a consequence of their particular learning experience.

For this reason we compare here the 'combined' knowledge of each of the four classes with respect to themes and attitudes treated in interviews. Then, in Chapter 5, we shall describe in some detail the teaching process observed in each class which can be associated with the classes' knowledge. This does not of course mean that here or later we claim that the 'process' of teaching is solely responsible for the 'product' of knowledge analysed here. For, on the one hand, in Chapter 4 we shall indicate the strength of other sources and influences and on the other we do not claim to have elicited in interview all the knowledge of French culture which might have been presented in class and retained by pupils; nor do we claim to present here the whole of what we did elicit. The picture can never be complete but we can sketch the main outlines. Factors such as personal experience, recall of acquaintances' accounts of France, and pupils' motivation need to be acknowledged when attempting to assess the provenance of information. Variations in recall of material presented in the classroom obviously modified class bodies of information. However, it was found that class differences were apparent in emphasis, accuracy and interest.

First, summaries of each class are presented without examples. These are followed by comparisons of the four classes across some main issues. Some sub-issues are then illustrated more extensively in order to offer some insight into the nature of the evidence and the range of views, and other sub-issues are summarised. Though it was noted that classes were at different stages of the course in their third year, information provided in the first two years was often recollected, in addition to recently covered material.

Attitudes

In order to facilitate comparison, a brief summary of class attitudes towards the French is presented first in anticipation of the analysis of attitudes in Chapter 3.

The statistical data presented in Chapter 3 shows that the summed attitudes of three of the observed classes were very similar in being at the top of the list of all 16 primary and secondary classes. Class 1 (the top set of Newfarm) occupies position 1 and Class 4 (the top set of Hillside) occupies position 2. Interestingly, Class 2 (the medium achievement class of Newfarm) occupies the third position in the ranking, which is obviously higher than those of all Hillside classes, except Class 4. The medium achievement class of Hillside, Class 3, occupies the seventh position.

It has already been noted that interaction with factors such as gender, may have affected class scores. In Classes 1 and 4 the number of girls far outweighed the number of boys. In Classes 2 and 3 the number of girls outweighed that of the boys in similar proportion, and yet they differed in attitudes expressed. It will be seen below that pupil perception of teachers' contributions to the cultural aspects of French lessons varied from class to class. However, the relationship of teacher input to pupil attitudes to French people, is complex. Several sources, such as classroom observation, interviews with teachers, and pupil perception, indicate, for example, that the teacher of Class 3 presented material about France with enthusiasm. This did not ensure that the sum of attitudes of this class was noticeably positive. Three primary classes occupied higher positions in the rankings.

Overview of class knowledge and perceptions

Class 1

The interviews for this class were generally quite extensive and most of the pupils spoke with ease, though information upon some of the topics was limited.

Main Issues

Food: As a group the class had extensive knowledge of the details of main meals — in few cases were sources specified. The basis of information on breakfasts was adequate, but very little was known about special meals and what was said appeared to be conjectural. The majority of the class were conversant with the reputation of French food, but some were unsure about French attitudes to food.

Jobs: Knowledge of jobs was limited and ideas upon types of jobs appeared to be derived from extrapolation from incidental textbook material. Examples given emphasised similarities with England and covered a limited range — such as retailers and factory workers. Opinions upon women's work were divided. Responses about working conditions appeared to be largely conjectural. Comments regarding the employment situation tended to be influenced by the television or be the result of comparison with local conditions.

Dress and physical appearance: There was no class consensus upon this issue. Some pupils referred to photographs in their textbook but most information was gained from acquaintance with French people.

French views of others: Diverse but not extensive opinions were expressed upon this issue and there was thus no apparent class consensus. Few sources were specified, and the subject of intercultural perception did not appear to feature in French lessons.

Sub-issues

Housing: It was generally known that there are many flats in France and they were usually thought to be small. There was no detailed acquaintance with French architectural or furnishing styles. Any detailed descriptions of individual styles of houses were the results of visits. Views upon comparative standards of living were diverse and not extensive.

Education: Information upon differences in the French school timetable was widespread but some inaccuracies regarding finishing times were apparent. It was generally thought that more homework is given in France but there was little knowledge of subject differences, of qualifications, primary and tertiary stages of education or teachers.

Politics: There was no class consensus regarding politics beyond acquaintance with the name of the President. Any knowledge appeared to have been gained from extra-mural sources, such as parents and television, but confusion about the political parties and the electoral system was apparent.

*History:*References were made by the majority to some of the following: Louis XIV, Napoleon, French Revolution, World War I and World War II, and occasionally to General de Gaulle. No information upon the French colonial past was given despite the introductory pages of the textbook upon regions of the world in which French is spoken.

Growing up: Pupils found this topic particularly difficult and opinions expressed were not extensive.

Religion: Though the majority of pupils were aware that Roman Catholicism predominates, opinions regarding church-going were divided, and some confusion regarding religion was apparent.

Leisure and the media: There was quite extensive recall of sports and activities available at youth clubs (football, discos, swimming and so forth). Pupils found consideration of adult activities much harder, suggesting some fragmentation (for example they knew in other contexts that the reputation of food is important, but they did not make any connections with this issue). No knowledge was apparent of youth activities such as *colonies de vacances, classes de neige,* nor of distinctive French sports, apart from the *Tour de France.* Impressions of pop music were gained from extra-mural sources and no pupil had acquaintance with French television or newspapers.

Geography: From French lessons the majority of pupils were acquainted with Paris, Boulogne, Marseille, two rivers, main mountain ranges and the fishing industry. No knowledge of topographical regional differences was evident. Geography lessons upon Marseille and district were recalled.

Languages: Pupils were unaware of linguistic connections between English and French, though some were aware of a few similar sounding words. Some were aware of different accents but did not name them.

Famous people in the arts and sciences; well-known buildings: The only connection with French art quoted was the Mona Lisa (known to be in the Louvre). There was no knowledge of major French artists or movements. There were occasional references to famous people (Curie, Pasteur, Sacha Distel) and to famous sights (Eiffel Tower, Arc de Triomphe).

Perceived role of the teacher: The majority considered they had learnt something about French culture from their teacher. For one of this group the subject matter learnt was diverse, but for most was confined to one subject area, principally cheese. One example of how to buy things was given and one example of encouragement to visit France was cited.

Perceived role of the textbook: Most pupils felt that more could be included in the textbook upon a wide variety of subjects — early life, school, sport, houses, geography, history, the arts and people. The textbook was thought to cover food, youth hostels, famous people (at the beginning) school times, stations, coping with going to swimming baths and using public transport, Boulogne and Paris and animals. The emphasis was thought to be on vocabulary and conversation.

Attitudes towards learning French: Only one of the twelve pupils interviewed claimed to dislike learning French in this class, though peers' attitudes were thought to be mixed. Reasons advanced were varied and apart from the usual instrumental and survival rationales, one pupil considered that the improvement of attitudes towards other peoples was an aim.

Class 2

Whilst pupils in this class had made least progress through their current course, the majority conversed confidently and made use of other sources.

Main issues

Food: Half the class were able to give reasonably detailed accounts of typical meals; the responses of the rest consisted of discrete details of different foods. Food was a topic being currently studied. Knowledge of the content of breakfasts was sound, whereas that of special meals was minimal, most pupils relying on conjecture. Few pupils were able to comment upon the reputation of French food, or the French attitude towards food.

Jobs: Knowledge of jobs suggested by the textbook was very limited, the consensus being that jobs would be the same as in England. There was little knowledge of women's work and no questioning of the images presented in the textbook. The textbook was not given as a source of information upon levels of pay, working conditions and unions, pupils making occasional use of other sources.

Dress and physical appearance: The opinions of the boys upon dress were generally positive, whilst those of the girls were both positive and negative. Only some differing items of physical appearance were noted, such as hair colour and length. The source of information was from seeing French people rather than the textbook.

French views of others: Opinions upon French views of others were approximately equally divided amongst the positive, negative, mixed and the 'don't knows'. Sources quoted were largely extra-mural, but some uncertainty was expressed and opinions were not extensive.

Sub-issues

Housing: The majority of pupils in this class, who had not travelled to or through France, had a somewhat idealised view of French flats and houses as 'bigger' and 'better' than English ones. The only information provided by the textbook related to details of housing such as the 'cave' and subterranean garage. No knowledge of regional differences or interiors was apparent.

Education: Pupils were aware that school times differed in France but inaccuracies regarding times of finishing were usual. By this stage pupils had acquired no knowledge of subject differences, teachers or stages other than secondary education.

Politics: No pupils were familiar with the French political system, and some opinions expressed seemed to be defensive.

History: Though the world wars were currently being studied in History lessons there was some confusion about relative roles. References were made to Napoleon, William of Normandy and Joan of Arc. Boys' recall of historical information was more extensive than that of the girls in this class.

Growing up: Growing up in France was considered to be the same as in England but responses were unsubstantiated.

Religion: Half the pupils questioned referred to Catholicism but had no further opinions upon the church.

Leisure and the media: Most of the pupils questioned thought that young people were able to take part in sports and visit youth clubs. Textbook information studied at the beginning of the year was the main source. No knowledge of particular French sports was in evidence, nor of adult activities. There was no acquaintance with the content of French media or books.

Geography: With the exception of two pupils, knowledge of French places was confined to Paris, Calais and Boulogne. Though the weather had been studied as a topic few pupils could recall regional differences.

Languages: Whilst a minority of pupils had noticed a few examples of words similar in both languages, there was no evidence of acquaintance with regional variations of French, or minority languages.

Famous people in the arts and sciences; well-known buildings: The majority of pupils recalled the names of two or more 'famous people' out of the following: Pasteur, Marie Curie, Cousteau, Sheila, Victor Hugo, Napoleon, William of Normandy and Brigitte Bardot. The source of these was the first textbook of the course with accompanying flash cards. No more recent sources or figures were quoted. The Mona Lisa was thought to have been painted by a French artist.

Perceived role of the teacher: The perception of the teacher's role as a purveyor of cultural information was generally limited, with one exception.

There was evidence that class motivation could have affected recall of what had been presented.

Perceived role of the textbook: The main units recollected from the textbook concerned food and transport, with some references to leisure, famous people and schooling. Some pupils made informed criticisms of the content, and interest in other possible issues was apparent.

Attitudes towards learning French: Just over half of the interviewees reported enjoyment of learning the French language in this class, though references to some difficulties encountered were made. Other responses were either mixed or negative. Several pupils stated that others in the class did not enjoy the subject. Attitudes to learning about culture were positive. Reasons given for learning French were for visits and getting a job.

Class 3

With the exception of one extensive interview from a boy in this class, girls were generally better informed or more interested in the material, or both, with the exception of politics and history.

Main issues

Food: Knowledge of typical meals and food was particularly extensive amongst the girls of this class, whilst adequate amongst the boys. Regarding breakfasts, the picture was reversed but generally accurate. Whilst special meals were problematic for most pupils, two thoughtful examples, influenced by visits, were found in this group. About half the class had formed opinions upon the distinctive reputation of French food, and attitudes towards it. The girls' responses were again more extensive than the boys' for this issue.

Jobs: Girls' examples of jobs were more varied than those of the boys. Visits were given as sources of information rather than the textbook. Where opinions were expressed it was thought that most French women were housewives. Opinions upon working conditions and pay were divided, but one pupil recalled observing the effects of a strike in France.

Dress and physical appearance: The majority of the boys saw French dress as the 'same' whilst girls made a greater number of differentiations both positively and negatively evaluated. Few opinions were expressed upon physical appearance apart from hair styles. Two thought that the French were more cheerful. The sources were visits and visitors, and, once, the textbook photographs.

French views of others: The majority of pupils in this class expressed tentative opinions upon this issue, several stressing similarity to English views of the French, or stating a somewhat neutral French view of England as 'alright'.

Sub-issues

Housing: Most references made to housing concerned details such as 'caves' and the number of flats. Two exceptionally good accounts of differences were given by girls who had visited France. Nothing was reported upon regional differences.

Education: Whilst pupils' recall of French school times was varied, a few pupils provided information upon subjects, homework, classroom and textbooks. Knowledge of the school system was confined to the secondary stage.

Politics: The boys' responses upon politics were very limited but superior to those of the girls, all of whom denied knowledge of the existence of the President, despite the history curriculum.

History: The boys recalled the names of several historical figures such as Napoleon, Joan of Arc, William the Conqueror and also Marie Curie and Louis Pasteur. The girls' attitudes towards history were extremely negative. Though they stated they had studied the French Revolution they candidly averred that they 'had not listened' as they did not like history.

Growing up: Few opinions were expressed upon growing up in France. One pupil indicated knowledge of festivals, and another considered life in French villages to be more favourable than in their English counterparts.

Religion: One pupil quoted her visit as a source of what limited information she had upon religion. One pupil only was aware of Catholicism.

Leisure and the media: The majority of the group were acquainted with sports in which young people could engage. A wide variety of other activities were suggested also, such as holidays, museums, discos, camping and restaurants. Information upon the length of holidays was inaccurate. There was some slight acquaintance with French pop music and television. Sources quoted were visits and the textbook.

Geography: Knowledge of places in France was limited to Paris and Boulogne, with the exception of one boy. Extra-mural sources (including articles in the paper) were quoted by one girl as informing her knowledge of industry in the North.

Languages: Most pupils were aware of the existence of different accents, sources being personal visits and those of an acquaintance. Knowledge of French books was confined to Asterix and a canine cartoon adaptation of the Three Musketeers for the television (Dogtanian).

Famous people in the arts and sciences; well-known buildings: Recall of famous people included Sacha Distel, Pasteur, Marie Curie and, more modernly, Platini. Several pupils referred to the existence of buildings, museums to visit and paintings, though could not recall the names of artists. The textbook was quoted as a source.

Perceived role of the teacher: The majority of pupils in the class felt that their teacher had provided information upon a wide variety of topics. The most enthusiastic accolades of a teacher were found amongst pupils of this class, whilst opinions were expressed upon the negative attitudes of some of their peers.

Perceived role of the textbook: The textbook was thought to provide information upon a wide variety of topics, though modified to some extent by recency of coverage. Only two pupils suggested adding many items to the textbook.

Attitudes towards learning French: Just over half the group stated that they enjoyed learning French (four girls and three boys). Others either stated a dislike of it or saw it as 'boring' though some enjoyed learning about French culture. Some pupils indicated that their peers did not enjoy the subject. The language was seen as useful for visits, travel, and increased communication with French visitors to England.

Class 4

Some difference in the interviews of boys and girls were found in this class in that a number of the girls were reserved and lacking in confidence about their responses. (These impressions were corroborated by the ethnographic report of classroom interaction (see Chapter 5) in which it was stated that many of the girls did not participate verbally in the class; the French teacher's assessments for year end reports substantiated this further.)

Main issues

Food: A third of the group had difficulty in recalling typical French meals; whilst others gave reasonably detailed answers, some responses appeared conjectural. Sources of information cited were personal visits and those of acquaintances. The group was familiar with the usual content of French breakfasts, but were unsure about special meals. The majority were aware of French food's reputation, from a variety of extra-mural sources.

Jobs: Whilst most pupils saw jobs as similar to ones in England, a minority attempted more detailed analysis. Pupils were unsure about the incidence of strikes, working conditions and pay. Women were thought to have paid employment. The textbook was not thought to provide much information upon jobs.

Dress and physical appearance: The majority of the class saw French dress as different, about one third seeing it as colourful; the opinions of others were diverse. Only a minority of pupils expressed opinions upon physical appearance. Visits and visitors were the only source of information given.

French views of others: Opinions on French views of others were not homogeneous with roughly equal groups seeing them as positive, negative and neutral. The few sources quoted were extra-mural.

Sub-issues

Housing: A variety of sources including the teacher and textbook were given for this issue, but visits remained the principal source. Details voiced were diverse and attempts were made to describe interiors and regional differences, but information upon these appeared sparse.

Education: This sub-issue was one which the majority of the group were able to describe in much detail. Information upon hours, subjects, homework, and lack of uniform was included; sources quoted were the textbook and a school visit. However some inaccuracies were apparent and little was known about primary and tertiary stages.

Politics: Whilst most pupils knew the President's name, no pupils could name political parties and some were unsure of the existence of a Prime Minister. Pupils were not familiar with current political issues (such as the sinking of a Greenpeace ship by French intelligence).

History: All pupils referred to France's position in World War II and most to World War I. About half recalled people or incidents connected with the French Revolution. The principal source was history lessons.

Growing up and Religion: Only one pupil from the group expressed a clear opinion upon growing up in France as 'different'. Few details of distinctive features or occasions were quoted. Whilst over half referred to the French being Christian, only a minority referred to the principal church.

Leisure and the media: The majority of pupils were acquainted with the kinds of sports which young people could engage in at youth clubs, but did not know of the range of extended holiday activities available. Few impressions of adult leisure were given. There was some familiarity with French pop music. Sources given were French lessons and their teacher.

Geography: All pupils except one were able to name a small number of places in France; Paris and Boulogne were the only two to be named frequently however. Whilst it was known that the South was warmer, no distinctive features of other regions were given. No sources were given.

Languages: A majority of pupils were aware that different accents exist in France but were unable to name them, or any minority languages. The source of information on languages was visits. Only a minority could name any similar or 'borrowed' words in English.

Famous people in the arts and sciences; well-known buildings: The textbook and French lessons were given as sources of information upon a common cluster of famous people. This information had been presented in the first year and did not appear to have been updated.

Perceived role of the teacher: Opinions about the role of the teacher were varied. Two pupils considered little extra information was given, and two saw his role as providing a variety of information on food, living and housing, the town hall, Paris and the telephone system. The overall impression was of discrete pieces of information.

Perceived role of the textbook: The textbook was said to offer information principally upon food, travel matters (cars, driving, signals and so forth) buildings and museums, Paris and Boulogne, education and the 'way of life'. Each of these were cited by several pupils. Camping, money and past times were mentioned by only one or two pupils each. It was thought that the textbook could provide more on a wide variety of topics, for instance, jobs, politics, people and places.

Attitudes towards learning French: All pupils stated that they were in favour of learning French mainly for travel reasons. Some diffidence about speaking French was expressed however, and some criticisms of certain styles of speaking were apparent.

A comparison of the four classes

Typical meals and differences in food

   Analysis of the four classes' knowledge of what might constitute a typical main meal of the day in France indicated that this question was the most comprehensively answered of all. In classes 1, 2 and 3, half or over half gave reasonably detailed accounts of possible meals, as well as including details of characteristically French foods (for example mussels and baguettes). Class 4 had the fewest reasonably detailed responses. In the case of this class factors such as their having progressed further through the course could have interferred with recall of details.

Other responses given in all classes consisted mainly of details of French food thought to be unusual but with little coherent presentation of what might constitute a typical meal. In all but Class 1 were found one or two pupils, however, who claimed not to know what might be eaten.

Class 3 appeared to be the class in which most of the reasonably detailed responses were found. However, on closer analysis an interesting difference between the boys and girls was found in that all the girls gave detailed responses whereas only one boy did. It was found when discussing French lessons that at least one of the girls in this class perceived an uneven amount of interest in French among fellow pupils which could, despite the best efforts of the teacher, mentioned by several, account for the discrepancy in responses.

There follows some illustrative quotations from each class. Examples from the two higher achievement classes are given first.

Class 1: (top French set, Newfarm)

I: Well if we start with the food, you mentioned cheese with every meal, could you tell me a bit more about what a typical French meal would be?
P: Well they normally have cheese first and then like the main meal just normally about the same as us, except a bit more healthy and for afters they just have coffee, stuff like that.
I: When you say healthy have you got something special in mind there?
P: Like, say we have fried stuff and all that they probably have something like vegetables and that and we'd have chips.
I: That would be a typical meal an every day meal then would it?
P: Yes, normally like dinner time and that. (101/8)

I: And then at midday?
P: Midday they have like the meal I told you before — no, midday they have a light meal and at teatime the other, they have like a snack, a sandwich or something like that.
I: In the middle of the day?

P: Yes. Then on the night they'd have like cheese and three courses or something like that, then for supper they'd have another light meal. (101/10)

I: And in the middle of the day?

P: I don't think that's too big just something like soup or something, like cake and stuff.

I: Yes. And then this meal in the afternoon?

P: Yes, like cups of tea or cocoa or something — just to keep you going till they have the big meal on a night where they have meat and two veg. or something like that.

I: Something like that — can you tell me what a typical meal would be?

P: I suppose it's mainly the same as over here like they eat chicken and beef — they don't all go around eating frogs' legs and snails and I think it's mainly the same as over here like they eat meat and chicken and vegetables.

I: What would you start with then?

P: I think it would be croissants and a drink and they have like cakes or something for afters, ice cream or something like that.

I: And the main part of the meal?

P: Something like chicken and vegetables and gravy.

I: And would it be the same preparation and like our way of eating, those things?

P: Do you mean the way they cook it?

I: Yes and the way they eat it as well.

P: They eat it differently I think. They have the bread on the table — they leave the bread on the table, they eat a lot of bread with the food.

I: And the preparation, would that be just . . .

P: Just the same as over here. (103/7)

I: This is about food which you mentioned — what would you describe as a typical French meal?

P: Probably an omelette or something or like delicacies like frogs' legs and snails. That kind of food.

I: What would you start with? What would a meal start with?

P: Probably a starter — they like raw vegetables or sometimes cheese. They like a lot don't they? Probably start on them. They eat cooked vegetables and then the meat without vegetables after that and then probably coffee or something.

I: Would you think of that as a special meal or just an everyday meal?

P: I think that would be their main meal on a night. Have a three-course. (104/11)

I; So the meals. What kind of meals would they have? What things are the French fond of?

P: Frogs' legs.

i: Frogs' legs,yes. That is the classic. All the French eat frogs' legs. Anything else?

P: Snails.

I: Yes, that is the other one. What about other kinds of things? They pay a lot of attention to eating so what kinds of things do they eat?

P: I don't know. They eat chips and things like that.

I: They eat chips. Sausage and chips?

P: Yes.

I: So if you went to a French family, you would say right let's get the sausage and chips frying, or would they have a different attitude do you think?

P: They would probably have a different attitude I think.

I: Normally at home I just have the one course. I have something like sausage and chips or fish fingers and chips, something like that. Is that the kind of meal you would expect if you were in France?

P: Well I think there would be some sort of dessert or sweet. (116/3,4)

P: Like they have their meal like we have our tea, like when we go home.

I: Yes. What do you think they have then?

P: Just the same as us like a meal. Then when we normally have our tea they have a snack and they have supper.

I: What do they have for supper?

P: Just . . . I don't know. We went to a French restaurant once and we had salad to start off with. Had all the different sorts of meats. Cold meat. Then we had a savoury pancake and we had cheese and ham and that and then we had a sweet one with chocolate on it, like, poured on chocolate.

I: Was it nice?

P: Lovely. (118S/7,8)

P: I don't know we saw some of them walking around the shops.

I: What about the food — coming back to the food then. You have done something about food in your textbook haven't you?

P: Well yes a bit.

I: Again how did that compare with the real thing: What were your expectations?

P: We just ate the same things over there as we do over here.

I: Did you see other people eating on the campsite and so on?

P: The only thing — we had steak a few nights and we thought it was steak but after about a fortnight we found out it was calf meat. It was very nice, we had it a couple of nights afterwards as well.

I: That was new to you. But there were other things which were new, small things perhaps in the food?

P: The chips were very skinny and things. I didn't like them. I like chips with plenty of potato in them. The beer was different as well.

I: In what way?

P: It just tasted different, little bottles and things.

I: Did you like it?

P: Yes. I don't like beer over here but I had a couple of drinks over there, not much, it was nice. (120/15)

Class 4: (top French set, Hillside)

I: Let's talk about their evening meal, what they call dinner. What time do they normally eat?

P: Normally about seven I think.

I: What time do you normally eat at home? I eat about 5.30 or something like that.

P: Yes about five or something like that.

I: So they eat a little bit later. Do they make more of their evening meal than we make?

P: Yes. Because they don't have as big a tea as we would have. They make more of a main meal on a night.

I: What kind of things do they have, do you know? I mean I normally would have something like sausage and chips or something like that.

P: Meat and vegetables, I would say.

I: Do they just have one course of more than one course?

P: I think they have dessert as well. That's what I had when I was in France.

I: Did you? Main course and dessert. Did you have a starter?

P: Yes sometimes, soup sometimes. Not everyday though. (241/15)

I: What about their midday meal, is that different?

P: . . . More or less just like what we have. Something like chips and that but not as good as what they have on a night. (241/17)

I: You mentioned you had a meal with the family what's a typical meal like?

P: I'm not sure whether it's a typical one but we had tuna fish and egg, some sort of egg, and then there was sort of chips and bacon, must have known that I liked it I think, and tomato and things like that. Probably just an English person coming sort of English things they gave me.

I: Yes. What would you think of then as a typical French meal?

P: Well I think of the French breakfast with the croissants and things like that, the best things about France I think, the breakfasts.

I: You wouldn't, would you be able to give me some idea about other kinds of meals?

P: Well, they eat chips I know that and I've had some of their pancakes, a crêpe sort of thing, they're nice, I don't know whether they eat them a lot but they're nice. They don't seem to have any wholemeal things — I don't know much about the French meals.

I: What about the times when the people eat, do you know anything about that?

P: Well it was late in the evening when we were eating the dinner and the morning was just about normal breakfast time for England and the dinner was just the same time because we didn't have proper French dinner there we sort of had whatever came like in the university thing we went to — no it was a youth hostel.

I: Youth hostel, yes. It was the middle of the day you said, dinner?

P: Yes. Sometimes we sort of had to go out into the town and get our own sort of packed lunch.

I: What about in a family is that the same kind of thing?

P: Well, I'm not sure about the family really, we didn't stay for dinner. (244/8,9)

P: ... and then they have the dinners at different times, a little dinner and then a little tea and a big meal at the end of the day.

I: What time do they have that then, the little dinner you said?

P: I think it's about 12 o'clock although it could be about one.

I: And then what do they have after that?

P: Like just sandwiches and cup of tea and things like that and children have chocolate, sweets and then about nine o'clock they have a big dinner and then go to bed 'cause they have to get up early. (245/6)

I: What do you think a typical French meal, say dinner, would be like?

P: The dinner on the night?

I: Well, yes, mainly, what they have.

P: Like bigger meat and like a Sunday dinner and I don't think they'd have like proper meat every night but you know, pie or chips or something.

I: Yes, so how often do you think they'd have meat in the week?

P: Maybe twice.

I: What would they have the other nights?

P: Maybe just like a big meal maybe just pizza or things like that

I: Yes. Do you think it's like English food on other nights or . . .?
P: No, maybe more like, more like the continent I think. (245/12)

I: Can you describe a typical French meal?
P: They have something to start with like soup or something like that, then meat and vegetables and different things. They have this sausage like salami thing and they have sometimes some sweet and they have wine and mineral water.
I: Why do they drink mineral water?
P: The water is not that good.
I: Is this the kind of meal you would expect them to have every day?
P: It would differ but usually about the same.
I: They would go to the same amount of trouble about it?
P: I think so. (246/8)

I: What did you try when you were over there?
P: . . . Croissants and French bread . . . the candy and chocolate. Just the fish, plaice and that.
I: Was that good the fish?
P: Yes, liked it . . . that's about it really.
I: What about the meats, did you try any of the cold meats or any of the cheeses?
P: Oh I tried a sausage thing that was nice.
I: What about the cheeses, are you a cheese fan, do you like cheese?
P: Yes.
I: Did you try many of the French cheeses?
P: No. (248/16)

I: The other thing you mentioned was meals.
P: Well, like they always, like when we cook our meat they always have the blood coming out of theirs.
I: Yes. What do you think of that?
P: Awful, 'cause I like well-done meat.
I: Yes. That's one thing, anything else?
P: . . . Not really.
I: What would a typical meal be like then?
P: They'd certainly have wine and French bread maybe like vegetables to start or something like that then the meat . . .
I: And you said that the meat would be prepared differently, what about the other things, what would the taste be like?
P: . . . Well my brother when he went abroad he said that it was very salty, they put a lot of salt on. (265/7,8)

Class 2: (middle achievement set, Newfarm)

I: And then through the day what would be the next meal?

P: They have, during the morning, they have a drink of coffee and they have a snack then there's — they have their lunch which, they have plenty of bread . . . they like have a canny big meal but the main meal's at the night.

I: What would a typical meal be like?

P: . . .

I: What would I notice about it?

P: . . . Taste different . . .

I: What would it consist of?

P: Sometimes they have snails and frogs legs or just . . . (131/9)

I: What are going to be the main differences there?

P: Well they eat different things like they have tomato salads and things like that — I've never had that, I don't like tomatoes anyway. And I don't think there's not many people in England eat tomato salad. We don't have sausages like salami very often.

I: Can you describe a typical French meal?

P: It's big, very, they have the like if they have cheese and crackers they have it before the dessert and we have it sort of after. And they have the big course and they just help themselves to what they want and things like that.

I: What would they start with then?

P: . . . Vegetables . . . like raw vegetables, soup maybe . . . maybe bread with some butter on or something . . .

I: and then?

P: Then for the main course beef, lamb or meats and vegetables with them maybe . . . potatoes

I: Would that be similar to us then?

P: Yes, I would say so.

I: What about to drink?

P: They have wine, coffee, tea, the same as us. Some of the children have hot chocolate . . . cider, beer, anything, they drink anything I think after their dinner.

I: What do you think of that as being a sort of everyday meal or a special meal, what you've just described to me?

P: . . . I think it's more or less an every day meal they have, that. (133/10)

I: But what about your trip to France, did that give you some information as well?

P: . . . Well when we went for a meal in a restaurant the woman came along with all these different kinds of meat on a like big plate thing and she put it down and we just got what we wanted, all the vegetables we wanted, drink . . . I think they're like different, they eat the stuff that we don't eat very often and we eat the stuff that they don't eat very often, like from what I hear they don't have chips very much I don't think. (133/12)

P: They eat bread with their evening meal and everything, they eat a lot as well I noticed. They have like four meals a day or something don't they? And they're weird, they eat lots of food, they eat lots.

I: Would there be anything else apart from food that I would notice as being special?

P: Don't know, don't think so, they drink wine with the meals and everything.

I: What would a typical meal be then?

P: . . . Breakfast, something like bread I think, bread and a cup of coffee, that's what they have and for dinner they have like meat and vegetables and for their tea they have something like a snack, like bread and crisps and cake and something like that and the evening meal is like meat and things like turkey and vegetables.

I: If you take one of those meals at midday or evening meal can you tell me a bit more, what would they start with and what comes first?

P: Mixed soup then a main course like meat and vegetables and they have like a dessert which would be a gateau or something like that. Cream cakes.

I: What would it be like, what would it look like? What would it taste like?

P: Soup is all right, and the meal. Have like pancakes and they have like chocolate put on, something like that. They are nice. Meat is the same.

I: The meat is probably the same? Prepared in the same way?

P: The vegetables are the same as well. (135/7,8)

I: Can you tell me a bit more detail then about the food? I mean if I am going to live with a family what kind of typical meal would I expect? expect?

P: Well they normally get a big full meal, like five course meal something like that.

I: Well what would I start with?

P: Probably soup or something.

I: And then?

P: Just the main meal and then a dessert and cup of coffee or something.

I: What would the main meal consist of?

P: Vegetables, meat sometimes you get salad. That's all.

I: Would there be anything special about the vegetables and meat compared with English food?

P: I don't think so.

I: So a fairly big meal then?

P: Yes.

I: Would that be an everyday meal then what you have just described to me?

P: Yes.

I: Have you had done this kind of thing in your textbook about food I mean?

I: Yes we are just doing it now, about food.

I: Well can you tell me a bit about what you are doing?

P: We are just like drawing food things and just copying up in our exercise book.

I: Well go on tell me a bit more. What food things?

P: Just drawing bowls with salad in and tomatoes and vegetables and fruit. That's all.

I: What is so special then about these things?

P: Don't know.

I: Are they like the English food then?

P: Yes. (152/5,6)

Class 3: (middle achievement set, Hillside)

I: . . . and then in the middle of the day?

P:. . . There'd be just the same I think just like ordinary dinners.

I: So what would I start with then?

P: . . . I don't know.

I: You've not done this in class or anything?

P: No.

I: What did you have when you were there yourself?

P: For dinner?

I: Yes, what did you have to eat, yes?

P: Chips . . . chicken . . . and ice cream for dessert.

I: Was that different from — I mean did it taste different, was it prepared differently?

P: Not really it was just the same.

I: Did you — where did you eat, in a restaurant?

P: Yes.

I: So that was very similar to what you had, what you would have here?

P: Yes. (162/8)

I: So you were saying that their food is different, that they eat some different things. Can you tell me what a typical French meal is like?

P: Their bread is different because they have long loaves and we have like sliced bread. They have a lot like jam and that at breakfast time and coffee.

I: So that's what you think they have for breakfast. What sort of things do they normally have for dinner do you think?

P: . . . Just the same as us most days apart from a Sunday, they will probably have something else.

I: What do you think they have then?

P: . . . Just something light because they have a lot for breakfast.

I: So on Sunday they have a lot, what do you think they have? Is that something else you have been told about that is different?

P: Um, yes.

I: So you say that most meals they have similar to English ones. Do you think they all sit down together or do they have it at different times say watching the tele?

P: More or less all together. (166/9,10)

I: You mentioned the food then didn't you, what would be a typical meal, say a dinner?

P: Probably have soup for starters and then you'd have fish or something for the main course and salad and you'd have some ice cream or something for the dessert.

I: And what would it taste like as a whole?

P: . . . It wouldn't taste any different than in England really.

I: And then in the middle of the day what kind of meal do they have in the middle of the day?

P: . . . I don't know they'd have anything, probably go to a café.

I: Yes, go to a café to eat?

P: Yes.

I: And then when would we have the kind of meal you were telling me about?

P: . . . About 7 o'clock.

I: Right, and in between, anything at all between midday and 7 o'clock?

P: . . . Children eat chocolate and bread.

I: Oh, yes. And drink, no?

P: . . . (167/6)

I: What sort of things have you heard about the food?

P: About the restaurants and that and about telephones.

I: What sort of things have you learnt about the restaurants?

P: The money and things and the menu, have to pay tips, things like that.
I: Do you always have to to that?
P: Not always. Like do different things.
I: I mean do you always have to leave tips in the restaurants?
P: Not always — it says at the bottom.
I: So it tells you if you have to. What sort of food do you think you could get at the restaurants? What do you think the main things are that they serve in French restaurants? What are they famous for?
P: Potage, things like that.
I: What else could you have apart from soup?
P: Salad, steak, things like that.
I: What about the desserts? Can you remember any of the famous desserts in France?
P: Yoghurt, gateaux, um . . . don't know any more.
I: What about the cheeses have you ever heard of any French cheeses?
P: No.
I: What do you think they normally drink?
P: Vin Rouge, um . . . beer and that, cidre.
I: That is the sort of thing you have in a restaurant. How do you think people eat at home? What would dinner or main meal be to a French family? What sort of thing would they have?
P: Don't know.
I: What do you think they would start with?
P: Soup. Don't know.
I: Do you think they would have more courses than an English family?
P: Yes.
I: So they might start with soup. What would they have next?
P: (says something like 'croquettes' but with an O — croquottes) I don't know it in French. Is it croucot or something?
I: Do you think they would have the same kind of meat as in a restaurant or not?
P: No. Don't know what they would have.
I: Do you think they would have a dessert or not?
P: Yes. (168/8,9)

I: Now you mentioned the food they eat, what do you think they normally eat for dinner? What do you think they'd start with usually?
P: . . . Soup just the same as us . . . chips and that . . .
I: What do you think they might have with the chips?
P: . . .
I: You had chicken I think do you think they have that often?
P: Some of them maybe . . . or beef, that sort of thing.

I: Yes.
P: Pork and that.
I: What do you think they might have after that?
P: Ice cream.
I: Yes. What would they drink?
P: . . . wine and coffee. (171/14)

I: Can you tell me something about the food? You said you would have to
    warn me about the food.
P: Some of the food can be horrible because when you go into it there are
    lots of noodles and shells and that put in it and I didn't like that. It
    seemed to be sweet soups because I had some I didn't know what it
    was. Like shells and spaghetti in the bottom with bits of meat dropped
    in. Seemed to be very sweet and I couldn't eat that.
I: What would a typical meal be like?
P: Well instead of having — usually they don't have all the meal on
    together. They have vegetables first and meat or something and they
    have a sweet . . . They have wine and cup of coffee and there would be
    ice cream at the end for the children. But they always have the meal set
    out like you have the vegetables first. Don't have all the meal shoved
    down together. That's what we found out.
I: Where did you eat?
P: First of all we ate in a place that they had set for us. We had all the meal
    shoved on together but when we sat down there was a woman across
    the way who had hers all specially set out and when we went past some
    cafés and they had all different plates set out with different food on.
    Like vegetables. I couldn't eat it like that but they seemed to like it that
    way.
I: What you have just described is that an everyday meal?
P: Sometimes just have sandwiches or short snack. They seem to be going
    more into salads now, healthfood. Everybody is going into that but
    usually salad or sandwich but if it is going to be a big meal there would
    be all the meats and different vegetables and that. (175/21,22,23)

   Direct attribution to information provided upon this subject in French
lessons was made most frequently by Class 2 pupils; for example in 154/6 it
is stated that they had 'just done food' though it was hard to recall what
had been 'done'. Pupils had been treated to chocolate on bread by their
teacher to elaborate upon textbook treatment of 'le goûter'.

   In Class 1 a third of the group recalled their teacher's contribution to
knowledge of food, by her provision of a variety of cheeses. Classroom

observation (for example 09/04/86 field notes) indicated that the teacher had discussed the large variety of French cheeses and their use in snacks such as a *croque monsieur*.

In Class 4 the main contribution to this item by the teacher was that meat in France was 'undercooked'; this view was mentioned by a quarter of the group, and was said to have come directly from the French teacher by one pupil.

The teacher of Class 3 was said to have provided information on a wide range of subjects. The only specific detail attributed to the teacher, however, when discussing this item came from one pupil, e.g. 183/12,13 quoted above.

Special meals

Only one or two pupils in each class were able to comment upon the content of 'special meals'. This was the phrase used in interviews to elicit perceptions of the difference between everyday food and eating customs and special occasions and festivities. Whilst some suggested that unusual foods, such as frogs' legs, might be served, few appeared to suggest that one feature might be the number of courses. Examples of some of the fuller responses were:

Class 1:

I: Yes. Basically the same. What about a meal say for a special occasion, like Christmas or a birthday? What do you think they might have then?
P: They might start off with . . . don't know what they start off with, don't know that much food. They might have frogs legs or turkey or a duck. Vegetables, potatoes. Wine. Pancakes or gateaux. Coffee. (102/13)

Class 2:

I: How would you imagine then a special meal, anniversary of some kind or whatever?
P: . . . Well for starters, soup again, some bread to dip in and that and they could have a choice of the meat what they wanted like in a sort of carvery in a restaurant or something like that, just say what they want and put it on the plate you know and all the more or less normal stuff, vegetables, have what you like.
I: But would it be just a question of more choice then, the difference

between that special meal and an ordinary meal? Would it be just a question of more choice for a special meal?

P: I think so.

I: What about Christmas and things like that?

P: Well I'd think it was more or less the same as ours, turkey and Christmas pudding and things like that. All the vegetables. (133/11)

Class 3:

I: When you say big meal — what would be a special meal for anniversary of some kind?

P: They would have all like decorated up. They would have vegetables done right and different meats on different plates. They would have the meat set out on different plates so you could put it out onto your own, they would carve it for you or something and they would have several different courses of meat and vegetables and have sweets and desserts and things like that and wine. The tall glasses of wine and coffee next to them. They have courses of things like that. (175/24)

Class 3:

I: So, so when you go into this expensive restaurant what will you get?

P: The best, like frogs' legs and all top things like that (inaudible) frogs' legs (inaudible) snails in France. They eat snails and frogs' legs and meat — they always have . . . meat, chips and peas on a plate, you know dress it up. If it's extra special they have trout and things like that and they put lettuce and stuff round it so it looks canny good and like you think well that's nice but you pay more for it (inaudible). (164/22)

Class 4:

I: What do you think of — what would you think of as a special meal in France then?

P: Snails.

I: Snails.

P: I wouldn't think of frogs' legs because they're expensive.

I: Yes. So a meal with snails is a speciality?

P: Yes.

I: Anything else, if you were imagining what a meal was — some kind of anniversary or if you have guests or whatever.

P: I think steak or something like that . . . (265/10)

All four classes were thus alike in finding difficulty with this item. Class 3 appeared to be most successful, with all three others producing mainly conjectural, brief examples. Classroom observation (13/01/86) indicated that the teacher had devoted part of a lesson to discussing Christmas and New Year celebrations such as 'le réveillon'.

Reputation of French food and French attitudes towards food

Whilst pupils were aware of the variety of foods available in France each class was similar in having a wide range of responses to questions upon the reputation of food, and French attitudes towards food. In each class, except class 2, were found about a quarter of the pupils who emphasised the care in preparation of food and the importance of food to the French. However, in each class also were found pupils with no idea, or who gave conjectural responses. The textbook was cited as a source only once:

Class 1:

I: Do you think they have a different attitude to food then to us?
P: Yes, what is it they say — they say we eat to live and they live to eat.
I: Yes. Where do you come across that saying?
P: It was in the French book I think. (101/12)

Other sources were used:

Class 4:

I: Do you think they feel the same way we do about food?
P: I think they take more care over it. How they prepare it and what they eat and the presentation.
I: Did you know that French food is supposed to be among the best in the world?
P: Yes.
I: Why do you think that is?
P: There is a chef where my Mum works. He used to live in Italy and he is always saying the French food is better. They take more care over it.
I: Do you know what the French think about English food?
P: No.
I: What does your Mum's chef think about it?
P: We overcook it. We boil our vegetables too long and we cook the meat too long. (273/13)

Observation of Class 3 (18/01/86) showed that the teacher had discussed at some length attitudes to food. It did not appear that the responses of this class indicated much recall of this subject.

Occasionally pupils without experience of France drew negative conclusions from acquaintance with French visitors to England.

Class 2:

I: What do you think the French think of English food?
P: Well I know when people come over here like they're fussy with their food like I want this and I want that as if to say this is my house and I can have what I want.
I: Yes, is that what happened to your friends when they had them or people you meet who had them?
P: Well that girl who came over with Maria was a little pig. (156/18)

Class 2 pupils had formed fewest opinions upon this issue.

Jobs

The conclusions of pupils in all four classes were similar for the issue of jobs and employment in general. The consensus was that the textbook provided only limited information upon jobs and that the types of jobs available were similar to those in England:

Class 1:

I: Can you describe — going back to the textbook you have been using for your course, can you describe the kind of jobs that people do in France?
P: Well there is mainly the same as in England I think, shop assistant, police officers, traffic wardens. Mainly the same I think.
I: There aren't any French jobs, I mean any jobs the French do that are different to the kinds of jobs that English people do. Are there more farmers in France, are there more factory workers?
P: No, I don't think so, just about the same. (116/12)

Class 2:

I: If you think of people working in France, what do you think of? What do you see them as doing?
P: Most of them work on market stalls. Like arcade things and ice-cream

stalls. That's all I really saw when I was in France. Mostly French people on these ice-cream stalls.

I: What about in your textbooks? What do people in the textbooks do?

P: Bus drivers that's all really. That's all we've covered. Like bus drivers and train drivers. Taxi drivers. (135/21)

Class 3:

I: To go back to the people themselves, in your textbooks what do they do — I mean what kind of jobs do they do?

P: . . . They're all different sorts of jobs like ours — builders . . . they have a lot of shop-keepers there . . . people who work in hotels . . . people like that and waiters, it's just the same as England really.

I: Do you not think — are there any jobs that they have in France that we don't have in England?

P: . . . Not that I can think of.

I: Do you see people working a lot in your textbooks?

P: No, not much.

I: What kind of things do they do then?

P: . . . Just shows you pictures of them shopping and laying the table and things like that, there's a couple of pictures of people running hotels. (167/20)

Class 4:

I: Let's move on to what people do in daily life again. What do people in your textbook, what sort of jobs do they have?

P: . . . We haven't really done that.

I: There must be some people, I don't know these textbooks, tell me there must be some people in the textbooks that you read about, French people.

P: They work in the ports . . . and offices and hospitals, but we haven't really learnt about that.

I: In the ports is that because of the place where your textbook is set?

P: I think so.

I: What do you remember about them?

P: Fishermen . . . that's all.

I: And are there jobs in France that people do which don't exist in England?

P: No. (253/22)

Though the industries of the region around Boulogne are introduced in the textbook *Action* Book One pp. 25–26, and described in detail in *Action* Book Two pp. 25–27 several pupils concluded that France is not as industrialised as Britain.

Class 4:

I: Going back to work you have been doing on the course then, what kinds of jobs do people do in France?

P: I think most of them are the same as ours but they haven't got as much mining and steelworks and not as industrial.

I: It's not as industrial. Are there more people involved in agriculture there?

P: I think so, a lot more fields and open spaces.

I: What other kinds of things do people do?

P: . . . Build machines and cars and that. They do a lot of things for Ford.

I: Is it fairly much the same as our country then?

P: Yes.

I: Except you said earlier you think it is less industrialised.

P: Yes. (248/21)

Class 4:

I: What's your impression of jobs in France, I mean what do people do in France, what kind of jobs do they do?

P: . . . Well don't think there's very many good jobs in France.

I: There aren't?

P: Yes, I don't think so.

I: Do you get, sorry.

P: No go on.

I: I was thinking about the standard of living, do you think that's the same?

P: There aren't many jobs so I think I wouldn't like to live there. Most of them are fishers I think, fish ports . . . (247/19)

The information provided on the pages mentioned is presented in English. It is possible that sometimes these pages are given for homework (as was noted by observation of Class 4). Visits to France provided some information upon work and working conditions but where visits had been made only to Boulogne the type of jobs observed were limited.

Class 3:

I: What sort of things do you imagine people in France — do they do jobs which we don't have or do they . . .

P: I don't know. I think they have more fishermen than we do, 'cause when the ban went on the food (inaudible).

I: When the what?

P: The ban. They give a ban to stop catching so many fish . . . France had a lot of ships like France was down in the dumps really with that on ban 'cause they weren't — all the prices went down for fish and that and people were just going off it but then when the ban went off a lot of French trawlers when we went a lot of French trawlers were at the docks and that but nearly every day when we went to the docks there was always a new boat coming in with a French name on and French people on it with big loads of fish on the trawlers and just letting — I think most French people have a lot of fishing and something to do with food and that. Some work in factories — big factories, French factories and most of them are business men.

I: Are there any jobs that they have that we don't have?

P: . . . Couldn't tell you. (164/36)

In only one case was a teacher quoted as a source of information:

Class 4:

I: What impression do you get about people's working life in France?

P: Well we've just sort of been told words of the working life they didn't say a lot about how they work and where they worked. We found out that the Town Hall isn't sort of a big building though it's sort of — the teacher talked about having the Mayor in a Portakabin, that stays in my mind.

I: Do your teachers tell you about other things, what kind of things do the teachers tell you?

P: He just sort of elaborates on points, things like that, tells us what he knows after he's been to French schools and things like that, probably his training and things like that. He told us loads about the traffic and when the rush hours would be and things like that 'cause all the French cars would come out at the same time in Paris and things like that. That's the sort of thing he elaborates on.

I: Do you find that's helpful, interesting what the teacher tells you?

P: Yes I find it interesting because he knows from first hand experience. Sometimes in the book you think well that could be wrong because things have changed now. Like 'phone numbers I think they've changed the dialling system or something like that but it is interesting, not talking, we don't have to do anything sort of speaking when he's doing it, we get away with it. (244/11)

(However classroom observation of 14/03/86 showed that the teacher in question was referring to one unusual instance of the town hall and went on to point out that the buildings were usually considerably larger.)

A few pupils recalled the existence of the wine industry and suggested jobs in viticulture as ones which would exist in France but not in Britain. Other suggestions were few in number ('Eiffel Tower attendant' and 'frog processor').

Class 1:

I: What do you think the main jobs are?
P: Like there must be doctors — the same as us really, like lawyers and everything.
I: Yes, do you think there are any farmers?
P: They've got as many as us but they seem to grow cattle more.
I: Yes, how have you heard about that?
P: 'cause there's like more like French cattle over there they seem to eat more meat than us. (121S/20)

Opinions upon whether women go out to work more in France than Britain were divided. In Class 2 few pupils were able to comment upon this issue. In Class 3 those commenting thought that women probably stayed at home. In Classes 1 and 4 however the majority of pupils concluded that French women do go out to work. One pupil suggested that an image of French women was presented in their textbooks:

Class 1:

I: What about women and going to work?
P: I don't think there's many go to work as they do here.
I: The women in your textbooks, what do they do?
P: They're all perfect housewives and that sort of thing.
I: The fact that you're smiling about that obviously implies that you're not too impressed by that.
P: No. It doesn't show you real life like really . . . (101/33)

Class 1:

I: What about the women?

P: They're more — I get the impression that they're more creative than English women. They're not just housewives and (inaudible).
I: What do you have in mind when you say that they're more creative?
P: They just are like, all the fashion designers are French and the top models and things like that.
I: And the ordinary women in your books what do they do?
P: Housewives.
I: They're housewives?
P: Yes.
I: You don't see them at work?
P: Yes, but you don't know what the work is, just go to work. (127/13)

Responses regarding levels of unemployment, strikes, trades unions and levels of pay appeared sometimes to be conjectural. What was clear in all classes was that extramural sources were drawn upon rather than the textbook.

Class 1:

I: What about their attitude to work, strikes and so on?
P: I don't think they get many strikes I don't know if they have unions over there, trade unions, but you never hear of many strikes over there.
I: Are there any jobs then over there which don't exist here, which are special to France I mean?
P: No I don't think so, no.
I: So on the whole your impression is that it's very similar jobs.
P: Jobs and that.
I: What about unemployment?
P: I don't think it's as bad as over here from what I've heard like about unemployment over in France — I don't think there's as much crime in the news over in France as well — not as much as there is over here anyway.
I: Do you watch the news a lot?
P: Yes, we do. (103/20)

Class 2:

I: Do you think that women work in France as much as they do in England or not?
P: I think they work more because like I've seen films and they've like shown cuts of all different things and one thing I have seen is like French women working in clothes factories and sewing away and

everything.

I: Do you think they have a better life than in England or about the same, the women, I wondered what you thought.

P: I think that, well I don't know because I think they think they've got a better life and we think we've got a better life. (156/22)

Class 3:

I: Do you think of France as having a good standard of living? Did it strike you that they were well off when you were there?

P: Yes, just all the stalls and that, the fish stalls and the docks.

I: What struck you about the fish stalls and the docks?

P: That they were all rich and that, like nearly all the coloured people had stalls and that.

I: What made you think that they were well off? Rich?

P: . . . Just they were flashing their money about.

I: Would you think of them as being better off than us then?

P: Yes, I think so. (161/25)

Class 3:

I: Do you think that the French ever have any strikes, have you ever heard of people going on strike in France?

P: When we went over there was something I think it was a strike at Calais, something like that. (171/25)

Class 4:

I: No. What are your impressions of work in France and people's attitudes to work, strikes and so on, unions and that kind of thing?

P: Don't think there's as much as in Britain although there's more unemployment here than I think there is in France.

I: More unemployment here?

P: Yes, and think they're just easy people, good people, they just go on get on with their lives.

I: Yes?

P: Not like some of us here in the North East with unemployment and things.

I: Yes, where there's a lot of unemployment.

P: Yes.

I: And the wages and the standard of living in general.

P: I think the French — the French wages — have to be higher though.

I: Was that the feeling when you went there — that they had a good standard of living?
P: No, most of them.
I: You don't get this kind of information then in your French lessons?
P: No.
I: Where does one get impressions from then?
P: Well from other people talking and listening.
I: And television, do you see much about France on telly?
P: Yes and when the French programmes are on you can always watch them.
I: Which kind of French programmes are you thinking of?
P: There's this French lesson on ITV I think it's called Action, I think. Where this frog comes up and everything. (247/20,21)

Whilst opinions upon types of work available were similar in all classes, pupils in Class 2 had least to say upon this issue. As they had progressed least far through the course and not many had had the benefit of going on visits to France, it was probably therefore harder for them to extrapolate from the type of information provided by the textbook. One possible textbook source was the recurrent presentation of advertisements for jobs for which French could be useful in France. Whilst these were referred to by their teacher (for instance field notes 05/03/86) it did not appear that pupils were able to transfer this kind of information to a general understanding of work available.

In Class 3 some difference between the gender groups was again found. The responses of the girls generally indicated more reflection upon this issue and in the absence of much textbook information they attempted to use what sources they had.

Sub-issues

Housing

For pupils in all four classes the textbook was thought only to have provided information upon the predominance of flats in France, and distinguishing characteristics such as 'caves' and subterranean garages. Visits could provide details of both exterior and interior design, but this was not necessarily the case; some pupils who had been on extended visits concluded that houses were 'the same'.

No obvious class consensuses of information, beyond superficial details from the textbook, cited above, were found. Therefore a few examples are given by class to indicate the diversity of responses found and their sources. Describing architectural features and distinguishing characteristics appeared to be difficult for a number of respondents.

In Class 1 the following were two of the more extensive responses:

Class 1:

I: What about the homes that people have? Keep imagining that I'm going to live —

P: I think their homes are a lot bigger than they are up here, mostly the houses over there they have like cellars and basements but over here like most people just live in like a council house on big estates. Most houses over there are like bought and different.

I: They're bought?

P: Yes.

I: So, well again I'd be interested if you can tell me in a bit more detail what your impression is of houses.

P: Like I say I think they are a lot bigger and they have a lot more rooms and cellars and basements and over here it's just like three bedrooms, bathroom, kitchen.

I: And what would the inside of the house be like? The furnishings?

P: Mostly the same as over here really.

I: And the outside, would that be.

P: I think most of their houses are made of wood I think and they paint them like white — a lot of them are white but ours are usually brick. (103/9)

I: What about the standard of living then, what is your feeling about that, are they better paid than we are?

P: They seem to go from living in very small houses and living quite poor to living in the large ones. There doesn't seem to be a middle.

I: Would you think of somebody — yourself and your family living in France — would you think of them as having the same standard of living?

P: There doesn't seem to be a middle one. We are not exactly rich but we are not poor. There doesn't seem to be that level. (120/24)

P: The size it wasn't in miles — kilometres. And there was a big sign when we first got off the ferry which had a picture of a housing estate then a number of how many miles to go and then some trees — how many miles to go and then a motorway and how many miles.

I: And if you follow your journey through your early days there?

P: We drove on the other side of the road. It was very confusing like the traffic lights and things.

I: As you were looking out through the window going through the towns and villages and countryside?

P: The countryside was very similar to ours. The houses and things were old and then we would come to a place with a lot of houses that were new. Then we went through like a holiday village and the houses were all funny shapes, they were awful.

I: I know the sort of thing you mean. The ordinary villages?

P: They just seemed to have a lot of old houses, then you would come to a place with a lot of new ones. They seemed to have a lot of little villages rather than big ones.

I: And the people in the villages, did they look different from the people in the towns?

P: No I don't think so.

I: Did you go through any large towns?

P: We went St. Levare (*sic*) but we just went to the supermarket there. They are just the same. (120/28)

In Class 2 travelling through France had provided information:

Class 2:

I: When you went to France, I mean obviously you saw something anyway it must have taken you a day to drive through, did it?

P: Yes.

I: Were there things — how did it compare with what you'd learnt about in French lessons?

P: . . . It's packed — like there's a lot of buildings like when we passed through Paris we saw the Eiffel Tower and we saw the post, that thing, like all the houses are really close together all like one big long row there's lots of railway lines there from where we passed and a lot of tunnels and subways and it was always busy there on the roads and they have a lot of signs up and canals at the sides of the — all the way through that went on for a long time, and ordinary things like that. (151/14)

Several pupils in the class thought that French houses were 'better' in some ways:

I: What would you say, what would you tell me?

P: It's a nice place, the weather can be a bit bad now and again, 9 hours sunny there. The beaches are canny nice. The French people are nice to you, polite and everything and the French houses are canny posh, better than round here like on their own like posh and like hardly any doors, like patios and things like that, it's nice. (135/6)

P: Well the windows and that are bigger than ours and like patios and modern like doors. Like garage down underneath them. Like normal bedrooms and normal kitchen and bathrooms. Just the same.
I: Would the furnishings then be the same?
P: Yes.
I: And the style of the house?
P: Maybe that would be different because they are more modern down in France. More modern furniture.
I: So they would be bigger and more modern than here? Would you think of the houses in towns as being different from the country?
P: Yes more like flats. Bit like the houses we have down here. Like blocks.
I: In towns?
P: In flats. In the countryside they have the beach, big houses.
I: You are thinking now of what you saw when you were in X?
P: Yes. (135/15)

I: Right now for somebody who lived in Paris what kind of house or flat do you think they'd live in?
P: . . . Pretty good.
I: What do you mean by pretty good? Would it be a big detached house?
P: Modern not like old-fashioned. (138/6)

Most pupils in Class 3 referred mainly to flats and 'caves'. Some pupils thought houses were big for a reason the provenance of which did not become clear.

Class 3:

I: What's their house or flat going to be like?
P: Big, 'cause they've got big families, most of them anyway and they're quite nice they've all got big bedrooms and big living rooms and a garage and if you live with them they've got like a basement where some people store home-made wines and things, French people anyway and . . . (164/17)

One girl who had visited France provided amongst the most detailed description of the whole sample upon housing.

I: What about the different regions of France, do you think of those as being different from each other?

P: No, just the buildings are different really some of them. Some are more traditional, some are just like flats, some are just normal houses.

I: Yes?

P: In the flats there is like younger people living there, they have like one piece of the garden below. That would be in a younger area but in an older area they would have houses that have like these wood things without windows — I've forgotten what you call them and they have more traditional like old men sitting outside in the garden with their pipes and berets on. They have their own bit of garden and do the garden and that and the women would be inside doing the cooking and come out shouting for them but that would be the older parts but Boulogne seemed to be older parts more than anything else. (175/12)

I: What about the sort of home in which I would expect to live? What would it be like inside the house?

P: If it's traditional they would have quite . . . box rooms in French, like French style. They have like funny wardrobes which seem to be different to ours — I don't know, you can tell it's foreign when you go in and the rooms seem to be more box shape and seem to be closer together. There are not as many rooms as in an English house. They have got everything in it but in a flat you are quite squashed but you have got everything you need. It's just like what you need for basics in a French house. When I went in there were just basics nothing — no special rooms fixed in for spare room or something. They just have all the basics, bits of fanciness like different ornaments to go on the side to make it brighter but they are quite cheerful the houses. (175/19)

As in the other classes knowledge of regional differences was rare. When probed upon this results were not encouraging.

I: What about the houses in different regions, do you think they are the same all over France?

P: In some places they will be bigger, like in the country because they have more space.

I: What about say in the Alps, what do you think the houses are like there?

P: They will be like bungalows.

I: What will they be made of do you think?

P: . . . Bricks and wood on the outside.

I: What, all round?

P: Wood on the outside and bricks on the inside. (166/29)

In Class 4 one pupil had visited an example of rural housing which he thought was atypical. His recollection of the visit was unusually vivid.

Class 4:

I: If we were to go back to the family, let's think about how they live, their home, what would that be like?

P: Well the home I went to was quite strange it was almost like a farm type, a small farm, it was in the sort of suburbs of the town and it was a bungalow and they had sort of chickens sort lots of dogs and things like that and it was almost a farm in the back garden. It seemed sort of, but it wasn't like our house, our house is sort of modern, it's got lots of modern things in their's was sort of more simple. I don't know if that's the same in all of France but just this part was all things like that. The toilet I noticed you had to turn the tap on to fill it with water then pull a lever and it emptied so it was strange.

I: Would you see that as being typical or . . .?

P: Well most of the toilets were just sort of like ours I think, the ones at the youth hostel were and that.

I: What about the house as a home do you think of that as being . . .

P: Well it was adequate but I wouldn't say it was — didn't have any luxuries as we do in England. It was a bungalow this one but from what I heard from some of the other people the houses were sort of just like ours really or bigger sometimes. It was just where I got picked to go.

I: Yes, and when you were in the place did you notice I mean what do the houses look like from the outside, the style?

P: They seem to have a lot of whitewashed sort of stone, not stone like concrete it looked like. It seemed more plain than ours when we have brick with the patterns and things like that theirs are quite plain. Most of them well a lot of them had shutters on.

I: So you'd see that they were a different style to ours?

P: Oh, yes they were a different style to ours. (244/13,14)

A girl who had also had experience of visiting France attempted to differentiate amongst styles, but drew unusual comparisons.

P: They'd have more, they wouldn't have like things hung up on the walls so much . . . they'd have more little things on shelves and that. That's about it just the same as ours.

I: Do they vary, again you've travelled through France — do the houses vary from region to region?

P: Yes, when you're in Boulogne it's just like fishermen's houses on the front and when you get down to Paris they're all big houses and when you get down to the South of France it's all a bit like this, a little bit quieter. (248/30)

Sources other than visits were quoted, for example:

Class 1:

I: How would you describe the style of housing in France?

P: Like in the cities it's already piled on top of the other same as it is here but I think it's a bit more like, more buildings in less space, like we've been looking at Boulogne and that and they had just a block of flats with about 10 storeys and that and that's just on the outskirts . . .

I: And the style? The architecture I mean?

P: The ones we've been looking at were about the same as ours except they were a bit like — our flats would probably be thin but in big massive blocks like the ones in Northern Ireland and that.

I: What do you mean by thin?

P: Like just one flat on top of the other but here they had like a row of three flats like and another three flats on top.

I: Right, yes. What about housing, as opposed to flats?

P: Housing's a different style 'cause like they have, they have rooms in the loft and that sort of thing and they have like different, different layout . . . (101/27)

I: And the standard of living in general, would that be the same?

P: I think so yes.

I: Where do you get this kind of information from, that interests me?

P: Well we had a French person over here on the French exchange that my brother took part in and he came over and brought photographs and that and then from the |*Action!*|Grade 2 book we use here, it has a lot of pictures.

I: So that is one source. And in the book, what sort of things are there in the book?

P: Well it shows you the French houses and everything and then there is a section of objects in the house and the different meals and everything. It shows you a lot of pictures in the books.

I: Do you also discuss these things in class?

P: Yes we discuss like we compare them both from English to French and see what the differences are between them.

I: Does your teacher then talk about France herself?

P: We had Miss Leyborne, she talked from her own experiences of being in France and taking part in exchanges and that and the same with Miss Saunders now. (104/8,9)

Pupils in Class 1 had studied the relevant units quite recently.

I: Do you think they have many flats in France?
P: I think they have a bit more than in England.
I: How've you learned about that?
P: We've been doing about flats and that in French.
I: Oh, have you? Was that recently?
P: About half a year ago.
I: Yes, and that's in your book is it, about their flats?
P: Well just like about the blocks and where the car parks.
I: Yes, does it tell you about inside the flats at all, what they're like?
P: Just like there's rooms and 3 bedrooms and just small kitchens.
I: Do you think they have a living room as well?
P: Yes, but like it joins the dining room.
I: Yes, so there's just one sort of room apart from the kitchen?
P: Yes. (121S/9,10)

Education

This was one topic in which class differences were noticeable in that Class 4 had studied units upon education not yet covered by other classes. From earlier years pupils in all classes had retained some information upon the differences in school timetables; these items of information had been added to from friends' accounts and visits to France, but varied widely in accuracy.

In Class 1 only a few details were presented.

I: And to go back to other things of every day life what about school I mean you mentioned school what would you be able to tell me about school? About the time it starts and things like that.
P: About 8 o'clock and it would finish like — start about 8 and finish about 1 I think and then you get the whole afternoon off as opposed to just starting at 9 and getting through till 4 in this country.
I: What do people do then in the afternoon?
P: Might go swimming I think or do their homework or play tennis or something in the summer. (106/10)

I: I was just going to ask you a little bit about schools that they go to because you tell me that they go a bit earlier. Do you know if they go to school every day?

P: . . . They don't go on a Wednesday . . . and on Sunday.

I: They don't go on Sunday?

P: No.

I: What about Saturday?

P: I think they go a half day.

I: How have you heard about that?

P: Just stories we've read in the French lessons.

I: You mentioned that they went early but I couldn't remember if you told me what time it was you thought they started.

P: About 8.

I: And what time do they go on till?

P: Three.

I: Do they get any free time do you think?

P: I don't know.

I: What about homework?

P: They still have to do like homework like us.

I: What about subjects do they get any subjects to do at school that you don't do, do you think?

P: . . . No, I don't think so, they might have a different language to do.

I: Yes, that's possible, what do you think they learn?

P: . . . Spanish or something like that.

I: Do you think there are any subjects that you do that they don't do?

P: . . . No.

I: What about holidays, do you think they have about the same amount of holidays as you?

P: Yes.

I: Not any more, or any less?

P: . . . They might have a few more.

I: What about in the summer?

P: I think it would be just about the same. (118S/27)

Some opinions regarding homework had been formed:

I: What sort of time do they start school?

P: I don't know about half past 8.

I: Have you ever heard what time they go on till?

P: Don't know I think it's 4 o'clock or something.

I: Yes. What do you think they do in the afternoon?

P: Just like do their homework which they have quite a lot of and say go out with their friends.

I: Do you think they have more homework than you or less?

P: They have more because they're at school for less time. (121S/8)

In Class 2 confusion about the timetable was just as prevalent. Interesting comparisons with English schools were drawn.

P: . . . like the schools have different sort of things get out at different times and different breaks and things like that.

I: Tell me a bit more about that —

P: Eat different things —

I: — about school.

P: — they go, I think they go to school on a Saturday as well and get a couple of days off through the week . . . the classroom is more, like you've got one desk to yourself, I saw a picture of a classroom in France and you've got one desk to one person and just different, it's just a bit plain, like the picture I saw just had a blackboard, desk, chairs, people working, that's all it had really.

I: Do you think the teachers would be different?

P: Not really, I don't think so, I think they would be about the same really, as the English. I mean they'll teach the same things probably.

I: They don't have any lessons other — that are different from ours?

P: Except they'll learn English, the language English and we learn language French. That's all I think different.

I: What about the time and breaks and so on that you were mentioning?

P: I think they have longer breaks than us, I'm not sure.

I: What time would they go to school?

P: Go to school? I think it's ten o'clock, so they've got a shorter day than us, shorter week and it's overall better I think, I suppose when you're at school in England, I suppose you learn more. It all depends what the attitude of the French is and the attitude of the English class. (133/7,8)

I: You've mentioned school already, what about what people actually do at school once they get there?

P: Just the same . . . except as us learning French, they would learn English or something like that.

I: And the school life, I think you said you thought the schools would be better?

P: Better teachers . . . school life, I suppose the school is probably bigger, well anything's better than this but the teachers would be better well some of them would be good and bad like this school but the schools would be better probably better equipped like than this one. (140/11)

In Class 3 a few more details of the secondary system became apparent, but some inaccuracies were evident.

I: What do you think their school day would be like?
P: It would be different on some days because some days they only go half days and we go whole days.
I: Which days do you think they go half days?
P: Saturday and Wednesday. (166/8)

I: What sort of things do you learn about the schools?
P: They have to buy their own books and things like that.
I: Is that in all schools?
P: I don't know, we have just done one or two.
I: What else have you learnt about schools?
P; A lot of them don't have to wear uniforms.
I: What do you think of that idea?
P: . . . Don't know.
I: Do you think it is a good idea or not? Do you like to wear uniform?
P: No. (166/42)

I: Have you ever heard anything about what time they start school?
P: Yes the teachers start at about 8 o'clock in the morning and finish at 12.
I: What about in the afternoon?
P: They don't go to school in the afternoon.
I: Who have you heard that from?
P: . . . Just some of my friends.
I: What, who have been to France?
P: Yes. (166/43)

A quotation earlier on Class 3's perception of the role of the teacher, indicated that the teacher had referred to having to buy books in France. (No. 183/35)

The majority of responses from Class 4 were detailed, and recall of material presented appeared to be more accurate than that of other classes. A few examples are given to illustrate this.

I: When you say the schools will be different, what had you in mind?
P: Well the fact that they don't wear any uniforms and can really do what they want and the times of school and things like that.
I: The times are different?
P: Yes, 'cause they start a bit more early and they have Wednesdays off,

stuff like that.

I: When you say they can do what they want what do you mean by that?

P: Well when we were reading the textbook it said that a lot of them smoked and things like that, I mean I know they do over here but it seemed as if everyone did over there.

I: Yes. What textbook was this then?

P: The *Action!* book three, 'cause we're doing about schools.

I: Do they tell you a lot of information about schools?

P: There was a couple of pages on it and it was just generally the time they went to school and what time they had off and the work that they did really, that's all it was.

I: And the work was that noticeably different?

P: No, not really it was about the same.

I: So going to school in France and going to school here would you feel that it's noticeably different or what it's like?

P: Just mainly the times and that's all.

I: What about the teachers, would they be different?

P: I don't think so, about the same. (265/6)

P: They would start earlier and get a few lessons but they would have free periods when they could just revise or do what they wanted. I think they have longer dinner breaks. When they come in they would stay in until about 5 o'clock or something like that.

I: On a weekly basis does that alter at all do you know?

P: I think they have Wednesday afternoons off. I think they go to school on Saturday mornings as well. (273/8)

I: Right let's go on to talk about schooling a bit. Imagine that you're going to a French school, what would it be like?

P: It would be a lot bigger than it is here. I think there would be a lot more rooms for specialist things.

I: What would the teachers be like?

P: I think they would be just the same.

I: The teachers would be the same?

P: Yes.

I: They would be no more strict or casual than the teachers here?

P: I think they might be a bit stricter.

I: What time would you go to school?

P: 8 o'clock.

I: And how much free time would you get?

P: I think about an hour and a half for the dinner break and they might have an hour free on a morning and an hour free on a night, afternoon.

I: Are there any subjects you wouldn't do in a French school?

P: R.E., you wouldn't do that.

I: How many days in the week do you go to school in France?

P: All of Monday and Tuesday, just Wednesday morning, all of Thursday and Friday and Saturday morning. (273/25)

I: No. What — do you know what young people do when they leave the secondary school?

P: . . .

I: Is there a system of training for them?

P: I think there's like a college place that they might be able to go to for about two years.

I: What qualifications can young people get in France similar to our GCSE?

P: I don't know. (273/26)

In no class were pupils aware of the differences in French school holiday length.

Whilst it was clear that Class 4 pupils had more recently covered material on schooling, observation of the class (29/11/85 field notes) indicated that the unit of schooling, written in English, was given for homework. This might account for some lack of recall of certain details. In *Action! Book 1*, information upon schools referred to French school councils; no pupils recalled this. Observation of Class 4 (12/12/85) showed that the teacher had referred to details of schooling such as 'nice long lunch hours', free periods and more homework. A further unit (studied 17/01/86), referred to differences in times of the timetable. The subject of education had therefore been covered quite extensively in this class.

Politics and history

In no class was knowledge of politics attributed to the textbook. In the two middle achievement classes (2 and 3), little was known beyond the name of the President, though even knowledge of this was not ensured. More detailed acquaintance with the French political system was found in Classes 1 and 4, but confusion regarding the roles of President and Prime Minister and their respective parties, was apparent. Boys generally gave more detailed responses upon politics than did girls.

Outside sources were all important, as is evident from this example from one of the best informed pupils:

I: Would you, I mean could you tell me anything about French politics?

P: It's just changed I think over there, the way, the voting system. From this last election they vote a new premier I think it is and just changed it — I can't remember what it's called.

I: Yes, I know what you mean.

P: Representation, personal representation.

I: Yes.

P: They've just changed it from the old system to that new system.

I: And can you tell me about the present situation then?

P: Proportional representation I think it's called, it's supposed to be a more fair system only the only thing is the like National Front can get voted in if they get a seat, like in the old system they wouldn't get voted in but there's a few National Front seats in France now.

I: And what else, I mean what other political parties are there, and who's in power?

P: Mitterand is like, I don't know what he is really — I don't know the name for him (inaudible) he's voted every eighth year I think it is, I don't know who the Prime Minister sort of person is. Is it Jacques Chirac or something?

I: And the system of I mean what's the relationship then between — what does the President do, what does Mitterand do?

P: They don't have sort of royal families so he's sort of half way he's like the head figure of the country, I suppose the head figure in this country is like the Queen or something. Like he's the head figure of that particular country, he represents the country at royal events and things like that.

I: With no political power?

P: Yes I think 'cause he doesn't have to be the same member of the party as the main party that rules over the country. I think the Prime Minister he's like a different — he's in a different party to what Mitterand is at the moment that's what all the controversy was about.

I: Right. Are you interested in English politics as well, is that why you're so well informed about French politics?

P: Yes, it's with watching the news a lot and my Dad's interested in politics.

I: Do you talk to him about politics then?

P: Yes. If I don't understand something like, like that new voting system in France that I didn't understand, I asked my Dad what it was all about and he explained it to me. (103/27)

Historical knowledge was more extensive also in Classes 1 and 4.

The following people and events were recalled in Class 1 (not in chronological order):

Louis XIV, General de Gaulle, the French Revolution, Louis XVI, Charles I, William the Conqueror, the Resistance, Marie Antoinette, World War I and II, and more improbably Louis IX.

Reasons for the French Revolution though studied recently inevitably varied in accuracy.

Class 1:

I: Do you ever hear anything about France in other lessons like history or geography?

P: We did . . . the only things we have done — we did the French Revolution. That's all.

I: When did you do that?

P: In history about five or six months ago.

I: Oh, yes, and what did you learn about that?

P: Just learnt all about big houses, Marie Antoinette's clothes, just the poverty.

I: Yes, so why do you think they had the Revolution?

P: . . . Just to get rid of the Ruler because he wasn't doing them any good. They were just living in poverty, they had no money.

I: So do you know how France is ruled now? Who is in charge so to speak?

P: Don't know who is in charge but it's a President.

I: Yes, so they have a President (inaudible) (102/31)

I: Have you ever learnt anything about the history of France? Not just in French lessons but in history as well?

P: . . . No, just about them being at war with Germany and . . .

I: Do you know which war or wars that was or those were? Which wars were they?

P: I think the First and Second World Wars.

I: Yes. Did you hear about that at school or at home?

P: At school.

I: In history lessons, because it varies you see in some schools people don't study it at all. When was it you heard about that?

P: We've done the French Revolution and I think it was a year last year and we've just finished the First World War.

I: Who did you study the French Revolution with?

P: Mrs A.

I: What was important about that?

P: . . . Don't know really.

I: Just wondered, why do you think they had it?
P: . . . To fight for their own lives but it just ended in them fighting each other. (118S/32)

Admissions of a lack of interest was sometimes expressed.

Class 1:

I: What do you know about politics in France at the moment?
P: Nothing.
I: Or do you know the way it works, the general institutions and things like that?
P: Nothing at all, but I don't know about any other country either.
I: What about English politics?
P: Oh, I know about England, you can't escape them.
I: Yes.
P: It doesn't interest me.
I: So you wouldn't want that to be in your textbook?
P: No, other children might but . . .
I: Not for you?
P: No. (127/20)

Information upon the World Wars was usually more accurate than upon other periods of history, due probably to other extramural factors, but confusion regarding many aspects of history was apparent.

Class 4:

I: Why does France have a President as opposed to a King and Queen?
P: Because I think because we used to rule them and they still took our Queen but they got their own President. (273/27)

An interest in history was not sufficient to ensure that all pupils regarded other countries sympathetically. For example a Class 4 boy stated:

I: You said that you'd heard about the Revolution is there anything else you've heard about the history of France?
P: Well the Battle of Hastings.
I: Yes.
P: That was, 'cause I was like on the French side then, do you know what I mean?

I: Yes.

P: I wanted William to win, but I wouldn't want them to win now if they came over.

I: Why's that?

P: Because they're not so nice now, they were like more important than Britain then, more civilised.

I: So they were more civilised then but when you say that they're not so nice now, how do you mean?

P: They don't really keep up with the times and they're not like, you know proper — nothing good 'cause they've got like a few television channels and they're not like good they're just like a few hours a day sort of thing, can't just have four big ones or something, got to have about eight little ones.

I: So you feel that they're a bit more old-fashioned, is that it?

P: Yes, they try to be modern and it always goes wrong.

I: It always goes wrong?

P: Yes.

I: What sort of things go wrong?

P: Well you hear things on Tomorrow's World about them but nothing's like — everything's been discovered and that and they're on about space things now but we know all those things so nothing's new.

I: So you mean they're a bit behind somehow?

P: Yes.

I: What happened in the Second World War?

P: . . . Well the Germans were going to conquer them weren't they, we had to help them but we shouldn't have.

I: Why's that do you think?

P: Well they wouldn't help us if we're ever going to get conquered, they'd just — well they'd want us to wouldn't they? (245/22)

In neither class was France regarded as a significant political power, though usually it was seen as occupying a similar role to that of Britain. It was not thought to be technologically advanced by another pupil in Class 4.

Class 4:

I: Do you think France has an important role to play in the world at present?

P: Not really because it doesn't seem to have any nuclear weapons or anything. (273/32)

In Class 2 references were made to Napoleon, the French Revolution and briefly to the World Wars. Though recently studied some confusion was apparent.

Class 2:

I: What about this century — the last war and the First World War? Do you know anything about France at that time?
P:. . .
I: In the Second World War and the First World War?
P: . . . Only that — learned they were in the war with Germany and Russia and Britain but not really.
I: Do you do anything about these things in other subjects in geography and history?
P: No.
I: You don't? What do you do in geography and history?
P: Geography we just learn about industry and places like forestry and ship-building and stuff like that and in history we are doing about World War I now — we are learning about World War I and Hitler and that but not much of the French just mainly about Hitler and we've been watching videos and that was it. (151/34)
I: What do you know of the history of France?
P: There was a Revolution or something. Napoleon was in it I think. People were killed in it. The Revolution.
I: What about this century, the wars in this century, First or Second World Wars?
P: Occupied by Germany. They were using France to get at England.
I: In which war?
P: The second. France was Britain's ally in the First I think . . . helped England in the second a bit . . . well you don't hear much about France and the history of it really. (133/27)

In Class 3 boys made more references to historical figures such as Napoleon, Joan of Arc and William the Conqueror. The source was clear.

I: What about history say, would you like to know a lot about French history? Have you done anything about French history?
P: No, we've done a bit about Napoleon, that's all.
I: Did you find it interesting?
P: Yes, quite interesting, yes.
I: Would you be interested in any more or do you think that's enough?
P: No, I think that's enough. It's supposed to be the French language what we're learning (161/33).

The attitude of the girls to French history and politics in Class 3 was unenthusiastic.

I: Have you heard anything about the politics in France?
P: No.
I: You know we have several parties in England do you think they have the same sort of system there?
P: Maybe — don't know.
I: About the President have you ever heard of him?
P: Didn't know they had one. (168/31)

I: But you haven't heard anything about how the French elections work or Parliament or anything? Have you ever heard about the President?
P: No.
I: Do you know why France has a President?
P: No, I've never heard of him.
I: You've not heard that they've got one. Do you think that they've got a Royal Family?
P: . . . Yes, I would think so.
I: Have you studied anything about France in history?
P: . . . No, not in our history lesson.
I: Not anything about the Revolution?
P: Oh, well, we've learned about that. I don't know I wasn't listening.
I: Not keen on history. Is that this year or last year that you did that?
P: This year.
I: Have you studied the Second World War or the First World War at all?
P: . . . Can't remember.
I: Not done that this year?
P: I think we have but I'm not interested. (171/31,32)

I: Could you tell me anything about the way the French parliament works as opposed to us, do they have a different way of electing their Presidents?
P: Don't know.
I: Why do they have a President?
P: To run the country.
I: Yes, to run the country. But why don't they have a King and Queen and then underneath them parliament?
P: Don't know.
I: Do you remember what happened in the French Revolution? Have you done the French Revolution?
P: We have but I don't like it, I never listened to it. (184/30,31)

Geography

Class 1 pupils gave the most detailed responses to questions upon the geography of France. This was probably attributable to both the geography curriculum of the class, and their recent coverage of a topic upon weather in French lessons. Observation of the class (17/12/85) showed that the teacher supplemented textbook activities with a quiz upon geography. A further lesson (20/01/86) was devoted to memorisation of maps of France. The following responses were among the most detailed of the whole sample.

Class 1:

I: Yes. The final thing is the question of geography would you put — what's your — if I show you a map of France would you — which I have somewhere here — would you point things out on that map to me. Would you be able — not as a test — what would you be able to put out on there?

P: Paris there, Marseille up there somewhere, this region, that's the Mediterranean, South of France, and I think that's where they go for their holidays down there, that's the Pyrenees, there's the river Rhone comes up there I think and there's the Garonne. I think that's down there. I think that's really all.

I: Yes, so you'd certainly know sort of few basic features of it. Is this something that you've done in class?

P: Yes, we done like the names of all the difference rivers and . . .

I: Yes, have you done anything about the regions geographically — economics of the regions and so on, and the industries.

P: . . . No. (103/40)

I: Do you feel that you know a lot about French geography?

P: I know the sort of land and everything and a couple of rivers and mountains and that and like in — I don't know much about the industry. I know a lot about Marseille and everything, we did that in Geography about the port in Marseille and everything and industries around there but would like to see more of it.

I: So some of this you have done in Geography lessons. Have you done some in French lessons?

P: Well we did the weather section, we ended up doing geography for the Alps and that but that was about it.

I: So you would like to see a bit more of that in the French lessons?

P: Yes. (104/25)

In Class 2 only two pupils gave responses which were at all detailed.

Class 2:

I: Right this is a map of France could you show me where the Atlantic Ocean is?
P: It's up here near England, is it?
I: Yes. Could you show me where Boulogne is?
P: Down here near Calais and that.
I: What about Paris?
P: About there.
I: Not bad, not bad. Where would the Alps be on that?
P: Alps. They're there aren't they or there's some mountains or something here.
I: Some mountains here.
P: There's something called the Central Massif or something. (138/34)

I: What about geography?
P: No — except North, South, East and West and that.
I: Yes. I have got a map somewhere. What would you be able to put on there?
P: Watch this — I can't think where they are. There is Paris somewhere up here somewhere, round here. Then there is Nice somewhere down here somewhere. Along that coast somewhere. Calais is along here somewhere I think. And then there is . . . Normandy . . .
I: What about some rivers and things like that?
P: Can't think. We did them but I can't remember what it was. We did them in geography actually. I don't know — does the Rhine go through there?
I: No it's on the border.
P: I knew it was somewhere near.
I: It actually forms the border with Germany. Here. So you have done something about French geography in geography lessons?
P: Yes. Just like where the rivers are and that. We did something about the trains. We did about Italy sinking and all that. Venice and all that sinking. (140/27)

Several instances of lessons including geographical subject matter were recorded in class observation (for example 04/12/85, 22/01/86, 03/02/86, 17/03/86, 19/02/86). A range of areas and place names were covered but few recalled by this class.

In Class 3 where the geography curriculum did not include France information appeared limited. Some knowledge of industries and regions had been gained from other sources.

Class 3:

I: What about these regions over here? Have you ever heard anything about these? This one that sticks out into the sea.

P: No not really I have just heard about Paris and Boulogne and that sort of thing.

I: Ever heard anything about the mountain area, the mountain regions?

P: I have heard about different skiing resorts or something.

I: Have you any idea which side or direction they might be?

P: Round here.

I: Yes, sort of middle towards the east. Have you heard anything about the industries — what they might be?

P: I think mainly farming. I'm not sure but I think there is iron or steel. I think I have heard that.

I: Have you any idea in which area they might be in? North or South?

P: I think they are in the Northern areas.

I: How have you heard about that, is that at school or on television?

P: No I have just read books, little articles every now and again about it. Bits in the paper mainly. (183/5,6)

Classroom observation (08/04/86 and 24/04/86) indicated that places such as Rouen, Lille and the Ardennes had been referred to in lessons. Extensive knowledge of regions and places in France appeared to be particularly difficult for Class 2 and Class 3 pupils to retain. The responses of Class 4 were the second most detailed group, though France was not studied in geography lessons. Though observation (13/03/86) showed that textbook material on towns and populations had been covered, knowledge of regions was limited.

Growing up and religion

All four classes were alike in having few opinions upon growing up in France and very little knowledge of religion in France. A few pupils in each class were aware that Catholicism predominates but some pupils exhibited confusion regarding religion generally. As this topic has been covered for the whole sample earlier in this chapter we shall not illustrate further here.

Language

No differences were found amongst the classes in pupils' knowledge of the relationship of languages. A few pupils could recall words which had been taken from either English into French, or vice versa. Some examples of a brief nature were found.

Class 2:

I: Do you know words that the French borrowed from the English recently?

P: Like when they play football like they like use our word football and it was invented over here.

I: Yes, what else, any others? How do you see the French, sorry, you were going to say.

P: Like tennis I think they say the same as us and all they have different — the same words as us 'cause maybe different countries have invented a lot and we invented them.

I: How do you think the French feel about pinching our words or having our words pushed on them?

P: . . . Not really pleased, they'd rather have their own words. (138/28)

Though the opening sections of *Action! Book 1* indicate where French is spoken in the world, and this issue is reiterated later in the course, most pupils did not appear, when discussing French history, to make any connections between the spread of the language and the past. This applied equally to their understanding of the connection between English and French, though the name of William the Conqueror was cited from time to time. Some connections were remembered:

Class 1:

I: Have you ever heard of any words which French has take from English recently?

P: Er . . . I've heard some English words in French but that's all.

I: Sorry, what did you say?

P: You get some — most English words come from French words.

I: Yes, how did you hear about that?

P: In history you get the — like taught about and things and they have French words instead of English and now they have the English words.

I: Which words can you remember?

P: Well café is the same as over here, in France . . . (121S/30)

.... Regarding how French is spoken in France several pupils were aware that there were different accents. The sources of this item of information were various:

I: What about the language that people speak in different parts of France?
P: . . . The language that they spoke with their accents and things was different from what I had learnt and heard on the tapes and things.
I: Was that a surprise to you then?
P: No because when you think about it in England we all speak different don't we? (120/29)

Class 3:

P: Yes, they won't like, they have like different accents and that you can't like get them in but some things that we use you can.
I: Yes, so do you think that they — how will it be in France is it going to be similar in France? Different accents and so on?
P: Yes, 'cause they seem to like roll their R's and things like that and I couldn't do that but it seems to be more jumpy than the speech like when they talk they seem to be like jumpy at the end to make a point a bit and you can't really get that but if you'd been living there for a while like a year or so you could maybe get it, otherwise you can't. (175/38)

Famous people in the arts, and sciences; well-known buildings

In asking pupils if they could recall the names of any famous people in the arts and sciences or any famous buildings, pupils in all four classes appeared to draw largely upon the same store of information, which had been presented to them in the first textbook of the course. Some of the same figures given by those questioned upon the history of France were cited. The major figures recalled therefore were:

Marie Curie, Pasteur, Sacha Distel, Sheila, Napoleon, Cousteau, Brigitte Bardot (once) and William the Conqueror.

The main buildings were:

the Eiffel Tower and the Arc de Triomphe (though observation of Class 3 and Class 4, 14/04/86 and 21/03/86, showed that a wide range of buildings and sights were presented).

For most pupils the list had not been added to. Football, however, was a source for one:

Class 3:

I: What about the French football team?
P: . . . Platini, I know him. I've heard about him.
I: Have you seen them play?
P: Yes. (163/24)

Recall of who did what was not always confident or accurate:

Class 2:

I: What about other things like paintings and scientists. Do you know the names of any famous painters or scientists or Louis Pasteur?
P: I've read of him he pasteurised milk . . .
I: Where did you hear about him?
P: In the first year — people like Sheila — like pictures of them.
I: Sheila?
P: Yes, this lady with the long blonde hair.
I: Oh, she's a pop singer you mean?
P: I don't know but like there was Napolean and this other fellow but I don't know and there was a fellow who was getting burnt on a stake.
I: Oh, yes, Joan of Arc?
P: Joan of Arc, yes.
I: What did you learn about all these people then?
P: Nothing we just had to remember their names. Like Miss used to like put — to test us and put our hands up and say the names and then . . . like I mean I know Napoleon was like in the war . . . and Louis Pasteur discovered pasteurised milk and Joan or Arc was burnt.
I: By? Who by?
P: I don't know. I've forgotten. We haven't really done it for a long time. (151/33)

Class 2:

I: Do you know any famous names?
P: . . . Marie Curie, Victor Hugo, Louis Pasteur. All of them ones.
I: What are they famous for?
P: Marie Curie is it platinum she took from the rocks. And the husband. She died of cancer or something. Louis Pasteur he was the first to pasteurise milk. He was named after it.
I: Victor Hugo?
P: He was a scientist . . . Sheila or something, she is a singer, I think.

I: Today.
P: Today?
I: She is a singer of today is she?
P: I think so I am not sure. (133/26)

Class 3

I: Do you know of arts in general, any famous artists and things like that, famous scientists?
P: They seem to be all over there. There seems to be a lot of artists there trying to work or something and there's paintings all hanging up in every room you go into.
I: In the houses you mean?
P: Yes, even in shops even you see paintings on the wall, they have them all over.
I: And do you know of any famous French painters?
P: Yes, they all seem to be called Louis in France. I can't remember half of them — I can't remember. (175/43)

The placing of a picture of the Mona Lisa in the textbook had caused confusion:

Class 1:

I: Do you think there are any books or paintings or music from France that are famous? Have you heard anything about those, either in school or on television?
P: There's quite a lot of them, well I know the Mona Lisa that's probably the most famous.
I: Yes.
P: There's a lot of painters in France.
I: Yes, do you know who painted the Mona Lisa?
P: No . . . I've forgotten now.
I: Yes, all right, but you've heard about it?
P: Yes.
I: Is it in France or is it painted by a Frenchman do you think?
P: Yes, it's painted by a Frenchman I think in France. (121S/32)

In Class 4 pupils had studied a unit on Paris quite recently and so knowledge of individual sights and buildings was slightly greater than in other classes. However, there was no increase in detailed knowledge of artistic, literary and musical figures or movements.

Class 4:

I: Can you tell me any famous paintings from France?
P: . . . The Mona Lisa and . . .
I: Is the Mona Lisa a French painting? Was it painted by a Frenchman?
P: . . . I know who painted it but I don't know what he was.
I: Who painted it?
P: Leonardo da Vinci.
I: Does that suggest French or does it suggest another country?
P: French I think.
I: OK. What about books, famous French books, French novels?
P: . . . I don't know. I don't know what that means.
I: What about d'Artagnan and his mates?
P: Oh, yes, I've heard about them.
I: Do you know who wrote the d'Artagnan stories?
P: No. (246/37)

Class 4:

I: Do you know any of the authors in France?
P: No I've just heard that they're good. (248/41)

It appeared that most knowledge therefore of selected famous French people had been acquired in the same way in each class, from the first textbook with attendant flash cards. Pupils were not acquainted first hand with the actual products of artistic and literary figures.

Summary of class knowledge

Although a simple count of instances would be inappropriate in summarising the comparison between the different classes, we have advanced under each heading an estimate of the amount and nature of the knowledge made apparent in interviews. The estimate is limited to little/ more comparisons which are valid within each topic but not across topics, so that 'more' knowledge of 'food' and of 'jobs' for example does not necessarily mean that there is a similar amount of knowledge of each topic, but only more knowledge than in other classes. For some topics despite individuals' knowledge no class consensus could be established and these are labelled 'none' in Table 2.5.

TABLE 2.5 *Summary of case study classes' knowledge by topic*

Topic	Class			
	1	2	3	4
food	m	m	m	l
special meal	n	n	n	n
food reputation	m	l	m	m
jobs	m	l	m	m
housing	n	n	n	n
education	n	n	l	m
politics/history	l	n	n	l
geography	m	n	l	m
growing up/religion	n	n	n	n
language	n	n	n	n
people/buildings	l	l	l	m

3 Pupils' Attitudes towards Foreign People

Introduction

This chapter deals with the question of the relationship between pupils' attitudes, language learning and other factors in their environment. The first part of the chapter relates the collection and analysis of quantitative data which might be expected to indicate statistically significant relationships among the various factors. In the second part this quantitative analysis is complemented by analysis of interview data on attitudes collected from the sub-sample chosen from each school class and representing the different levels of ethnocentricity measured by an attitudinal test. Thus the framework for the second part is provided by quantitative data. It serves both to validate the quantitative data and 'fill out' the statistics with pupils' statements and opinions analysed qualitatively.

Operationalisation of 'Attitudes' and Other Variables

It was important to keep clear the distinction between attitudes towards French as a school subject — which has been investigated on other occasions (APU, 1985; Schools Council, 1981) — and attitudes towards foreign people, and French people in particular. For this reason, existing tests were avoided. The concept of attitudes towards French people was operationalised as pupils' level of ethnocentricity with respect to a specific national group: the degree to which they feel well or ill-disposed when confronted with the notion of, say, 'the French'. Although one solution might have been to devise a measure to suit the particular problem in a way that existing work in social psychology might not, it was important to avoid the danger of turning the research into a project on attitude testing.

Consideration was given to tests which measure degrees of agreement/disagreement with given statements (see Robinson & Shaver, 1973), but

145

such tests raise significant ethical problems, particularly when working with children. There is a danger of introducing immoral ideas. For example, one measure of British ethnocentricity offered statements such as 'I do not think that immigrants should come into this country' (Warr *et al.*, 1967: 271). It seemed improper to appear to legitimise such statements by presenting them to children in a test. Furthermore this, and other tests using statements, raised problems of reading ability, particularly for primary school pupils. Other measures, such as situational attitude scales (Sedlacek *et al.*, 1971) which combine social distance techniques (Bogardus, 1925) and the semantic differential (Osgood *et al.*, 1957) raised similar problems.

Measures of cultural imagery as used in cultural attitude scales (Zirkel & Greene, 1976) might have been worth pursuing if the project had been centrally concerned with developing and validating tests. For example, it would have been necessary to establish an image that the particular people we were interested in, i.e. the French, themselves recognise as portraying an element of their culture. This would then be presented to the pupils in question in order to measure their degree of familiarity and agreement with the particular image.

Eventually, we turned to the notion of the semantic differential in its original and developed forms (Osgood *et al.* 1957; Snider & Osgood, 168; Stager & Osgood, 1964; Maltz, 1969) because in measuring meanings of words, the semantic differential appeared to focus on our principal concern. We were interested in measuring pupils' concepts of foreign people, their concept of 'the French' or 'the Germans' etc. It was decided therefore to combine the semantic differential with the notion of social distance, of how familiar the subject wishes to be with a particular group. This was done in the context of our knowledge of the case-study schools. The schools are closely linked with their communities. Some of the pupils are from small villages, often relatively isolated and with a clear sense of identity. Others are from the small towns in which the comprehensive schools are situated. It was necessary therefore to bear in mind how self-contained and limited their experience of other people might be; this was certainly a view of pupils' experience which teachers held. More positively, however, this social and spatial dimension of the children's social worlds allowed a measure of social distance (Bogardus, 1925) to be built into the instrument devised to measure ethnocentricity without raising ethical or technical problems.

A series of scales was constructed starting with the individual and moving to measurement of how pupils felt about their 'friends', 'people who live near them', 'people who live in Newcastle' (i.e. a focal point in the region, some distance away), 'the English', and then people from other cultures. In addition to 'the French', 'the Germans' and 'the Americans' were included; 'the Germans' because the concept provided a basis for comparison with another European people, and because German is frequently taught in schools; 'the Americans' because of the omnipresent media influence from North America and the potential comparison with people not speaking a foreign language. The test was piloted using a five-point scale and, as a consequence of the piloting, the scale was changed to seven points. Pupils said they wished to put their crosses between 'a bit' and 'fairly'. They found it difficult to say things about themselves but were much clearer and more confident about saying things about the English or the Americans.

(In the course of piloting the ethnocentricity test, conversations with groups of pupils were recorded, as they were asked to comment on the tests and on other aspects of the research. From these conversations a list of statements was made and pupils in the case study schools were asked to agree or disagree. They were also offered the opportunity to write their own statements. This was a supplementary questionnaire which might have been used as a validation and triangulation of the ethnocentricity test or as a basis for discussion in interviews. In the event it was used only to supplement other factors in the selection of interviewees and for occasional discussion of sources in interviews.)

It was axiomatic to the research that the influence of language teaching should be considered in the context of other factors which might affect pupils' attitudes and perceptions. It was necessary therefore to devise a questionnaire which would collect information about other sources of influence to which pupils might be exposed. In addition information was sought on the usual social dimensions of gender, socio-economic status, home location, and achievement in relevant school subjects; this information was provided by the schools.

In developing the questionnaire three broad areas were included: family, foreign travel and the mass-media. Questions about the family background asked whether pupils had foreign relations, how much knowledge of languages parents and siblings had, what languages other than English were spoken in the home and so on. Questions on foreign travel were divided into those dealing with travel with the family and those referring to school-organised journeys. Questions on the media referred to television, comics and so on.

The range of information was potentially very wide and consequently the questionnaire very long. It was necessary therefore to take care with the presentation of the questionnaire and with the clarity of the instructions. It had to be interesting in itself to make it accessible to primary as well as secondary pupils, and again the question of reading ability had to be considered. In the event, most pupils had little information about such issues as foreign relations and completed the questionnaire in approximately half an hour. Some pupils had to be helped with reading and it was important to have a number of adults present to make sure problems could be dealt with. The piloting of the questionnaire in primary and secondary schools clarified some of these points.

Tests and questionnaires were administered in the teaching groups concerned. In the case of secondary pupils, French lessons of 70 minutes were made available and both tests and questionnaires could be completed by almost all pupils within this period. A second visit was made in each case after responses had been checked and pupils were asked to complete any gaps or clarify any uncertainties. This meant that there was only negligible loss of subjects through incomplete data; the minor losses arose from a few pupils moving away from the area in the course of the project.

In the case of primary pupils, it was decided that to administer both test and questionnaire would be too demanding on their concentration. Permission was readily given for school work to be stopped on two occasions and, on a third occasion, missing information was collected as for secondary pupils. Again there were only minor losses.

As pointed out in Chapter 2, the validity of the ethnocentricity test was checked against pupils' statements in interviews. For both age groups the correspondence between the semantic differential scores and attitudes expressed in the interviews was reasonably clear bearing in mind the breadth of the categories used for allocation to an ethnocentric group. It was noticeable that the greatest correspondence was found amongst those categorised as non-ethnocentric, only one case, from amongst the juniors, being unequivocally negative. In the other two groups there were pupils who expressed both positive and negative views about the French.

Amongst the secondary ethnocentric group the majority were negative, whilst amongst the junior groups there was less obvious association. It would not be surprising if the attitudes of the younger age group exhibited inconsistency. A number of the junior pupils' responses to being asked to generalise about a people were wholly non-evaluative, referring to aspects of life or behaviour; a few were unable to answer the question.

The percentages for each age group are given below in Tables 3.1 and 3.2. Responses were broadly categorised into Positive, Negative and

TABLE 3.1 *Association between secondary pupils' semantic differential scores and attitudes*

Secondary age group	Positive	Negative	Mixed
Most ethnocentric group	2 (9.5%)	10 (47.6%)	9 (42.8%)
Medium/neutral group	10 (47.6%)	5 (23.8%)	6 (28.6%)
Non-ethnocentric group	12 (70.6%)	0 (0.0%)	5 (29.4%)

who? What age?

TABLE 3.2 *Association between junior pupils' semantic differential scores and attitudes*

Junior age group	Positive	Negative	Mixed	Non-evaluative	'Don't knows'	
Most ethnocentric group	9 (33.3%)	7 (25.9%)	3 (11.1%)	3 (11.1%)	5 (18.5%)	27
Medium/neutral group	10 (37.0%)	5 (18.5%)	4 (14.8%)	6 (22.2%)	2 (7.4%)	27
Non-ethnocentric group	19 (65.5%)	1 (3.4%)	3 (10.3%)	5 (17.2%)	1 (3.4%)	29

Mixed for the secondary pupils, the first two implying unequivocally positive or negative responses. The majority of responses were positive, approximately 51% of responses being classifiable in this way, with ambivalent responses making up 30% and unequivocally negative responses making up 28% of the total.

Some of the instances of responses which do not accord with the semantic differential scores are illustrated in the text. Given that the semantic differential test makes use of constructs which do not derive from the pupils, and that the grouping of them into three categories was of necessity broad and unable to allow for the complexities of the test completion, the use of the semantic differential test appeared to have fulfilled its purpose. Factors such as inconsistency of attitude could not be controlled for in the intervening period of one to two months between administration of the tests and the commencement of interviewing.

Perhaps most importantly, where extremely negative and hostile attitudes were expressed in interviews, these came from those in the most ethnocentric group and never from the non-ethnocentric group. In one case where a secondary pupil had been categorised as ethnocentric, having a very low score, yet expressed amongst the most positive feelings about the French, there were grounds for thinking that he was one of those occasional informants who find amusement in not completing attitudinal tests in accordance with their own opinions, but rather in response to some other perceived pressures.

It was found that both age groups tended to focus upon the same kinds of issues when talking about the French. Discussion of the kinds of constructs used spontaneously will be introduced later in this chapter.

Levels of Ethnocentricity: Selection of Dependent Variables

All three tests measuring pupils' attitudes towards other peoples, namely the French, the Germans and the Americans, were used as dependent variables. These were compared also with pupils' views of the English. Whilst the substantive focus of the project is upon young peoples' perceptions of the French and French culture, a useful comparison is provided through inclusion of the attitude measures for other peoples. For each target people, only those factors termed 'evaluative' by Osgood *et al.* (1957) were used (the potency and activity factors being considered to relate more to other aspects such as potential behaviour rather than to attitudes towards others). Thus for each individual a score was given for each of the dependent variables; this score represented the mean of the sum of their evaluative factor scores. There being a possible total range of sums of evaluative scores of 6 to 42 from measurements on the six evaluative factors, the range of mean scores stretched from 1 to 7.

It was found that the distributions of scores for the three dependent variables differed somewhat. Whilst it was not found that attitudes towards others were particularly negative or hostile, it was clear that attitudes towards the Americans were the most positive of all three other peoples. Attitudes towards the Germans tended to be somewhat polarised, whilst those towards the French were the most evenly distributed. For the purpose of the main part of the project only analysis of scores for the other peoples are used; in order to provide a comparison with views of their own people the mean score for the English was also calculated; it can be seen that scores for views of the English are the highest of the four groups. The means are given in Table 3.3

TABLE 3.3 *Mean scores for the three dependent variables*

Group	Mean score
French	4.308
Germans	3.728
Americans	4.911
English	5.33

Relating Levels of Ethnocentricity to Independent Variables

Information collected by means of the questionnaire was above all focused on potentially interesting experiential variables: the language learning experience of pupils and their families, the incidence of having relations of other linguistic backgrounds, experience of other countries, personal contact with people of other nationalities, in particular the French, and images of France and the French.

For information on the background of each pupil, age group and gender were selected as two other independent variables. Information was provided, where possible, by the schools upon socio-economic status, the location of the home, the school class, and set for French for the secondary school class, and achievement levels in the basic skills.

Analysis of the sample and description of background variables selected for analysis

The size of the sample totalled 401. The two age groups selected were, it will be recalled, one from the secondary age range at the end of their third year of secondary education, and one from the primary age range, seen during their first term of their fourth and final year. At the time of the questionnaire administration the secondary school sample ages ranged therefore from thirteen years eight months to fourteen years seven months (average age fourteen years one month). The primary school sample ages ranged from ten years two months to eleven years one month (average age ten years seven months). The size of each group is given in Table 3.4.

Gender was included as one of the independent variables as research into related areas in language teaching has found some association between

TABLE 3.4 *Age groups*

Age group	No. of pupils	Percentage
Secondary	208	51.9%
Primary	193	48.1%
Total	401	

attitudes towards languages and gender (e.g. Burstall *et al.*, 1974; Powell, 1986).

It was thought of interest to examine whether any relationship obtains between attitudes to other peoples and gender. The number in each gender group is given in Table 3.5.

The number of girls in the whole sample was greater than that of the boys; this was due to chance factors in the secondary school intake for the relevant year; the primary school sample was not so affected. The breakdown by age group is given in Table 3.6. The proportion of girls to boys in a number of the classes was thus made uneven; the details are given below under the description of school classes.

TABLE 3.5 *Gender groups*

Gender	No. of pupils	Percentage
Boys	178	44.4%
Girls	223	55.6%
Total	401	

TABLE 3.6 *Distribution of gender by age groups*

	Boys	Girls	Total
Secondary sample	82	126	208
Primary sample	96	97	193
Total	178	223	401

School class (rather than school) was chosen as an independent variable partly as a consequence of classroom observations (see also Chapter 5). The sample was drawn from two secondary schools and their main feeder schools. In Newfarm the two classes studying French were selected from the third year, in Hillside six classes were studying French. (Of the eight classes available four were selected for long-term classroom observation, two from each secondary school. Cf. Chapter 5). Eight primary school classes, one from each of the eight 'feeder' primary schools, were selected. The two age groups were thus drawn from the same two catchment areas.

The majority of pupils in each class completed the questionnaire and the semantic differential tests. A small minority either refused or were absent. The numbers completing both instruments are given by school class and gender in Table 3.7.

Information upon the socio-economic status of the parents of pupils was collected with the assistance of the staff of the schools concerned. Information was not however available for all participants and it was only possible to classify some according to global categories. Thus for the purposes of preliminary analysis two categories were created, one, group 1 corresponding to the Registrar General's classificatory categories of III Manual, IV and V, with the addition of the long-term unemployed; and the other, group 2 corresponding to the Registrar General's categories of I, II, and III Non-manual. Details are given in Table 3.8.

As the proportion of pupils drawn from Group 1 (the skilled, unskilled and long-term unemployed) was much greater than that of pupils drawn from Group 2 most classes reflected this distribution. Two classes only did not conform to this pattern. In Class 1 Newfarm the numbers of known backgrounds were similar (14 in Group 1, 13 in Group 2 and three unknown). In one of the primary schools, 'Chase Grove' only two were from Group 1, whilst 27 were designated as Group 2, with three being unknown.

A slightly larger proportion of pupils known to be in Group 2 was found amongst the primary school sample. Details are given in Table 3.9. Percentages of each group as a function of the known sample are given.

A slightly larger proportion of boys than girls were found to come from Group 2 background. Details are given in Table 3.10.

The two secondary schools were situated in towns, Newfarm in a new town and Hillside in an old town, in areas of comparable socio-economic range. Most of the pupils from Newfarm and its feeder schools, 'Beech-

TABLE 3.7 *Size of school classes and gender groups*

Classes		Boys	Girls	Total
Secondary School				
Newfarm	1 highest language set	7	23	30
	2 third language set	9	18	26
Hillside	4 highest French set	10	24	34
	8 second French set	16	14	30
	6 third French set	15	11	26
	3 fourth French set	7	18	25
	5 fifth French set	7	12	19
	7 sixth French set	12	6	18
	Total	82	126	208
Primary School[a]				
Newfarm 'feeder' schools:				
	Beechmead	11	10	21
	Chase Grove	16	16	32
	St James	12	13	25
Hillside 'feeder' Schools:				
	Lilac Street	10	20	30
	Rockington Heath	12	10	22
	Market Garth	12	16	28
	East Wheatham	20	9	29
	Eccleston	3	3	6
	Total	96	97	193

[a] *Note:* the name of each primary class given is that of the school from which it was drawn. The names of the primary schools are fictitious in order to preserve anonymity.

mead', 'Chase Grove' and 'St. James', lived in the new town. Pupils at Hillside and its feeder schools (the remaining five primary schools) lived either in the old town or in its neighbouring villages. The numbers for each location are given in Table 3.11.

It was also decided to include some measures of the pupils' achievement levels in the basic skills and in French (the latter for the secondary

TABLE 3.8 *Socio-economic status*

Group	Category	No.	Percentage
1	Skilled manual, partly skilled, unskilled, long-term unemployed	252	62.8%
2	Professional, intermediate, skilled—non-manual	109	27.2%
	Unknown	40	10.0%

TABLE 3.9 *Socio-economic groupings of the two age groups*

	Primary		Secondary		Total
Group 1	112	62.9%	140	76.5%	252
Group 2	66	37.1%	43	23.5%	109
Total	178		183		361

TABLE 3.10 *Socio-economic groupings by gender*

	Boys		Girls		Total
Group 1	106	67.1%	146	71.9%	252
Group 2	52	32.9%	57	28.1%	109
Total	158		203		361

TABLE 3.11 *Location of homes*

Location	No. of pupils	Percentage
Old Town	154	38.4%
New Town	153	38.2%
Villages	92	22.9%
Unknown	2	0.5%
Total	401	

age group only). As no standardised test results were available for the whole sample, teachers' assessments of pupil achievement were sought. These were based partly on tests used by individual schools (such as reading tests), partly on recent school examination results, and partly upon course work. As teachers' comments tended to reflect use of terms such as 'above average', 'average' and 'below average' it was felt that a three category scale, using those constructs, was most appropriate and feasible, given the variety of schools, classes and the two discrete age groups.

Measures of achievement in French were confined to the secondary school sample. School examinations determining the assessments of pupils took place shortly after the administration of the questionnaire, and before the completion of the secondary sample interviews.

Measures of achievement in two main areas of curriculum, common to both secondary and primary schools, mathematics and English, were also collected. Figures for the numbers in each category are given in Tables 3.12, 3.13 and 3.14.

TABLE 3.12 *Assessments of pupil achievement in French (secondary sample only)*

Achievement in French	No. of pupils	Percentage
Below average	49	23.6%
Average	66	31.7%
Above average	93	44.7%
Total	208	

TABLE 3.13 *Assessments of pupil achievement in Mathematics*

Achievement in Maths	No. of pupils	Percentage
Below average	125	31.2%
Average	133	33.2%
Above average	143	35.7%
Total	401	

TABLE 3.14 *Assessments of pupil achievement in English*

Achievement in English	No. of pupils	Percentage
Below average	98	24.4%
Average	155	38.7%
Above average	148	36.9%
Total	401	

(It will be noted that proportions in each group are weighted slightly in favour of the average and above average categories. This may be attributable to a number of factors: firstly, no pupils in the secondary school sample were interviewed from what may be termed remedial sets of streams, as the pupils in these sets did not study French; secondly, teachers, contrary to some received opinions about teachers' expectations, tended in some schools to give very favourable assessments to their pupils. As noted above, teachers' assessments and school test results were the only forms of information available. In this respect it may be the case that teachers' assessments are made in terms of pupils' achievements within\their teaching group rather than in the context of the whole year group. It was evident from conversations with teachers that there is a form of relative assessment which had to be taken into account, and teachers were asked to make their assessments for our purposes in terms of the whole year group.)

Questionnaire analysis: pupil experience variables

Seven variables derived from information provided by pupils on the questionnaire were chosen for the first analysis of the data. These are described below with their frequencies.

For the purpose of the first analysis a variable was created to compute the incidence of pupils familiar with *relations who spoke a language other than English*, either all or part of the time. This was chosen in distinction, for instance, to having foreign relations (who might or might not have been seen) and in distinction to having English relatives, who had gone to live in another country. The aim of this particular variable was to identify pupils with active experience of languages other than English in the family, as distinct from those learnt at school or privately by parents and siblings.

The number of those so identified represented a small proportion of the sample. Figures are given in Table 3.15.

The next variable measuring pupil experience concerned *family language learning experience* — that is the incidence of foreign language learning, both current and in the past, of participants' parents and siblings. (It was not necessary to include pupils' own structured language learning experience as a variable as this was accounted for by the age group

TABLE 3.15 *Acquaintance with relations of other linguistic backgrounds*

No acquaintance with relations of other linguistic backgrounds	358	89.3%
Acquaintance with relations of other linguistic backgrounds	43	10.7%
Total	401	

variable.) It was found that the majority of pupils had parents or siblings who had language learning experience. For the purposes of first analysis for this (as for all the pupil experience variables) global categories were used, it not being considered necessary at this stage to provide a more differentiated list of categories. The details of family language learning experience is given in Table 3.16.

TABLE 3.16 *Family language learning experience*

No family language learning experience	147	36.7%
Some family language learning experience	254	63.3%
Total	401	

The next four variables concern pupil experience of visiting France and other countries. The first of these was to identify which pupils had *visited France for any form of visit* (school visit or extended family holiday). The figures for the two groups, those with experience of France and those with none, are given in Table 3.17.

TABLE 3.17 *Experience of France*

No experience of France	269	67.1%
Experience of France	132	32.9%
Total	401	

The number of pupils in the secondary age range with experience of France was much greater than that of primary school pupils; this was partly attributable to the incidence of school visits arranged by the secondary schools. The figures for the age groups are given in Table 3.18.

TABLE 3.18 *Experience of France of each age group*

	Primary Age group		Secondary Age group	
No experience of France	164	85.0%	105	50.5%
Experience of France	29	15.0%	103	49.5%
Total	193		208	

As some of the pupil experience of France had been gained through school visits of brief duration, another variable was derived from the questionnaire; this was designed to differentiate those pupils who had had *lengthy experience of France* from those who had been on one or at the most two, weekend trips to France. (Those pupils who had had both experience of family holidays, of more than one weekend's duration, and of school visits were classified as having much experience.) The figures for each group are given in Table 3.19. All but one of those with 'little' experience were secondary school pupils, as only one of the primary schools organised school visits and these were not to France although the school had organised French trips in the past, at the time that some of the secondary school pupils were attending the school. (One primary school pupil was found whose sole holiday experience had been one weekend to France and was thus classified as being of 'little experience'.)

TABLE 3.19 *Length of experience of France*

None	269	67.1%
Little (1–4 days)	62	15.5%
Much (one week or more)	70	17.4%
Total	401	

A wide range of *countries other than France* had been visited either for family holidays or for longer school visits of either a week or a fortnight's duration. (A list of all countries visited is given below.) It also included pupils who had lived in other countries; no pupils had lived in France. The figures for those with experience and those without are given in Table 3.20.

It was decided to create a variable from the two preceding variables to identify pupils with *any experience of foreign countries*. The issue of foreign

TABLE 3.20 *Experience of countries other than France*

No experience of countries other than France	222	55.4%
Experience of countries other than France	179	44.6%
Total	401	

TABLE 3.21 *Length of experience of foreign countries*

None	166	41.4%
Little	32	8.0%
Much	203	50.6%
Total	401	

experience was considered likely to be of potential interest and significance; thus several variables were devoted to investigation of this area. For
the experience of foreign countries (France and other countries outside the
United Kingdom) a scale was created similar to that used for the length of
experience of France. The figures are given in Table 3.21. It can be seen
that nearly 60% of the sample had some experience of foreign countries,
when the values of the two categories 'little' and 'much' are totalled.

Not surprisingly, the number of secondary school pupils who had
visited foreign countries was somewhat higher than that of primary school
pupils; however a substantial minority of the younger group (45%) had
been abroad, in many cases several times. The figures for the age groups
are given in Table 3.22.

It was found that a large number of different countries had been
visited by both age groups in the sample. School visits and exchanges had
been arranged principally to France, Germany and Austria by the secondary schools, and one primary school had arranged a school skiing visit to
Italy. A small group of children had experienced living abroad, due to their
fathers' work. The substantive experience of foreign countries was gained
through family holidays.

In order to illustrate the range of countries experienced a list follows
of all those said to have been visited. Those countries at the beginning of
the list represent the countries most frequently visited:

France, Germany, Austria, Spain, Tenerife, Italy, Belgium, Greece,
Switzerland, America, Barbados, Portugal, Tunisia, Yugoslavia, Holland,

TABLE 3.22 *Length of foreign country experience of each age group*

	Primary		Secondary	
No experience	106	54.9%	60	28.8%
Little experience	1	0.5%	31	14.9%
Much experience	86	44.6%	117	56.3%
Total	193		208	

Malta, Norway, Canada, Cyprus, South Africa, Morocco, Denmark, Thailand, Hong Kong, Sweden, United Arab Emirates, Bulgaria, Poland.

It was found that the total amount of experience of other countries in each class varied considerably. An index was created for each class to assess the variations. This was done by totalling the number of different countries visited by each individual in each class, and dividing this by the number of children in each class. A list follows below in Table 3.23, ranking the classes in order of relative amount of experience. It will be seen that one primary school with a small number of fourth year pupils occupies the first position due to the fact that two children had travelled to eight countries, due partly to their fathers' employment, and partly due to a family interest in world tours. The secondary school pupils of Newfarm had less experience of other countries than the pupils of Hillside. It will be seen that some variation exists amongst the classes of Hillside. Whilst many of those in the lower French sets had been abroad much of this experience came from the short week-end breaks arranged by the school to Boulogne. Pupils in the higher French sets had more experience of both family holidays and school visits.

The index in Table 3.23 was designed merely as a measure of individual and class experience of different countries. An index of the total number of holidays taken would be even higher as a number of pupils had visited the same country more than once. The information has been presented in some detail for the purposes of characterising each class, school class being one of the independent variables.

The final variable derived from the questionnaire concerned pupil *contact with French people*; this variable was designed to identify pupils who had had extended personal contact, such as having French visitors in the home, or penfriends. The frequencies for the two groups, those with and those without contact, are given in Table 3.24.

TABLE 3.23 *Class experience of foreign countries*

School	Total number of countries visited by individuals	Number of pupils in class	Index of class experience
Eccleston	19	6	3.16
French set—Hillside:			
Class 4 highest set	76	34	2.2
Class 6 third set	55	26	2.11
Class 8 second set	53	30	1.76
Chase Grove—Primary	43	32	1.34
French set—Hillside:			
Class 5 fifth set	24	19	1.26
Class 3 fourth set	28	25	1.12
Market Garth—Primary	30	28	1.07
French set—Hillside:			
Class 7 sixth set	19	18	1.05
Lilac Street—Primary	31	30	1.03
French set—Newfarm:			
Class 1 highest set	29	30	0.96
Class 2 third set	22	26	0.84
St. James—primary	11	15	0.44
East Wheatham—primary	12	19	0.41
Rockington Heath—primary	9	22	0.40
Beechmead—primary	8	21	0.38
Total	469		

Results

All the independent variables described above, the measures of both background and experience, were tested independently to see what relationships obtained between them and each of the three dependent variables, views of the French, the Germans and the Americans.

As it was found that one of the assumptions for the use of parametric tests, that of the homogeneity of variance, could not be satisfied for all

TABLE 3.24 *Personal contact with French people*

No personal contact	341	85.0%
Some personal contact	60	15.0%
Total	401	

variables, both parametric and non-parametric tests were used, and the results of both these are given below (Table 3.25 seq.) A summary of the results is given first in Table 3.25 with details of the most appropriate test only given.

It can be seen that only a small number of variables were found to be significantly associated when tested individually with attitudes to other peoples. It will be seen below (pp. 181–87) that there was some interaction amongst a few of the variables. Further, association of any variable with one dependent variable did not necessarily entail association with the other dependent variables. Whilst, as was stated above, attitudes were not generally speaking found to be extremely negative, the dependent variable of attitudes towards the Germans was found to be most frequently and most strongly associated with independent variables. The independent variables found to be most strongly associated with attitudes tended to be those measuring pupil background rather than experience of other countries and languages. Thus it can be seen that gender, school class and age group are more significantly related to attitudes than are the experiental variables. Socio-economic status was found to be associated only with attitudes towards the French. Of the experiental variables having foreign relations, family language experience and experience of countries other than France were found to have some association with attitudes.

Background variables

Age

Age was found to have a complex relationship to pupil attitudes. It has been noted above that the attitudes expressed towards other peoples were not particularly negative or hostile in general. The younger age group showed more negative attitudes towards the Germans and the French, whilst having more positive attitudes towards the Americans. The group means for each dependent variable are given in Tables 3.26–3.31.

TABLE 3.25 *Summary of results (univariate analysis)*

Independent Variables	Dependent Variables		
	Views of the French	*Views of the Germans*	*Views of the Americans*
Age	T = −1.22 p = 0.22(s)	T = −3.27 p=0.001(s)***	T = 1.14 p = 0.26
Gender	T = −4.77 p<0.001(s)***	T = −4.9 p<0.001***	T = −2.38 p = 0.02(s)*
School Class	H = 36.12 p = 0.002***	H = 67.92 p<0.0001***	H = 16.48 p.0.35
Socio-economic status	T = −2.22 p = 0.03(s)*	T = −1.59 p = 0.11	T = 0.75 p = 0.45
Home location	F = 0.41 p = 0.66	F = 2.72 p = 0.07	F = 0.93 p = 0.39
Achievement in French	r = 0.04 (n.s.)	r = −0.06 (n.s.)	r = −0.07 (n.s.)
Achievement in Mathematics	r = 0.0003 (n.s.)	r = −0.04 (n.s.)	r = −0.06 (n.s.)
Achievement in English	r = 0.02 (n.s.)	r = 0.04 (n.s.)	r = 0.008 (n.s.)
Acquaintance with relations of other linguistic backgrounds	T = −0.03 p = 0.97	T = −0.25 p = 0.80	T = −1.93 p = 0.05*
Family Language Learning Experience	T = −1.42 p = 0.16	T = −1.92 p = 0.05*	T = −0.9 p = 0.37
Experience of France	T = 0.25 p = 0.8	T = −0.18 p = 0.86(s)	T = 0.49 p = 0.62
Length of Experience of France (scale)	r = 0.004 (n.s.)	r_s = 0.006 (n.s.)	r = −0.02 (n.s.)
Experience of countries other than France	T = 1.64 p = 0.1	T = −0.85 p = 0.39	T = −0.24 p = 0.81
Experience of abroad: France plus other countries (scale)	r_s = −0.08 (n.s.)	r_s = 0.08 (n.s.)	r = 0.01 (n.s.)
Personal contact with French people	T = 0.25 p = 0.8	T = 0.59 p = 0.56	T = −0.72 p = 0.47

(s = separate variance estimate)

TABLE 3.26 *Age and attitudes towards the French (parametric)*

	Group means of scores for the French
Primary school age group	4.22
Secondary school age group	4.39

$T = -1.22$ (separate variance estimate) n.s.

TABLE 3.27 *Age and attitudes towards the French (non-parametric)*

	Mean rank of scores for the French
Primary school age group	195.28
Secondary school age group	206.31

$U = 18968.0$ n.s.

TABLE 3.28 *Age and attitudes towards the Germans (parametric)*

	Group means of scores for the Germans
Primary school age group	3.46
Secondary school age group	3.97

$T = -3.27$ (separate variance estimate) $p < 0.001$

TABLE 3.29 *Age and attitudes towards the Germans (non-parametric)*

	Group means of scores for the Germans
Primary school age group	180.27
Secondary school age group	220.23

$U = 16071.5$ $p < 0.001$

TABLE 3.30 *Age and attitudes towards the Americans (parametric)*

	Group means of scores for the Americans
Primary school age group	4.49
Secondary school age group	4.84

T=1.14   n.s.

TABLE 3.31 *Age and attitudes towards the Americans*

	Mean rank of scores for the Americans
Primary school age group	206.75
Secondary school age group	195.67

U=18963.0 n.s.

Thus whilst a slight difference in means was apparent between the two age groups, it was only for attitudes towards the Germans that the results reached a level of significance. It was noticeable that, though the differences in means found for attitudes towards the Americans, did not reach a level of significance, for this people the mean of the younger age group was higher than that of the older age group. This was a reverse of their relative positions regarding the French and the Germans. It will be seen that complex interactions could have affected the results.

Gender

Gender was found to be one of the variables most frequently associated with the variance in attitudinal scores. The group means for the girls were higher for all three target peoples, the French, the Germans and the Americans.

It was found that not only were overall means and ranks of scores higher for girls than for boys in all the attitudinal tests, but the variances of the girls' scores were smaller than those of the boys. The difference in scores between the girls and boys regarding the French and the Germans is particularly clear. Though less significant, a similar trend is apparent regarding attitudes towards the Americans. However in this case the group mean for the boys (of 4.73) is above the medium of the range of scores, whereas for the French and the Germans, the group mean is somewhat lower. This suggests that of the three target peoples only the Americans are positively perceived by boys; the girls scores reflect the trend of boys' scores, in that the same order of preference from Germans at the bottom to Americans at the top, is preserved, with slightly more positive appraisals reported.

TABLE 3.32 *Gender and attitudes towards the French (parametric)*

	Group means of scores for the French
Boys	3.94
Girls	4.60

T=−4.77 (separate variance estimate) p<0.001

TABLE 3.33 *Gender and attitudes towards the French (non-parametric)*

	Mean rank of scores for the French
Boys	173.12
Girls	223.25

U=14884.5 p<0.0001

TABLE 3.34 *Gender and attitudes towards the Germans (parametric)*

	Group means of scores for the Germans
Boys	3.31
Girls	4.06

T=−4.9 p<0.001

TABLE 3.35 *Gender and attitudes towards the Germans (non-parametric)*

	Mean rank of scores for the Germans
Boys	169.77
Girls	225.93

U=14287.5   p<0.0001

TABLE 3.36 *Gender and attitudes towards the Americans (parametric)*

	Group means of scores for the Americans
Boys	4.73
Girls	5.05

T=−2.38 (separate variance estimate)   p=0.018

TABLE 3.37 *Gender and attitudes towards the Americans (non-parametric)*

	Group means of scores for the Americans
Boys	188.85
Girls	210.70

U=17684.0   n.s. (p=0.06)

School class

It was not possible to use parametric tests for analysis of school class differences in scores for the French and the Germans, owing to an absence of homogeneity of variances. Thus only non-parametric results are given in Tables 3.38–3.40.

Attitudes towards the French and the Germans were thus found to differ amongst the classes. Table 3.41 summarises the comparative

TABLE 3.38 *School class and attitudes towards the French*

Classes	Mean rank of scores for the French	Order of ranking
1 First language set Newfarm	255.87	1st
2 Third language set Newfarm	235.23	3rd
3 Fourth French set Hillside	216.86	7th
4 First French set Hillside	238.01	2nd
5 Fifth French set Hillside	185.26	11th
6 Third French set Hillside	169.87	14th
7 Sixth French set Hillside	179.25	13th
8 Second French set Hillside	148.10	15th
9 Beechmead	120.36	16th
10 Chase Grove	203.05	9th
11 Lilac Street	179.78	12th
12 St. James	228.74	5th
13 Rockington Heath	207.09	8th
14 Market Garth	219.11	6th
15 East Wheatham	189.16	10th
16 Eccleston	229.25	4th

Kruskal Wallis H=36.1191 (corrected for ties)   p=0.0017

positions of each class, regarding each of the peoples. The positions for the classes regarding the Americans are included for the purposes of comparison, though differences amongst the classes regarding the Americans were not found to be significant.

As school class serves both as a descriptor of a collection of pupils receiving similar teaching (*pace* individualised methods) and as a descriptor of an aggregate of individuals having a variety of backgrounds and experience, interaction amongst factors is likely to obtain. Gender is one factor to be considered (see Table 3.4.) Another factor could be experience of foreign travel. (For instance it is noticeable that the primary class occupying reasonably high positions regarding all three peoples is the class with the greatest per capita amount of experience of foreign travel.) It can be seen that positions regarding the three peoples vary. The junior age group, with only one exception, Chase Grove, have higher (or at the least

TABLE 3.39 *School class and attitudes towards the Germans*

Classes	Mean rank of scores for the Germans	Order of ranking
1 First language set Newfarm	269.25	2nd
2 Third language set Newfarm	284.06	1st
3 Fourth French set Hillside	185.26	9th
4 First French set Hillside	222.22	6th
5 Fifth French set Hillside	237.55	5th
6 Third French set Hillside	179.90	10th
7 Sixth French set Hillside	211.78	7th
8 Second French set Hillside	171.85	13th
9 Beechmead	175.81	12th
10 Chase Grove	242.14	4th
11 Lilac Street	146.37	14th
12 St. James	135.86	15th
13 Rockington Heath	178.23	11th
14 Market Garth	245.25	3rd
15 East Wheatham	122.91	16th
16 Eccleston	202.00	8th

Kruskal Wallis H=67.9248 $p < 0.0001$

equal) positions when ranked for their American scores when compared with their French and German positions.

The two secondary classes from Newfarm have high positions regarding the French and the Germans; both have high proportions of girls in them. However, Class 2 is much more positive about the Americans than is Class 1.

The classes rated highest in achievement in French at Newfarm and Hillside are the two highest in their regard for the French, however, it will be seen below that generally achievement in French does *not* co-vary with attitudes to the French.

Socio-economic status

Little association was found between socio-economic status and attitudes, though some differences in direction of preferences was found. Only

TABLE 3.40 *School class and attitudes towards the Americans*

Classes	Mean rank of scores for the Americans	Order of ranking
1 First language set Newfarm	188.23	12th
2 Third language set Newfarm	246.83	2nd
3 Fourth French set Hillside	214.54	7th
4 First French set Hillside	201.06	9th
5 Fifth French set Hillside	183.08	14th
6 Third French set Hillside	186.92	13th
7 Sixth French set Hillside	193.11	11th
8 Second French set Hillside	154.02	16th
9 Beechmead	215.52	6th
10 Chase Grove	176.28	15th
11 Lilac Street	195.20	10th
12 St. James	215.26	5th
13 Rockington Heath	216.77	4th
14 Market Garth	219.88	3rd
15 East Wheatham	204.33	8th
16 Eccleston	274.42	1st

Kruskal Wallis $H = 16.4775$ n.s.

in the case of the French, when using parametric tests, did results achieve a level of significance. The results for all three peoples are given in Tables 3.42–3.47, in order to illustrate the differences in directions of relative preferences of the two groups.

It might be argued that the association of socio-economic status and attitudes towards the French could be affected by possible increased *experience* of France of the financially better off Group 2. However, as will be seen below a greater amount of individual experience of France did not ensure significantly more positive attitudes.

Other background variables

It was not found that any of the other background variables (home location and achievement in French, Mathematics and English) were significantly associated with attitudes towards any of the peoples when considered independently. However some significant interactions with other variables were found. These are reported below.

TABLE 3.41 *Relative positions of school classes regarding attitudes towards other peoples*

Classes	French	Germans	Americans	Rank according to experience
1 First language set Newfarm	1st	2nd	12th	11th
2 Third language set Newfarm	3rd	1st	2nd	12th
3 Fourth French set Hillside	7th	9th	7th	7th
4 First French set Hillside	2nd	6th	9th	2nd
5 Fifth French set Hillside	11th	5th	14th	6th
6 Third French set Hillside	14th	10th	13th	3rd
7 Sixth French set Hillside	13th	7th	11th	10th
8 Second French set Hillside	15th	13th	16th	4th
9 Beechmead	16th	12th	6th	16th
10 Chase Grove	9th	4th	15th	5th
11 Lilac Street	12th	14th	10th	9th
12 St. James	5th	15th	5th	13th
13 Rockington Heath	8th	11th	4th	15th
14 Market Garth	6th	3rd	3rd	8th
15 East Wheatham	10th	16th	8th	14th
16 Eccleston	4th	8th	1st	1st

Experiential variables

Relations of other linguistic backgrounds

Having relations of other linguistic backgrounds did not affect attitudes towards other peoples to any significant extent. The only people for which attitudes were more than minutely more positive were the Americans. (It should be noted that this cannot be attributed to pupils having for example *American* relations, as American relations were treated for the purpose of this variable, as being of the same linguistic background.)

Thus it can be seen that acquaintance with relations of other linguistic backgrounds, which were predominantly European (for example German, Dutch or Scandinavian) did not make a great difference to attitudes. However, the trend is for those with such relations to be *slightly* more positive about other peoples; it is possible if this type of study were replicated with a variety of populations, more differentiation might become apparent. It was not always possible for the younger age group in

TABLE 3.42 *SES and attitudes towards the French (parametric)*

	Group means of scores for the French
Group 1 (RG groups IIIM, IV, V)	4.23
Group 2 (RG groups I, II, IIIN–M)	4.55

$T = -2.22$ $p = 0.027$ (separate variance estimate)

TABLE 3.43 *SES and attitudes towards the French (non-parametric)*

	Mean rank of scores for the French
Group 1	174.70
Group 2	195.57

$U = 12145.5$ n.s.

TABLE 3.44 *SES and attitudes towards the Germans (parametric)*

	Group means of scores for the Germans
Group 1	3.66
Group 2	3.94

$T = -1.59$ n.s.

TABLE 3.45 *SES and attitudes towards the Germans (non-parametric)*

	Mean rank of scores for the Germans
Group 1	175.31
Group 2	194.15

$U = 12301.0$ n.s.

TABLE 3.46 *SES and attitudes towards the Americans (parametric)*

	Group means of scores for the Americans
Group 1	4.93
Group 2	4.82

T=0.75 n.s.

TABLE 3.47 *SES and attitudes towards the Americans (non-parametric)*

	Mean rank of scores for the Germans
Group 1	183.61
Group 2	174.98

U=13077.5 n.s. (p=0.4703)

TABLE 3.48 *Relations of other linguistic backgrounds and attitudes towards the French (parametric)*

	Group means for the French
No relations of other linguistic backgrounds	4.3073
Relations of other linguistic backgrounds	4.3140

T=−0.03 n.s.

TABLE 3.49 *Relations of other linguistic backgrounds and attitudes towards the French (non-parametric)*

	Mean rank for the French
No relations of other linguistic backgrounds	200.98
Relations of other linguistic backgrounds	201.20

U=7688.5 n.s. (p=0.9905)

TABLE 3.50 *Relations of other linguistic backgrounds and attitudes towards the Germans (parametric)*

	Group means for the Germans
No relations of other linguistic backgrounds	3.7209
Relations of other linguistic backgrounds	3.7837

T=−0.25 n.s.

TABLE 3.51 *Relations of other linguistic backgrounds and attitudes towards the Germans (non-parametric)*

	Mean rank for the Germans
No relations of other linguistic backgrounds	200.43
Relations of other linguistic backgrounds	205.77

U=7492.0 n.s. (p=0.7751)

TABLE 3.52 *Relations of other linguistic backgrounds and attitudes towards the Americans (parametric)*

	Group means for the Americans
No relations of other linguistic backgrounds	4.8684
Relations of other linguistic backgrounds	5.2698

T=−1.93 p=0.05

this sample to recall with accuracy the provenance of some of their relations; where doubt existed it was likely that they claimed to have no such relations.

Family language learning experience

Family language learning experience was found to be associated only with attitudes towards the Germans, where those with some experience

TABLE 3.53 *Relations of other linguistic backgrounds and attitudes towards the Americans (non-parametric)*

	Mean rank for the Americans
No relations of other linguistic backgrounds	197.35
Relations of other linguistic backgrounds	231.37

U=6391.0   n.s. (p=0.0687)

had a higher group mean. It was found generally that family language learning experience resulted in there being higher group means than where there was no family language learning experience, but for attitudes towards the French and the Americans an accepted level of significance was not found. Recall of parental language learning experience might have proved difficult for some of the sample. (See Tables 3.54–3.59.)

TABLE 3.54 *Family language learning experience and attitudes towards the French (parametric)*

	Group means for the French
No family language learning experience	4.18
Some family language learning experience	4.38

T=−1.42   n.s.

TABLE 3.55 *Family language learning experience and attitudes towards the French (non-parametric)*

	Mean rank for the French
No family language learning experience	187.49
Some family language learning experience	208.82

U=16683.0   n.s.

TABLE 3.56 *Family language learning experience and attitudes towards the Germans (parametric)*

	Group means for the Germans
No family language learning experience	3.53
Some family language learning experience	3.84

$T=-1.92$ $p=0.05$

TABLE 3.57 *Family language learning experience and attitudes towards the Germans (non-parametric)*

	Mean rank for the Germans
No family language learning experience	186.90
Some family language learning experience	209.16

$U=16596.0$ n.s.

TABLE 3.58 *Family language learning experience and attitudes towards the Americans (parametric)*

	Group means for the Americans
No family language learning experience	4.84
Some family language learning experience	4.95

$T=-0.9$ n.s.

Experience of countries other than France

Having experience of countries *other* than France was found to *lower* the group mean of attitudes towards the French; an increase in the group means of attitudes towards the Germans and the Americans was also found though results did not reach an acceptable level of significance. (See Tables 3.60–3.65.)

TABLE 3.59 *Family language learning experience and attitudes towards the Americans (non-parametric)*

	Mean rank for the Americans
No family language learning experience	194.6
Some family language learning experience	204.7

U=17728.0   n.s.

TABLE 3.60 *Experience of countries other than France and attitudes towards the French (parametric)*

	Group means for the French
None	4.41
Some	4.18

T=−1.64   n.s.

TABLE 3.61 *Experience of countries other than France and attitudes towards the French (non-parametric)*

	Mean rank for the French
None	211.57
Some	187.96

U=17523.5   p=0.04

Other questionnaire variables

The questionnaire variables, which were not found to be significantly associated with attitudes towards *any* of the other peoples when analysed independently, were experience of France, length of experience of France, length of experience of foreign countries (France and others) and personal contact with French people.

TABLE 3.62 *Experience of countries other than France and attitudes towards the Germans (parametric)*

	Group means for the Germans
None	3.67
Some	3.80

T=−0.85   n.s.

TABLE 3.63 *Experience of countries other than France and attitudes towards the Germans (non-parametric)*

	Mean rank for the Germans
Non	196.69
Some	206.35

U=18911.5   n.s.

TABLE 3.64 *Experience of countries other than France and attitudes towards the Americans (parametric)*

	Group means for the Americans
None	4.89
Some	4.93

T=−0.24   n.s.

Whilst it was not expected that experience of France and French people would necessarily influence attitudes towards the Germans or the Americans, it might have been hypothesised that such experience would ameliorate attitudes towards the French. This was *not* found to be the case. Whilst not achieving an acceptable level of significance, extended personal contact with French people slightly *reduced* the group means of attitudes towards the French. However, some interesting interactions amongst the independent variables were found; these are reported in the next section.

TABLE 3.65 *Experience of countries other than France and attitudes towards the Americans (non-parametric)*

	Mean rank for the Americans
None	196.89
Some	206.09

U=18957.0   n.s.

Interaction amongst independent variables

Analysis of variance was carried out to examine what, if any, interaction obtained amongst the independent variables. Clearly only variables which conformed to the assumptions of homoscedasticity could be entered, and therefore in certain cases only small proportions of the variance were accounted for. Whilst acknowledging these limitations, the results are given below as it is argued they shed some interesting light upon the differential effect of experience.

Views of the French: whole sample

Analysis of variance for the dependent variable, views of the French, were carried out initially for the whole sample and then separately for the sub-sample of the secondary age group only. For the whole sample the variables suitable for inclusion in the analysis were the incidence of relations of other linguistic backgrounds, family language learning experience, general experience of France, experience of countries other than France, home location, personal contact with French people and also type of experience of France. It was not possible to include both 'general experience of France' and 'type of experience of France', as the latter variable represents a scale of the former. Also the variable 'type of experience' was less useful in analysing the experience of the younger age group than that of the older age group as the category 'little experience' catered largely for those who had been only on short weekend school trips. Therefore the variable 'general' experience of France was selected in preference to 'type of experience' for analysis of the whole sample.

It was clear from initial analysis of the data, that none of the afore mentioned variables was significant as a main effect. There were no significant two-way interactions, but two significant three-way interactions were found. These were firstly relations of other linguistic backgrounds with family language learning experience and general experience of France, (F = 3.638 p = 0.05) and secondly, relations of other linguistic backgrounds with general experience of France and personal contact with French people (F = 5.922 p = 0.015). Details of the group means are given below in Tables 3.66 and 3.67.

Whilst the variables, 'relations of other linguistic backgrounds' accounts for all non-English speaking nationalities and not solely the French, it might have been argued that having such relations might increase scores for views of other peoples. However, it is noticeable that that group representing the *maximum* amount of exposure to France, to family language learning experience and to personal contact with French people has the *lowest* group mean (3.63). The highest group mean is found for the group with *no* experience of France, but with family language learning experience and with relations of other linguistic backgrounds (4.66).

TABLE 3.66 *Interaction of variables: relations of other linguistic backgrounds, family language learning experience and general experience of France*

	No family language learning experience	Some family language learning experience
No experience of France:		
No relations of other linguistic backgrounds	4.16 (N = 85)	4.36 (152)
Relations of other linguistic backgrounds	4.00 (7)	4.66 (23)
Some experience of France:		
No relations of other linguistic backgrounds	4.20 (50)	4.42 (67)
Relations of other linguistic backgrounds	4.63 (3)	3.63 (10)

F=3.638   p=0.05

TABLE 3.67 *Interaction of variables: relations of other linguistic backgrounds, general experience of France, and personal contact with French people*

	No experience of France	Some experience of France
No personal contact:		
No relations of other linguistic backgrounds	4.33 (N = 214)	4.27 (93)
Relations of other linguistic backgrounds	4.38 (25)	3.94 (7)
Personal contact:		
No relations of other linguistic backgrounds	3.92 (23)	4.52 (26)
Relations of other linguistic backgrounds	5.10 (5)	3.80 (6)

F=5.922　p=0.015

Again it appears that what would appear to be optimal, that is maximum experience of France, French people and relations of other linguistic backgrounds is *not* associated with a high score (3.80). The group with the highest group mean is that with personal contact with French people, with relations of other linguistic backgrounds but without experience of France. (It is of course not possible to assess the amount of variance which might be attributable to other factors such as gender in this form of analysis.) These results amount therefore to only partial explanations but it is argued that they are worthy of note, in that they indicate that factors which might be thought to ameliorate or raise scores do not necessarily do so. Therefore one might conclude that regarding some peoples, the quality of experience is important and thus use of the interview data is invaluable in illustrating differential experience.

Views of the French: secondary sample only

It was decided to examine whether the addition of the variable, achievement in French, would account in interaction for any of the variance. As achievement in French was not a variable applying to the primary school sample, only those from the secondary sample were included in this analysis.

The variables entered initially were therefore relations of other linguistic backgrounds, family language learning experience, experience of countries other than France, home location, personal contact with French people, achievement in French, and general experience of France. No significant two-way interactions of significance were found when achievement in French was added. However, it was found that the significance of two main effects was modified when just the secondary sample was considered. These were home location and experience of countries other than France. The group means for these two variables are given in Tables 3.68 and 3.69.

It thus appears that for the secondary sample the scores of the pupils from the new town were higher compared with those from the old town and the villages. It should be noted that almost all those living in villages

TABLE 3.68 *Group means for the variable: home location (secondary sample only)*

Home location:	Old town	New town	Villages
	4.22 (103)	4.85 (54)	4.19 (49)

F=3.483   p=0.033

TABLE 3.69 *Group means for the variable: experience of countries other than France (secondary sample only)*

No experience	Some experience
4.58 (105)	4.17 (101)

F=4.898   p=0.028

lived in those surrounding the *old* town; only two children attending the secondary school in the new town lived in a village.

Experience of countries other than France

Whilst it appeared that going to France made no significant difference to views of the French, those with experience of countries other than France had lower group mean than those with no experience.

As the experience of France of the secondary school sample could be differentiated into three groups — much experience, little experience (comprising only short weekend school trips) and no experience, another analysis of variance was carried out, substituting the variable type of experience of France for experience of France. In this case it was found that there was a significant two-way interaction between type of experience and having relations of other linguistic backgrounds. The group means for these are given in Table 3.70.

It appears that where there was no or little experience of France, having relations of other linguistic backgrounds can enhance the scores for views of the French, whilst for those with much experience the opposite obtained. However in view of the small size of the sample of those with relations of other linguistic backgrounds it is possible that other factors such as gender, which could not be entered in the analysis, might have modified the scores; thus no clear conclusions can be easily drawn.

TABLE 3.70 *Interaction of variables: type of experience of France and relations of other linguistic backgrounds*

| | *Type of experience* | | |
	None	*Little*	*Much*
No relations of other linguistic backgrounds	4.50 (91)	4.11 (56)	4.46 (38)
Some relations of other linguistic backgrounds	4.62 (12)	4.73 (6)	3.07 (3)

$F=5.889$ $p=0.003$

View of the Germans: whole sample

The six independent variables entered for analysis of variance regarding view of the Germans were socio-economic status, relations of other linguistic backgrounds, experience of countries other than France, family language learning experience, home location and gender. In this case two of the background variables, socio-economic status and gender conformed to the assumptions of analysis of variance and thus a greater proportion of the variance is accounted for. A brief table of the significant main effects and interactions is given below (followed by analysis of the groups concerned.)

TABLE 3.71 *Significant interactions regarding views of the Germans*

Main effects	$F = 4.279$	$p < 0.001$
Socio-economic status with relations of other linguistic backgrounds	$F = 5.280$	$p = 0.02$
Socio-economic status with experience of countries other than France	$F = 4.110$	$p = 0.04$
Experience of countries other than France with family language learning experience	$F = 4.369$	$p = 0.03$
Socio-economic status with home location and gender	$F = 5.161$	$p = 0.006$
Socio-economic status with relations of other linguistic backgrounds and home location	$F = 3.654$	$p = 0.027$
Relations of other linguistic backgrounds with experience of countries other than France and home location	$F = 4.657$	$p = 0.010$
Relations of other linguistic backgrounds with family language learning experience and gender	$F = 7.894$	$p = 0.005$

View of the Americans: whole sample

The independent variables suitable for inclusion in this analysis of variance were age, socio-economic status, relations of other linguistic backgrounds, family language learning experience, experience of France and other countries and home location. Only the variable having relations of other linguistic backgrounds, was found to be a significant main effect as in the preliminary analysis of the data (those *with* relations of other linguistic backgrounds had higher scores for their views of the Americans). The only significant two-way interaction was found to be between socio-economic status and home location ($F = 3.0$, $p = 0.05$).

TABLE 3.72 *Interaction of variables: socio-economic status and home location for views of the Americans*

	Old town	New town	Village
Group 1 (skilled and unskilled, long-term unemployed)	4.87 (108)	5.15 (88)	4.72 (56)
Group 2 (professional, intermediate and non-manual)	5.23 (31)	4.60 (52)	4.76 (26)

$F=3.0$ $p=0.05$

Socio-economic status and home location

As stated before scores for the Americans of all groups are clearly noticeably higher than for the other peoples considered. In the above interaction the highest group mean was found to be that of Group 2 living in the old town; however, children from Group 2 in the new town had the lowest group mean of the sample.

Discussion

Using the instrument the semantic differential to measure young peoples' attitudes towards a selection of peoples indicated that for the sample in question, young people do differentiate amongst groups perceived, and that a number of different factors may modify their attitudes. Whilst it has always to be recognised that any alteration in the procedure of measurement may produce very different results, certain similarities obtain between this and other groups studied; where dissimilarities exist these results may be illustrative of other aspects of interest, such as socio-cultural norms of the groups selected for study.

Whilst it was not the substantive intention of the project to investigate the unitariness of the phenomenon of ethnocentrism or prejudice, by employing tests aimed at tapping attitudes towards different peoples it was possible to draw some conclusions upon this related issue, which was further illustrated by the interview material. Some early studies of ethnocentrism such as that of Adorno *et al.* (1950) argued that if a person is ethnocentric he or she will dislike all 'out-groups'; a concomitant of this position was thought to be that the 'in-group' would be therefore held in very high regard. However more recent work in social psychology has indicated that certain peoples are more frequently the target of negative attitudes, whilst conversely, other peoples, such as the Americans are frequently favourably perceived (see for example Lambert & Klineberg, 1967; Jahoda, 1962; Johnson *et al.* 1970).

In the sample under consideration in this study it was found that attitudes towards the sample's own people, the English, was uniformly high. Of the three other peoples selected the Americans were clearly the preferred people followed in a somewhat neutral position by the French, with the Germans occupying the third position. As negative views of the English were extremely rare no clear indication that positive regard for one's own group was related to low regard for an 'out group' could have been detected; this finding was in tune with that of Ray & Lovejoy (1986) who did not find the kind of relationship posited by Adorno.

A number of reasons have been advanced in the past for the popularity of the American people, such as putative similarity, attributable partly to children's perceptions of linguistic and ethnic similarities. Liking of the similar and fear of the unknown has been thought to be the rationale underlying people's choices in a number of studies both in the field of ethnocentrism and other areas (Allport, 1954; Byrne, 1971). Perceptions of others have been thought for some time to be modified by availability of information about them (Johnson *et al.* 1970). The present sample's views of the Americans would appear therefore to be similar to other reported findings. The position of the Germans in the scale of preference was also similar to that in other studies; it was found however that this was modified by the age of the sample. Whilst it has been argued by some (e.g. Lambert & Klineberg, 1967) that with age children become more proficient in the use of stereotypes current in their social group, it appeared that views of the Germans became more differentiated and less hostile with the older age group. This might be partly attributable to increased experience provided by holidays, school visits and language lessons which might gain ascendancy over television and other media (e.g. boys' comics) as a provider of images. Perceptions of similarity might thus be enhanced, as was found in Stillwell and Spencer's study (1974).

For the people with which the project is principally concerned, the French, age was not found to modify attitudes. The clearest division, which was also found regarding the Germans, was between the gender groups. In this the present sample differs markedly from many of the groups inter- views in Lambert & Klineberg's large-scale comparative study in which more groups of boys were found to have positive views of others than girls.

Another factor which was found to be associated with views of the French (though not to a significant extent with views of the Germans) was socio-economic status. This was a factor also found by Lambert & Klineberg cross-culturally to enhance views (though his use of the term 'affection' for other peoples seems somewhat unusual). However, it has to be noted that in the present study information upon socio-economic status was not available for approximately 10% of the sample and though helpfully provided by schools could only be classified in terms of global categories. Further research into the effects of socio-economic status would be needed before attaching major importance to this factor.

It might have been supposed that experience of France and other countries would enhance views of other peoples. In a related field, the study of racial prejudice, it has been suggested by Katz (1983) that it might be argued that fear of the unknown, if there be such a phenomenon, might be reduced by contact. Whilst somewhat complex interactions were found amongst variables for the present sample, no main effects were clearly attributable to the variables designed to tap experience. This might appear at first glance surprising if it be assumed that all children on first making contact with another country travel with no preconceptions about the country or its inhabitants, but no *tabula rasa* for travel purposes can be guaranteed. Each individual is likely to have received ideas about countries from parents, siblings and friends as well as the media. Indeed it was noticeable that those people perceived most positively, the Americans, according to the semantic differential, had not been any more frequently encountered than people of other nationalities. This point will be further illustrated by analysis of the interview material. The data gathered by means of the semantic differential and questionnaire was intended to try to assess the role of experience and to suggest areas of enquiry for the in- depth interviews. The results obtained appear to indicate that what might seem at first sight to be 'obvious' factors, such as experience of other countries, family language learning experience or acquaintance with rela- tions of other linguistic backgrounds or nationalities, do not necessarily enhance views of other peoples, but must be considered as part of a matrix of factors. Even maximum possible experience of other countries and peoples did not clearly enhance views of other peoples. Had it been possible to enter all factors in the interactional analysis, yet other combinations, drawing upon the background variables, might have been indicated. However, it is argued that from these results yielded, the minutiae of experience and its totality, and interaction with individual and socio-cultural background need always to be taken into consideration when researching the complex field of national attitudes. Thus the analysis of results from use of semantic differential, whilst indicating some interesting parallels with and divergences from other studies, needs to be considered in conjunction with the interview material, for it is at the level of the individual that some of the processes leading to the expression of attitudes can be more usefully observed. In completing the semantic differential participants were being invited to make extempore generalisations, even if differentiated to some extent, about other peoples. In-depth interviewing facilitated the embellishment or elaboration of their views, so both approaches need to be taken into account in arriving at a description of young people's views of others.

Exploring Attitudes in Interviews

As pointed out in Chapter 2, the interviews, which were primarily focused on establishing pupils' perceptions, were also used as a means of gathering statements of attitudes. We saw earlier in this chapter how such statements were first used as a means of validation of the ethnocentricity test, and we turn now to a closer analysis of the statements themselves. We indicated in our account of the method of dealing with interview transcripts — in Chapter 2 — that a sub-corpus of, in this case attitude, statements is created from the whole set of transcripts and then analysed by hand. Given that the central purpose of the research is to examine change in attitudes and perceptions over time, sub-corpora of attitudes towards the French were created and analysed in terms of age and level of ethnocentricity. As a basis for comparison further sub-corpora were created of attitudes towards the Germans and Americans. We consider first the older pupils.

Secondary pupils

Most ethnocentric group

Though the attitudes of this group were not uniformly negative and in

many cases were ambivalent, the most vehement expressions of dislike
were more likely to be expressed by this group than by any other. Certain
types of response suggested that stereotyped views were either being
repeated or had provided a framework for the interpretation of incidents
when meeting French people. For instance lack of patience, sometimes
coupled with an absence of friendliness, was sometimes said to be an
attribute of the French:

I: And what did you think of it? [France]
P: Thought the place was alright but I didn't like the French people.
I: No, why was that?
P: They didn't have any patience.
I: No, were you staying with a family?
P: No it was like a hostel.
I: Did you go for a weekend or for a few days?
P: A weekend.
I: Whereabouts was it?
P: Boulogne.
I: And what sort of people did you meet? Was it people running the hostel
   or people in the town?
P: People in the town and running the hostel.
I: When they were impatient, how were they impatient?
P: Like looking round the shops and not buying anything they would just
   throw you out. (Class 7 boy, school visit experience) (256/19)

This kind of incident was recalled by a number of those who had been on
school visits to France:

I: What would put you off living in France?
P: Don't like the food much and sometimes people can be a bit nasty —
   they're not friendly really.
I: What gives you these impressions then?
P: Like if you go into a shop there they say to you what do you want
   instead of can I help you and stuff like that.
I: Where have you come across that?
P: When I was passing through France on the school trip. I went in the
   shop there just having a look round, post cards and stuff like that, and
   the shop keeper like going round and I asked him — in French — could
   buy — if we could buy, if we wanted anything to buy but we were just
   really looking. (Class 2 boy, family and school holiday experience)
   (143/20)

In these cases it was of course possible that other factors were involved of which the interviewees did not seem to be aware and which could have prejudiced initial reactions towards them. Firstly, if obviously, the size and frequency of school parties could have adversely affected reception in shops. Secondly, whilst the pupils perceived the French as unfriendly they were perhaps ignorant of the possibility that they might have been expected to greet the shop and café owners on entering any establishment; thus their lack of overtures could have aggravated reactions to them. Thirdly, though café life is often documented as a feature of French life in textbooks teenagers under the age of sixteen are not necessarily allowed to enter them unaccompanied and so they could have been infringing a by-law. Whilst not the entire picture it would be unfortunate if those for whom school visits could be beneficial should through lack of preparation return with negative attitudes towards the French.

Even within this group however the opposite view of helpfulness and friendliness could be found. Referring to an incident also encountered on a school visit this Class 4 boy had a different view of what had been interpreted as harassment by others; he also noted the use of trying to make verbal contact:

> all he wanted to do was see who they were cos they were English, they were different and sort of he started talking as we walked past 'cause we were lost and told us where the hostel was and took us back to the hostel, all helpful. Just if you talk to them, not if you sort of shout at them in a loud voice and try and get over in English they ignore you but if you try to talk to them in French they'll help you as much as they can. (244/22)

In this group there was one boy (Class 8) whose semantic differential score did not seem in accord with his opinions. This was probably due to chance temporal or peer groups factors. Through longer experience in France he had gained a contrasting view of French friendliness and it was a theme to which he kept returning, for example:

I: Say you could choose to be any other nationality, not English, what would you choose to be?
P: French.
I: Why's that?
P: They get on with everybody. A lot friendlier.
I: You mean amongst themselves or with other countries?
P: Just like amongst themselves, when we went over they were always going in and out next door and a few doors down and saying hello to everybody. (301/3)

and:

P: They always talk to everybody. If there was somebody down the other end of the yard when we went to school there and they would run down the other end just to say hello. Weird. (301/3)

and:

P: The main thing is that they are a lot more friendly. No matter what anybody says about them. I would still go on holiday there because it is a good country. (301/28)

Only occasionally did it appear that hostile impressions of the French were based upon genuinely serious incidents. It was perhaps not surprising, if unfortunate, that the same boys (Class 6, school visit experience) had had their visit to France marred thus:

P: I don't like the French people.
I: No. What in particular don't you like about them?
P: When we were over Boulogne we got jumped on by some lads.
I: Yes I'd heard that some of you had been. Were you one of the ones that was jumped on?
P: No I went in this shop and D. tried to pay for something and they tried to get the money off D. and me and M. ran back and told Mr. X. (221/8)

The details of this incident were repeated by a number of interviewees and so sadly the network of acquaintances helped to turn the memory of one occasion into a description of how the French in general might behave.

Another source of information about one French age group was of course the exchange visit. This had happened more recently in Newfarm school, than at Hillside. Several pupils recollected their impressions of the French pupils who had visited the school, sometimes unfavourably. It should be borne in mind however that these pupils were on an exchange with an older class, not the class from which the interviewees were drawn and thus were separated by at least one year. The opinions expressed by those in this ethnocentric group, who remarked upon exchange pupils, were amongst the most forcefully expressed, for example:

I: What's your impression of the people then?
P: Just a bit loud, a bit too much really for me.
I: Where do you get that information from?

P: When they came over for the French exchange they were like that and from what I can remember when I was there they were always shouting. (101/6)

One of the most vehement expressions of all came from a Class 2 girl, with no experience of France:

I: Have you met any French people over here or when you were in Spain?
P: I didn't meet any when I was in Spain but when I was in — when some of the French people came over here they all like walked around the school, lashing out with dirty looks and everything. I just don't like the way they look at you, they look at you as to say what are you looking at — I don't like them. (156/6)

A few pupils in all groups referred guardedly to others who were known not to be well-disposed towards French people. In one case the interviewee hinted at a defensive type of reaction:

I: Why do you think people might not be friendly to French people?
P: Just because they're different, they're a different nationality and they don't know them.
I: Yes. Do you think many people feel like that?
P: . . . Not really, some are different and try to get to know them.
I: So you think that it's not specially because they're French but because they're a different nationality?
P: Yes.
I: What do you think most English people would think of say Germans then?
P: . . . Don't suppose they like them really either because they're a different nationality. (Class 8 girl, family and school visit experience) (322/18)

Parents' and friends' experiences and attitudes were sometimes influential:

I: Yes. What do you think most of your friends think?
P: I don't think they like the French. I don't think I would like to go there.
I: No. What do you think the main things are that they wouldn't like about them or is it impossible to say?
P: . . . I think most people think they are dirty. Unfriendly.
I: When you say dirty do you mean what the things they wear or the streets or what sort of things?
P: Just don't wash, like that.

I: What is that everybody in the towns or the country?
P: Just about everywhere really.
I: Is that something that some people have said?
P: Yes. (Class 1 boy, no experience of France) (102/17)

Another member of his class expressed the following opinion when discussing history:

I: You said that you'd heard about the revolution is there anything else you've heard about the history of France?
P: Well the battle of Hastings —
I: Yes?
P: — that was, 'cause I was like on the French side then, do you know what I mean?
I: Yes?
P: I wanted William to win, but I wouldn't want them to win now if they came over.
I: Why's that?
P: Because they're not so nice now, they were like more important than Britain then, more civilised.
I: So they were more civilised then but when you say that they're not so nice now how do you mean?
P: They don't really keep up with the times and they're not like, you know proper — nothing good 'cause they've got like a few television channels and they're not like good they're just like a few hours a day sort of thing, can't just have four big ones or something, got to have about eight little ones.
I: So you feel that they're a bit more old-fashioned, is that it?
P: Yes, they try to be modern and it always go wrong.
I: It always goes wrong?
P: Yes.
I: What sort of things go wrong?
P: Well you hear things on *Tomorrow's World* about them but nothing's like — everything's been discovered and that and they're on about space things now but we know all those things so nothing's new. (Class 4 boy, family visit experience) (245/22)

Later he modified his conclusion thus:

P: They are not really backward I am sure.

However, the general tone of his interview was negative regarding the French, even to the extent of stating:

P: . . . Well the Germans were going to conquer them weren't they, we had to help them but we shouldn't have.

I: Why's that do you think?

P: Well they wouldn't help us if we're ever going to get conquered, they'd just — well they'd want us to wouldn't they? (245/22)

Whilst this kind of conclusion was rare it should be remembered that this interviewee came from the top French set of his school. He was interested in learning French and other languages for largely linguistic reasons and appeared extremely co-operative to his interviewer. He did not appear to consider the possibility that anyone might construe his opinions as socially undesirable.

Medium ethnocentric group

Amongst the medium ethnocentric group there was a marked increase in the number of favourable comments made about the French and a diminution in the number of clearly negative comments; almost one third of the comments were however ambivalent. The same kinds of issues were as important for this group as for the most ethnocentric group. The principal concern was with whether French people were generally impatient, unfriendly and unhelpful or their opposites, opinions being roughly equally divided.

The influences upon the formation of the more negative attitudes in this group were chance occurrences and the media. The most strongly expressed opinion in this group came from a Class 5 boy with no experience of France. In the estimation of the interviewer the general tone of the interview suggested that this participant was something of a 'character', who sought consciously to amuse and referred to himself as having his 'own theories'. His opinions are quoted, however, as being illustrative of a particular kind of reaction which, if left undetected, could militate against class teachers' efforts to ameliorate pupils' views of other peoples. The second extract in particular indicates the persistence of stereotypes and is an exemplar of how they can become evident in the most unexpected places. He had met French people on holiday in a different part of the country:

P: And they always used to pretend they used to own the place and things like that.

I: Yes?

P: So I didn't get on very well with them.

I: No?

P: They seemed as if they wanted to look as if they owned the place.
I: Yes. What did they do?
P: They used to boss you around and things like that and say don't go on there and like boss you around. (Class 5 boy, no experience of going to France) (195/4)

Later, discussing housing he concluded that few French people had 'very good gardens':

P: I don't reckon they'd have much patience with it. Like with England like nearly every house has a garden so they're much more like patient so they're always like plodding over it but the French would like get sick after a couple of minutes, hard digging and things like that.
I: Why do you think they're impatient?
P: . . . It's like when they do have a traffic jam over in France like, all these people blast their horns where we just take it, like 'cause we're used to it but over there they get impatient.
I: Do you think most people are impatient?
P: No not really. Like if you're used to traffic jams you can take it like. Say like when they have like traffic jams over there they're not used to it see so they like just miss each other but when they do have one they get impatient and that and drive around like maniacs and the police are trying to undo the traffic jams and that. (195/22)

The final statement is a deduction from an earlier premise that as France was large there were few traffic jams, a contrast to the habituation of the English to traffic jams.

Unexplained incidents from school visits and other holidays again influenced views. One Class 3 girl considered the French as generally similar to the English but saw some as bad-tempered or, in her terminology, 'grumpy':

P: Well we went down like a back street from the main street and there was this man getting into his car and as we were passing the car we like looked and he was pointing his finger and all sorts, we just ran. (171/43)

Sometimes there was an automatic assumption that the English were always innocent in any awkward situation. One Class 7 girl considered that most English people would see the French as 'nasty' and referred to an incident in which a holiday coach on which she had been travelling had broken down and needed a spare part. As the coach driver reportedly had not been provided with funds by the company all the holiday makers had had to provide the cash before the garage owner would mend the coach:

P: Like on the bus they knew we couldn't go without that piece they knew that the piece cost a hundred and twenty pounds, they had no consideration. (295/14)

This might appear a trivial incident but it is included to illustrate the not inconsiderable number of adverse comments which could be usefully explored in class by those teachers who wish to broaden pupils' perspectives.

From the same group there were a number of expressions of more positive attitudes:

I: What the routine's going to be like. What would you say?
P: That you'd enjoy yourself and that the French people are very nice and that the life's different but it's better I think. (Class 2 girl, no experience of France) (140/5)

From experience of family holidays a Class 5 boy concluded:

P: They are very clean. Helpful. Like if you are lost and ask someone where you were . . . they would tell you where you were. (192/13)

Another boy in the same class with no experience of France had a positive view of the benefits of the Channel Tunnel:

P: Because I would like to know the French a bit better than I do now.
I: You think the Channel Tunnel would make that easier?
P: Yes. I think we would get more French people possibly living over here. (193/18)

Impressions gained from school and friends could influence views favourably. In the following example there is an implicit reflection upon life in this Class 5 girl's environment:

I: What sort of things have you been told?
P: . . . Just that they're friendly and they don't pick on you as much.
I: As much as?
P: English. (200/35)

When asking pupils for their views of how the French view Britain a number of pupils referred to a mutual lack of understanding which could cause antipathy:

P: Don't think they like us . . . 'cause we are not used to them . . . we don't understand them talking and they don't understand us. (294/16)

This Class 7 girl, with no experience of France, concluded that 'it would be alright' if linguistic barriers were removed.

Again pupils referred to others not liking the French and the following example is illustrative of unusual caution:

I: After all the time you have learnt French, what do you think of French people generally?
P: I don't know them maybe if I met one I might.
I: What sort of things have you been told about French people in schools?
P: I don't think many people like them. Some people get on with them.
I: What — the people who have been don't like them?
P: Some get on with them, 'cause some of them talk in English.
I: Why do you think the other people didn't like them?
P: Maybe because they are a different culture. (Class 3 girl, no experience of France) (168/34)

A Class 8 boy with no experience of France thought that many of his friends in class disliked the French but agreed that this was an issue never discussed with their French teacher. (This class was one with one of the lowest overall means for the semantic differential for the French.)

Some pupils reasoned that antipathy felt by the British would be reciprocated:
P: . . . because they think the same as us and we think they are stupid and things. (288/11) (Class 7 boy, no experience of France)

Amongst some pupils this assumption of reciprocity was replaced by one of a more tolerant if somewhat 'backward' nature:

P: They can only be human. I might get to meet a few, some I might not like, some I might like, can't tell. They have all got different personalities.
I: Would there be a nationality which you prefer from what you know of them? Obviously you have to generalise. The French or the Germans or Americans?

P: Like as I said before I think all nationalities as I said are only human so they are all going to be roughly the same. (Class 2 boy, no experience of France) (132/25)

Non-ethnocentric group

Amongst the interviewees' responses drawn from the non-ethnocentric group there were no extremely hostile comments, whilst there were a few ambivalent or mixed responses. The majority were clearly favourable and well disposed towards the French.

The majority of the comments were again concerned with friendliness, helpfulness and so on, but for this group it was the positive end of the spectrum which was represented. One Class 2 boy with family visit experience saw the people as 'more friendly' and recommended an outgoing strategy which contrasted with the reactions of some pupils who on school visits had admitted to keeping themselves to themselves:

P: . . . Well just expect friendliness from people and advice like don't be afraid to ask people where to go things like that. (135/5)

and then:

I: What about being in a family, a French family?
P: In a French family? . . . Join in a little bit like some people are sort of shy, aren't they, sort of get like in there and be friendly with them. (133/5)

and later:

P: Yes. I got along when I was there like. There was lots of French people that spoke English. That was like helpful but even when the people didn't speak English it was good. I didn't feel left out or odd. I felt well I will have a go and I can only try my best.
I: Yes. They were friendly when you did that?
P: Yes. (133/34)

Family holidays again could influence attitudes:

P: They are quite friendly, because I have been to France before and enjoyed it. My Mam and Dad didn't though because we were camping, and they were helpful, came round all the time and helped us clear up. They were just nice in all the shops and that. (Class 4 boy) (248/5)

A Class 6 girl, of brief school visit experience, summed up the French as 'pleasant' and 'well-mannered'. Whilst this was not a topic upon which many interviewees spoke some of those who had visited French families recalled that certain conventions were observed, such as greeting people in the morning and upon leaving them.

When discussing the perceptions of some of those in the most ethnocentric group of people's reactions to them it was argued that some of these pupils might not have been aware of some of the societal conventions. Though the course used does lay stress upon the observation of certain codes of behaviour, references to 'manners' were few.

A Class 6 girl who had school visit experience of France saw the French generally as 'quite nice, quite friendly', but concluded 'they keep themselves to themselves a bit though as well'. This kind of statement seems not dissimilar from the comments made upon English 'reserve' by others, and again is something which could provide a useful starting point for the discussion and comparison of cultures.

There was some suggestion that the course used did not actually tell pupils what French people are like and that pupils would be interested in more information upon social aspects:

... Well the textbook doesn't tell you everything about France really. I mean it only says about the sort of food they eat. It doesn't say like how they eat it, well it says how they eat it but ... and how they travel about and things like that and it doesn't really say they're nice people it just says what they eat and how they travel about on the trains and on the buses. It doesn't really tell you about the attitudes of them really. (Class 2 boy with extended experience of France) (133/14)

Whilst the writers of textbooks would probably hesitate to include bland generalisations about a people, they might also find it somewhat surprising that what is thought to be the more 'human angle' of modern textbooks is seen as inadequate by some consumers. More surprising too perhaps is that after three years of studying the language and culture one Class 8 boy (with no experience of France) found it hard to comment upon whether he would rather be French or English because he did not know what being French 'is like'.

The conclusion that the French are 'just the same as us' was a frequent rather brief assertion by pupils in all groups, when asked to sum up or make some sort of conclusion about the French.

In some cases there could have been an implicit assumption that 'just the same' meant similarly 'nice' or similarly diverse in characteristics. Occasionally the assumptions were made explicit:

P: The people I've seen and met, they're all nice, just the same as us. (Class 8 boy, family and school visit experience)

In this case English standards are unequivocally regarded as the norm.

Primary pupils

Most ethnocentric group

The responses of the most ethnocentric group exhibited a greater deviation from their semantic differential scores than did those of the corresponding secondary groups and negative responses were not from the majority. The attributes ascribed to French people and the types of concerns made evident in the primary pupils' interviews were similar to those of the secondary pupils, the emphasis being frequently upon helpfulness, friendliness, patience and their opposites. Other attributes, sometimes unsubstantiated and possibly mainly imaginary, were also included:

P: I don't think they'll be very nice 'cause . . . they might smell and things .

I: What else would you say?
P: . . . The people might not be the same — like they might not — they might be . . . have a nasty attitude and things and they might get in bad tempers and . . . I don't like people who get in bad tempers . . . (Class 13 girl, no experience of France) (491/18)

Sometimes the rationales provided for disliking a people by this age group appear idiosyncratic yet powerful enough to help form attitudes:

P: I don't really like France and that.
I: Why don't you like the French people very much?
P: The way they dress and the way they are, I just don't really like them.
I: How do French people dress then?
P: Well in short trousers. (Class 10 girl, no experience of France) (378/10)

Later in the interview she again said that she did not like them, and summed up the French thus:

P: Well . . . don't really know just that they're much different to us and they do different things and I see them as they're always arguing and I don't know. (378/21)

For this age group lack of familiarity with the French language could of course exacerbate any misunderstandings. Chance incidents could from time to time shape attitudes powerfully:

Sometimes they can be friendly and sometimes they can't because when I was travelling to Spain the first time and we stopped at this café on the way back, there was like my Dad behind us and my two brothers and there was Mam behind me and I was in front. There was these two French ladies in front of us all and like our Barry slipped and pushed my Mam and my Mam pushed me into one of these old ladies and she turned round and she said go back to papa and like shouted at me and that and I never liked them since. (Class 13 boy) (475/3)

However, in summing up he decided:

Quite a lot of exciting places. A lot of people. Friendly and kind. A lot of welcoming places and a lot that aren't. (475/21)

The sources of information which helped form attitudes for those with no experience of France included films and television. In some cases pupils recalled impressions gained several years before:

I: You don't like French people, why don't you like the French people?
P: 'cause I can't understand the language and I think they're rude.
I: They're rude, why do you think they're rude?
P: Because like I've seen films and things about when they're like — they've got onions around their necks and they're drinking beer and they're drunk and that.
I: And they're rude?
P: Yes.
I: Who are they rude to?
P: The English people.
I: English people?
P: Yes, 'cause once a man made a song about Margaret Thatcher and all the English people and I thought that was rude 'cause it told you all the words in English. (Class 13 boy, no experience of France) (478/3)

For this boy the French therefore could not be 'posh':

P: Because like to be posh or something you don't drink a very lot and you've got to like eat proper food. (478/8)

In the first year he had seen a number of films which had given him the impression of 'battered' streets and 'rude' people. These impressions had been retained despite his mother's experience:

P: She said they were very well mannered and things like that and I said that I don't believe it. (478/29)

Some knowledge of French industry had led him to add another attribute to the already unprepossessing picture:

I: If you had to say in a few words what you think French people are like, what would you say?
P: Um . . . I think they are rough mannered, they weren't well behaved and they drink too much.
I: Yes . . . and you think that — what gives you the impression that the French are drunken people?
P: Well 'cause through France they make beer and wine and stuff like that. (478/31)

then:

I: Have you seen pictures of them drinking too much?
P: Yes.
I: Where did you see these pictures?
P: Once there was a picture in the paper and he'd like — he'd been drinking too much over the limit and then he went and took some drugs and he died. (478/31)

Within the same group a more positive attitude towards learning French and about France was evident though in the following example the motivation was candidly instrumental:

I: Do you think it is important to learn how people live as well as language?
P: Yes because you will know the traditions and all the things you need to know. When you go there you will know the traditions and you will be able to please people. (Class 9 boy, no experience of France) (347/32)

He explained:

P: Well if you don't please people they will go round saying he is awful.

One of the reasons for discrepancies between the semantic differential scores and the attitudes expressed in the interviews could be a general inconsistency of attitudes which age, might modify even further. Another factor could be interviewing experiences as possibly in this case:

P: It is a nice country, I like it. I think a lot of people like France and a lot of people have written nice things about it.
I: What are you thinking of there when you say that?
P: Like a lot of people like them and when they say — some people were here talking about France — they would say 'people say it is a nice country' because they do. They say 'that's a nice country, I like it there'.
I: Who are you thinking of now? Who says that kind of thing?
P: The one that lives just round near the shop. I went up there — like I was going to the shop and I met this woman, she is called Barbara and near the shop she said she liked it there. I said had she been there and she said 'well I have been there but my son-in-law has been there as well, that's what I was saying in the shop'. She was getting her groceries. (Class 12 girl, no experience of France) (453/14)

Whilst the tone of many of the extracts in this group has been negative there was a sizeable minority who expressed positive, if brief, opinions about the French. They were described as 'alright', 'nice', 'friendly' by several in this group, but these comments were usually in the form of summing up statements with little substantiation. One Class 10 boy who had met French people when in Italy chose an unusual epithet to describe them as 'quite jolly' (361/13).

Medium ethnocentric group

Amongst this group there was a slight decrease in the number of negative attitudes. Most of the pupils in this group emphasised similar characteristics to those in the most ethnocentric group, the emphasis being upon kindness, helpfulness and their opposites. This Class 10 girl had family holiday experience of France:

I: What do you think I should know about what it [France] was going to be like?
P: . . . Nice. Probably the food would be nice and they would be kind to you as most French people are. (379/6)

She summed up the French thus:

> Kind . . . helpful with directions and things like that. (379/26)

Inevitably there were some pupils who could not articulate their reasons for disliking people. The following Class 10 boy had no experience of going to France but his family had had a French guest to stay. He decided 'I just didn't like him'. In summing up the French he decided they were 'just the same as us'. Unless a pupil qualified this type of statement it was not possible to assess whether this was a non-evaluative statement possibly referring only to, for example, physical characteristics, or an evaluative statement implying similarity in being for example 'pleasant', 'unpleasant', or similarity in diversity of characteristics.

Elements of the stereotype of the French as 'impatient' were again evident:

P: Just that they are fussy and I don't think they are very nice people to live with.

I: Do you think of them as being different from us then?

P: Yes.

I: How?

P: I don't know — like we sometimes take our time but they like never take their time and are like rushing around a lot and like saying they want this and want that and putting them back. They don't know what they want because they are rushing around. (Class 11 girl, no experience of France) (424/10)

The issue of 'politeness' was again mentioned, the source being second-hand, and in this case containing an unexplained component:

P: . . . They're not polite . . . some of them don't like the British . . . that's all.

I: Where have you heard these things?

P: My sister says they're not polite.

I: So she had some bad experience of them did she when she was over there?

P: Well they were polite sometimes but she had some good arguments with the — on the market when she went. 'Cause they were selling this elephant that she was buying my Mam and she said it cost too much and she was arguing with him to give her it about 30 pence cheaper. (Class 9 boy, no experience of France) (350/25)

Again this kind of incident might appear trivial but could also be seen as formative; at the least this kind of perception could be usefully used educatively. The following girl had a stereotyped view of French apparel and a strangely negative assessment of the people which might conceivably prejudice future attitudes towards learning French:

> Horrible and dirty. The food is quite nice and I think they always wear onions around their necks. (Class 12, no experience of France) (456/ 32)

The problems of not knowing the language characterised some of the responses concerning introductory questions upon staying with a French family. Some of the primary pupils shared the secondary pupils' views of the use of being able to speak French, though this might be expressed in more ingenuously instrumental terms:

P: I think they have a different accent to us English people and they might always be unpleasant to English people 'cause if an English person spoke French they'd be kind to them and that 'cause they might have thought that he was French too. (Class 13 boy, no experience of France) (479/41)

He explained further

P: Because they might not like the sound of what they're saying and one father might find out that an English child might have been picking on his son.
I: Have you ever heard of that happening or do you just think that would happen?
P: Might happen. (479/41)

(This was one case where it was possible that recent events in his personal history might have been projected onto the matter under discussion. Obviously any research undertaking could be so affected, but methodologically it is worth bearing in mind that there is an argument that the younger the group the less likely their powers of being objective.)

For some pupils with no experience of France generalising about the French was not particularly easy and so responses were speculative taking the form of 'might be nice' and 'would be nice'. Some pupils like their older counterparts concluded that the French were 'more or less the same as us' but only a few were able to expand upon this:

I: Are they likeable people or . . . ?
P: Some of them are, some of them aren't. (Class 10 girl, family holiday experience) (388/22)

Whilst this kind of response is brief and the interviewee needed help in arriving at it, there are grounds for concluding that her perception of the French is at least more differentiated than some in this age group and suggests an underlying appreciation that diversity is an attribute of all cultures.

Non-ethnocentric group

Whilst a few ambivalent responses were given by this group only one wholly negative response was given, and most of the responses were unequivocally positive. Interestingly in addition to referring to attributes such as 'friendliness' and 'kindness' pupils in this group had noticed other diverse characteristics. Again however the types of assessments could suggest that what was most salient for some in describing the French was how the French were thought to behave towards the self:

P: Like if you go into the shop and like you don't know what to say 'cause you can't pronounce the word or something and like you can't talk to them very much they'll help you pick things up and try to show you like that's what you want and you go through all the things till they find out what you want.
I: Who's told you this?
P: Well my Mam when she went in this shop when we stopped at this service station like we were trying to tell them what we wanted 'cos it was French people in. (Class 13 girl, experience limited to travelling through France) (484/31)

Some of the lengthiest passages come from pupils who perceived both positive and negative aspects. Two pupils in particular spoke at great length upon their views of the French; only selections can be included here. In the first case this Class 10 boy who had been on holiday to France gave the most extended comment upon impatience coupled with helpfulness:

It would be very difficult because they get very, their tempers get very quickly and if you can't understand them like they get in tempers and get very cross and they get very mad and when — if you're making a lot of noise they go mad and just leap around shouting at you and go and complain to people and stuff and get in really hot tempers and the policemen, if you've done something wrong and he starts getting mad and bipping the horns at you and stuff, it's not very nice and people shouting at you and they can really get into hot tempers and they're friendly and they want to help you all the time but when you ask them for directions they try to — and when you ask them to help you they're so keen to help you that they forget where you're going — they're friendly, they want to help you all the time but they just can't because they give you the wrong directions, they're so keen to help you. (367/8)

He had noted other aspects of French life:

They're very friendly, very friendly and . . . I think they always want to get their own way though and . . . I think they're proud of their country and they like to keep everything neat and tidy and the trees in straight rows and everything — make sure there's nothing out of place. They're tidy people, they like the country and they're very friendly. (367/9)

About staying with a French family he reasoned:

. . . you'll try more foods with them 'cause we're too frightened to say no or they'll get in tempers and . . . they're alright I think. (367/10)

he also recalled:

The French ferry drivers — I'm scared of them for — 'cause they look so big and they were telling some people off for being stupid, clinging on the rails and stuff and they seem very fierce. (367/14)

Finally he suggested another characteristic from an incident which could be merely trivial or could embody what some see as French attitudes to authority and related bodies:

I think the French are very daring 'cause we were on the campsite and I hit the ping pong ball over the fence and it was a big fence and it was the owner's private house, big gates all the way round, and he sneaked in the fence and got the ping pong ball out . . . (367/25)

Though somewhat fearful this boy concluded:

I enjoyed playing with the French children though 'cause they're very, they want to play and they'll do anything to play with you. (367/25)

A unique perspective upon perceived contrasts between France and Britain was provided by a boy who had recently moved to the North of England but whose relations came from Bangladesh. The main source of his information came from an older relation at secondary school with whom he had discussed France. He had also met French people when travelling by air. Some of the terms he used to describe the French differed markedly from those of others:

> I would say go there and have a holiday but never stay there because it is not very civilised and all that as England. I would like to go on a holiday but I would tell them I would warn them about the unclean-ness there and all that and I would tell them not to stay there. (Class 11 boy) (409/5)

From having heard a little about French schools he concluded that people were not helpful:

P: Because they look like strict people — rough. Harsh.
I: When you say rough and harsh how do you mean?
P: Say you ask them a question. You ask them what this was or something. They would probably say work it out yourself. Don't ask me. That's what I reckon. (409/14)

His relation's experience in France caused him to contrast France sponta-neously with America:

I: Would you be interested in going to France yourself?
P: Quite interested to go there but my brother told me — my nephew told me once when he was walking down the street the people aren't very kind. This lad swore to him when my nephew was walking down. He never said hello or anything. While as in America if you walk down somewhere they probably say hello how are you and all that. While in France they just don't bother. (409/24)

However he drew an interesting and unique distinction between superficial or overt characteristics and others 'inside':

I: If I were to say — in a few words what do you think about 'the French', what would you say?
P: Mean but reasonably well thought. Good mind, they have a good mind but its just the outside of them. You can reckon they are really bad outside but the inside of them I think will be quite good. So they are not all that bad really. (409/45)

He explained:

> Say somebody really really likes you but inside they really hate you.
> They really want to kill you but you just act to them like 'hiya hiya'
> and talk to them a lot but inside you are really burning, you want to
> kill them or something. Just like that. Like the French. They are bad
> outside. They might be unkind outside but inside they have a good
> heart. (409/45)

He recalled meeting a Frenchman on a plane:

> He was questioning me, then I started questioning him. What is it like
> in France, how is it? He said in France it isn't like in Bangladesh, it is
> not as hot as there but gets more money than that. Said in a kind way.
> I thought that person was quite good and I would like to meet him
> again if I can. (409/47)

Unlike the rest of the primary interviewees he was able to make use of
a more international perspective and whereas for most pupils France was
implicitly contrasted with England, for him France and England were
positively contrasted with Bangladesh and a number of other countries,
and both were viewed as less successful than America, about which he had
heard much from other relations.

Experience of staying in a 'gîte' rather than on a campsite enabled one
pupil to form positive impressions of the French which contrasted with
those of some older pupils who had only been on short visits:

P: Like they say . . . au revoir a lot and hello and good morning and . . .
they've like got good manners and . . . (Class 13 boy) (492/4)

However some aspects of daily life being different was enough to
cause him to attribute strangeness to the French, English behaviour
presumably being the norm:

P: The young people weren't that different but the old people like they
were — they had queer ways.
I: What do you mean?
P: Its queer like 'cause you're . . . like the right and left side of the road
things, like they go on the right side and we go on the left side.
I: What else is queer?
P: . . . The countryside like they've got like orchards and things 'cause
they've got like more sun and we haven't . . . (492/15)

Despite experience of France elements of the stereotype remained or were confirmed, though some confusion became apparent:

> Mostly they wear berets and like sell onions and things and mostly they ride bikes and they have like . . . little like bikes, like motor bikes, they have little motor bikes with little motors and . . . mostly they're Jews . . . and the houses are different sometimes inside, four poster beds and things . . . (492/23)

and finally:

> Er . . . they're kind, they've got good manners and mostly have like a tan, like 'cause they've been sun bathing and that . . . they wear hats and that for the festival and things and they mostly go to church . . . and they're Jews and . . . can't remember anything else. (492/23)

Some pupils in this group saw the French as 'different'; in this case reference was not to psychological or personalistic attributes:

I: OK. If I asked you to say in just a few words about what French people are like what would you say?
P: They're probably different to us.
I: They're different to us, what sort of ways are they different?
P: Like they eat different food and sell different things to us and . . .
I: So if you were a French girl instead of an English girl how do you think you might be different, do you think you would be a different person?
P: Mm.
I: How would you be different?
P: 'cause I'd be talking French and I'd have to get a job — a different job.
  (Class 11 girl, no experience of France) (428/20)

One pupil, who had a half French aunt saw the French as 'friendly' but 'different'. Again the differences were cultural rather than personal: as she referred to 'the clothes, the language'.

The responses of this group regarding the French appeared to be more diverse and in some cases possibly more complex than those in the other two groups. Though there were some ambivalent responses the overall impression was of favourable attitudes. In one case only were the interviewee's reported attitudes unequivocally negative and thus not in accord with his semantic differential score. In this particular instance what was interesting was not so much the instability of attitude expressed but the fact that triangulation with other material was possible. The pupil in question stated that neither he nor his sister liked the French though his parents did. Despite careful probing by the interviewer he was adamant that he had no French relations. His older sister had already been interviewed and had given a very favourable account of how she saw France. In addition she revealed that they had a number of French relations. Sometimes having access to other material can help to confirm researchers' findings; in cases such as this questions are left unanswered.

Attitudes to the Germans and the Americans

A brief comparison of pupils' attitudes towards French people with their attitudes towards other peoples was carried out. Their views of the Germans and the Americans formed the main basis of this comparison but incidental material upon other peoples mentioned spontaneously was also analysed.

The amount of time devoted to this part of the study was much smaller than that devoted to perceptions of the French and thus only tentative conclusions can be drawn. However in reviewing the kinds of constructs which pupils used in their descriptions of other peoples two rather opposing points emerged. Firstly the principal concern of a large majority of pupils was with whether other people were 'nice' and/or 'friendly'; in this their judgements were based on the same criteria as those used for the French. Secondly, when negative comments were made about the Americans the most usual description was that they were 'big-headed' and 'show-off'. For the Germans there was a diverse range of descriptions both positive and negative.

America was the country most often chosen as a desirable place to visit partly because of some well known sights such as Disneyland. When asked what nationality they would like to be if not English, being American was most often chosen and though some pupils resented any suspicion of 'showing-off' attributed to wealth, other pupils were attracted by opportunities across the Atlantic. It was seen from the semantic differential tests that the Americans were the most favourably perceived, followed by the French, whilst views of the Germans were polarised.

Since the principal focus of the study is upon perceptions of the French, the terms 'ethnocentric' and 'non-ethnocentric' have been used to denote levels of prejudice principally regarding the French. However, it became clear from both the semantic differential results and from the interviews that pupils did not express the same kinds of attitudes towards all peoples and thus differentiated amongst them. Thus any one pupil might view one people positively and another negatively, whilst holding ambivalent views of a third. Also possible combinations could be found including negative views of peoples other than the English, and positive views of all other peoples mentioned. Early studies of the concept of ethnocentrism and prejudice such as those of Allport (1954) and Adorno *et al.* (1950) suggested that ethnocentrism was a unitary concept, that is if prejudice existed there would be prejudice against all 'out-groups'. More recent work such as that of Ray & Lovejoy (1986) has argued that no major correlations obtained amongst views of different peoples or with other aspects such as patriotism. In this study it was clear that pupils did differentiate amongst peoples. The most common combination of responses was the type where an ambivalent assessment of one or more peoples was combined with positive or negative attitudes towards the remaining peoples (for example having an ambivalent attitude towards the French, a negative attitude towards the Germans and a positive attitude towards the Americans). Many types of combination were represented, as were also combinations of two positive and one negative attitude and of two negative and one positive attitude. Several interviewees were found who expressed unequivocally positive attitudes towards all three peoples. No instances of unequivocally negative attitudes towards all three peoples were found in the interviews but as this was not at the centre of our study questioning upon this area was not uniform and could form a useful basis for future research. It was clear that extreme prejudice against all 'out-groups' was not a phenomenon found amongst this sample and in designating some attitudes as negative this does not imply that they were all violently hostile. As will be seen below many were at the level of seeing others as 'big-headed' or 'forward'.

The combinations of scores on the semantic differential tests were analysed also. Rather than carry out correlated tests on the scores alone it was decided to see on how many occasions all three scores fell into the most ethnocentric category, the non-ethnocentric category and so forth, as this kind of data yields more information upon whether individuals differentiated amongst the peoples concerned than could correlational analysis. It was found that in the large majority of cases, approximately 80%, the attitudes expressed did not fall within the same broad categories. In approximately 11% of the cases all three peoples were favourably perceived, in approximately 6% of the cases all three peoples were negatively perceived, and in approximately 3% of the cases all three attitudes fell into the medium category. Of the 6% whose scores came into the most ethnocentric category it was found that there was variation amongst the scores in that they were not all necessarily at the lowest point of the scale, and some were at a point falling only just below the parameters for the middle category.

Some interesting class variations were found when analysing the combinations of scores. The two classes with the highest number of all positive non-ethnocentric scores were Classes 1 and 2 (the two Newfarm secondary classes), with seven in each class. Of the junior classes the class with the greatest number was Class 15 (Market Garth). A greater number of non-ethnocentric combination was found amongst the secondary sample than the junior (27:17). The numbers of combinations of most ethnocentric attitudes were similar in both age groups (12 secondary:13 junior) with one class in each — Class 8 and Class 15 — having five pupils who expressed similar attitudes to all three peoples.

A brief selection of the types of statements made about Germans and Americans is given below.

The Germans

From meeting German visitors at a friend's house a Class 15 boy decided that he would say:

. . . they were very joyful and playful and nice friendly people.

Many pupils of both age groups were unaware of twentieth century German history, and some, like the following Class 11 boy with no experience of going abroad retained this image of the Germans:

P: Because the Germans fight. They seem to like war and that.
I: Do you read about that kind of thing? Do you read comics and so on?
P: No.
I: Where do you know about Germany then?
P: Because I have seen it — I have heard about it because my Mam tells me and that.
I: What does your Mam tell you?
P: About when it was the Second World War, things like my Grandad used to drive tanks and my other Grandad used to polish the guns and all that.
I: I see, so she has talked to you about it has she? Have you talked to your Granded or is he dead?
P: One of them is.
I: Have you talked to the other one?
P: Yes.

I: Talked to him have you, what does he say?
P: He just tells us stories about when he was like in the army. (407/2)

Others did not share this view:

> No. I don't think that's fair on the Germans or us any more to blame
> the war on anyone. 'Cause it's over now and I wasn't — I'm glad the
> English won or we'd be in German hands just about now but I don't
> like war I don't want there to be a war again. That's why I'm not
> saying anything about it. I don't take sides I mean I am English but
> I'm glad the English won but I don't think of the war and Germany
> any more, I would probably like the Germans as the war was ages ago
> and there's nothing going to stop me making friends with a German or
> something just because of the war, it's silly that 'cause it's over now
> and there's nothing between the two countries now they're not going
> to have a war again, not now in 1986 or 1987. I don't think there's
> nothing wrong with the Germans. (Class 14 girl, experience of going
> abroad) (515/27)

The same judgements upon the diversity of individuals were as apparent
when talking about the Germans as when talking about the French.

> . . . They're nice and there's some good people among them.

Then:

I: . . . When you say there's some nice people among does that mean that
   there's some that aren't?
P: Yes, I think there'd be a few that are aren't.
I: What makes you think of that?
P: 'Cause not everyone can be good, there has to be someone that's not
   very nice.
I: Yes, but would that be the same for the French then?
P: . . . Yes. (Class 14 boy, no experience of going abroad) (502/22)

In the absence of personal acquaintance with German people, many
pupils had recourse to television images:

I: What about German people? Could you say in a few words what they
   are like?
P: Evil.
I: Why are they evil?

P: Because on the films I have seen they just go round killing people and making wars.

I: Anything else?

P: They get the soldiers to work for them and they don't really want to. Then they kill all of the English people. That's all. (Class 12 girl, no experience of abroad) (456/33)

It appeared that the television was also a source of material more recent than the Second World War:

> That other programme, on holiday in Spain . . . and he's always like saying that the Germans are bragging. (Class 5 boy, with experience of abroad) (197/37)

The Americans

The Americans were favourably perceived by the majority of pupils, American was one of the most preferred nationalities and America was a country which many pupils wished to visit. The country was seen as rich and powerful:

> I really reckon the Americans are brilliant. Really good. But I think in one way they are quite bad. Because Russia is trying to stop and make peace while they want to fight because they have most of the power haven't they. In space, Star Wars, nuclear missiles and everything. While Russia just has one particular missile or something. Not as powerful as America so I reckon America in one way are good and one way bad . . . Most people go to America as well to earn money because they are one of the biggest, richest countries in the world really. If you think of America and Saudi Arabia, two of the richest say. I think for oil Saudi Arabia is better but for money I think it is definitely America. (Class 11 boy) (409/48)

The source of much of the information was the television but some had met Americans:-

P: Yes, I met one and she's nice and my Uncle was telling me when he was abroad they are all very nice to you and that, better than others.

I: Who were they better than?

P: . . . Like French people and that. (Class 6 girl, no experience of abroad) (236/1)

When Americans were not liked it was usually because they were thought to 'show-off' or be big-headed:

P: Oh well the Americans are forward.
I: What do you mean by forward?
P: Like they think they're it like.
I: You don't think the French think that?
P: Not really no. Americans like seem like I'm from America I'm great, like that. They think they're good 'cause they are from America. (Class 2 boy, experience of abroad) (138/39)

The negative images which the younger age group had of the Americans were similar to those of the secondary pupils:

They are pretty arrogant and have different accents and ride round in big cars and that. Lots of stars live over there. (Class 15 girl, no experience of abroad) (552/28)

Whilst the negative images tended to be more strongly expressed than the positive, these are in the context of generally favourable attitudes towards the Americans. Some pupils felt that there was a special relationship between England and America:

I: Which country do you think it would be best to come from?
P: . . . America.
I: Why do you think it would be best to be American?
P: Because Americans like English people better. (Class 9 boy, no experience of abroad) (341/3)

Discussion

From the extracts included in the sections upon the French, the Germans and the Americans it can be seen that there was a wide variation amongst the responses, ranging from the discursive and the reflective to the brief and unsubstantiated. For many pupils, particularly those without experience of the relevant countries, being asked to summarise and to generalise were not easy tasks. However the majority were able to respond in some form, only a small proportion not being able to answer at all. Those with little extensive experience often relied upon relations' and friends' accounts of other cultures. These of course could become exaggerated or modified in both transmission and recollection. Some consensus amongst responses did obtain, however, despite the above reservations, and thus one is able to conclude that both age groups had begun to form impressions of other peoples which, in the case of the three target peoples, were distinct. Thus there was an overriding emphasis upon whether other peoples were 'friendly', usually on an individual rather than national basis, but thereafter characteristics were attributed differentially.

For the French the other characteristics sometimes mentioned were 'noisy', and 'polite/impolite'. In these emphases the pupils did not necessarily construe their experiences in a different way from adults, but not all were able to locate chance impressions within a broader perspective.

For the Germans and the Americans the most common terms used were the rather bland 'nice' or 'not so nice as . . .' some other people. For the Germans 'friendly' was again a common epithet, whilst Americans were seen as 'show-offs' often with their money. For both peoples a variety of other terms was applied, but usually only used by one individual. For the Germans these included 'funny, joyful, playful, big, strong, horrible, mean — with a mean look, rougher than the French, normal, suspicious, awful, evil, noisy, pleasant, not bad and very wise'. For the Americans the following were used: 'posh, rich, stupid, brilliant, funny, tall, crazy, noisy, strong, violent, forward, quiet, better than others and upper class'.

The evaluative constructs which Osgood found to be most common were rarely used. Osgood's evaluative constructs consisted of the following: 'pleasant/unpleasant, sweet/sour, beautiful/ugly, good/bad, clean/dirty, valuable/worthless'. Of these 'pleasant' was used once by the interviewees, terms such as 'nice' being far more common. 'Nasty', 'horrible' or 'not as nice as' were used in preference to 'unpleasant'. 'Good' was used twice but 'bad' was not used by itself, but only in the phrase 'not bad' which in terms of English culture can be indicative of more than a neutral position, that is even quite approving! Being 'dirty' or 'clean' was mentioned by a small number of pupils but it did not appear to be a salient issue. The kinds of adjectives used most often by pupils in this study reflected largely interactional behaviour, or how the people were perceived to behave towards them or their acquaintances on an individual basis.

When terms such as 'pushy', 'arrogant' and 'showing off with their money' were used, it is possible that some subcultural factors were being added to any English heterostereotypes in that economic factors in the region might have produced amongst some a certain resentment against those appearing to be more wealthy. That pupils were aware of difficulties of gaining employment locally and of concomitant lack of money was evident from one oft-repeated reason for learning French: that one might be able to find a job in France. Many pupils knew also of friends and relations who had left the area to go to Australia.

One noticeable difference between the two age groups was that amongst the juniors some pupils described other peoples in terms of physical and behavioural differences rather than in terms of personalistic attributes, with their concomitant evaluations. The majority of the juniors did however respond in a similar way to the secondary pupils. Where the object of perception is an individual, or group of individuals, rather than a nationality, social cognitive research, such as that of Brierley (1967) and Peevers & Secord (1973), has shown that it is usual to find an increase with age in the capacity to construe others in terms of personalistic or psychological rather than physical attributes. Lambert & Klineberg (1967) found a similar increase when the objects of perception were nationalities.

The understanding of nationality has been argued by Katz (1983) to develop long after that of gender and race, concepts of which are established in the pre-school years. Like the understanding of religious groups, perceptions of nationalities are not thought to be of major interest until the junior school years. Thus for the younger age group of this study's sample the acquisition of concepts of nationality would probably have been quite recent. The focus of the study was upon peoples to whom the English are relatively close geographically, and of whom images are frequently presented by the media. Had other peoples been chosen from countries with which most pupils were less familiar the information might have been much reduced. Lambert & Klineberg's cross-cultural studies indicated that amounts of information available about peoples varied widely.

Whilst the present study is not cross-cultural, some interesting parallels with Lambert & Klineberg's findings were found. Given of course the usual complexity of such large scale works, they found that America was generally positively regarded, that France occupied a similarly favourable position to that of Britain, both coming after America, that Russia was not popular and that ambivalent attitudes towards Germany were evident. The reasons given for the positive attitudes towards America were, amongst most nationalities questioned, the personal qualities of the Americans. For a minority it was the style of living and wealth which were the reasons given for desired American nationality. In the present study life style and wealth were reasons which predominated in both the pro and anti-American groups.

The types of constructs used by the wide groups of nationalities questioned bore some similarities to those used in this study, though emphases differed according to the nationality questioned (for example the

French were concerned about what Lambert & Klineberg termed the 'cultural' category). However as Lambert & Klineberg used very global categories under which a number of what might appear to be disparate qualities were subsumed, direct comparison is not feasible. For example, whilst we agree that the evaluations subsumed under the category heading 'good' are positive, the following adjectives were included under this heading: 'are friends, nice, kind, friendly, with us in war, welcoming, generous, truthful'. Other major categories used were 'peaceful, ambitious, intelligent, and cultured'. A few of the adjectives included under this heading were occasionally used by our sample such as 'fashionable', 'polite', 'modern', 'quiet', but others such as 'refined', 'reserved', 'cultivated' and 'modest' did not form part of this sample's repertoire. There were few references to the items of which the other favourable evaluative descriptions consisted. Similar conclusions could be drawn also about the unfavourable evaluative descriptions, only the categories of 'aggressive' and 'uncultured' (which included 'impolite' and 'rude') being at all similar. No English sample was included in Lambert & Klineberg's study, so it is not possible to draw a direct comparison with this earlier work, but it is possible that we might have a culturally-specific consensus regarding what aspects of other nationalities were seen as important by the English, as was the case for the nationality groups questioned by Lambert & Klineberg.

Lambert & Klineberg concluded that the group which received the greatest amount of information from the media, the Americans, did not appear to be adversely affected by the images transmitted in that they scored most highly on their assessments of 'affection' for other peoples. In assessing these conclusions one would need to take into account the nature of the available television programmes which could easily have presented less stereotyped images than those prevalent in the British media twenty years later. One interesting age difference was found by Lambert & Klineberg in that their youngest age group of six year olds from most nationalities made much greater use of parents as sources of information than did the ten and fourteen year olds who relied to a greater extent upon the media. In the present study information and attitudes transmitted by parents and friends were very evident whilst television was also a potent force. Whilst teachers were obvious sources of information for the present sample, a lack of recall of teachers' attitudes towards peoples similar to that found by Lambert & Klineberg was apparent. There may of course be pedagogical reasons for this but it was clear that pupils did not refer, in discussing attitudes, to any stances which teachers claimed they took with the purpose of ameliorating views of the French. However it is possible to contend that the increase in information alone about the French, received by the older age group of this study, was sufficient to ensure that rigid stereotypes were not held, in contrast to Lambert & Klineberg's claim that they found an age-related increase in stereotyped views of other peoples. Clearly other factors, such as increased capacities for differentiated conceptualisation, may also have affected the views of the older age group. Further research could usefully include analysis of control groups of secondary school age not being taught French.

Lambert & Klineberg also found that the younger the age group the greater the likelihood that differences would be construed in terms of physical rather than psychological attributes, and following Vygotsky concluded that the true ability to perceive differences would precede the recognition of similarities. However no suggestion was made by Lambert & Klineberg that any, of for example the older age group, had begun to attempt a more integrated assessment. For Lambert & Klineberg the underlying assumption appeared to be that to state that others were 'just the same' was the most laudable response which, while not wishing to detract from the putatively sympathetic aspects of this type of response, could also suggest a quick closure strategy indicative of a lack of reflection or perception.

One other interesting similarity found between the present study and that of Lambert & Klineberg is that a similar lack of diversity of positively evaluative descriptions was found when compared with the negatively evaluative descriptions. In this, judgement of whole nationalities does not differ from most of the findings of social cognitive research, for instance that dislike of someone usually produces greater diversity of description than does the liking of someone. The reasons why this should be so are not clear. It is possible that the amount of arousal caused by negative feelings is greater than that caused by positive feelings apart from in certain well-documented situations, and therefore negative feelings lead to greater concentration upon aspects which are actively disliked, whereas if one's response is positive the inclination is not usually to define why. In the context of the pupils' own experience recall of negative encounters was usually more vivid than that of positive ones. Details of who said what to whom in these situations were legion whereas descriptions of the liked were usually bland and not extensive.

From the present sample certain types of responses were apparent and could be grouped under the headings given below, which, whilst ordered, do not imply a stage sequence of development, in that it is conceivable that different target nationalities could elicit different responses. Responses therefore indicated that the individual:

(i)   Knows that the people concerned are of a 'different nationality' and uses perception of physical differences only to conclude that they will be 'different' in other characteristics.

(ii)   Concludes that the people concerned differ in one or more attributes of a personalistic rather than physical nature. No similarities are mentioned.

(iii)   Perceives the people as 'just the same' . . . (except where appropriate for their language). This usually implies a positive evaluation, i.e. as good as us, and is distinct from (iv).

(iv)   Perceives the people as similar to 'us' in having a diversity of characteristics both positive and negative.

It would of course be possible to posit another type of response in which a more integrated conception of for example the interaction of culture and personality was articulated but in terms of the present sample this remains hypothetical. Whilst we acknowledge the influence of Harvey, Hunt & Schroder (1961) upon the above typology, it is always necessary also to bear in mind more fundamental factors such as pupils' capacities of recall when asked for extempore appraisals of peoples gathered in the unusual setting of the interview.

Much work has been done upon the functions of stereotypes and the intermediary role of information by Tajfel (1973), Johnson et al. (1970), Stillwell & Spencer (1974) and it is not proposed to draw any comparisons with their work except to consider the role of information provided by schools in this study. As was stated above, factual information was perhaps adequate to prevent the growth of stereotyped views about the French, but whilst most interviewees did not display extreme hostility towards the French, it is argued that there was enough somewhat negative material which teachers could use in discussing stereotypes. It was clear moreover from teachers' interviews that it was not usual for teachers to make use of pupils' own experiences in France, though they subscribed to the aim of ameliorating relations between peoples. The actual provenance of some of the more stereotyped images, such as the media and encounters on school visits, could form useful discussion material, and could also illustrate the diversity of perceptions. It was after all argued by Tajfel (1973) that, in order to reduce the incidence of stereotypes, more attention should be drawn to intra-cultural diversity than to intercultural differences and similarities.

4 Sources of and Influences on Pupils' Perceptions and Attitudes — the Pupils' Views

Introduction

Having described pupils' attitudes and perceptions in the preceding two chapters, we turn now to the question of the sources for and influences on pupils in these respects. It was an assumption in the research design that such sources and influences are not confined to the classroom. This assumption was supported by the findings of the statistical analysis of Chapter 3, that 'background' factors associated more strongly with attitudes than did 'experiential' factors. In this chapter we continue that rough distinction by considering sources and influences from outside school separately from those within school and particularly within the teaching of French. We consider pupils' own views on this issue as a complement to the statistical analysis and to the account of classroom processes produced from observation and ethnographic analysis, which will be the subject of Chapter 5.

Sources and Influences From Outside School

Primary pupils' views

It was assumed already from interviewing experience that primary teachers do not constitute an important source, and this was subsequently confirmed in analysis of transcripts. It was also apparent from analysis of perceptions by topic — such as 'dress and physical appearance' — that the membership of a particular school class is not significant in this respect. The experience of a stay in France on the other hand is influential. It was decided therefore to select material according to degree of ethnocentricity, to see whether there is any discernible pattern in the sources of information of different ethnocentricity groups. Clearly any such pattern would be most evident in the 'ethnocentric' and 'non-ethnocentric' groups and, since selection according to these two groups alone already produced large corpuses of material, it was decided to use it as the basis for analysis.

Although different categories of sources had been used for inserting keywords in the transcripts, all the material was included in the corpus, irrespective of category, and new categories established from the new text: books, films, television, parents (and other adults), foreign visitors, other foreign contacts, siblings, visits by self, visits by siblings (usually school trips).

As a first stage an approximative quantitative analysis shows some marked differences between the two groups. The N group ('non-ethnocentric') corpus consists of statements from 30 pupils with 161 references. The E group ('ethnocentric') corpus is made up of statements from 29 pupils with 102 references. Three categories account for most of the difference: 'siblings' combined with 'visits by siblings' and 'visits by self'. There are 6 and 5 references respectively in the E group and 24 and 26 references respectively in the N group. The accounts given by siblings are not always positive, whether it is with respect to the impressions they give of the French language or the stories they tell of their visits to France. Similarly pupils' own visits to France do not always result in positive experiences. Yet it is striking that the N group have more experience, both personal and vicarious, and much if not all of it is positive. The statistical analysis does not use the same categories but the factor 'family language learning experience' did indicate higher group means in attitudes towards French, Americans and Germans, although only in the last case was any acceptable level of significance achieved. This factor includes however parental learning as well as siblings' learning of foreign languages.

Similarly there is no significant statistical relationship between experience of France and attitudes. In analysis of interaction between variables it was concluded that what might be assumed to be an optimal combination of experience of France, French people and having relations of other linguistic backgrounds is not necessarily so, and that the quality of experience is likely to be important. The quality of pupils' visits as general sources of information is also variable, as will be seen below. On the other hand the quality of visits is likely to be more directly related to the amount of knowledge pupils have, irrespective of whether the visit has influenced their attitudes. The quality of the visit, as far as knowledge is concerned, is rather a question of the detail and accuracy.

Still in terms of quantity, another striking feature of both corpuses is the number of references to television: 24 in the E group and 31 in the N group. Books by comparison are mentioned only 8 times in the E group and 9 times in the N group. There are also 5 E group and 9 N group references to films, some of which overlap with television although three pupils mentioned seeing the film 'Le Ballon Rouge' at school. Finally there are 11 E group references to parents and other adults, 1 reference to a visitor from France, and 4 references to other forms of contact, e.g. penfriend. The comparable figures for the N group are 13, 2 and 3 respectively.

After this approximative quantitative overview, the second stage of analysis involves a close reading of the different categories of extracts. It becomes apparent that even within the large categories — siblings, visits, television — there is no pattern which might differentiate the groups' attitudes. The information they receive is sometimes encouraging and sometimes not, and in some cases it is not possible to interpret what effect it may have had. For this reason the categories will be presented as a combination of material from both groups.

Television and films

Information and images gleaned from television by pupils fall into three broad categories: news presentations, comedy programmes and other light entertainment, and holiday and cookery programmes. At first sight the first source might be assumed to be representative and factual, but many pupils say that France is not mentioned on the news, and those that do remember something report events which are likely to give a bad impression. By chance, about the time of interviewing, there had been reports on English television of student demonstrations in Paris and terrorist bombings. Some pupils were asked if they had seen this and said not. Others spontaneously mentioned it when asked about television in general:

I: You've heard that, about bombs in cars?
P: Yes. Underneath cars and when people start the cars they blow up.
I: Tell me a bit more about that, what is it you've heard exactly?
P: Like people in France have a different religion than us and if there was an English person went over and he was rude to the French people they'd probably put a bomb underneath his car or in his exhaust and probably blow up.

I: You said a different religion to us, what religion are they then?

P: They're French religion and we're British religion, they speak different and we speak different.

I: And we are — what are we, Church of England things like that do you mean?

P: Yes

I: What are the French then?

P: I don't know really.

I: This about putting bombs in cars where have you heard that, have you seen that on television or on the news or something?

P: On the news like when there's people been gunned down and shot and all that, it sometimes — it might tell you about France if there's been an explosion in France and that I like to hear about France and other countries.

I: When was the last time you heard about France then?

P: Can't remember 'cause it's on like, like on the news at 10 o'clock you hear all different stories about France and what's happening in different countries. (561/20; 562/21)

and:

I: News programmes, do you watch the news?

P: Yes. At the moment — I think it is in France — there is students going around doing marches and things like that and they have got against something but I don't know what they are against.

I: But you have seen that on the tele?

P: Yes.

I: What did you think when you saw that?

P: They have a lot of students because there was about half a million and there was hundreds of them and I didn't understand what they were marching around for. They had a lot of banners, things like that and they were jumping off things and climbing up things and I know that a few of them were arrested. That's all I know about it. (452/16)

The second category, comedy and light entertainment, is dominated by the caricatures and stereotypes of the programme *'Allo 'Allo*. It is difficult to estimate what effect this has, since it is set in a past which for some pupils at least is rather hazy:

I: Have you ever seen any programmes about France?

P: I watch *'Allo 'Allo*.

I: What sort of ideas does that give you about France?

P: Er . . . men on their bikes with strings of onions around their necks and stripy tee-shirts.

I: Yes, are there many of them in this programme because I don't often see it?

P: No, it's just a comedy programme.

I: Yes. But are there many on bikes or is it just one?

P: Just shows you sometimes.

I: Who else takes part in it, who else is on *'Allo 'Allo*?

P: Er . . . well there's these two French like waitresses in a café and they wear frilly aprons and things and that's it, I don't know what else.

I: Do you know when it's set, when it's supposed to be from, what sort of years?

P: It was in the war or something.

I: Yes. Do you know which war it was?

P: No. (555/5)

There is none the less some reinforcement of stereotypes:

I: No. If I say to you The French what comes to your mind, in a few words?

P: People riding bikes with onions round them.

I: Oh. And what gives you that impression?

P: 'Cause on like programmes I've seen one programme and all of the French have them round, 'cause that's what they had in *'Allo 'Allo*.

I: Oh, yes, you've seen that have you?

P: Yes.

I: Yes, what else have you seen?

P: That's all. (564/20)

Other programmes mentioned are *Fawlty Towers* and *Grange Hill* (and even '*Auf Wiedersehen, Pet* that French thing that was on' — another example of confusion of everything foreign and/or a pupil wanting to be helpful to the interviewer). The onion-seller stereotype seems to be frequently reinforced elsewhere on television too:

I: But from the ideas you have from television and elsewhere, what sort of things would be the same and what would be different?

P: I would say the food was different. They have different things to us. They usually have onions. So do we like but they have onions all round their necks on string on the tele.

I: What was that on?

P: I don't know. I think it was on *Blue Peter*.
I: They showed somebody with onions round their neck?
P: Yes riding a bike. (341/8)

I: Anything else you've seen, any French film or programmes about France, or even adverts?
P: Yes, when . . . it's about this drink and a scene of a Frenchman with slippers and a drink and a man on a bike wearing a stripy jumper and onions.
I: So is that what makes you think that the man on the bike was French?
P: Mm.
I: Because he had a stripy jumper on and everything?
P: Mm.
I: Do you think there's many people like that over in France?
P: Mm. (428/17)

Cookery programmes and holiday programmes, the third category, add more to the stereotype. In this case it can be more positive in effect:

P: I like the French, I think the food might be OK, I've never ever tasted it before but I think they're good cooks, they know how to cook better than what the Spanish do.
I: You've heard that have you, that they're good cooks?
P: Yes, 'cause like if you turned on BBC2 sometimes on Sundays you might watch them and all that. On BBC1 there's all singing and that like this woman with a red thing on her head and playing music and that.
I: Like (inaudible) Indian.
P: Yes.
I: But what about BBC2 what were you telling me about BBC2 then?
P: Oh, like they tell you how to cook in French and different regions.
I: Right. So what — that's what you would say about the French then?
P: Yes.
I: Anything else?
P: No. like I think — I don't like onions but I think they like peeling onions 'cause their eyes never start to water. (561/28)

I: Is there anywhere else you learn about France that you can think of?
P: This programme called *Food and Drink* on BBC2 . . . er . . . I've forgotten what it's called . . . it was called *Food and Drink* . . . er . . .
I: And what do you learn about France from that then?

P: Like they make like recipes of France and drinks and like they say
  French words that you don't know about but you know that they're
  French 'cause like Mum and Dad tells us some of them.
I: What sort of impression of French food do you get from that, from the
  recipes?
P: Sometimes it's like queer and sometimes it's like — really you don't
  know what you're eating when you're there.
I: Does that put you off?
P: Sometimes . . . (492/20)

Advertisements for French cheese are another source which completes the
picture of France being a country of wine and cheese and *haute cuisine*, a
picture which, unlike the onion-seller, corresponds to the autostereotype.
Recall from the holiday programmes is vague. Images of the Eiffel Tower
and skiing and a general impression of it being 'nice' are all that remain:

I: What about other programmes which are set in France or give infor-
  mation about France. Have you seen any of those?
P: I have seen a holiday programme. That is about it.
I: That was in one of the holiday series?
P: Yes.
I: Can you remember what it showed you about France?
P: It showed you most of the towns and showed you the sights.
I: Can you remember what they seemed like?
P: It seemed nice and interesting. (347/31)

A similar projection of the French autostereotype is reinforced by television fashion programmes; at this age it is perhaps not surprising that only
two pupils mentioned it, for example:

I: What's your impression of French people then?
P: Funny . . . they wear like different clothes to us, things like that.
I: What's different about their clothes?
P: The way they dress. A lot of them wear suits the men and the women
  wear fancy dresses and things like that.
I: Do you think if you saw a group of people in town here, without hearing
  them speak you would be able to pick out the French people?
P: No.
I: You wouldn't.
P: No.
I: But you think of them as wearing different clothing to us?
P: Yes.

I: What about the question of fashion. I mean French fashion is quite
famous isn't it? Again can you tell me what your impression is of why
French fashion is so well known?

P: Because the women they wear dresses and they have all things that
dangle down on it and patterns, nice patterns on them and the people
who make them are clever. Through making all different clothes, they
get well known and make a canny bit of money.

I: Where have you heard about this, have you seen things?

P: Yes.

I: Tell me about that then.

P: There was a thing on the tele a few days ago and I watched that and
they had a lot of French clothes on and things like that.

I: What was it exactly?

P: A fashion show. (452/15)

On the other hand, it is evident from Chapter 2 that pupils do have much to
say about physical appearance and modes of dress. The apparent contra-
diction may be a consequence of compartmentalisation of their views.

Although some pupils said they do not watch televison very often and
even more said they do not watch news or holiday programmes, there is no
doubt that the impact of the television image of France is to provide a
stereotype which is sometimes negative and sometimes in harmony with
French people's projection of their autostereotype. In the secondary
schools, the use of television as a teaching aid with programmes made for
languages classes was not significant. It is difficult to know, then, whether
this could counteract the general effect of television, although the programmes which accompany the *Action!* textbook provide a tourist view
point just like the textbook itself as we shall see in Chapter 5.

As for films, on television or at the cinema, they appear to have little
effect on pupils' images of France. They mention war films, especially *The
Longest Day*, but when asked what they remember of the setting, they had
nothing definite to say. Occasionally, they had glimpsed French films on
television, with sub-titles, but had not watched them before turning to
another channel. One pupil was quite clear about the impression he had
from films, however:

I: You don't like French people, why don't you like the French people?

P: 'Cause I can't understand the language and I think they're rude.

I: They're rude, why do you think they're rude?

P: Because like I've seen films and things about when they're like —
they've got onions around their necks and they're drinking beer and
they're drunk and that.

I: And they're rude?

P: Yes.

I: Who are they rude to?

P: The English people.

I: English people?

P: Yes, 'cause once a man made a song about Margaret Thatcher and all the English people and I thought that was rude 'cause it told you all the words in English. (478/3)

The film *Le Ballon Rouge* was mentioned by two pupils:

I: What do you think the school might be like?

P: . . . A lot different to what it is here.

I: A lot different, how might it be different?

P: The kind of — how they organise things like they might not have three play times like we do here, and they don't have to be in school by a certain time, come in when you want.

I: You think you can just go to school whenever you want to?

P: Well I've heard in a certain hour, where you can go in the afternoon and if you're naughty there you get chained up in a room or something.

I: Do you, where did you hear that?

P: This French programme where there's no speaking and they did the boy with the red balloon and he goes to school one day and they all just go in at different times and he's naughty and the headmaster takes him round to a room and he locks him in.

I: And this is a French programme, was it? When did you see this?

P: I've seen it twice, when I was nine, 'cause I'm ten now, about a year ago and I once saw it when I was little.

I: And you saw that at home did you?

P: No, at school. (531/4)

The power of the visual image speaks for itself.

There is only one other mention of school as a source of information and it can be included here for convenience:

P: We did a project on France in my other school and we had to learn a little bit of the language so my Dad told me some and the teacher told me some.

I: So what did you do for the project?

P: We had to write facts about France. It wasn't in the file, it was just on a piece of paper. Out of some drawing paper we made a small book about

France.

I: That was the whole class was it?

P: Yes. I wrote two stories in the book, I wrote some French words down and some facts about France.

I: You found out some of those things from your Dad did you?

P: Yes.

I: Your Dad speaks French?

P: No but he picks up French easily. He is good at it. (373/24)

Books

Books do not seem to have a wide influence but for some pupils they are a source of information which is largely historical or geographical. These historical episodes are mentioned: Joan of Arc, Louis XIV and this account of the Burghers of Calais, including an illusion to Rodin and *Blue Peter*:

I: Where do you get your ideas then, I mean you obviously get — you've seen a lot 'cause you've been on holiday is there anywhere else you get your ideas about France from, do you watch things on television about France?

P: . . . Stories.

I: What kind of stories?

P: Like . . . about this man and the thingy, I think he's in the castle but they don't get reinforcements, the only ones in the castle and they've been so long so they have to have six executions I think 'cause the king doesn't like it that they've been in the castle so long about a year they've been in the castle . . . er . . . so like they come out and get six executed but the queen, his wife, she doesn't want them to be — go dead 'cause like she's kind but the king had a cruel heart sometimes and . . . she asked the king if they could be her prisoners and she'd keep them to prevent them being dead, put them out of trouble.

I: Do you remember the name of the story?

P: . . . No.

I: I don't recognise it.

P: I've forgotten. This one had a sculpture, the one I was talking about before, he like did like a sculpture of the six ones that were dead, that were going to be dead.

I: Was it the six Burghers of Calais?

P: That might have been it.

I: Yes, I think that's what it is. So you had that story then did you?

P: Yes.

I: Where did you have that?
P: It was in this like story book.
I: Was it at school or was it one you just read yourself?
P: It was one I read myself it had like tales of different countries, it was called I think, *Tales of* (inaudible) or *Tales of France* and it told you the story on *Blue Peter* as well.
I: The same story?
P: Yes, I had the book. (492/19)

Atlases are the source of geographical information, particularly pictorial atlases, supplemented by holiday brochures or postcards sent from France by friends or family:

P: Well there is bigger families because the Aunts and Uncles live in the same house and the Grandmas and Grandads live in the same house and other cousins live in the same house.
I: Has somebody told you that or did you see that on the tele?
P: I've seen that in a book.
I: Can you remember what the book was about?
P: It was all about France.
I: So it said in the book that they all live together.
P: Yes.
I: Was that a book in school or a book you have at home?
P: At home (347/15)

Otherwise, books can also be another source of stereotypes:

I: What do they wear then? What do you think of them as wearing?
P: . . . I've seen them in books with stripy tops with onions round their necks, I've seen them.
I: You've seen them in books?
P: Yes . . . and . . . I've seen some — some of them wear hats in the book but maybe that's just to keep the sun off the heads . . .
I: Which book was this then?
P: It was one out of the library, it was about a girl who went to France and she didn't like it. (491/11)

P: No. Ah there is this book that I've got but it's like, it's called (inaudible) and it's like just frogs as soldiers and all that and it's in France.
I: Frogs?
P: Yes.

I: Skitting them.

P: Right, yes. Making fun of them then. I don't know at the time but there's mice and things like that, they're just animals in it. (548/19)

Parents and other adults

Information from parents and other adults is fragmentary and disparate. It is both positive and negative, and often tangential. In some cases the adults' experience has been very limited, for example passing through France on a coach journey to Spain, but there are a few who seem to have more substantial experience, although pupils are often confused and confusing about different countries:

I: And you said your father worked in France?

P: Yes.

I: And he lived there for a bit?

P: Yes.

I: Do you know what he did there and why he was living there?

P: Because my Uncle was in the army in Germany and my Nana and my Granda and my Dad lived in that house with him.

I: Oh, I see.

P: So they moved to France 'cause he had to go to France or something and then he went to Germany.

I: So they did France before your Uncle went to Germany?

P: Yes.

I: I wonder if it was near the German border. And he hasn't said anything to you but your Mother has.

P: Yes.

I: And she told you that it was big?

P: Yes.

I: And they liked it did they?

P: Yes.

I: That's why they went back on holiday?

P: Yes, 'cause my Gran died there and my Mum likes to go over there. (535/1)

P: Well there's grape vines and things there.

I: How have you heard about those?

P: Saw it on postcards and things 'cause my Nana and Grandma have both been there and stayed in a French hotel.

I: Yes. And they sent you postcards?

P: Yes.

I: What did it look like?

P: Well it has like little towns and villages and things on and the houses and a lady and she brought us a doll from France back and it's got a long dress and a little apron.

I: Yes.

P: And a French hat on, it's like a long tube thing.

I: Yes, that sounds interesting. What's it made of I mean is it sort of lace or is it . . .

P: Mm, it's lacy and the dress is made of different kinds of materials.

I: Yes, what sort of colours?

P: Bright colours, like red and blue and things.

I: Do you know which bit of France that would be from?

P: Belgium.

I: Oh, right. So your Aunt brought that or your . . .

P: Nana.

I: Nana, right. (555/5)

There is also one interesting effect of the schooltrip:

I: OK. So can you think of anywhere else you might have learned about France, you know quite a lot about France don't you really when you think about it, can you think where you've learned most of it from?

P: I've learned most of it off my Mum.

I: Your Mum.

P: And Dad.

I: What's she said to you about?

P: Well she went there for a school trip and a couple of weeks ago she got out the old photos and showed us.

I: Did she?

P: And like she was telling us about them.

I: Did she like France?

P: Yes, she likes it.

I: Does she speak French?

P: A little bit.

I: Has she said anything to you about learning French when you go up to the comp?

P: Yes and like that's how she got the little booklet.

I: So she's encouraged you quite a lot?

P: Yes.

I: And she tells you about France does she?

P: A little bit, yes.

I: What does she tell you, what sort of thing?

P: Er . . . well she just tells us things I've told you like it's a nice place and that. (484/29)

Perhaps inevitably, parents also talk about French food. One pupil was impressed by a 'fish thing' which his mother had bought. 'It had garlic in and things like that' (452/12) whereas another mother had tried snails and frogs' legs in an English restaurant: 'She liked the snails but she thought the frogs' legs were awful' (552/7).

Other influences from adults range from a chance conversation overhead in a shop to a mother's friend or neighbours who have been to France and tell snippets of information:

I: Do you think of France as being an important country in the world?

P: It is a nice country I like it. I think a lot of people like France and a lot of people have written nice things about it.

I: What are you thinking of there when you say that?

P: Like a lot of people like them and when they say — some people were here talking about France — they would say 'People say it is a nice country' because they do. They say 'That's a nice country, I like it there'.

I: Who are you thinking of now? Who says that kind of thing?

P: The one that lives just round near the shop. I went up there — like I was going to the shop and I met this woman, she is called Barbara and near the shop she said she liked it there. I said had she been there and she said 'Well I have been there but my son-in-law has been there as well, that's what I was saying in the shop'. She was getting her groceries.

I: Did she tell you about it?

P: I wasn't really talking about it with her because we were just outside. She had all of her groceries so she couldn't stay long anyway. She just said she had been there before. (453/14)

And of course there is always what 'my Auntie says':

I: Right. What about — the things that you said — where do you get your ideas from? You mentioned food and you mentioned the way people dress. How do you know all these things if you have never been? That's what I am interested in as well.

P: My auntie has been and she has tasted the frogs' legs and that. She told me what it was like.

I: Right. Tell me more. What did she tell you?
P: . . .
I: Can't you remember? Is it difficult to remember?
P: . . . (551/11)

Contact with French people

Although pupils go on holiday to France, their contacts with French people are very limited even in France. One pupil seemed to know a French family well and has some idea from 'Uncle Robert':

I: You think of them as being hard-working, again what gives you that impression?
P: Just like they work hard . . .
I: What makes you think that?
P: Um . . . 'cause like my Uncle Robert the French person says that they work harder than Britons.
I: What else did he tell you?
P: He says Maggie Thatcher's a load of rubbish.
I: Does he — well he must — does he talk to you a lot about France then?
P: Mm.
I: Tell me what else he tells you.
P: He says that . . . like there's a lot of nice country in France in the south.
I: Anything else?
P: No.
I: Try to remember what he tells you.
P: He says that the French government's no good . . .
I: Right, so when do you see him then?
P: Well I haven't seen him for a long time, they were going to come over to England and stay with us last August but they never.
I: They didn't come?
P: No? (563/16)

Another had a chance meeting with a French boy on holiday:

I: What's it like going to school in France?
P: I was talking to a French boy and he says it's . . . he says it's OK, he says he likes it. He used to live in England but he lives in France now.
I: Is it any different then from school in England?
P: He says there's not much difference, apart from the schools are bigger, a lot more complicated and I think the French are very daring 'cause we were on the campsite and I hit the ping pong ball over the fence and it

was a big fence and it was the owner's private house, big gates all the way round, and he sneaked in the fence and got the ping pong ball out . . . 'cause they do some weird things to us and we do some weird things to them, I think.

I: What are you thinking of?

P: 'Cause I was saying 'Do you want to play cricket?' and he was going 'What's that?' And he was — he was saying 'Do you want to play ballmanac?' or something and I didn't know what he meant and he said 'Do you know what that means?' And we played some good games but weird names for them. I enjoyed playing with the French children 'cause they're very, they want to play and they'll do anything to play with you. (367/25)

There are other examples of chance contacts but they remain rare. As for visitors from France, they are even rarer. One family has an English friend who lives in Nice and visits from time to time. There is also a very limited influence from school exchanges:

I: Have you met any French people?

P: Yes. A person stayed at our house called Florence.

I: Tell me something about that.

P: About like what do you want?

I: Well who was she, when was that?

P: It was about four years ago when my older sister was at school and she didn't like the food that we ate and we normally eat in the kitchen and we have a dining room table and all the time we had to sit at the dining room table 'cause that was the good table. She didn't like the pro-grammes we watched but she liked the drinks and she liked the dogs, she liked the people that were here and that's all.

I: Why was she in your house then?

P: Because my Nicola went to France and they could pick who ever wanted to go back with them and she picked Florence.

I: Nicola's your sister?

P: Yes.

I: Right and this was with school was it?

P: Yes. (564/9)

Unfortunately Nicola did not enjoy the exchange much either: 'She said there was litter all over and that there was lots of fights all the time' (564/9).

Siblings and other children

The potential influence of older siblings and other children is recognised by one pupil:

I: Have you talked about learning French with your mates?
P: Mates?
I: Friends here.
P: Friends. They don't really note France really. They are not interested. Well there is two or three people who are interested, a couple of the brainiest in our class, they are interested in languages. There is another one in our class he has a brother who is learning French so he is interested. It is mainly if you know someone who knows French in your family you seem to get interested while if you don't know anything about it you are going to get bored. You won't be interested.
I: So you are looking forward to learning French then?
P: Yes quite a lot. (409/44)

We already noted above the difference in the number of times siblings were mentioned by the two groups. As elsewhere, the effects can be both positive and negative, so the quantity has to be analysed with respect to quality too. One of the negative comments can be juxtaposed with a very positive one:

P: They eat frogs' legs and all that.
I: They eat frogs' legs. Anything else?
P: No.
I: How often do you think French people eat frogs legs?
P: I don't know.
I: Do they eat them a lot?
P: Probably.
I: Would you like to try them?
P: No.
I: You wouldn't, why not?
P: 'Cause they're all slimy and that.
I: Has your sister tried them?
P: Yes.
I: She has, what did she think?
P: They're horrible.
I: Did she not like them?
P: No. (428/3)

P: My sister says she would like to live there.
I: She would?
P: Get a job, yes.

I: Why did she say that?
P: She says you can't get very much over here.
I: She really liked France, did she?
P: Yes, she liked France.
I: Do you think you might like to move over there and get a job?
P: No.
I: No. So she hasn't persuaded you yet?
P: No.
I: OK.
P: She tells us French jokes.
I: Does she?
P: Tells us French jokes.
I: And do you understand them?
P: She like, she told them in English. She says there was this English man
   and he went in a French bar and goes 'Have you got any frogs' legs?'
   and he goes 'Yes, hop it'.
I: Oh, OK.
P: I don't know the other one what she said.
I: It's just as well. (476/8)

The advantage of interviewing seems to include learning new jokes!

Siblings' and others' visits to France are perhaps the most powerful
influence. On the whole the impressions given seem to be positive, but the
basis for the account is often very limited:

I: What would you think about France as a place to go on a holiday?
P: Well my friend's been in the class and she says it's a nice place and she
   says they all ride bikes.
I: What else?
P: . . . She says most of them speak English and most of them don't speak
   a different language.
I: In France?
P: Yes.
I: So would you like to go yourself, from what she's told you?
P: Yes, I think so.
I: But not too sure?
P: No. (491/4)

I: So say somebody was going to go to France for the first time and they
   came to you and asked you about it and you had to tell them what you
   think it's like what would you say to them?

P: I'd say it was good but there's like some streets what seem dirty from what I've heard any way and like it's quite big 'cause there was one street what I saw, massive, and well.

I: When did you see that?

P: . . . Joanne 'cause she's been, last year, no maybe sometime this year or last year, can't remember.

I: What? Did she send you a picture do you mean or did she show you a picture?

P: No, she showed us 'cause she brought her like photos back, she went with the school.

I: Oh, I see.

P: And she was showing us.

I: So you saw some photos of France from her. Some of the streets looked dirty did they?

P: Well not all of them, there was just like one where like there was — well it wasn't quite, it wasn't really dirty there was just a bit, it didn't seem very clean. (559/6)

An example of a negative account from a school camping holiday demonstrates that poor weather — 'it was cold and everything' — puts the interviewed pupil off any thought of going to France (501/3). Yet in another case, the opposite was the case:

P: He said it was a nice place because he went with the school and the places he stayed they were nice people he stayed with and they were always friendly to you and it was sometimes hard to understand but it was good. (566/1)

Perhaps the most effective influence is from the pictures and presents which are brought back; the most unusual one mentioned was breakfast:

I: What about breakfast. Have you ever heard anything about French breakfasts?

P: Well I have had a French breakfast before.

I: What was that, what did you have?

P: It was like in a tin, like popcorn. I don't know it was packed in a tin and you didn't put milk in it you just ate it.

I: Where did you have that?

P: My nephew brought it just for a little treat. (409/14)

Visits to France

'Visits' to France range from a brief stop for coffee on a coach journey to Spain, through camping and *gîte* holidays, to visiting a French family. Although the nature of the visit clearly influences the kind of contact and observations pupils make, the effect on their perceptions can be just as strong whatever the length of stay:

I: Is there anywhere you would not like to go? On holiday.
P: . . . France.
I: Why is that?
P: Because it is like — just like — I don't like the people there. Sometimes they can be friendly and sometimes they can't because when I was travelling to Spain the first time and we stopped at this café on the way back. There was like my Dad behind us and my two brothers and there was Mum behind me and I was in front. There was these two French ladies in front of us all and like our Barry slipped and pushed my Mum and my Mum pushed me into one of these old ladies and she turned round and she said go back to Papa and like shouted at me and that and I have never liked them since. (475/3)

I: Do you think their food is . . .
P: It is very nice. It is better than the English food.
I: Have you ever tried any?
P: Yes. Once. We were travelling and stopped at this big restaurant on the bus and I don't know what you call it but we had these sort of chips, fish in a sort of sauce thing and some French bread and it was nice. Can't remember the name of it. The French bread we had at the end there was like flies all over it. We had to go back to the bus.
I: It was hot?
P: Yes very hot. (475/10)

On longer contact more complex events shape pupils' perceptions and, in some cases, their misunderstandings:

I: What would it be like to be in France, with a French family, what would be the same and what different?
P: It would be very difficult because they get very, their tempers get very quickly and if you can't understand them like they get in tempers and get very cross and they get very mad and when — if you're making a lot of noise they go mad and just leap around shouting at you and go and complain to people and stuff and get in really hot tempers and the policemen, if you've done something wrong and he starts getting mad and bipping the horns at you and stuff, it's not very nice and people shouting at you and they can really get into hot tempers and they're

friendly and they want to help you all the time but when you ask them for directions they try to — and when you ask them to help you they're so keen to help you that they forget where you're going — they're friendly, they want to help you all the time but they just can't because they give you the wrong directions, they're so keen to help you.

I: This happened to you did it?

P: Yes, we kept asking and there was an English person with a group of boys who were youth hostelling and the English person and he was being stupid and the French person was telling us more about the stuff than the English person.

I: Telling you more about where to go and things like that?

P: Yes and pointing here and telling you to go down there and things and the English person was just laughing. (367/8)

P: We like got a map — we got a brochure and ordered the house.

I: Oh, I see so you were actually living — hired or rented a French house?

P: Yes.

I: Right, so what would I notice then inside a French house, what would be different?

P: They've mostly got like crosses and things 'cause they're mostly Jews and they've got loads of crosses in the markets and towns.

I: In the houses as well?

P: Yes and they're mostly, they've got . . . like, they might have three farm houses or four on a farm . . . (492/5)

Apart from the fact that the E group has very little experience of visits, already noted above, the only emergent pattern is the increase in detail of observation due to length and degree of contact. The ideas and images elicited are also a consequence of the topics raised with pupils according to the interview schedule. None the less, spontaneous observations arise such as the characterisation of French people evident in the above account of asking for advice and directions. Another quotation is also an illustration of the omniscient Auntie, and the difficulty the interviewer has in teasing out the sources of pupils' generalisations:

I: A moment ago you said you liked the Spanish people more than the French, what made you say that?

P: 'Cause like the Spanish don't shout a lot like the French do 'cause some of the Spanish are very kind — like last time I got a melon free. I get all drinks free when I go on holiday, it's good, but if you're in France they wouldn't give you anything free.

I: And when you say they shout a lot what were you thinking of, was it something that happened?

P: 'Cause if there was a store they would be all shouting but when I went to Spain they weren't shouting a lot, they were just talking and giving prices to things and all that, it was good.

I: And was this in the market place then?

P: Yes, on the market day and that.

I: What gives you the impression that the French people shout a lot then, what makes you say that?

P: Because they always — like if we shout it sounds loud when they like if they go — I can't explain it really — if they shout they make a big racket, it sounds horrible.

I: And you heard this when you were there did you?

P: Yes, there's a lot of shouting. When you go through France like if you go off the bus you'll hear you're near to a store, they're always shouting and that.

I: And this is what happened to you is it?

P: No, 'cause my friends go on holiday, this is what my auntie Irene told me, this is what it's like, sounds horrible and that. Nasty. (561/17)

Apart from food, pupils notice a wide range of phenomena:

I: Do you think the women go out to work?

P: A few.

I: Is that more than England or less?

P: Less.

I: Why do you think that is?

P: I don't know. I didn't see many ladies in the shops.

I: Oh I see. They were mainly run by men? (351/21)

I: I know when you go to secondary school you learn much more about all these things. I just wondered if you had ever heard anything about what sort of school days people had. Would it be like going to an English school?

P: I think they start earlier and finish earlier as well.

I: What sort of time do you think they start?

P: Something like 7 o'clock.

I: Do you know that from going to France or is that something you have read?

P: I learnt it from going.

I: You saw people setting off for school did you? Do you think they wore a uniform or not? You have a uniform don't you?

P: I don't think they did. (377/10)

I: You mentioned the house, what houses are like. Can you paint me a picture in words of a French house?

P: A French house is rather big. It has vines and things in the garden because they grow their own wine and things like that. They would have quite a few plants and if it was like the villa we went to they would have like a sort of farm at the back because they would need all the food mainly.

I: So you lived in a villa?

P: Well we had a holiday in a villa with nearly the whole family. It was huge the villa. (427/9)

The quality of the descriptions pupils can give seems to depend as much on the individual and his/her good fortune as on the amount of experience. However one pupil who talked freely about a number of topics — dress, employment, houses, leisure — had spent a holiday in a *gîte*, on a farm. She was the one who noticed the crosses in people's houses and in the country-side. She also saw a wedding:

I: Do you think it would be different, different kind of ceremonies and different — when babies are born they're baptised and . . .

P: Oh they trail round, we saw this wedding and it was trailing round the streets and everybody was following them 'cause they'd just come out of the church I think and they were like following the bride and the bridegroom.

I: Well what was so special about that, don't you see that here?

P: They don't walk round or anything in the streets in our country, they just go to the church and then go back to the house like for a like banquet or something. (492/17)

When asked to summarise her impressions 'in a few words', she starts with the stereotype and adds her own details:

Mostly they wear berets and like sell onions and things and mostly they ride bikes and they have like . . . little like bikes, like motor bikes, they have little motor bikes with little motors and . . . mostly they're Jews . . . and the houses are different sometimes inside, four-poster beds and things . . . Er . . . they're kind, they've got good manners and mostly have like a tan, like 'cause they've been sun-bathing and that . . . they wear hats and that for the festivals and things and they mostly go to church . . . and they're Jews and . . . can't remember anything else. (492/23)

The fragmentary and erroneous nature of even the latter pupil's impressions and views, who has more experience and power of observation than most, is the basis upon which secondary school French is developed. The contribution of teacher and textbook to the overall image is crucial, but teachers are not always aware of the need to work with and work on the images pupils bring with them. The stereotypes continue to be influential and secondary pupils continue to be exposed to influences other than school and it is to these that we turn next. Before we do so however one other 'external' influence should be noted:

I: So you're looking forward to learning French are you?
P: Yes.
I: What do you think it would be like, have you got any brothers and sisters who are learning French?
P: No. I've only got a young sister.
I: Has anybody every spoken to you about learning French — talked to you, you know, told you what it's like?
P: There's these two ladies that came and questioned us and give us these sheets.
I: Which two ladies were those?
P: I think they were from Durham. (492/7)

Secondary pupils' views

In the case of secondary pupils it quickly became clear that their much greater experience, as a group, of France and the French way of life was a significant source of knowledge. It might be argued that this source was 'within school' rather than external insofar as much of that experience was the consequence of visits and exchanges organised by school staff. We have chosen to present it here first because it is in practice impossible to be always sure whether a particular experience was school-organised or not and second because pupils appear to perceive the school trip as separable from their work in French lessons. Furthermore there is only a little evidence from observations that school trips were integrated and exploited in lessons, for a number of reasons. Because of the importance of personal experience of the foreign country, we shall present pupils' accounts according to some of the issues which were the framework for interviews.

Experience of France

Whilst statistical analysis indicated that the experience of visiting France was not clearly associated with attitudes towards French people, it was apparent from the interviews that in many cases staying in the country could result in enhanced imagery of French culture. Inevitably, however, there were those who, despite the experience, saw many aspects of French life as 'the same'.

In the course of the interviews many pupils stated spontaneously that their visit was a source of information, in other cases pupils were asked directly how their experience had added to their store of knowledge. As attributions to sources of information were not always made, analysis of the aspects of French culture noticed cannot be exhaustive. However it was noticeable, perhaps unsurprisingly, that items of food eaten or refused were most frequently recalled. References to food encountered were made almost twice as often as to the next most frequent topics — housing and perceptions of French people. Visits to France provided information upon other aspects of French culture too such as education, jobs and physical appearance. Pupils also recalled sights seen in Paris and Boulogne and recounted vividly the experience of speaking French in a French context. Several pupils remarked upon shops and shopping and transport. Only occasional references were made to other aspects of French life such as the media, religion, leisure, books and perceptions of growing up in France. Comparisons with textbook information upon transport were also drawn by some pupils.

Food

Recollection of meals experienced in France was often vivid:

I: Yes, but what about your trip to France, did that give you some information as well?

P: . . . Well when we went for a meal in a restaurant the woman came along with all these different kinds of meat on a like big plate thing and she put it down and we just got what we wanted, all the vegetables we wanted, drink . . . I think they're like different, they eat the stuff that we don't eat very often and we eat the stuff that they don't eat very often, like from what I hear they don't have chips very much I don't think. (133/12) (Class 2 boy)

Often there was confusion between what was thought to be 'French' or 'English' food:

P: Some of the French people we saw them eating their food. They had different meals. They had like some proper English meals when we

went. Some of the French didn't like it. Putting different sauces on and
that to try to improve the taste I think.

I: Where was this?

P: In the café we were at that the school took us to. There were some
French people in and they were having chicken and chips and didn't
seem to like the chicken so were getting like apple sauce and parsley
sauce and just putting it all over even on the chips. I don't know
whether they liked it, they didn't seem to. They walked out and paid for
it but I don't think they ate any of it. (175/26)

The same pupil vividly contrasted an image presented in the textbook with
an experience in France:

I: How much of this did you know from the textbook?

P: Not that much. I didn't know about the food. They described some of
the cakes but there seemed to be a lot more when you went into a cake
shop. There was more than anything. It was just full of cakes but I
didn't expect that much. I knew there were cake shops. We went in this
big one it was completely cakes. Didn't realise until I went in. There is a
lot more than you think. (175/27)

On being asked about possible improvements to the textbook she made a
number of suggestions amongst which was:

> Where are the best places to go, where the weather is. I think that
> could help because sometimes you can go to France and it is raining. I
> expected it to be sunny like it is in the textbook but it isn't always that.
> They seem to make it appear more exciting than it is but they could
> put like a bit more truth in it and say about the weather at times,
> different months. We went and it was raining. The first day we were
> there was rather dreary. All the clothes shops and that were shutting
> down, most of the shops were shut when we went the second time.
> (175/28)

Evaluations of food were varied, from 'I love it' (233/9) to 'You'll have
croissants with coffee in a bowl, which is unusual' (247/12), to: '. . . the
meat wasn't very nice, I didn't eat much of it.' (310/14). In the last instance
the meat was said to be 'raw'.

Some pupils who referred to their experience in France as a source of
information had been on the short weekend trips to Boulogne. The
majority appeared to have had the same menu. It was not seen to differ

from English fare:

I: What did you have when you were there yourself?
P: For dinner?
I: Yes, what did you have to eat, yes?
P: Chips . . . chicken . . . and ice cream for dessert.
I: Was that different from — I mean did it taste different, was it prepared differently?
P: Not really, it was just the same. (162/8)

Similarly another pupil recalls:

P: Just had — it was mainly the same. We went out for a meal and I had chicken and chips and it was just the same. (228/10)

    Pupils experiencing this short break did not appear to feel that they had eaten 'French' food:

I: What did you think of the French food when you were there?
P: I didn't have none really. (246/12)

    Some pupils had positive attitudes towards foods disliked by others:

P: . . . I liked most of it.
I: What did you have?
P: Like the steak was rare, I liked that and the drink and all that.
I: What did you drink?
P: Wine most of the time.
I: Did they let you walk in the bar then?
P: Yes and we had some, like in the Youth Hostel we had some beer out of there.
I: Did you?
P: Yes, teachers didn't know though.
I: What did you think of French beer?
P: It's nice. (217/10)

    One pupil was able to see that his own tastes need not determine the norm but was unwilling to take any risks:

P: You could have steak, beefburger I think, something like that and chips but the beefburger was like, in the middle it was like, rare, raw like, if you cut into it the blood ran out of it 'cause that's what they're used to like, cook it like that. So I just had chicken and that. (298/12)

Housing

Details of housing differences were recalled quite frequently from both extended visits to France and from passing through the country to other destinations. It was evident however in interviews that, whatever the source of information, be it textbook or visit, pupils often appeared to experience difficulties in articulating perceived architectural differences:

> In some of the houses they had something like a bathroom in their own bedrooms like some had a sink in their own bedrooms and they had a main one . . . They had more bedrooms than some houses do in England and that, the houses are much bigger and . . . kind of a funny shape like they are all went in different — like the houses went up and down and stuff like that. (151/15)

When prompted one girl attempted to describe regional differences:

I: Do they vary, again you've travelled through France — do the houses vary from region to region?
P: Yes, when you're in Boulogne it's just like fishermens' houses on the front and when you get down to Paris they're all big houses and when you get down to the South of France it's all a bit like this, a little bit quieter. (248/30)

One pupil had noticed differences in interior fittings:

P: You would notice the different furnishings, carpets the way that they decorate, the lights — the plug system might be different — little things like that, the toilets, showers, the baths things like that. (283/10)

When asked if he had perceived differences in external styles, he indicated how attention to new experiences can be distracted:

I: And did you notice the different architectural style?
P: . . . No, not really. There might have been, but see with us being all excited I just looked. (283/10)

One girl who had been on the weekend visit to Boulogne had made use of a chance to see inside a French house:

P: It's just like what you need for basics in a French house. When I went in

there were just basics nothing — no special rooms fixed in for spare
room or something. They just have all the basics, bits of fanciness like
different ornaments to go on the side to make it brighter but they are
quite cheerful the houses. (175/19)

She explained how this had happened:

I: Well how did you go into a French household? Was it a house or flat?
P: It was a house — well we were asking this woman the way and she
   seemed to want us to come in so while she was pouring something out
   we stood and looked all over and had a look around. Then she showed
   us to the supermarket.
I: What did she offer you?
P: She said would you like a cup of coffee and we said no because we
   wanted to go to the supermarket to meet up with some of our other
   friends. She looked as though she was alone in the house and she
   wanted to like talk to speak to us but she shows us to the supermarket.
   She was a very quick walker. We had to try to run to keep up with her.
   She seemed to be quite alone and she had some cats with her. She was
   nice and the house was nice and tidy and everything in its place. (175/
   20)

For pupils who had spent longer in France conclusions could vary
widely according to the nature of their experience:

and the French houses are canny posh, better than round here like on
their own like posh and like hardly any doors, like patios and things
like that, it's nice. (135/6)

and expanded upon this:

P: . . . Well the windows and that are bigger than ours and like patios and
   modern like doors. Like garage down underneath them. Like normal
   bedrooms and normal kitchen and bathrooms. Just the same.
I: Would the furnishings then be the same?
P: Yes.
I: And the style of the house?
P: Maybe that would be different because they are more modern down in
   France. More modern furniture. (135/15)

From Hillside one pupil had compared his visit to a French home with
those of his friends, and though he thought it was typical did not view

France as modern:

> Well the home I went to was quite strange it was almost like a farm type, a small farm, it was in the sort of suburbs of the town and it was a bungalow and they had sort of chickens sort of lots of dogs and things like that and it was almost a farm in the back garden. It seemed sort of, but it wasn't like our house, our house is sort of modern, it's got lots of modern things in their's was sort of more simple. I don't know if that's the same in all of France but just this part was all things like that. The toilet I noticed you had to turn the tap on to fill it with water then pull a lever and it emptied so it was strange. (244/13)

He contrasted the information presented in French lessons with his experience:

> Well in the class we've done more about the cities and things like that not the smaller villages so we sort of saw a different type of France it was more — can't say primitive — but sort of less technological because in the cities it was just like England, apart from like the old buildings and things like that but I suppose if the textbook concentrated on different parts of France we'd get to know more about that. (244/14)

Attitudes towards French people

In considering the effects of experience of France on attitudes, it is useful to take the three levels of ethnocentricity separately. For, in general, it was noted above that interview statements corresponded with ethnocentricity rating.

In this first example from the non-ethnocentric group, the pupil made an interesting distinction concerning the way he had been received in different parts of France and also indicated his ability to perceive other people's experience from their own viewpoint:

> Well the people, I don't think they were that different but they were a lot more friendly to us when we were in the North and down the South they've obviously got a lot more used to tourists and they were just taking us as part of everyday life and that wasn't quite as nice as being up in the North. (310/35)

His later conclusion is also a clear indication of correspondence with his test rating:

> The people I've seen and met, they're all nice, just the same as us.

In the following example it is noticeable that though the pupil realised subsequently that her interpretation of an incident might have been at fault — again an indicator of the capacity for self-appraisal and seeing oneself from another viewpoint — she still remembered the French person involved as 'funny':

> Well I think just from people I've met when I've been there they're quite nice, quite friendly and they keep themselves to themselves a bit though as well. The older people are maybe a bit sort of funny sort of like, I don't know really I just always remember when we went to France one time we were driving along in the car and there was like a sort of zebra crossing and there was an old man waiting to go over and we stopped to let him go over but he wouldn't go like across the road but we didn't realise at the time like how they work and that and he was sort of waving and we were waving him on all the time and he wouldn't cross the road, they're just very, I don't know sort of very quiet, the old people. They're quite friendly though I think. (233/5)

In one case a girl drew a distinction between the generations:

> Well . . . some of them have more younger people, some more older people in and the older people just sit and watch you, that's not so bad but the younger people tend to run after you and say 'Are you foreigners?' ask you questions and things. They seem to go on at you all the time but there is like different parts. Like round Boulogne there was one half that seemed to be more old people than younger people but when you went down the beach at Boulogne it seemed to be younger people so we tried to keep away from that and stay in the towns. (175/11)

Her experience of France was more limited than that of the first boy quoted and was symptomatic of the particular problems which appear to arise from visits to the Channel ports. She had experienced difficulties in shops in Boulogne:

> When you go in the shops, they try and get you to buy things but instead of saying 'Will you buy?' they say 'Go on buy it' like pushing you to buy it and if they want you to move out of the way they don't

ask you, they just push you around. You seem to get pushed around
an awful lot instead of them asking you they seem to push you a bit. If
it wasn't that I think I would like to be French but otherwise no.
(175/ 9)

Amongst those rated as of medium ethnocentricity experience of
France had resulted in a variety of conclusions. There was a tendency
towards describing the French with rather bland epithets such as 'nice' or
'all right'. In one case views were clearly influenced by an English
perspective:

> Well French people are quite polite I think. That has made it better I
> think. Like the French people have learned to speak English well. I
> like that about it. (218/21)

Accounts of visits by those rated as ethnocentric were more explicit
and definite in expression than the medium group, as might be expected.
For example, the epithets used in this account of experiences gained from a
junior school visit are more extreme. A tendency to some defensive
reactiveness might have affected his conclusions about some, but not all
people encountered:

P: The French fishermen were nice as well, they gave us a couple of crabs
each. Just gave us them . . . for our teas.
I: What do you think the French think of other people? I have been asking
you about the French, but what do they think of us?
P: Some of them can be pretty nasty. Like you ask them a question and
they snap back at you and just tell you which way and probably turn
away and talk to someone else. Pretty hard — like I was in this market
and I asked this lady what the price was for this necklace. She told us
the price and just turned away and started talking to this other French
lady. I just walked off. In the markets you can like bid with them. If you
have only like ten francs and you think it is like twelve francs, they just
give you it for that money. (135/16)

Shopping appeared to be a fertile area for misunderstanding and
subsequent hostility:

I: What would put you off living in France?
P: Don't like the food that much and sometimes people can be a bit nasty
— they're not friendly really.
I: What gives you these impressions then?

P: Like if you go into a shop there they say to you 'What do you want?' instead of 'Can I help you? and stuff like that.

I: Where have you come across that?

P: When I was passing through France on the school trip. I went in the shop there just having a look round, postcards and stuff like that, and the shopkeeper like going around and I asked him — in French — could buy — if we could buy, if we wanted anything to buy but we were just really looking. (131/4)

The junior school experiences were remembered on several occasions more positively than the shorter secondary school visits to the Channel ports:

Like some of them stood and stared like when they heard us talking but most of them like sort of wanted to speak to us like on the beach and that and there was some French girls and some of the boys played football with the French boys like the English against the French, they were friendly. (118S/18)

This pupil when older had concluded that French pupils visiting their school had been 'snobby'. It is not impossible that interaction might be construed differently according to the age at which it took place.

Dress and physical appearance

From class case study analysis, in Chapter 2, it was found that the textbook was not an extensive source of information upon dress and physical appearance. Pupils relied to a much greater extent upon their experience of French people seen in England as well as France. No consensus regarding French appearance emerged from the diversity of experience of France. One Newfarm pupil gave what was probably a positive evaluation:

I: So how would you — or can you describe a typical Frenchman?

P: Happy. Dressed well . . . Good.

I: Dressed well?

P: Yes, they are always dressed well.

I: What does that mean? They are dressed up?

P: Well sort of, when I went to France you walked down the street and everyone looked smart. All the French people that we passed looked smart.

I: Does that mean that they were wearing formal clothes? Suits and things or what?

P: Well not so much suits. More casual, like shirts and trousers or jeans. Pair of shoes.

I: But smart?

P: Yes.

I: And the young people the same?

P: Some of them.

I: Not all of them?

P: No. Most of them are fashionable. Bright colours, walking down the street. (133/21) (N group)

A pupil from Hillside contrasted the textbook image with experience:

They are not that much different at all but they think they are better dressers. That is what it says in the textbook but there was no evidence of that in France. Apart from a lot more clothes shops around the main city areas. (310/20 (N group)

For one no differences could be perceived:

They wear all just things like shirts and that, just like what we wear. (206/20) (N group)

For another, whilst young peoples' jeans were similar in both countries, other clothes seen were a source of surprise:

P: But I noticed that some other people dressed different, in different places.

I: And what was different about those people then exactly?

P: Well just the colours that they wear — that we wouldn't dream of. Something like gold, well some people wear gold I mean not like them. I think I've seen a woman in a shop wearing a gold suit, I don't mean gold I mean gold . . . (283/22) (N group)

A junior school visit to France had been sufficient to negate a stereotyped view of French dress for one pupil:

No, they're just the same, people say that they go round with berets on and stripy tops and all that but they don't, not when we were there. (118S/25) (E group)

One boy drew a distinction between formal and casual dress:

Well I think when they're dressed up smart they're dressed the same I think but they seem to wear a lot of flat caps I saw in the place where I was at but I'm not sure again whether that's typical of France or just the region. (244/19) (E group)

Spoken French

Experiencing spoken French in France was seen to differ from the usual classroom discourse:

P: It was hard to understand. From what I have found out there was some dialects or some accent or something but you could pick up words and put together some of it but some you couldn't understand at all.
I: What did it feel like? What was your reaction when you hear real people speaking real French?
P: I felt it wasn't anything like what we do in class. It didn't sound like that at all. It sounded a lot different. (310/11) (N group)

Some found the experience a positive one:

P: I enjoyed it (Boulogne).
I: What kind of things did you enjoy about it?
P: . . . When we were like outside anywhere talking to the French people and things like that. I enjoyed it. (228/5) (M group)

One pupil thought the context helpful:

P: . . . it was easier than speaking to someone English in French because they knew what they were doing, they were helping you and sometimes encouraging their English so they were saying English words. (244/22) (E group)

He summed up the contribution of the visit:

It didn't make a lot of difference to the language but it sort of put into practice — a lot more real not just sort of dead language when we had to speak it and use it properly, not just to the teacher and things like that. It makes it a lot more interesting. (244/30)

He added:

P: The trouble is we had to sort of stay inside as well as sort of doing just class work and that sort of spoiled it. You're in France why not go out and speak French but you couldn't do that all the time. It was interesting though.

I: Would you make that part of the French course if you could — everyone could go?

P: Yes, I would but I'd make it more sort of practical speaking instead of doing normal class work 'cause while you're in France you may as well do as much as you can practical. It did help my French a lot. (244/30)

Education

Only a small number of pupils had experienced the French schooling system first hand. Impressions were, however, not extensive:

P: Well the school was quite good, like it wasn't as big as ours though, seems though they had more art and things up on the wall and things like that.

I: What about the lessons they were doing?

P: I looked at a woodwork lesson and it was — I went into and it seems they were doing pretty free for all not sort of told what to do, they weren't getting stopped like we do and go on and work properly. (244/7) (E group)

There were no clear judgements upon teachers:

I: Did you get any feeling that they were — the relationships between the teachers and pupils were — what they were like?

P: Well when I was in the woodwork lesson they — one of the pupils was talking to the teacher so they must be able to talk to them there, but as I say we didn't see much of the lessons. (244/7)

For another pupil of similar experience teachers were seen as 'just the same'.

For one pupil an item of information presented by the textbook was vividly exemplified during the week-long visit to France; referring to shops he said:

P: They are open on Sunday but I don't know about Saturday morning because I couldn't believe it when they woke us up to go to school. (301/6) (E group)

Jobs

Whilst some pupils stated that one reason for learning French was in order to be able to work in France, it was found generally that few had extensive information upon the work structure of France. When in France some pupils had observed markets and other retail outlets:

> Most of them work on market stalls. Like arcade things and ice-cream stalls. That's all I really saw when I was in France. Mostly French people on these ice-cream stalls. (135/21) (E group)

One pupil when prompted drew a conclusion about women's work:

I: Do you think that women work as much as in England or more?
P: More.
I: Why do you think they work more?
P: When we went there was like streets and every house had like washing out on the line.
I: So they do more housework?
P: Yes.
I: Do they go out to paid work more?
P: No. (201/16) (M group)

Growing up

Sometimes recollections were elicited by probing questions:

I: Do they have special birthdays in France, compared with the way we do in England, where we just have the one birthday?
P: Yes 'cause when I was in France last year, I can't remember what it was called, they had a special day, it wasn't a birthday or anything and we used to sing this song. (248/38) (N group)

Books

One rare example of recall of one type of French literature came from holiday experience:

I: Yes, have you seen any Asterix?
P: I've seen some of the books and comics, Asterix comics.
I: Oh, I see, in shops in England or in school?
P: Like when I went to France they were in the shops and at the airport

and that. (197/10) (M group)

Religion

P: . . . they [the churches] were nice, like, built up houses but there didn't
seem to be that many people there but they were always nice and tidy
but some people I don't think really believe in religion or they don't
seem to be going to church or anything.
I: Do you know which religion it is?
P: I don't know. I don't know much about it. (175/51 (N group)

Other sources — introduction

Apart from French lessons and visits to France the most frequent
sources to which pupils attributed their information were the television and
friends' and relations' accounts of France. School history lessons provided
information upon a limited range of periods. A variety of other sources was
also given but much less frequently than were these main sources. The
minor sources included penfriends, magazines, books, the radio, French
visitors seen in England and geography lessons.

By selecting examples according to type of source quoted it is not
possible to illustrate the differential use of information made by individuals. Some pupils were found who recalled about a dozen different
examples of information sources; at the other extreme were those who had
noted few extramural influences. Several of the pupils whose responses
indicated use of a wide range of sources came from Class 1 and Class 4, the
highest achievement classes. In Chapter 2 it was found that the amount of
information attributed to the French teacher was not extensive in these two
classes; these pupils appeared to supplement their school-based knowledge
by making use of an impressive array of extramural sources.

The principal sources of information are described first below, followed by the minor sources.

Television

Whilst many pupils concluded that they had not observed much
material about France on television as large a number conversely gave it as
a source of information for a variety of topics. Many different types of
programmes were cited; of these the news and related documentary
programmes were most frequently given.

Much of what was recalled from the news related to politics, but was not necessarily extensive:

I: And on the news, do you notice much about France?
P: There was about a few months back about the fans but after that it's been not much just saying when our prime minister talks to theirs and all this but not much. (310/30) (N group)

The following example is unusually lengthy:

P: The government seems to have a lot more influence than it used to, you never used to hear much about the French government but now you do and different things it's involved with . . . it seems recently that it's actually come forward and you can see it's not really all that different from other governments, it's not something totally different, they have the same faults as other governments and that they're not something strange.
I: Are you thinking of some of the people just now?
P: I was thinking about the 'Rainbow Warrior' I think it was called that was blown up and there was documentary on the television a while back where the government were trying to cover up for it and saying that they hadn't anything to do with it and that it couldn't have been anyone from France when in fact it was and I suppose that's what most governments do I know they do over here. (326/32) (N group)

What could be gained from television programmes was often seen to be modified by the wishes of parents. In one example the interests of the father were made clear, and it is possible to hypothesise that where the news is watched it is because of parental wishes. It will be seen below, in discussing films on the television, that parental wishes could exert an opposing influence. This extract regarding the news is taken from the interviews of the medium group:

I: Would you, I mean could you tell me anything about French politics?
P: It's just changed I think over there, the way, the voting system. From this last election they vote a new premier I think it is and just changed it — I can't remember what it's called.
I: Yes, I know what you mean.
P: Representation, personal representation.
I: Yes.
P: They've just changed it from the old system to that new system.
I: And what can you tell me about the present situation then?

P: Proportional representation I think it's called, it's supposed to be a more fair system only the only thing is the like National Front can get voted in if they get a seat, like in the old system they wouldn't get voted in but there's a few National Front seats in France now.

I: And what else, I mean what other political parties are there, and who's in power?

P: Mitterand is like, I don't know what he is really — I don't know the name for him (inaudible) he's voted every eighth year I think it is I don't know who the Prime Minister sort of person is. Is it Jacques Chirac or something?

I: And the system of I mean what's the relationship then between — what does the President do, what does Mitterand do?

P: They don't have sort of royal families so he's sort of half way he's like the head figure of the country, I suppose the head figure in this country is like the Queen or something. Like he's the head figure of that particular country, he represents the country at royal events and things like that.

I: With no political power?

P: Yes I think 'cause he doesn't have to be the same member of the party as the main party that rules over the country. I think their Prime Minister he's like a different — he's in a different party to what Mitterand is at the moment that's what all the controversy was about.

I: Right. Are you interested in English politics as well, is that why you're so well informed about French politics?

P: Yes. It's with watching the news a lot and my Dad's interested in politics.

I: Do you talk to him about politics then?

P: Yes. If I don't understand something like, like that new voting system in France that I didn't understand, I asked my Dad what it was all about and he explained it to me. (103/27)

Sometimes pupils became aware of political figures though they were not particularly interested:

I: Where do you get this kind of knowledge from?

P: My Dad mostly because he's pretty interested in all politics and just off the news because my Dad watches it non-stop.

I: Do you discuss it then with him?

P: Yes, about ten minutes after the news we just talk about things and that.

I: Do you find it interesting?

P: Not really, not much. (101/21) (E group)

When discussing issues related to employment several pupils recalled items subsequently attributed to television news:

> I don't think they get many strikes I don't know if they have unions over there, trade unions, but you never hear of many strikes. There was one about the farmers a few weeks ago I think but that was about the milk quota I think it was. I don't think you get many strikes over there. (103/20) (M group)

One pupil whose membership of the most ethnocentric group was one of the few anomalous examples, contrasted the image presented on the television with his experience in France. He also indicated the attitudes of some of those around him, which might have contributed to the lack of consistency in his views:

P: There was a lot on the telly about farmers and all that but I couldn't really believe it like what the farmers were doing because they are so friendly over there. Like here — my Dad's best friend he doesn't like them at all, he won't go over. His wife bought some French yoghurt and he wouldn't have it in the house, he was going mad.

I: Do you think they are like that about France — people that haven't been or people that have been as well?

P: No I was like annoyed really the way he was going on about them because they are nice. (301/18)

I: Do you think you learn much about France from the television?

P: It depends like, when there was a lot on the news about the French farmers and that everybody took the English side but it wasn't all the French people that were doing that it was just some of them. I didn't really believe what they were doing because they are not like that when we go over. They all welcome you and everything. It's nice. (301/23)

The dating of some events was not always clear:

P: I know a bit ago there was the students on strike because of different things I don't think they were happy at the way things were but you don't really hear much about the workers going on strike like the miners strike, nothing like that.

I: What are you referring to the students what was that?

P: It was quite a while ago where they were all out and rioting, it started off as a demonstration and they were rioting it was quite a long time ago though.

I: Before your time?

P: I know there was something a few years ago but it wasn't on the scale of the one quite a long time ago.

I: So who's told you about that?

P: I think it came up on the news when they — I don't know whether it was a documentary or the news — something about France and this came up and I think it was mentioned in the house before. (326/25) (N group)

When analysing the class case studies in Chapter 2 it was found that boys in Classes 1 to 4 appeared to be more interested in, or have more knowledge of, politics than girls. All the extracts quoted above, with the exception of those from pupil 326 (p. 261), are from boys' interviews. Whilst this is not a comprehensive account the extracts were chosen for being the most extensive. (It is possible that greater exposure to television amongst boys, which has been demonstrated in past surveys such as those of Brown (ed.) (1976) still obtains and could influence the amount recalled. A number of girls in this study stated that they watched little television, preferring to go out or listen to pop music.)

About one fifth of the secondary interview sample referred to films on television as a possible source of information. However as will be seen below, interest in French films was not always evident.

Inevitably some of the films watched were war films and may not have been of French origin. In some cases they provided images of one period of French history. One extensive example came from the non-ethnocentric group:

P: . . . you see a lot of French films on other channels and the world war films tell you a lot about France.

I: Do you mean the feature films or documentary films?

P: Well both I would think.

I: So the films give you some information about France then do they? Do you find that a helpful way of finding out about France?

P: Yes.

I: What kind — can you give me a concrete example of a film that you have seen. Can you think of one of them at the moment?

P: . . . I think *Winds of War* had one in I just saw a clip of that. That was last year and then there was one recently and that was based in France and how it affected this French town.

I: How the war affected it?

P: Yes. Like the Jews living in it and everything.

I: So what do you remember about the French town then? What did you see of the French town?

P: There is a lot of artists. It was about artists. Saw the shops, like bakeries and everything, meals in the houses and area around.

I: Did the buildings strike you particularly?

P: . . . What they were like then, they were similar to the old Georgian houses I think what we have. They were similar to them. I suppose they are now but the modern day ones are different, more like ours. (104/ 26,27)

Few pupils from the most ethnocentric group recalled any films, either ones based on the war or other types.

Though examples given were not numerous, those reporting some interest in films other than war films, came from the non-ethnocentric group. Some films seen were not modern. In the following example the pupil refers also to another unusual television source, but it is included here, rather than below, in order to pursue the style of the interview:

I: Do you ever see French films on television?

P: Yes on late night on channel four yes, but they're always in black and white.

I: Yes, but they are in French with sub-titles?

P: Yes, I watched them once and read the writing — I recognise some words like Je m'appelle. Sometimes, once it was on television and I sort of tried to write the words how they said it — wrong spelling but — like when I watched the Eurovision song contest the song 'J'aime, J'aime la vie' I asked Miss what that meant and she said I love life. I was trying to sing the words. But it's hard like if you compare — if you really want to learn discussion, if you didn't have the sub-titles on the French I wouldn't be able to understand it.

I: Does it give you some idea of what France is like to watch these French films?

P: Yes there's a lot of countryside from the films I've seen. Lot of countryside, lot of bikes. I suppose that's it.

I: When you say they're black and white does that mean they're mainly old films you see?

P: . . . Don't know. Some of them maybe just in the forties. They're in black and white though. I've never seen one in colour. (151/31)

The combination of dated subject matter and sub-titles diminished the interest of many, though some pupils persevered:

P: I think if there is like a film on and you have shots in France, you can sometimes get some information from there.

I: Can you think of anything in particular? Do you watch films at all on telly?

P: Yes.

I: Including French films?

P: Well — I think I have watched one or two of them but I found it hard to understand. I had a go at like listening to what they were saying then I tried reading the sub-titles but I wasn't too keen on it.

I: You found it hard going?

P: Yes.

I: But did that give you some idea of what the place is like?

P: Yes.

I: Or not?

P: It gives us an idea.

I: Can you remember anything specific from any of the films?

P: No.

I: About the setting where they were or things like that?

P: It was in like a town but didn't look like a modern one. Like an old one. It was by the seaside or had a port.

I: What makes you say it was old, what struck you as being old about it?

P: Well there was not a lot of people about and they had shutters on the windows and little window boxes.

I: Did the houses look old then?

P: Mm and a few of the cars were old.

I: Well it might have been an old film in that case.

P: Mm it was in black and white. (313/37)

Within the non-ethnocentric group, as well as the other two groups, several pupils were unenthusiastic:

P: I've watched a couple but not, I wouldn't, say there was a French film at night, I wouldn't go home and say I'm watching a French film, if it's on and there's nothing else on I'd watch it.

I: Yes, but you wouldn't go for it especially. Do those films give you any impressions of what life is like in France?

P: No.

I: No?

P: 'Cause I just think they're acting. See like things like 'East Enders' if I was, well I'm not saying there should be, but there could be one like in French just them instead of us. (283/30)

Unlike their interest in the news, no parents were reported as showing an interest in French films; the opposite was more usually the case:

I: What about French films have you ever seen any on the television?
P: My Mum always turns them off 'cause she can't understand them, 'cause they're all sub-titles. (293/25) (Medium group)

French films on television, therefore, were not favourably perceived. It should be noted that many foreign films shown on English television are transmitted late at night and thus not viewed by these age groups, for even those with more flexible bed-times had to contend with lack of parental interest. As sub-titles were seen as a drawback no evidence was given of these late films having been videotaped. Selective use of this material could perhaps be made by French teachers.

At the time during which the interviews were carried out English television was transmitting at least two television comedy programmes which made use of stereotypes of other peoples, such as the French and the Germans. It was found that secondary pupils did not refer to these series extensively whereas junior pupils did. Thus it is possible that secondary pupils both watched these programmes less, and treated the images presented less seriously:

I: . . . are there other sources on television that you see about France?
P: On the Schools and Colleges once there was a programme on the exchange and that showed the English going over to France and different things and then of course the children's programmes like *Grange Hill*, they covered it.
I: And there is the famous *'Allo 'Allo*, did you see that?
P: Oh yes — good.
I: Did that tell you anything about France?
P: It told me about the café and that's about it . . . (104/29) (N group)

Another pupil refuted the images transmitted:

I: Do you think that is very realistic about the French?
P: I don't think it is that realistic but it's funny.
I: What kind of things do you like about it?
P: I like when René is talking to the Resistance and things like that. And you get this kind of English accent which is slightly frenchified.
I: How realistic do you think that is?
P: Not at all.
I: Do you think the French act like the people in *'Allo 'Allo*?
P: No. They are totally crazy in *'Allo 'Allo* (116/10) (M group)

However whereas pupils did not take the images of the French presented in comedy series too seriously, stereotypes of the Germans were not necessarily challenged:

P: My Mum says the Germans are not very nice.
I: Who said that?
P: Just like everyone. On the telly and that and in comedies and that they are always picking on the Germans.
I: Do you ever see that programme called 'Allo 'Allo?
P: I've seen it once or twice.
I: What do you think of that? Some people get ideas from that. I haven't really seen it much.
P: It's about — he is French and don't like Germany.
I: Do you think it is true to life or do you think it is not?
P: A little bit. It may be in the war and that. (197/37)

Holiday programmes were an obvious source of some information about France. The areas shown differed from those presented in the textbook, and the images were generally positive if not extensive:

P: It shows you what it's like in France.
I: What is it like, from these programmes?
P: Sunny and there's lots of people . . . and it's just . . . it's a nice place . . . (253/19) (M group)

Similarly:

P: When I'm in at home, off school, it usually comes on the telly.
I: Yes . . .
P: And holidays abroad . . .
I: They tell you in holiday programmes on television?
P: The South of France and places like that. (164/11) (M group)

Apart from the news, films, comedy series and holiday programmes, pupils attributed ideas about the French to a number of different types of programme. It was not clear in all cases which programmes were thought to be responsible; ideas were attributed generally to the television.

Friends' and relatives' accounts

Friends' and relatives' accounts of their experiences of French culture were frequently given as sources of information. Clearly it is not possible to assess to what extent these accounts were accurately recalled. It is not possible either to assess how salient other people's views were in comparison with information gained through visiting France or from French lessons. The types of information and perceptions transmitted from others covered a range of items which consisted principally of factual information relating to France, information and opinions about speaking French, comments upon food and perceptions of French people.

For some pupils the kings of information about France passed on by friends differed from that presented in the textbook:

P: There was like a lot of things to see . . .
I: What kind of things?
P: Castles, Manor houses . . . about the submarine pen at St. Nazaire. (120/37) (N group)

Most information passed on came into the touristic category:

P: I would like to go to Paris and see . . . the life there.
I: Yes, I was going to say are there any bits you think would be more interesting to go to?
P: I think Paris because there would be a lot of variety. I like to see places of interest.
I: What have you heard about Paris?
P: Well my Mum has been to Paris and she says it is quite nice. Look at the ruins and monuments. She really enjoyed that. (183/4) (N group)

and:

P: 'Cause like in the South of France I think it's supposed to be really hot but in Boulogne it's just like here but a bit warmer . . . I only know about the South of France 'cause my Uncle's been to South of France before last year . . . 'cause my Auntie went. She says there's a lot of flies and that — a lot of flies about. That's what she said — she said she didn't like it 'cause there was a lot of flies and that. That's all I know about the South of France. (164/28) (M group)

Perceptions of similarities were sometimes transmitted:

P: . . . I don't know really . . . they liked France and . . . a lot of them they wouldn't like to live there but they'd like to go back and things like that and just generally were surprised at the fact that it was so much like England. (265/25) (N group)

Others noted details thought to differ:

P: . . . My brother said they [the houses] looked a little bit different 'cause he visited a French family and . . .
I: He visited, your brother?
P: Yes, and he said the general appearance, he doesn't know how to explain it but it looked — you could tell it wasn't an English house, it definitely looked foreign but inside it was just the same as an English house.
I: He found it difficult to pin it down what it was that was different, that made it foreign?
P: It's just like the general appearance of it, you know, it wasn't like any make of house over here. (265/13) (N group)

Information about the French language was quite frequently transmitted amongst friends and relations. Attitudes towards learning languages could also be influenced by members of the family:

I: Do you enjoy learning French?
P: Yes.
I: Have you always liked it from the beginning?
P: Yes, 'cause when I started taking French my Mum used to say how she enjoyed it and she used to teach us the odd word now and again and by the time I'd reached the secondary school I couldn't wait to start French and I really enjoyed it.
I: So your mother speaks a fair bit of French does she or, learned French at school?
P: She did but she's a bit rusty now. (256/27) (N group)

Comments were not always positive:

I: What do your parents think about you learning French?
P: My Mum says it's really a waste of time in this country 'cause she doesn't think we'll be able to go over to France any time. (292/37) (M group)

Those who had not been on school visits could gain impressions from their friends' experiences:

I: What are the impressions they give you, your friends who have been to France?
P: They say it is pretty funny because of trying to understand the French

and that. Trying to work out how to buy things and that. (304/22) (M
group)

   Another Class 4 boy, who enjoyed learning French but disliked
French people, quoted a friend's opinion of the French language, derived
from an unusual source:

I: What about French films have you ever seen any?
P: I don't know, Chris has and he says like they're not as good — they
    don't have so many words as the British so they can't like express
    themselves very good.
I: Is that a friend of yours?
P: Yes. 'Cause he went to see Indiana Jones and the Temple of Doom in
    France, I don't know why 'cause he couldn't understand any of it.
I: Was it dubbed in French do you mean?
P: Yes it was French sound.
I: But there weren't as many words?
P: Yes, he said he knew a lot of them like so that shows you how bad it
    was. (245/32) (E group)

   Opinions upon food were, not surprisingly, transmitted to some
pupils. They had inevitably heard of relations' consumption of frogs' legs,
and perceptions of taste could be passed on:

P: It tastes — different — like what people said as well, that puts you off as
    well and stuff like that really. (131/16) (E group)

Some relations were more adventurous:

I: And what would you think of the taste of French food?
P: I love it.
I: You've had some, have you?
P: I think so, well my Mum's cooked bits of things like that, she likes
    experimenting and I like it, I think it's better than what we have — a big
    plate.
I: You think of it as being fancier?
P: Yes, I think they sort of present it a lot better as well. (233/9) (N group)

Others' attempts were not successful:

P: There are lots of French cheeses.
I: Have you not had any of those?

P: Miss, one week my Mum got one but it was very strong and nobody could eat it. (293/8) (M group)

Evaluations of French people made by friends, relations and even acquaintances were recalled:

P: . . . it's just French people laugh a lot and that.
I: How do you know about this?
P: Just my grandma has been.
I: Oh yes, what did she tell you about it?
P: It is a nice place. (166/18) (M group)

Some pupils did not usually accept the views of others, for example:

P: Don't know about like whether they're friendly or not but I've heard, they say they're not very friendly but you don't know what to believe.
I: Yes, where've you heard from?
P: Just people who've been on holiday and that.
I: Yes. Are you thinking of people who've been from school or . . .
P: No, older people like my Mum and Dad's friends. (101/17) (E group)

Others, in particular two in the most ethnocentric group, did not appear to question paternal views:

I: What do you think your parents think of French people?
P: Well, I'll tell you something, my Dad hates French people. I think I take after my Dad any way but my Mum she likes the French. (156/35) (E group)

It is also evident that parental influence can be stronger than school:

[the French teacher] says Paris is good but I've heard from my Dad that it's big and nobody will help you find your way — back in London you can ask someone. (245/26)

Other minor sources

Other sources were only referred to by a small number of pupils in each case. Some pupils had met French people in England, and though the instances, apart from exchange pupils, were not numerous, the resultant impressions could be quite vivid:

Sometimes I was with my parents and my Uncle and my Aunt and other times I was on my own like and I made some friends and we had them over for Christmas once and we had like our dinner — we asked them if they wanted a French meal or an English one and they said an English one so we made them an English one and we had like soup and then we had our vegetables and our pudding and that and then we had our Christmas pudding and we set fire to it and they all went — look at it, its on fire look it's burning, quick put it out! We were all laughing at them 'cause they hadn't seen that done before — they were shocked when they saw it go on fire . . .

I: Were these friends from Boulogne?
P: Yes from my Uncle's like street, around there, there was one lass and two boys. (208/34)

Of the minor sources, printed material such as magazines and comics, were the most frequently cited. These referred to a variety of aspects of French life:

I: What's so special about it? [French food]
P: . . . Don't know really it's just probably the way it tastes and the way it looks and everything, they've probably got more variety I think really, they use more like when there's salad — I was just reading in a magazine — with salad we just like have the lettuce and that but they have a whole range of different things like vegetables and things like that. (233/19) (N group)

Fashion was an obvious subject for a few:

I: Have you ever heard anything about French fashion, Parisian fashion, not just the sort of clothes for everyday wear, but expensive fashion?
P: Miss they do a lot of like fashion shows and things like that.
I: How have you heard about that?
P: Miss in a book and a magazine.
I: Is that something you have at home or at school?
P: At home.
I: Can you remember what the magazine was?
P: *Just Seventeen.*
I: Oh, yes. What were the clothes like?
P: Miss, some of them were like way out. (293/16) (M group)

Boys too could be aware of this aspect:

I: What about the high fashion, Parisian fashion? Do you think that influences us?
P: Yes. Yes, I think most people like look in magazines and see them and say 'wouldn't mind having one of them' and go on holiday and get one for coming back and show it off to people.
I: Is that mainly women's fashion you are thinking of or is it men's as well?
P: Mainly women. Mainly *Vogue* and magazines like that. Like women just look at them. (135/19) (E group)

Textbook material on house interiors could be supplemented from the same source:

I: Did you see any pictures of French interiors of houses anywhere?
P: Yes in a magazine and that.
I: Yes some people seem to see more magazines than others. Can you remember which ones those were?
P: Just one about decorating your house.
I: Was that one you had at home or at school?
P: At home. My Mum got it when she was decorating. (298/8) (E group)

Apart from textbooks and supplementary books used in French lessons, pupils did not refer to many books as sources. The following was an unusual example from a girl in a middle achievement class (Class 3):

P: I've got a book at home called (inaudible) and I've been reading that for a bit but there are some words I can understand and some I can't but it's like good to read it then you can understand it, the book, it's quite good.
I: Is this a book you've borrowed from school?
P: No this book's my own and it's about a man trying to kill another man, something like that.
I: Where did you get that?
P: My Gran, she's been buying some French books for us but this one was the only book I could read.
I: That's an unusual thing for your Gran to be doing.
P: Yes, Mum wants to get us like into languages and my Gran like, she likes to learn as well. I was supposed to be learning my Mum to speak French as well but she's alright — I sometimes try and help her out. I get this book out and I read it to her and see if she can tell us what it means — I have to sometimes check up though. (175/45) (N group)

The sources read were not always specified but could be illuminating:

I: What do you think they think of us as a nation or as people?

P: I don't really think they like us really 'cause I don't know they just think we're sort of very loud maybe — I don't know about like the food and the wines and that they must think we're a bit thick, sort of just picking up the nearest bottle of plonk you find and things like that and eating anything.

I: What gave you that impression?

P: Just reading different things and that. (233/16) (N group)

A few pupils knew of the Asterix books, but they were thought by some to be 'hard' and no impressions of France were attributed to them.

In the secondary schools pupils were encouraged to write to pen-friends. Some pupils had made contacts whilst in primary schools:

I: What kind of things did you write about then?

P: About what it was like in France and places.

I: This was before you learned French, so you had some idea before you started. What kind of things did he tell you?

P: It was hot, nice places to go things to do things like that. (137/22) (N group)

Others had made French friends when on holiday abroad. The following example is taken from an interview with a boy in a low achievement set who had a very positive attitude towards France:

I: Say you had to choose to be a different nationality, not to be English. What whould you choose?

P: I'd like to be French, I think I like French best because I've got a French penpal.

I: Have you?

P: When I was in Spain I met him on holiday and I like the French.

I: So you like them a lot do you?

P: Yes.

I: What sort of things have you heard about France from him?

P: Just where he lives and he sent us some leaflets about his town and that.

I: Yes. Whereabouts does he live?

P: Can't remember, near Paris. 70km from Paris but I can't remember exactly. (197/6) (M group)

The radio was only cited as a source of information when pupils discussed pop music:

P: Music seems to be always on the (mind) the pop music always seems to be jumpy. If they do any slow music they always have the same tune but the music's rather like ours in a way but the pop music isn't, the classical is but the pop music isn't.

I: Where have you heard French music?

P: On the radio sometimes, sometimes you get them on the telly when you're doing French, then the music seems to be jumpy but like so that the crowd can sing along with their music, we really can't with ours, some of the music you cannot sing along with it but they seem to like have music to sing along to and clap hands to and things like that so that it's quite different to ours. (175/41) (N group)

Another unusual example of attempts to listen to French radio was:

P: . . . I've listened to some French music before and it seems to have a different tone . . . it's hard to explain . . . you know it's not English . . . if like there's no speaking I wouldn't know like but . . . the kind of music it was but it certainly isn't English there's a certain difference but don't really know what it is.

I: What kind of music is it you're talking about then?

P: Pop music.

I: Pop music?

P: Yes 'cause I managed to tune into some French and there was a definite difference between French and English.

I: So you listen to the radio do you?

P: Yes.

I: The French radio?

P: Sometimes. (295/23) (N group)

Information about and evaluation of French culture were therefore gained from a wide, if uneven, range of extramural sources. Whilst pupils attributed the majority of their knowledge to French lessons, it was noticeable that some pupils drew upon numerous extramural sources. Use of some of those available, for example television, was not always optimal and could perhaps benefit from guidance or monitored use. If it is desired that pupils receive a particular impression of French life from their French courses in schools, it has to be acknowledged that they exist within a network of other sources of information, the potential of which does not appear to be discussed readily in the classroom.

Sources and Influences Inside the School

It will be recalled from Chapter 3 that an independent variable termed 'school class' — referring to pupils' membership of a specific teaching group — was found to associate with ethnocentricity score. It was suggested that this variable has to be treated with care as it no doubt reflects a composite factor: the nature of a school class is for example influenced by the ratio of boys to girls, by the range of experience of other countries of the pupils in it, by the range of socio-economic background of the pupils and so on. None the less this variable also reflects teachers' intuitive grasp of the relationships which influence and are influenced by the teaching process. Furthermore, classroom observation — see Chapter 5 — also suggested that the teaching style with respect to cultural information and attitudes expressed differs from class to class. For these reasons we present pupils' views about the influences and sources within French teaching on the basis of the class to which they belong. In anticipation of the fact that classroom observation was eventually focused on four third year classes, which in turn form the basis of our discussion of models of cultural studies teaching in Chapter 6, the following account presents the views of the pupils in those four classes only.

Class 1

Seen from the pupils' viewpoint the function of the teacher is to supplement and enrich the information provided by the textbook. Twelve pupils were interviewed in total. All but one of the eight pupils asked about what the teacher had told them agreed that they did receive supplementary information. She contrasted German lessons where 'every so often we will read a bit about the German family' with French lessons where 'I don't think I have learned anything about France' (120/34) but says the French teacher talks about France 'not very often' which suggests that it is the contrast with German which influences her reply, not the absolute lack of teacher information.

The teacher first of all supplements the textbook:

It tells you everything you just get more bits from the teachers who have been to France. (127/18)

but also improves on the textbook:

Probably learn a lot from the teacher than I do from the textbook because they've usually had like more experience and that and they're easy to understand than just reading it 'cause if somebody tells you it sticks in your mind rather than just reading it. (127/12)

Furthermore the teacher can provide experience which the textbook cannot. Three pupils spontaneously referred to a lesson in their first year of French which had clearly stuck in their minds as was suggested above. The teacher had provided a cheese-tasting occasion:

P: Yes, they tell us like about all different foods and Mrs X brought in a lot of cheeses and that . . .

I: Is this in addition to what you learn from the textbooks?

P: Yes, we were just, just when we'd started learning about how to ask for food and how to go into cafés she brought all, about 15 different French cheeses in.

I: You found that interesting then?

P: Yes, never realised there was so many — there's about hundreds of different types. (101/29)

The textbook remains however the guide in the sense that it determines the topic and the order in which topics are taken. Within the textbook guidelines, the acquisition of language is determining:

I: Do you do more language than about France?

P: We do about France and then it mingles with about France when we learn about the language, the vocabulary and that.

I: Do you do about the country without bothering about the language and learning the words?

P: No, not really.

I: It's all connected with learning the language is it?

P: Yes. (128/19)

One pupil was also asked whether she had any preference within the dichotomy which the interviewer had established between 'language' and 'France':

I: Which do you prefer?

P: . . . Learning about it better, 'cause I'd like to find more about the place rather than how to say 'Where's the toilet?' and things like that, I'd rather learn about the place. (127/18)

Although it is the interviewer's distinction, she appears to recognise it even though she puts it in terms of language functions 'how to say' which have a specific realisation "'Where's the toilet?' and things like that."

If we now turn directly to pupils' perceptions of the textbook, they demonstrate both how dominant the book can be and how some pupils are able to take a critical view, apparently without the help of the teacher. First, the general view of the book is summed up by one pupil as follows:

I: And how do you learn about the thing you've been telling me about, the food and so on, how's that done?
P: Well we have *Action!* group French and different chapters are on different subjects, like one chapter could be on the sort of food they have, another chapter on how to pay the round on a bus and another chapter would be about the table and what to expect on the table, and it's mostly either meal times or transport.
I: When you say one chapter is on — what does it consist of then, the chapter on transport say?
P: It consists of the vocabulary that you would use, the phrases translated into English as well, and then there'd be some pictures and there would be a conversation or some facts about it and then there would be say another conversation but with some bits missing bits about it and then some more information and maybe a game, an educational game sort of thing, that you can play and —
I: When you say information, what kind of information is there?
P: It tells you in English what to expect sort of thing on the bus and how to say things and sort of thing you would say on the bus and wanting to go — just generally telling you about the thing. (106/12)

The reference to pictures is confirmed as significant by others who mention the pictures when asked about their sources of information:

I: So that is one source. And in the book, what sort of things are there in the book?
P: Well it shows you the French houses and everything and then there is a section of objects in the house and the different meals and everything. It shows you a lot of pictures in the books.
I: Do you also discuss these things in class?
P: Yes we discuss like we compare them both from English to French and see what the differences are between them.
I: Does your teacher then talk about France herself?
P: We had Miss X, she talked from her own experiences of being in France and taking part in exchanges and that and the same with Miss Y now.

I: So that adds a lot more to it does it?
P: Yes. (104/9)

Again the teacher's own experience enriches the textbook image.

   The relationship of textbook image to reality was pursued particularly with one pupil who had just returned from a holiday in France:

I: Well that is interesting as well because what I am interested in is because you have just been, what you thought you were going to see from what you had learned from your textbooks.
P: I expected a lot of buses and trains but there wasn't. I hardly saw any trains and I hardly saw any service buses. I think I only saw a couple of bus stops as well.
I: Anything else that you were surprised about?
P: I knew I would see them carrying French loaves about but I didn't expect that they carried them about like on the backs of bikes and they were just walking down the street with them. Things like that. (120/12)

Here it is evident that particular images ('carrying French loaves') differ and also that the choice of topic, the emphasis given and the ordering of topics within the book are signficant. The emphasis on means of transport confirmed in the summary above, has an effect on expectations about the whole 'street-image' not just on knowledge of how to function linguistically, and especially as a tourist, on French transport. One interview theme was particularly revealing. Pupils were asked about how people earn their living in France:

I: Do you have any impressions from your textbooks about what people do in France? What the men do in your textbook?
P: . . .
I: I mean there are presumably characters in your textbook?
P: Yes. They just like work — the first year book we had characters, a family, but I can't remember what the man did.
I: What about the women, what do they do?
P: They seem to be just housewives.
I: So do you get any real impression of what work is like in France from the textbooks?
P: The men seem to do most of the work. (120/22)

In fact, since the topic 'work' had not been treated as such by the textbook — and therefore not by the teacher either — pupils have a less conscious fund of 'information' about work but none the less an awareness of what people do is present. One pupil explained what kind of impression was available, simultaneously pointing to the cause of the particular image; the 'tourist' view, propagated by the textbook:

I: The other thing that interests me is what people know about the work that French people do. For example your textbooks, the jobs that are described there if there are any?
P: No.
I: No? What do you see people doing for work?
P: From what we saw, it was more as if you were a tourist. There was more in department stores and everything so the only jobs there were like shop assistants and everything. That's about it. (104/21)

The particular issue of women's occupations was discussed with pupils and it is already evident from an earlier quotation that they are thought of by some only as housewives because of the textbook image. One pupil was critical:

I: What about men going to work?
P: I don't think there's many go to work as they do here.
I: The women in your textbooks, what do they do?
P: They're all perfect housewives and that sort of thing.
I: The fact that you're smiling about that obviously implies that you're not too impressed by that.
P: No, it doesn't show you real life like really . . . (101/33)

In general, it appears that pupils can learn French for three years — after which some will not continue — and are given no firm knowledge about how French people earn their living. They have to draw conclusions from their experience of their own culture and tend to assimilate French culture to their own, despite the underlying uneasiness about the relationship of textbook to reality:

I: Let's go on to what people do in their everyday life in respect to work. Do you get it in your textbook? What do people do? What kind of work do they . . .
P: Mostly in offices and factories, mostly in occupations that there are over here, not all that different.
I: Are you thinking of the men now, or the women?
P: I think there's a lot of French housewives I don't think many French women go to work.

I: That's the impression you get from your textbook?
P: Yes.
I: Are there any jobs in the textbook you could name or tell me about?
P: No, not specific jobs. (103/19)

Class 2

In general the pupils in this class say initially that they get little from the teacher and that what they do have is supplementary to the textbook. However opinions about the amount of teacher information are divided and are probably influenced as much by the basic motivation of pupils as by the amount or quality of teacher information. The ambiguous attitude to teacher and subject is evident in the following quotation, a girl with a high ethnocentricity score:

I: What about the teacher what has she told you about France?
P: She doesn't tell us nothing just read the book, copy things down have tests. She's a good laugh, I like her but she starts shouting and everything at us. She's dead canny. My Mam knows her.
I: So she hasn't told you much about France itself, did she ever at any time?
P: Yes, she has done but I can't remember really. She's talked about the sports they do and the fashion. (156/40)

This can however be contrasted with the following:

I: She tells you as well?
P: Yes, a lot, yes.
I: What kind of thing does she tell you?
P: Like about the meals, like some things what aren't in the exercise books, she tells us.
I: In the textbooks?
P: Textbooks. She tells us like little bits about it. Some learn a lot more from Miss Leyborne than from the books.
I: More from her. Can you give me a few examples of what things that she would tell you that's not in the books?
P: Like it didn't describe the 'goûter' there very well in the book. So Miss Leyborne was telling us all about it. (140/14)

This description of the 'goûter' was mentioned spontaneously by another pupil (133/24), suggesting that it had made a distinct impression, although it may also have been a recent lesson and remembered for that reason. Another effective measure which depends on the teacher's efforts rather than the textbook is the deceptively simple device of making material available for pupils to consult:

I: What about French newspapers, have you ever had a look at those?
P: We've had a look at Miss' books before and magazines.
I: What sort of magazines does she bring in?
P: Like women's magazines. Like we can get 'Woman' and things over here.
I: Oh yes. Does she bring them in often?
P: No. She has always got them in like her drawers and that in the classroom. (146/32)

This is mentioned by just one pupil.

Finally, one pupil made an interesting point about the way in which the teacher supplements the textbook information; she not only gives more detail but also talks in a more subjective way about French people:

P: . . . Well the textbook doesn't tell you everything about France really. I mean it only says about the sort of food they eat, it doesn't say like how they eat it, well it says how they eat it but . . . and how they travel about and things like that and it doesn't really say they're nice people it just says what they eat and how they travel about on the trains and on the buses. It doesn't really tell you about the attitudes of them really.
I: Would you like to have more of them in your textbooks?
P: Yes. (133/14)

Here the implication is that information about people as they think and feel is missing from the textbook and that the teacher is in a better position to give the evaluative accounts missing from the book.

The themes in the book mentioned by pupils in this class repeat those in Class 1. 'Transport' and 'food' are most frequent, followed closely by 'youth clubs' and 'sport'. Again pupils have no clear ideas about employment and the work of women. Other topics mentioned are 'famous people', 'shops' and 'houses.

Employment in the book and in reality was contrasted by one pupil:

P: Most of them work on market stalls. Like arcade things and ice-cream stalls. That's all I really saw when I was in France. Mostly French people on these ice-cream stalls.

I: What about in your textbooks? What do the people in the textbooks do?

P: Bus drivers that's all really. That's all we've covered. Like bus drivers and train drivers, taxi drivers.

I: What about the women, what do they do?

P: Haven't done that. Not in the textbooks we haven't. (135/21)

This quotation also indicates how even exposure to reality may provide only a limited view. The contact through a holiday visit is restricted and although pupils may well extrapolate from their own culture to surmise that there are other jobs than these, the effect of this direct experience is evident in the way the pupil grasps at personal experience as the first stage of response. A similar effect is found in the next quotation where vicarious but reliable experience of friends is evident:

I: Where do you get the information that you do have?

P: Well most from the textbook but from friends who've been to France and just a bit from the textbook that's all.

I: What kind of things do your friends talk about then, what do they particularly remember?

P: Talk about the food, mainly about the food and the people there.

I: And what's the general impression that they give you?

P: They say it's — the other thing I don't like is the people but they say it's clean like, they like the place, there's some good sights there in France. (131/12)

Both these boys are rated as ethnocentric and in the latter quotation there is an indication of how an underlying dislike of the people is juxtaposed with friends' statements about 'the place' without being influenced by the good report.

This characteristic of cleanliness can also be gleaned from the book as the following quotation shows, although the pupil, of medium ethnocentr- city rating, expresses some scepticism about the book's bias:

P: From what I have seen of them — look pretty smart. Even if they have got a tee-shirt on — when you see them in textbooks they haven't got any stains down the front. They are always dead clean. I don't know whether that is just because they are out of textbooks and they got people to pose or whether it is true or not. I think they definitely have less litter over there than here.

I: Less litter?

P: Yes we just drop litter anywhere. Whilst the French care about the country. (132/14)

As for family life, there are impressions of large houses gained from the pictures in the book — again reinforcing the importance of pictures and their potential to be misleading:

I: The houses are bigger — you have mentioned that already, is that something you have seen in the textbook?
P: Yes. About how many rooms. They have basements and everything and bigger rooms I should think. I am just thinking.
I: Have you seen this in pictures in textbooks or been told this or what?
P: Well Miss was telling us a lot and there was some photos in the book about a typical French house. (140/31)

The family as such however seems to be missing as is most evident to a pupil who had used a book centred on family life:

I: Anything about family?
P: No, like when I was in the first year I was in a different class, a higher class, then I got moved down. In the first year we used this book that was much better than the *Action!* books we use now.
I: Why was it better?
P: It described the family a lot more and the home life and stuff like that. (140/15)

This same pupil, when asked about relationships between parents and children, referred to the textbook and had drawn her conclusions:

I: Is this something you've got from your friend who was there? What did she say?
P: No, from the textbook like it described how they're a close family, they look like it any way.
I: Did she tell you anything at all about that kind of thing?
P: Not really. (140/19)

One summarising comment suggests not only that pupils are left to surmise that, unless specific differences are mentioned, France is essentially the same as England. Assimilation to existing perceptions is tacitly encouraged by the textbook in particular and, as noted in classroom observation, (see Chapter 5), is unchallenged in the classroom in general:

P: . . . You have like at the very beginning of the first year they have these

people, there was a boy called John and this other girl, his sister, and
they're like always through just give you information about different
places they go.

I: Go on then, what information?

P: Well like when they go to the discos and youth centres, places like that.

I: Do you remember any of that? Can you tell me any of it?

P: . . . Club des jeunes it's like a — where you play ping pong, table tennis
and hockey, they say that it's the same over here in a way, apart from
the food. (151/12)

Class 3

The overwhelming impression from interviews in this class especially
in contrast to the first two, is that pupils' knowledge comes from the
teacher. She supplements the textbook as others do by giving more detail
on the same topic but she also talks about her own experience and her own
views of France and French people. In Class 2, one pupil welcomed the
teacher's subjective approach because it gives a more human impression of
French people. In this class there is clearly a feeling that this is what the
teacher does well. It is above all the anecdotes she uses which seem to
make an impression, since several pupils mention the same incidents
related by the teacher and remember them in some detail. An important
source of the teacher's experience is, say pupils, her visits with schooltrips
to France; they note and appreciate her enthusiasm and knowledge and
contrast it with other teachers'.

The latter point is evident in the following quotations:

but she knows a lot more I think about France and that than Miss X
and she can learn by — I think she goes a lot of times and she goes
with the school trips and that about every year and first and second
years. So it's twice a year really. (164/41)

and she brings us — teacher brings a lot of like things to show us and
maps and other things so we can understand — she doesn't like just
say that's a stamp there and show it round the class holding it in her
hand — she passes it round so we can have a look at that and she
explains everything. (164/38)

Not only does the teacher bring things into the classroom as in other
classes, but this pupil at least appreciates the chance to handle them. The

importance of the teacher's explanation is evident too and is expanded, in contrast to the textbook, by another pupil:

> I can understand her more than the textbook, 'cause she describes people well enough and in the textbook they seem to be more like us really, but like when you go over they seem to be different. I can understand her more than the textbook. (175/37)

and later in the interview:

> Oh yes, Mrs Johnson, she was quite good at French and she seemed to tell you everything about the textbook like you read it out of the textbook and sometimes it's a bit boring like — there's nothing in it really it's just the same like we talk about the same things and the same units and they don't describe it that well. (175/37)

There are two points of interest here. First, the general impression given by the textbook is that, unless differences are made explicit, France is no different from England; this emerged in Class 2 also and we shall return to it below. Second, this pupil and others agree that the book alone would be boring.

In addition to bringing things into the classroom the teacher uses the technique of talking about her own experience, sometimes to great effect. One pupil recalls with enthusiasm even if with some confusion, some account of travelling in France — in contrast to the lack of interest in 'Transport' evident in other classes:

> Say we have to go somewhere and we can't afford to fly we get a bus and we go through France and then he says right I'll drop you off here and there'll be another one along shortly to pick you up in the middle of the road in the middle of Paris (unclear). You're going to have a day's trip around France and then he'll say (unclear) and try to do something and if he does something you can't understand like you remember that Mrs Johnson told you that that happened to her and she said something and that got her out of it and you say thank god Mrs Johnson takes us for French at school, so you know what to look out for — learn by other people's mistakes, so I think that's very good. (164/39)

Other pupils also remembered the anecdote which lies behind this.

The effect of this teacher's techniques and the style involved varies from pupil to pupil. Of the nine pupils asked about the teacher, six found what she says and does interesting and better than the book — and in some cases preferable to 'language'. The others tended to be indifferent and in one case sceptical:

> Yes, she talks a lot about places she's been to and she tries to get us interested but like I said sometimes not a lot of people are interested. (183/27)

There is no apparent relationship between degree of ethnocentricity and comment on style. The three who were more negative in their comments (171/41, 177/22, 183/27) are of three different levels of ethnocentricity.

Although the pupils prefer the teacher's explanations and stories to the textbook, they none the less recall a lot of topics from the book: restaurant, post office, hotels, transport, cafés, pets, houses — as in other classes the impression is houses are big — sport, food and one mention of Paris. There are several further indications of the assimilation effect mentioned above. Since the world of work is little mentioned or illustrated the textbook gives an impression of similarity with England with respect to employment:

> They're all different sorts of jobs like ours — builders . . . they have a lot of shop keepers there . . . people who work in hotels . . . people like that and waiters, it's just the same as England really. (167/20)

A more general statement from this pupil who has not been abroad at all indicates that he is left with an assimilated image:

I: What kinds of people are they that you learn about?
P: . . . just typical French people who live in the house.
I: Do you see anything of daily life, what kind of impression do you get of the daily life in the textbook?
P: Just the same as ours, they have their meals at slightly different times but not much different. (167/22)

When the textbook image is compared with reality as experienced on a schooltrip to Boulogne, there is in the account not only the discrepancy noted elsewhere, but the special problem of visiting a place which is overwhelmed by English school children:

P: They seem to be friendly people but they ask a lot of questions, seem to be asking you a question to everything you say but they seem to be friendly from the textbook and it must be nice and clean and lots of places to see, so that is the impression I get.

I: What places for example?

P: They had about Boulogne in it before I went. I read up about that and it is a nice clean town, lots of people help you and people are really friendly. They show you about but when I went they seemed to be pushing you about more than anything else and the younger people were a bit funny with us. It was near enough good example to set from before I went so I knew it would be like that. (175/13)

The reference to people asking a lot of questions suggests that the predominance of exercises with the language of social transactions can also colour the image of people themselves. Another quotation reveals how significant one passage from the textbook can be. When asked about the relationship between parents and children this boy, who has not been abroad, said:

P: . . . I don't know really but I just think they'd be a lot stricter 'cause of the textbook. I've read things about what they have to do — like we read a passage once about a girl she had to be in for half past nine I think it was.

I: You read it, yes?

P: Yes.

I: Is there anything else that you would find about French parents?

P: . . . No, only they're stricter but the same as all parents. (167/37)

Thus the assumption is that things are 'the same' unless a specific difference is emphasised, consciously or not, by the textbook writer.

Similarly the choice of pictures can be very signficant for a girl who has only been on the school trip to Boulogne:

I: Does it [the textbook] give you impressions of other parts of France?

P: Some places tend to be more like fishing areas and for the old people to go fishing. The fishermen it's just by the coast. It just seems to be that. When you go in the middle it just seems to be all statues here and there but I guess that's it just statues and sea.

I: Statues of what and where?

P: French people doing different things like (unclear) pound note or something of a French person and they have got a statue of him. Called Louis something and they seem to have statues everywhere of anybody

who has done anything good and they are all round really. Big houses
and that so that is all you seem to see. They show you statues and places
to go but they don't tell you much about the area and the people but
they tell you like what's on and where to go and to see, things like that.
(175/14)

Class 4

The main emphasis in this class is for the teacher to supplement the
textbook, as others do, with further factual information. He pays particular
attention to differences between England and France and in some cases
gives his own evaluation of French culture. Pupils appreciate the first-hand
experience of the teacher and contrast the style of teaching with that which
is purely 'language', although the amount of extra information is limited by
the time available.

The conditions in which cultural knowledge is passed on are captured
by one pupil quite explicitly, not just with respect to the present teacher, in
his phrase 'if we've got time on our hands':

I: Do you discuss this kind of thing with your teachers? Not just the
   present one but in the past?
P: . . . We have done, yes, like we did about Christmas, and . . . a bit
   about the houses but not a lot but something. If we've got time on our
   hands then they explain it a bit more in depth. If they've been in France
   then they explain what their attitude was about their own experience
   and so on.
I: How do you find that kind of information from the teacher compared to
   the book?
P: A bit better 'cause like you know the teacher and you don't know the
   person who writes the book so you're getting first hand information
   which relates to a person that you know. (265/14)

Here too the pupil's sense of the significance of first-hand knowledge is
evident. The teacher appears to contrast this with the textbook:

Yes I find it interesting because he knows from first-hand experience.
Sometimes in the book you think well that could be wrong 'cause, and
sometimes he tells us it is wrong because things have changed now.
Like 'phone numbers I think they've changed the dialling system or
something like that but it's interesting, not talking, we don't have to

do anything sort of speaking when he's doing it, we get away with it. (244/11)

The last few words also reveal that in this class the contrast between language 'work' and cultural 'relaxation' is felt by pupils and is worth comparing with the teacher's attitude.

The same pupil none the less has a second, more pedagogical reason for liking the teacher's accounts of France:

I: What about other teachers that you had earlier, did they tell you?
P: One of them did, my first year teacher did but there's one teacher — I don't think I should mention any names — but she wasn't, she didn't sort of teach very well she sort of just gave you things like verbs and sort of learn that and then she just tested you she didn't tell you as much about, like the other teachers do.
I: So you think that bit extra that teachers tell you valuable, do you?
P: Yes, I like listening to things like that because I mean France seems quite an interesting place. It's totally different in some respects, isn't it? (244/12)

This is a similar statement to those found elsewhere but especially in Class 3, where pupils were particularly aware of the teacher's own experience and enthusiasm — and her teaching techniques, including the introduction of things from France into the classroom.

This class has also been given the opportunity to experience things from France but, perhaps because of injudicious teacher choice, the occasion was not completely successful:

I: Have you heard much French pop music?
P: Yes, we heard one in the lesson it sounded like '70s.
I: Who was it.
P: Sheila.
I: What Mr Clarke brought one in did he?
P: Yes. Everyone laughed.
I: So what did they think of it on the whole?
P: They thought it was — one or two thought it was all right but a bit like 'Abba' things like that.
I: So it seemed a bit dated did it?
P: Yes.
I: A bit 1970s. (245/31)

The unrelenting demands of modernity especially in pop music are known and feared by many teachers! The teacher's own comments too can also be remembered more vividly than he perhaps intended:

I: What impressions do you get about people's working life in France?
P: Well we've just sort of been told words of the working life they didn't say a lot about how they work and where they worked. We found out that the Town Hall isn't sort of big building though it's sort of — the teacher talked about being the Mayor in a portakabin, that stays in my mind. (244/11)

On the other hand we meet again the power of the world outside the classroom to contradict what the teacher says:

I: What about what the teacher's told you about France or other countries, in French I mean?
P: I don't know.
I: What sort of thing?
P: He says it's all right but I — he says Paris is good but I've heard from my Dad that it's big and nobody will help you find your way. Back in London you can ask someone. (245/26)

As for the textbook in general these pupils agree broadly with others. They mention the same range of topics, and otherwise accept the implication in general that France is the same as England. In one case this is made particularly explicit with respect to the account of school life. Again in this passage it is evident that where a difference is mentioned it is remembered but the real significance of the difference is not clear to the pupil who assumes that the essential character of school is 'the same' and that the differences are superficial:

I: When you say the school will be different, what had you in mind?
P: Well the fact that they don't wear any uniforms and can really do what they want and the times of school and things like that.
I: The times are different?
P: Yes, 'cause they start a bit more early and they have Wednesdays off, stuff like that.
I: When you say they can do what they want what do you mean by that?
P: Well when we were reading the textbook it said that a lot of them smoked and things like that. I mean I know they do over here but it seemed as if everyone did over there.
I: Yes. What textbook was this then?
P: The *Action!* book three, 'cause we're doing about schools. There was a

couple of pages on it and it was just generally the time they went to
school and what time they had off and the work that they did really,
that's all it was.

I: And the work was that noticeably different?

P: No, not really it was about the same.

I: So going to school in France and going to school here would you feel
   that it's noticeably different or what it's like?

P: Just mainly the times and that's all.

I: What about the teachers, would they be different?

P: I don't think so, about the same. (255/6)

Most comparative educationists would agree that schools in France are
different and might use the two facts mentioned by this pupil to illustrate
fundamental differences in attitudes to pupils, the role of teachers and the
nature of schooling. The pupil is left with a superficial view of schools in
France which does not challenge or alter his existing concepts of what
schooling is or might be.

   Two interesting comments are made about the material which accom-
panies the textbook. The television programmes were rarely used in either
of the schools but pupils have sometimes seen them by chance, not
necessarily associating them with their textbook. This pupil implicitly
confirms the influence of pictures in the textbook already noted and
contrasts them with the television programmes:

P: Like on Sunday morning when there's nothing to watch and you get this
   action telly or something like this where it tells you and news programmes I sometimes watch.

I: And you watch that?

P: Yes, it's quite interesting because they tell you what they're going to say
   in English then the speaker says it in French and you get to know what
   that is. I think they're interesting those programmes on a morning
   'cause they tell you a lot about France and things like that. They say a
   picture's worth a thousand words, a moving picture must be worth
   hundreds of — instead of looking at still photos in a book, black and
   white and things like that. You see people reacting and things like that
   not just faces staying still. Sometimes have video programmes as well at
   school but that's only — we've had two I think since the first year.
   That's when you realise you've got some grasp of French when you
   know what they're saying on the television. It's quite good. (244/28)

The influence of these programmes cannot however be assumed to be automatically positive as the comment on another kind of auxiliary material, the audio-recordings, shows. In this case the pupil was attempting to explain why she is 'not keen on the way the French talk':

> When they speak in French, like all the tapes we have at school, the women are always high pitched and the men are always low pitched and grumpy and they always sound like that, I don't know whether the real French people are like that but it's got a picture in my mind that they are so. (265/18)

Finally, one pupil summed up, unwittingly, the tourist-orientation of the textbook when talking about her family holiday:

P: I'm getting them to read the thing about camping, there's a big unit about that it's going to take the whole family to read that for this year's holiday.

I: From the textbook?

P: Yes. It's a useful textbook really the way they set all of the sort of — they put things you already know in the vocabulary lists just so that you get started and learning more things you don't know, a few words, quite interesting. (244/13)

In one way, of course, her last comment supports the viewpoint taken by the textbook but our textbook analysis in Chapter 5 will show the inadequacy of tourism as a basis for learning.

5 The Effect of French Teaching — Observations in the Classroom

Introduction

This chapter is based on an ethnographic description of foreign language teaching in the two secondary schools. Its focus is the 'cultural' content of foreign language lessons, that is, a study of the knowledge or information about France to which pupils are exposed in the French language classroom and the processes involved. It will be recalled that the research design took into account the assumption that language teaching is only one of many sources and influences. This proved to be the case, as earlier chapters have shown. With respect to language teaching however the research was designed not just to trace and measure the degree and kind of influence involved but also to attempt to establish how that influence operates. This was done in order to provide a basis for applications of the research. For whatever the nature of classroom influence and its relationship to extramural sources of influence, classroom processes are more susceptible of change — in a relatively controlled environment — than are the 'background' processes in the family, the media and the non-school environment in general. Having said this, we do not underestimate either the problems of changing classroom processes nor the prior problems of analysing those processes as they exist at present. Our focus on what many teachers perceive as incidental to their main concern with *language* teaching, may well lead to difficulties in innovation procedures for changes in classroom processes. One of the purposes of producing a book for practising teachers as a companion to this present volume is to prepare the ground for innovation. The second problem is of more immediate import. The lack of previous empirical research which is both classroom-based and concerned with cultural knowledge meant that we had to develop our own approach, and it is to this issue that we turn first.

Research in the foreign language classroom

Much foreign language classroom research has been undertaken with the eventual aim of describing the most effective ways of teaching foreign languages, as Allwright (1988) has recently shown in his review. Mitchell (1985) reviews what she calls 'process research' in foreign language classes by making the distinction between 'global' and 'single issue' research studies. Global studies have attempted to describe, usually through systematic observation, interaction in the foreign language class. A recent example of this, particularly relevant because of its focus on British secondary schools, is Sanderson's (1982) attempt to characterise good foreign language teaching. The limitations of this kind of approach stem from its imposition of a structure upon observations from the outset; it can only verify or quantify what the reseacher already thinks may be the case. Sanderson, for example, stated that a number of features of classroom life were deemed important but the method of research meant a selection had to be made and even those features selected were researched very briefly. One of the features used in his scheme for observing classes was 'relates language to target culture'. Such a feature is clearly of interest in our research, but a quantification of the feature cannot explain how or where the relationship occurs, which is a much more fundamental and interesting issue. In recognition of the complexity of the foreign language class many researchers, says Mitchell, have focused upon single issues in the hope that eventually a full and indepth picture will result. However the issues investigated to date have tended to be specifically concerned with the teaching of *language*; for example, how errors are handled, how teachers talk to pupils and teachers' use of the native and foreign language in the class. We have found no study focusing upon talk about other cultures.

The use of qualitative ethnographic techniques to study language teaching has been a relatively recent development. Allwright (1988: 171–94) describes 'the "conversation analysis" perspective' as beginning in the early 1980s but the work he cites is again focused on *language* learning rather than culture. We do not of course imply by this that there is no link between the two, as we shall point out below, but the lack of concern with that link and the exclusive focus on linguistic issues means that this earlier work is of little help to us.

We decided therefore to develop our own approach to the teaching of French in the two schools following basic ethnographic principles of observation. One important aspect of this is that analytic categories arise out of the observations and fieldnotes rather than being imposed in advance. One reason for our choice was that the analysis of the 'cultural content' of lessons might be carried out using similar procedures to those appropriate to analysis of the foreign culture itself; the ethnographic analysis of cultures in the social anthropological tradition might provide a useful analogy. There was a second reason too. The close conceptual and practical links between teaching language and teaching culture — despite teachers' perceptions of a distinction between 'language' and 'background' studies — required the sensitivity to detail and interpretative power of qualitative analysis. An approach which, for example, relied on pre-determined categories of 'culture teaching' would not do full justice to the relationship between language and culture and hence between language teaching and culture teaching.

Data Collection

There were two broad initial aims for the ethnography:

— To describe the culture-content of foreign language lessons, that is the nature of the information about France to which pupils were exposed. It was intended to compare this account with an account of what pupils know about France, derived from interviews, and thus begin to analyse the contribution of teaching in comparison with other sources of information.
— To characterise different teachers in terms of their culture-teaching 'style'. This might allow us to describe a relationship between specific teaching styles and pupils' perceptions or images of another culture. It might then form the basis of proposals for change in teaching processes since it is more effective to modify existing practices and perceptions than to introduce and attempt to impose new proposals without taking account of current procedures and purposes.

In fine, the aims of the classroom-based research were exploratory and descriptive. A method of enquiry was therefore chosen which would allow the researcher to observe different kinds of teaching as far as possible without preconceptions, and to describe them while taking for granted as little as possible. The aim was to produce a holistic account of the situations observed. Observations were guided only by the working hypothesis that the cultural content and mode of its delivery would be worthy of observation. The aims listed below are those arising during the process of observation and refer not to that process but to the ethnographic description which was its outcome:

1. To describe the nature of the cultural information expressed in the classroom and the range of situations and methods of expression.

2. To differentiate between one teacher and class (style) and another in terms of (1), and more general characteristics which may contribute to (1), e.g. teachers' perceptions of the class, or class characteristics.
3. To produce a typology of teaching styles with reference to cultural content.

With respect to the first aim listed, it quickly became apparent that foreign language teaching in the two schools was structured by the use of a textbook, the same in both cases. This provided a degree of conformity in the cultural content of lessons. Information about France was almost exclusively derived from *Action! Graded French* (Buckby, 1980, 1981, 1983) or in response to information in the textbook. Thus descriptions of the cultural information to which pupils were exposed are a combination of textbook analysis of information covered by each class, and additional information individual teachers introduced.

Although the explicit contributions of pupils to the culture content of lessons was considered potentially significant at the outset, in reality pupil contributions very rarely extend beyond a question to the teacher about an aspect of French life.

As a consequence the ethnographic study comprises three dimensions: observation — including audio-recording — of classes, analysis of the textbook, and interviews with language teachers. The latter were supplemented by many informal discussions with teachers before and after classes, and by interviews with other teachers — especially of geography and history — on the nature of their subjects' potential contribution to pupils' knowledge of France and French culture. Since the focus of this project was upon the cultural studies included in foreign language teaching, the numerous dimensions of classroom activity which would have to be included in order to provide a whole account had to be 'bracketed out', i.e. they are recognised as present but put to one side. In this respect we follow the trend described by Mitchell in her review referred to above.

Fieldwork

Fieldwork was undertaken in the two comprehensive schools over a period of ten months. Observations of teaching were conducted during eight months, whilst two months were spent in interviewing teachers, collecting information about the schools and language departments and analysing syllabuses and textbooks.

During the first months of fieldwork, first, second and third year classes were observed at all achievement levels (sets) and with seven different language teachers. Initially it was hoped that this would provide an account of the previous experience of the third year cohort who were the focus of the study. Eventually it was decided that since different 'styles' of teaching depend on the particular combination of a teacher and a class, it would not be possible to 'reconstitute' the history of the third year in any useful fashion. It was decided therefore to concentrate on teaching currently experienced by the third year cohort. Even so, some classes were not accessible, either because the teacher was not prepared to have the researcher observe that particular class, or because two potentially interesting classes were being taught at the same time, sometimes in two different locations. Ultimately, after two or three months, four classes were chosen for observation over a long period; these became the case studies.

A considerable number of lessons were observed, varying from 9 to 15 lessons a week depending on the stage of the fieldwork. Table 5.1 summarises the extent of observation of third year case-study classes.The researcher sat at the back or side of the class and took notes. In some cases teachers were persuaded to allow audio-recording of their lessons. The researcher then talked informally to teachers after lessons, although this was often difficult as teachers often had to hurry to another class directly after the observed lesson. The information gleaned on these occasions was then supplemented by pre-arranged semi-structured interviews with every teacher — those in the case studies and others — after the observation period was complete. These interviews were recorded and transcribed.

TABLE 5.1 *Lessons observed in case-study classes*

School/class	No.	Period
Newfarm		
Class 1	22	4.9.85–23.4.85
Class 2	19	10.9.85–23.4.86
Hillside		
Class 3	19	12.11.85–22.4.86
Class 4	21	28.11.85–25.4.86

Defining concepts and establishing definitions

As the classroom observation was to describe what contribution to pupils' knowledge of France is made by exposure to French teaching, the first question raised was what is to count as knowledge about France and French people. In the design and analysis of interviews with pupils, this was operationalised in terms of themes about which pupils were asked to give accounts. In preparation for the classroom observation aspect of the project we also considered the main characteristics of anthropological definitions of culture, that it is:

— shared common knowledge among a given group of people
— acquired and not inherited; neither is it a static body of knowledge to be acquired as a whole but it is always changing and developing
— recipe knowledge; that is, knowledge used to interpret experience and inform a social behaviour.

For two reasons, a definition of this order was not suitable for the classroom observations. Firstly, for the day to day research a more concrete operationalisation was needed as it was the manifestations of culture as they appear in the classroom with which we were concerned. Secondly, we were concerned not only with the definition of culture as 'knowing how' but also with 'knowledge that', about France and the French people, including its geography and art for example, as well as its social institutions. What was central to the observational study was the definition implicit in language teaching. Indeed it was part of the purpose of the observational study to elucidate that implicit definition. It appears that, in the elementary and intermediate stages of language learning with which we are concerned, culture is defined as information which is additional or 'background' to linguistic knowledge and skills and with special attention given to knowledge and behaviour required to use the language learnt in a culturally specific and appropriate manner.

Thus the working definition of cultural knowledge in the classroom was a very open one: information expressed verbally or otherwise, explicitly or implicitly, about France or the French people, as indicated in Figure 5.1. Our distinction between explicit and implicit information is not however as clear-cut as Figure 5.1 might suggest. Some information is explicitly presented as information, for example a teacher talking about the French school day. Other information is less obviously stated as such but is embedded in other classroom talk or experience. For example, cultural information may be implicit in a linguistic expression, but the focus of pupil and teacher attention is on an aspect of grammar. The distinction between

Information

	verbal	material
Explicit	A	C
Implicit	B	D

FIGURE 5.1 *A working definition of culture in the classroom*

information expressed verbally and that expressed in other ways, which we shall call 'material', is more evident. 'Materially' expressed information is present for example in textbook pictures or cultural artefacts introduced into the classroom by the teacher.

Examples of the four resulting contingencies might be:

(a) *Explicit-verbal*: any talk or text about France or the French way of life which is the focus of the lesson at a particular time.

(b) *Implicit-verbal*: repeated use of culture-specific words in language exercises, reinforcing the words and their attendant images.

(c) *Explicit-material*: exposure to pictures of France or items from France which are central to the lesson and to which pupils' attention is drawn.

(d) *Implicit-material*: exposure to pictures of or items from France, used for language-focused activity.

Another very important kind of implicit information — which we have also noted in pupil interviews — is the assumption that in some ways France or French people are the same as England or the English because no distinction or direct comparison is made. In a situation where the two cultures are constantly being compared and contrasted, what is not said is as significant as what is. For example, the implication of talking about the French schooling system very briefly and not mentioning the system of discipline may lead the class to assume it is probably no different to their own. Similarly the direct comparison of vocabularies can lead to assumptions about the similarity of the referents in the two cultures. There is evidence that this is the case from interviews with pupils who, when asked about an aspect of French life not well known to them but which had none the less been mentioned in class, would assume that it is 'the same really'.

In short, in observing the classes our purpose was to note and describe anything to which the classes were exposed which could contribute to an image of France or the French people being either the same as or different to English people.

Data Analysis

Analysing observations

The analysis of fieldnotes and audio-recordings was carried out by hand, although we did experiment with computer-aided analysis using a text-analysis program. The procedure was that commonly used in qualitative research: themes and topics were identified from the data as a consequence of repeated close reading during and after the period of observation. An 'etic' level of analysis and description will be provided below in the form of accounts of the principal characteristics of the four case-study classes. At this level the purpose is to describe the teaching procedures observed and illustrate them with extracts from the fieldnotes. We shall however also link these accounts with analysis of interviews with the four teachers and in so doing begin to move the perspective to the 'emic' level, i.e. to consider the characteristics of the teaching process from the viewpoint of those engaged in it.

The next stage of our analysis relates the specific characteristics of the four case-studies within an overall abstract system. That system comprises a number of 'emic' features of the culture teaching observed. The aim is to establish a means of characterising a specific teaching approach in terms of the system comprising the features. At the moment these features, arising as they do from specific cases, are a means of generalising the analysis across the four cases. We do not claim that the system is valid beyond the four cases, although it would of course be interesting to test their wider validity and potential use as a basis for analysis of other teaching approaches.

Analysing the textbook

It was evident from the early stage of observations that the textbook plays an important role in determining the nature of the cultural information presented in the classroom. Furthermore, as pointed out above, it happened that as a consequence of LEA policy the same textbook was used in both secondary schools in the study. This provided some common ground useful in the ultimate analysis. On the other hand the precise nature of the impact of the textbook might have become even more evident had there been two different books to serve as a contrast between schools or classes.

Various ways of approaching the textbook were considered and it is clear that a straightforward content analysis of the textbook associated with Holsti (1969) and Berelson (1971), and with a strong tradition in social research, would be useful for identifying dominant themes and characters in the textbook. However it would fail to convey the textbook image in a holistic way and the combination of traditional content analysis and a literary approach was developed.

Holsti and Berelson describe the process of content analysis as 'any technique for making references by objectifying and systematically identifying characteristics of messages'. Usually, a sample of the items to be studied is taken, and categories of interest are formulated, indicators of these categories are then identified and it is these (which may in fact be the same as the categories) which are described and quantified. The precise method largely depends upon the research interest and can range from the counting of specific words, to a less rigid description based on a general reading. Kirschner (1972), for example, uses a three-fold approach to textbook analysis identifying the topic (role of females) in the contents list of each textbook. This gives a very general impression of the importance of the topic in the book and highlights the important issue of not only quantity of material on the subject under consideration but also its presentation. A topic which is included in the contents list, and presented as a chapter, is almost certainly going to be of importance in the text.

Risager (1986 and 1987) proposes an approach which has been developed particularly for the analysis of foreign language textbooks. Her criteria are expressed in terms of 'realism' by which she refers not simply to accuracy and comprehensive coverage in the depiction of the foreign culture in textbooks but, more importantly, to the degree to which the reader may perceive and accept the image presented — no matter how complete or partial — as being realistic. Thus Risager combines a descriptive and evaluative approach, since the requirement of 'realism' implies a specific philosophy of the purpose of language teaching, to the effect that it shall provide the opportunity for social criticism.

Our approach will combine 'content analysis' with Risager's approach. The first stage is to provide a descriptive account, based on a systematic reading of the three volumes of the textbook and some quantification of content, in order to highlight the major themes. By developing an analytic scheme from the textbook, rather than imposing one upon it, we shall describe the overall image in the textbook. The second stage involves the evaluative element. The image presented will be considered against the criteria implicit in the textbook writer's stated aims and, secondly, in the light of the criteria for realism suggested by Risager.

Language Teaching in Two Secondary Schools

The schools and their language departments

There are a number of physical differences between the two schools ('Hillside' and 'Newfarm' are pseudonyms) which also suggest differences of ethos.

Hillside is a large school with about 1,050 pupils which includes a sixth form and is situated in the centre of a small industrial town. The school is an amalgamation of grammar and secondary modern schools and is as a consequence located on two sites about half a mile apart. The lower school, previously the secondary modern, houses the first and second years and is the smaller, more pleasant, of the two buildings. The upper school previously the grammar school, is an older building, more imposing and impersonal in style but quite well maintained. Thus our cohort of third year pupils had just moved to the upper school. Teachers at Hillside, although having their own rooms for French, did not necessarily teach all their French classes there. For example, two teachers had their own rooms in the lower school which meant their teaching in the upper school was in other, general purpose classrooms. This has implications for organisation and planning of lessons and the extent to which the teacher can influence the surroundings in which she or he teaches the subject. There is then little sense of a 'language department' in a physical location in the upper school. There is also a degree of flux in the composition of the department, which comprises four main language teachers and one helping out from the English department. The bulk of the language teaching is in fact done by just three of the teachers. In short Hillside, and particularly the upper school, has a detached, impersonal and more traditional atmosphere which contrasts with the smaller and newer school, Newfarm.

Newfarm is a small, friendly school with about 550 pupils, with no sixth form; it is situated on the edge of a new town. Its buildings are modern, purpose-built, bright and well maintained. The school has a good reputation in the area. The language department at Newfarm consists of only two teachers, a head and one other, each with their own adjacent rooms which physically constitute the language department. The teaching is fairly equally balanced between the two and both teach French and German, and no other subjects. Newfarm has, as a consequence of its size and situation, a friendly and individual character.

Characteristics common to language teaching in the two schools

Teaching style is complex and difficult to define. No two teachers or teaching situations are exactly the same. The styles described below are all very different and those features which most clearly differentiate teacher styles in relation to cultural studies are described later. However a number of more general characteristics which relate to the nature of foreign language teaching are common to all the teachers in the study and may also be shared by many others. This section describes the shared view teachers have about cultural studies and foreign language teaching. It also gives some insight into the experience of France on which they seem to base much of their cultural studies teaching.

In contrast to the different styles of teaching there are common views expressed by teachers concerning the role and importance of cultural studies in foreign language teaching. The teachers in both schools were all very clear about the importance of including cultural information in their language teaching and regarded recent moves in this direction in language teaching in general as positive. There are broadly two justifications teachers gave for including cultural information. The first relates to pupils' development as human and social beings: the importance of learning about ways of living other than their own to promote tolerance and a less restricted view of life. The second is linked with the management of the lesson and maintaining children's interest in the language. Teachers in the study generally expressed both but with different emphasis.

The question which immediately arises is of course to what extent their views — and their practices described below — are 'representative'. There are two kinds of representativeness involved: 'representative' of those teachers' usual beliefs and practices when not involved in a research project whose general focus they knew, and 'representative' of other teachers in the profession in general. It is of course possible, and even likely, that the 'Hawthorne effect' was in operation in this situation as in many others. In one sense this does not matter, for it is the practices as observed in the particular year of the research which we wish to link with the particular views and effects noted among pupils in that same year.

Even if these are not fully representative they provide a basis for analysis of the relationship between teaching and pupils' views. It is however unlikely that, whatever views were expressed by the teachers, they could or would maintain inhabitual practices over a long period — a school year — during which they were being observed. This is the advantage of indepth observation and qualitative analysis. As to the degree to which they represent the profession as a whole, the absence of other observational studies focusing on the teaching of culture means that there is no basis for discussion of practices. However, as we shall see below, teachers in our study expressed a strong commitment to the value of teaching culture. In another study it was found that of 59 teachers in Scotland interviewed about their teaching practices and beliefs only one fifth mentioned 'the development of cross-cultural knowledge and understanding' as one of their objectives in language teaching (Mitchell, 1988: 21).

By contrast teachers in the present study frequently talked about the importance of cultural information for widening children's horizons or reducing their prejudices. This view is, however, premised upon several others: for example on the view that the children in their language classes are not already open-minded and well informed, and that this situation can be remedied by filling the information gap. Teachers did generally describe their pupils as being poorly informed and in many cases prejudiced. One teacher said:

> They haven't any idea at all. They think the French eat frogs and snails all day. They honestly do. They think the Germans are Nazis and run about in uniforms giving Hitler salutes because they got it off comics. They don't associate them with any human qualities whatsoever and it all has to be knocked out of them. They really have enormous prejudices against French and German people.

Another teacher echoing the general view said:

> Children are very quick to say 'that is stupid' but you have got to try to explain to them that a French person may find what we do stupid and it is just a difference and not necessarily an inferiority.

Thus generally teachers believed their pupils have a limited and false view of other cultures. Various explanations for this were suggested: the media (TV, comics and papers) and older relatives who perpetuated the propaganda of their time. Some teachers also seemed to believe the particular areas in which their children lived added to the problem. One expressed this view, and the importance therefore of talking about other cultures, very clearly:

You have to try to get across to them that you are dealing with human beings and that they are just human beings in a different way of life and in fact quite a lot of things that the kids find odd or difficult are the things that are not really linguistic but cultural and you have to explain it is a way of life that you are dealing with and it isn't just that the language is different but they have a whole different history and background and upbringing which I think is as useful as anything to teach to, what, 50% of these kids who are never really going to make useful language. But if they can come out at the end of it with a sort of tolerance towards foreigners in general without actually thinking that because they are foreigners doesn't mean they are horrible, you have probably achieved something. Regrettably I doubt we are doing much because there is such an ingrained intolerance of foreigners in this area. I mean I think the idea is certainly true we ought to be teaching them to accept that people are different and not everybody is born and brought up in — well even Hillside. I mean some of them would probably think it was foreign to come from Birmingham or London . .

and later:

I'm sure teaching French to kids in Kent with day trips to Calais or Boulogne must be a totally different experience. I mean some of them if they want to, can go to Dover and look at the damn place. You know for these kids it could be a million miles away.

Although there is an assumption that informing pupils about or giving them experience of other peoples can potentially change their view, this teacher and others were cautious about any significant changes.

A second justification is probably easier for teachers to measure and relates more specifically to the language lessons. This is the view that cultural information contributes to language learning by capturing pupils' interest, contextualising language learning or filling the lesson when children are felt to have exhausted their language learning potential for that occasion:

I think the difficulty is they can't see a purpose in French, living here in Hillside. I have got to give them an example of a situation where it is going to have a use.

This particular view suggests a specific functional type of information as the following quotation from a different teacher shows:

. . . There are not very many of the children in the school who will take a language as an academic subject when you think about it. They will

probably need it for when they are going on holiday and I think that is
the sort of think you should aim for really. Being able to go into a
shop, being able to book into a youth hostel or hotel, or campsite.
Things like that . . . once that they have the basis of that then you
might get children wanting to know more.

However, not all the teachers took such a functional view but still
believed this cultural 'background' to be important. The following teacher
takes a broader view:

You can't have French language without there being a culture
attached to it. Without there being a country where it is spoken,
otherwise you would just be learning French in a vacuum and I think
that is what a lot of people have done in the past — just learnt French
in a vacuum. I think I did. I hadn't the foggiest idea what France was
actually like even though I was quite good at French verbs. I think if
you can tie the two together and bring some sort of meaning to what
you are doing then, in theory anyway, they will get a lot more out of it.

This teacher makes explicit what others imply when talking about
culture in language teaching: that the two are linked; that the language
class is an appropriate place in which to talk about the culture. The
language becomes meaningful in its culture. However there is also the issue
of culture being of interest to children — for some children more interesting than the language. Teachers believed children in lower ability groups
are more interested in the culture than the language (in some cases because
the language becomes too difficult). Teachers were not however in agreement as to whether lower or higher ability children were more interested in
general. Some teachers found higher ability children most interested
although inclined to worry about the language and they believe this is
because pupils are aware that ultimately they will be tested in linguistic
ability. One teacher identified different kinds of interests between the
ability groups, the high ability groups being more interested in general
customs, the lower in information directly relevant to them and their
particular needs. Despite these differences there is a shared view that
ability influences a pupil's interest but in general all children are interested
in learning about other cultures to some extent. This can be used to
improve their language learning or increase their interest in the lesson
more generally:

. . . Even in the difficult classes, if you start and talk about something
that is relevant to their lives that they do in France or Germany which
is different, especially if you talk about schools, they really like to
listen to the differences in schools and school day.

Although pupils are interested in other cultures some teachers said that it was generally 'snippets' of information which occurred naturally in the course of the lesson. There was a view that lengthy prepared material about French culture would fail to maintain pupil interest. Teachers either prepared very little cultural information or more commonly not at all:

> I don't prepare any cultural information at all because I think if I went and said, right we are going to talk about schools in Germany today or the schools in France, I think they would just start talking amongst themselves and maybe catch half of it, but if you come across it, especially say come across it in a book, and you say 'Ah, yes but you see the French have 2 hours for lunch' Ah, but why? You see they all start to talk and I say 'Oh, yes, they get this three course meal for dinner' — this sort of thing, 'And all the bread is free' — they latch on to that. 'You help yourself.' They love that, they'll listen to that but that is enough. Just tell them about that then go on with the rest of the lesson and if something else crops up — it's bitty but they build up their own picture.

Only one was observed to have organised cultural information to any extent, other than what was in the textbook. She talked about the time taken to prepare authentic materials and how this made their use in a large number of lessons impossible.

The lack of planning means that classroom information is opportunist, arising out of a section in the textbook or a pupil question for example. Teachers believed however this approach is most useful, not only because children prefer it but because it is the general view which is more important, rather than any specific information. Teachers were asked whether there was a core of information they tried to teach. Their response was generally similar to the following:

> I wouldn't say there is a core of information. I think the most important information is that which appears naturally in the course of what you are doing. I don't think you should really or can really say suddenly 'Right we are now going to have a lesson on what the French do at Christmas', say, or what the French family life is like. I think it emerges as you teach. If you are talking about staying in a youth hostel or staying in a hotel in France then the system emerges during the course of the teaching because then they can tie the two together and they can see well yes — that is how the French do it — that is how we do it . . . I think the things have to be tied together and you wouldn't just separate them out.

Returning to the problem of pupil ethnocentricity another said:

I think it is more a case of whenever you get any signs coming through of these irrational prejudices you try to suggest tolerance to them to discuss the difference from a Frenchman's point of view if you like.

It was mentioned above that teachers were cautious about the influence they had on their pupils' perceptions. Perhaps one reason for this is that they are aware of limitations the classroom places upon them. Teachers felt that the most influential factor in influencing a pupil's view would be direct experience of another culture by visit or exchange. This made the country more real to them and increased their interest. The substitute for real experience is second-hand experience and again teachers had found that classes enjoyed hearing about France from someone who had actually been there:

> . . . it makes it a little bit more interesting for them rather than taken out of textbooks. Like this (far) away never never land that they never go to.

A number of teachers made this comparison between the textbook and their own reports. Another said:

> . . . any textbook is really by nature limited in what it can tell you about France. You can't really put over the feeling of France in a book. Pictures help and letters and descriptions and tape recordings and things like that all help but I think it depends an awful lot on the teacher as well, to sort of add extra bits and talk about their own experiences. Children like to actually see someone in the flesh who has actually been there.

Given the general recognition of the significance of information and knowledge of France, teachers were asked about their own experience of the country, on the assumption that this is a significant source of their own knowledge. It is this 'stock of knowledge' upon which they draw to complement or criticise information given in the textbook. All six teachers teaching the third year French classes were interviewed. It transpired that although some teachers had visited France very many more times than others, the teachers' experiences of France were very similar in kind. Their experience was very much centred on visits to or work in French schools or, secondly, brief holidays in France. Usually it was a combination of the two. There are however variations between teachers within this commonality of experience which are reflected in their teaching styles. The parameters are the extent of their contact with France, length of their stays, and whether they studied for French degrees. It is interesting that of the four case-study teachers only one graduated in French.

Another feature which the two schools and their teachers have in common, and which is of significant influence upon 'teaching style' is the textbook they have chosen to follow. This is the *Action! Graded French* course (Buckby, 1980, 1981, 1983) which was designed to be taught in the new 'communicative' approach to language learning and has a clear emphasis upon preparing pupils for holidays in France. The choice of textbook is perhaps more significant in language teaching than in any other school subject. Even the most creative of teachers in our study charted a course through the series of textbooks topic by topic. At the very least it provides a strong core around which he or she builds lessons. Very few of the lessons observed were conducted without opening the textbook and many lessons consisted of a series of exercises from it. The fact that all the teachers used these books therefore suggests a certain similarity of lesson content as far as knowledge of French culture — and language — is concerned. The textbook provides an overall structure to the information children receive about the language and culture. These common features are then modified by a degree of 'unstructured' information to which pupils are exposed over and above the textbook content or from another part of the textbook, an earlier part of the course.

It has been implied in our discussion that the flow of information is in one direction — from teacher to pupil. Another common factor in the teaching observed was that this is indeed how lessons were conducted. It is plausible that some of the pupils in the study had more direct experience or knowledge of the French way of life, history or geography than some of the teachers. However, pupil talk about France was noticeable by its absence. Pupils did not contribute to the cultural knowledge with personal experience but tended to recall cultural knowledge from their earlier language learning. It was not within the scope of this project but further research might explore whether the constraints of the lessons mean that pupils have little or no opportunity to talk; see for example the work of Edwards & Westgate (1987) or Mehan (1979) who explore the structuring process of classroom interaction.

Finally, we should mention another kind of common factor in the teaching in the two schools: the 'external' influences of changes in language teaching taking place in Britain as a whole. The research was carried out at a period when the schools were preparing for implementation of a new public examination — the General Certificate of Secondary Education. This is taken by pupils at the end of the fifth year if they opt to continue language learning beyond the third year. This examination is, for the prsent, the culmination of major revisions of syllabus and teaching methods locally and nationally. The adoption of *Action! Graded French* had been a symptom of the acceptance of these changes in both schools. It could however be argued that at the period of research the schools were still in the midst of change and this too has implications for the generalisability of the study. On the other hand the significance of the study against the background of debate outlined in Chapter 1 is all the greater because the schools in question were affected by the general change and the move towards new interpretations of the nature and purpose of foreign language teaching.

History and geography

Although it is possible that any number of school experiences, including other subject lessons, could influence pupils' perceptions of other cultures it was not possible to be exhaustive in the investigation. The research was concerned with cultural information in language teaching and this could stand on its own. However the syllabuses of Geography and History courses in the first three years in each school were discussed with the respective heads of departments.

The geography of France was not studied at all in 1st, 2nd or 3rd year at Hillside school although in the first two years there may have been a brief mention of EEC countries (1st year) and French colonies (2nd year). A 'regional approach' was adopted to Geography but France was not included. Children opting to study Geography in 4th and 5th year would study France.

At Newfarm, France was not studied in the first two years but in Year 3, three to four weeks were spent studying Europe and France in particular. This included physical maps and focus upon Paris, Marseilles and two inland waterways. This was taught to all achievement levels (sets) although the textbooks used varied and upper sets studied in more detail. This suggests that by the end of their third year, classes at Newfarm had some formal geographical information about France in addition to that learned in French lessons whereas at Hillside they did not.

Turning now to History, it was reported that the French Revolution figures prominently in the syllabuses of both schools. All pupils learnt about it in their third year, apart from low achievement sets at Newfarm. The low achievement pupils instead learnt about Wolfe, Clive and Florence Nightingale. Previous experience had taught the head of history at Newfarm that lower streams find the Revolution too difficult. At Newfarm, those who studied the French Revolution spent about half a term on it, and also studied the Russian Revolution. At Hillside pupils studied the conflict between France and Britain in the eighteenth century (Wolfe and Clive) and the French revolution, spending less time on each. Both schools had some textbooks in common but also used others. All children learnt about the first and second world wars which involved some information about the role of France and included some mapwork. In addition to this there are various brief references to France and the French throughout the history courses of both schools although nothing in detail.

Although only the syllabuses of Geography and History courses were studied, it is likely that, as in French teaching, the individual styles of the teachers, and the characters of the classes will influence the lesson content and form, thus the account given here is limited and relates only to reported information and resources.

Analysis of the Textbook

An overview of content

It is important to remember in the analysis of any text the specific function(s) it was designed to perform, and the audience for which it is intended (Holsti, 1969). The *Action!* textbooks are specifically intended for the teaching of French language, in a classroom context, to 11–16 year olds. In addition, the author states they are intended,

> To develop an understanding of, and to foster positive attitudes towards, countries where French is spoken and to speakers of French (Buckby, 1980: 3)

In this analysis we shall only be concerned with Books 1 to 3 since those are the ones used with the classes and pupils under study. It might be argued that this does a disservice to the textbook because the total image is presented in five books. The fact remains however that for most of the pupils studied here — and in general throughout English schools — the 'total' is reached after three years when they opt out of French classes.

Action! embodies the new 'communicative' approach to language teaching and as such emphasises the learning of the language for clearly defined purposes. These are outlined in the general objectives for the textbook. The communicative approach, together with Buckby's commitment to fostering positive attitudes towards the French, have very definite implications for the image of France portrayed. Buckby hopes to equip children with the necessary knowledge to be able to visit France with a school or his/her family. This knowledge consists of language and skills for coping with situations likely to arise during a visit, ranging from finding a place to stay to coping with a breakdown in the car. Such situations can be seen in the selection of geographic location, characters and situations, and also in the general presentation.

The presentation of information in *Action!* takes several forms:

— black and white photographs of people, places or items from France
— simple sketches, drawings and cartoons varying from small cartoons to maps and drawings of items for language exercises
— English (or French in Book 3) text presented as factual, or as talk by characters in the book. This can cover several pages or a few lines and includes geographical, historical and cultural (customs and habits) information. It also ranges from personal descriptions by characters used in the textbook to more general impersonal accounts.

Each textbook is divided into a number of units — each addressing a different aspect of French life. As Kirschner (1972) states, the way in which an author organises the textbook into chapters and the content of each chapter illustrates his or her priorities, what he or she sees as the important subject-areas to cover. The *Action!* textbooks are divided into situations in which a pupil could find him or herself on a visit, such as ordering a meal, asking the way, or introducing him or herself to a family. This is particularly clear in the units devoted to French food of which there are 11 — the greatest number on any one theme. The first mention of food is in Book 1 where there are six units devoted to buying or ordering and paying for food in either a café or a shop. The range of foods is at this stage quite limited, in keeping with the café situation. In Book 2 the range of foods is widened and the situations are in the home. In Book 3, food is presented in a restaurant in keeping with the focus of Book 3 on Paris.

Thus the situation and general content of *Action!* dictate the content of more specific cultural information. Books 1 and 2 vary from Book 3 not only in that the location changes from Boulogne to Paris but in their more general presentation. Whereas in Books 1 and 2 two children living in France give a personal insight into French lifestyle, albeit briefly, in Book 3 the commentary is on the whole anonymous and detached, much more the outsider's view.

Themes in *Action*!

Analysis by theme is the most appropriate means of analysis of the text since Buckby's approach in *Action*! is a thematic one. Throughout the books specific problems of a visit to France are addressed ranging from asking directions to finding a place to stay and booking in. Each problem is addressed by providing the relevant vocabulary and phrases and brief information about the theme in general and specific situations which could arise. This creates a feeling that the visit is 'problematic', consisting of a number of difficulties to be overcome.

The main themes can be described as:

(a) Geographical and historical information (including the weather and weather maps)
(b) People and interactions (French people, including famous French people; the French family; appearance; clothing; talking about oneself; greeting others)
(c) Food and eating (at home, in cafés and in restaurants)
(d) Using services (travel, public transport and other communications)
(e) Leisure (including places to stay on holiday and leisure activities)

Minor themes:
(f) Housing
(g) Schooling.

The division between main and minor themes in the textbook is a quantitative one. 'Housing' and 'schooling' are confined to two units whereas main themes have six or more units devoted to them. The themes are not always mutually exclusive, e.g. 'buying clothes' involves 'personal information' and 'shopping' and may also be sub-divided by locations and activities. 'Using services' has a situational dimension, e.g. a café, and an activities dimension, e.g. playing pinball.

The themes can also be sub-divided according to the way in which they appear in the book. Themes other than 'people and interaction', and 'geographical and historical information' tend to be confined to specifically allocated units, which can all be described as relating to contemporary French society and are of an instrumental nature. The first two themes also have units allocated to them but are also present in a more pervasive way. Finally, an image of French people in particular is formed throughout the book as a consequence of the pictures which accompany many different themes and of the language exercises which also have an implicit message about French people.

Let us consider each theme and its main content in turn.

(a) Geographical and historical information

Most of the geographical and historical information in the textbook is provided in the context of Boulogne in Books 1 and 2, and Paris in Book 3. These locations are described in some depth and dominate the view given of France; they also have implications for the textbook content as a whole, to be described later. The two locations are presented as interesting places to visit. There are two densely presented pages on 'Boulogne-sur-mer' near the beginning of Book 2 and then various references to and pictures of the town throughout Books 1 and 2. Paris is presented in Book 3 quite extensively, from a visitor's point of view, through four sections called 'Paris Touristique'. These take the form of description of a guided coach tour around Paris, highlighting famous sights and including some historical information about each. These pages are set apart from the rest of the text, as they are presented on a different colour paper and constitute the major source of historical and geographical information.

Before the introduction to France however, the first part of Book 1 is set in French-speaking Canada, with the emphasis upon people and interaction rather than geographical and historical issues. Also at the beginning of Book 1 other French-speaking countries are introduced very briefly. The geography of France as a whole is briefly covered in units about travel in France and the weather. Other than the pages of tourist information mentioned above, there is very little historical information about France; the emphasis of the book is a contemporary one. Thus most of the historical information relates either to Paris or to famous French people, treated in the next section.

Finally there is the question of the implicit image of France present where the main emphasis is in fact on other matters. Throughout the books language exercises are illustrated with pictures of existing places or buildings in France, but largely linked to the locations already mentioned. In short, the textbook does not present France as a country, but rather two cities, Boulogne and Paris. This means that the dominant image is northern, urban and touristic.

(b) People and interactions

French people are all presented positively, as attractive, smiling and helpful. They can be divided into several groups:

— central characters (Books 1 and 2 only)

— minor characters
— officials
— famous people
— passers-by or 'extras'

Central characters: In Book 1 we are introduced to Jean and Catherine Lavigne who travel from Quebec to Boulogne and introduce us to friends, family, French customs and to parts of Boulogne. They are used throughout Books 1 and 2 but not in Book 3 which takes a more anonymous approach. It is through these characters then that an image of France seen from the viewpoint of young people is portrayed.

Minor characters: With the exceptions of brief introductions to parents and grandparents the minor characters in all three books are young people around 11–16 — although slightly older in Book 3.

Officials: The officials in the textbooks comprise police, traffic wardens, ticket collectors etc. There are many pictures and brief references particularly to the police and apart from central characters they are the most frequently occurring image in the books.

Famous People: Famous people include historical figures (Jeanne d'Arc, Napoleon, Louis XIV), sport and media personalities (Jerome Gallion, Sacha Distel, Sheila), prominent scientists and inventors (Marie Curie, Louis Pasteur, Louis Bleriot), writers (Victor Hugo and Jules Verne) and one political figure, General de Gaulle.

Passers-by/Extras: Other visual images are of incidental characters in photographs, passers-by, shop-keepers, school children.

Most of Book 1 is centred on two issues: the English pupil learning to greet a French-speaking person and ask directions and, secondly, being able to talk about him or herself, family and interests, with special emphasis given to children's pets. The utility of being able to speak in French is also stressed by showing how many countries speak French and the sort of jobs speaking French can lead to. The image which emerges is one of French people being very helpful and friendly. It is also part of this image that people are very polite; they all, even children, shake hands and use the polite form of address — *vous* — to strangers, always saying Mademoiselle, Monsieur or Madame.

The interpersonal interaction in Books 1–3 is on the whole one to one, uninterrupted, successful and unemotional. As an exception to the general tone, the equivalent of one page toward the end of Book 3 (pages 126/7) suggests how to argue, and insult another person's clothing. Interestingly the illustration is a drawing of two boys arguing over a pencil. This is less aggressive in tone than would be the realism of a photograph. The vocabulary has a ratio of 2:5 for insults as opposed to compliments. Otherwise, the lack of any expression of emotion, particularly negative feelings, is a common feature of most textbooks as described by Risager (1986). There are at least two possible outcomes of this. First, there is a general impression gained from the textbook that all French people are placid, unemotional and positively disposed towards each other and strangers. This might lead, secondly, to the impression that the characters are less credible to the reader. This rather bland image of French people counteracts stereotypical views of the French but it is also contrary to common-sense knowledge of people in general. We shall return to this in our discussion of the 'realism' of the textbook below.

The visual effect of the textbook is attractive and it includes many pictures and photographs, largely black and white. However, the use of the latter can have a detrimental effect since the photographs, particularly of people, quickly become out-dated and give an old-fashioned view of France. In addition drawings and cartoons tend towards caricature and are therefore prone to portraying stereotypes.

(c) Food and eating

Food is a dominant theme throughout textbooks 1–3, and units describe buying food and eating in situations ranging from the picnic to the restaurant. There are a total of eleven units where food is the central theme and they include the following titles:

'Going to a café'
'More to eat and drink'
'Buying Food'
'Buying more food'
'Food, glorious food'

There are 76 pages within these eleven units about eating and drinking (not to mention other references throughout the rest of the books), which abound with photos, drawings and menus.

In Book 1 a limited number of foods and drinks are introduced and are generally snacks such as 'frites', croissants or sandwiches, with coca-cola, 'jus d'orange' and so on. This is in keeping with the café setting. There is also a picture and description of 'un croque-monsieur'. In Book 2 the range of food is widened and the situations are in the home. Book 3 describes eating in a restaurant. In Book 2 there is also a historical account of the

Quiche Lorraine, and a map of speciality foods of different regions in France.

Otherwise the emphasis is upon buying and asking for or refusing food politely. There are sections written in an impersonal style in which pupils are encouraged to try French food whenever the occcasion arises. These sections also include attempts to counteract stereotypes by stating, for example, that the French do not eat frogs' legs (and snails) all the time. As a consequence of this and the emphasis on snacks, the food illustrated in *Action*! seems very familiar to the English viewpoint.

(d) Using services

Since the emphasis of the textbook is upon enabling students to visit France, a large proportion of each text is devoted to using a variety of services. These include public transport and other communications, and also shopping, although most of the shopping described relates to food. There are units devoted to travelling by bus, coach and train, sending a telegram and using the post office. In Book 3, there are also three units concerned with driving in France. 'Using services' accounts then for nearly one quarter of all the units in Books 1–3.

Information consists of maps and diagrams, signposts and photographs of the means of transport or communication, tickets and people undertaking journeys or making phone calls. The procedures of undertaking a journey or making a phonecall are described in detail: knowing where to go, what do do, asking for information. It is in this area that the instrumental nature of the information is most obvious. It may be noted in passing that the provision of such detailed information about French services introduces pupils to matters which they have probably not yet met in their own culture.

(e) Leisure

Leisure is another well-represented theme, ranging from camping and youth hostelling in France to watching TV. Also described are various sports, including café-games, more home-based leisure activities such as reading or listening to records, and going to the cinema. Not only is leisure dealt with in specific units but the whole contents of the books, as already stated, are directed towards holiday-making in France. People seen in work situations are almost exclusively in the service industries (transport, shops, hotels). There are three very minor exceptions to this, a picture of a man in a picket line, another clocking-in at work and a woman typing, buried among a number of other pictures (Book 3, p.84). Employment is only very briefly discussed, under 'education', in terms of what children hope to do in adult life.

Minor themes

(f) Housing

Although the emphasis of all three texts is upon visiting rather than residing in France, there is some mention of housing. In Book 2 in the 'Living in France' unit, different types of housing are described in France (including Paris) and in other French-speaking countries (Belgium, West Africa, Switzerland, Canada, Martinique). The main differences expressed are that French people tend to live in flats, often rented and that most houses have 'une cave'. There are a number of photographs of interiors presented in the form of advertisements. In Book 3 (Unit 7: A Mon Avis) there are more advertisements for houses and some discussion of three people's housing needs. Housing is thus represented more as buildings and interiors rather than as homes with people living in them.

(g) Schooling

There are two units in Book 3 which deal with education in France; prior to this schools in France are not mentioned. The first unit looks at French schools and the second puts the English pupil in the position of showing French people around a British school. The emphasis in the second unit is clearly upon language learning. In the first unit the number of years spent at school is compared with other countries. Further to this there is information about the different schools in France, the school week, the daily timetable, the system of discipline, assessment, lessons studied and free time. This unit is probably the most extensive in informational content in any of the three books.

The textbook image

The analysis so far has been largely descriptive using a thematic approach because the textbook itself is structured on themes; the analytic categories were taken from the object of analysis itself. We move now to the question of evaluation. An evaluation has to be related to a particular view of the aims of cultural studies in foreign language teaching and there are many different views, (see Byram, 1989, for an overview). Initially however when the author of a textbook makes his/her own view explicit, it is also possible to evaluate the book according to those criteria and to ask to what extent it fulfils the author's stated intention. Having done this we shall then turn to an approach described briefly above, in which Risager has developed a scheme for the evaluation of foreign language textbooks based on theory of literary realism.

The 'royal visit' image

As we pointed out at the beginning of this analysis, it is the author's stated intention to 'foster positive attitudes towards countries where French is spoken and to speakers of French'. He is not alone in this for he takes this formulation from documents which were to become part of the national criteria for the teaching and assessment of foreign languages. In principle, then, all textbook authors and teachers should pursue this aim, and when we turn below to a more critical evaluation of the textbook it is in the full knowledge that the critique should in some respects be directed more at those documents and their authors rather than at the textbook writers and teachers who comply with national criteria. In accordance with these, the first three books of *Action!* do present a positive image of France and French people. The emphasis is at all times upon being able to enjoy a visit to France and communicate with French people at home or abroad.

The country is presented positively mainly through locating the textbooks in Boulogne and Paris, real places that children may visit, or have heard of, where there is apparently lots to do and see. This place-of-interest view of France is portrayed through descriptions, pictures and characters' accounts. It is supported by the text's concentration upon leisure activities, travel and eating out and is strongest in the third textbook where the image of Paris as a cultural and tourist centre is stressed. The description of Boulogne in Book 2 is similar in that it is presented as a nice place to visit, but there is also brief reference to the town's industry, even though the impression is given that this consists largely of fishing.

The positive view of French people is most strongly portrayed through pictures, throughout all three books, of smiling, attractive people, who are on the whole young. People offer help and directions generously and particularly in Book 1 there is a great deal of hand-shaking and greeting. Any negative aspects of the image are due to the inevitable dating of photographs. A book which relies heavily upon photographs for a dynamic and contemporary approach unfortunately quickly becomes out of date.

In short the image portrayed can be compared to a royal visit. For only a royal visit would run as smoothly, without glimpsing less attractive or more mundane features of French life.

The only exception to this approach is the treatment of French driving. The topic is part of the general tourist orientation and reflects the pre-occupations of French authorities with road accident statistics. On the other hand the topic is dealt with from the viewpoint of the outsider and in a way which reinforces stereotype responses to the ways of another culture. One of the characters, Jean Lavigne, who is an outsider insofar as he has arrived from French-speaking Canada, states:

> While I've been finding my way around Boulogne I've been amazed at the speed of the traffic . . . . There are crossings marked on the roads with white lines, but don't expect the cars to stop for you if you want to stay alive! (Book 1, p. 33)

A development of the concern about motoring in France comes at the end of Book 3, where there is one unit about breaking down in France, and another about a car accident. This is a departure from the general carefree approach to France.

Two other images stand out from the rest of the textbook insofar as they suggest dangers and problems, when seen from an English viewpoint: a poster warning against the danger of importing rabies from abroad takes up a whole page of the book, and, second, there is a repeated image of the policeman carrying a revolver, although it is stated that policemen are generally helpful.

Although the overall image is, we have suggested, unlike any which anyone but royalty might meet, there is an attempt to avoid stereotypes. People are presented as being very similar to people in England and the volume of pictures of 'ordinary'-looking characters outweighs the occasional stereotypes such as Coco — the frog hand puppet — and those to be found in the cartoons (examples Book 1, p. 82; Book 2, p. 49; Book 3, p. 181).

On the author's own criteria, then, the books appear to be satisfactory. The image which is presented is almost entirely positive and it is assumed that this image will also 'foster positive attitudes', although the link between 'positive image' and 'positive attitudes' remains unproven.

The 'real' image

If we turn now to Risager's criteria, it will become evident that her aims in promoting cultural knowledge are not simply instrumental or attitudinal but also encompass socialisation through foreign language learning, a view which we share and develop elsewhere (Byram, 1989). According to Risager, for an accurate view of another culture, positive and negative aspects are important and it is clear that *Action!* emphasises a positive France and neglects negative features. Risager argues that for cultural studies to be realistic, the universe must be:

(a) balanced, comprehensive;
(b) at micro and macro level;
(c) positive and negative.

The requirement of balance and comprehensiveness does however raise difficulties. Since the perceptions of any one person at any one time depend upon their position in society, past experience, and immediate situation, the requirement would be best fulfilled with a number of different perspectives. The degree to which this can be accomplished depends on time and resources available. It is nonetheless possible to require an orientation towards balance in whatever circumstances pertain.

Action! cannot be described as balanced or comprehensive for a number of reasons. These include the age and social identity of the characters predominating in the textbook, and the situations in which we find them. *Action!* does not attempt to be balanced by, for example, presenting a wider age range and different viewpoints from different ages. Nor does it offer any attempt at a comprehensive view, for example by dealing with a range of social classes, ethnic groups or social and cultural institutions. The author's declared aim of preparing for short visits, making contacts and going on holidays and exchanges appears to preclude this.

Another consequence of the tourist orientation is the concentration on peripheral, micro-social events. Since the tourist does not come into contact with the central social institutions of a society, social interaction portrayed in the textbook is in situations which are not part of the French person's own experience of their society. Furthermore, the tourist needs no knowledge of macro-level dimensions of the foreign society, for example of its political or economic structures or of the role of religion in French society, and their effects on the lives of the members of society. The accounts of the industrial structure of Boulogne — the only attempt to include this kind of information — are limited to the presentation of isolated facts and figures which are unrelated to any structural dimensions of French society or to French people's experience of them.

Risager's criteria are essentially a requirement that the textbook or course should be 'realistic'. In a literary sense 'realism' can be defined in terms of authors' portrayal of places, situations and people which are believable because they are recognisable from readers' own experience. The presentation that the textbook gives of France is in this view a question of the presentation of a perspective or section of life which is recognisable as real. The characters must be credible, the places and the institutions must be possible. Even if the requirement of comprehensiveness is relaxed, the account must be true. Literary realism is often a function of the setting of the novel or play. A novel is given a degree of realism by explicit reference to actual places or people, to historical events or institutions. This is the force of setting a language teaching textbook in an existing town and portraying the setting with photographs and as we saw above *Action!* does attempt to provide this kind of realism.

An evaluation according to these criteria can thus accept that there has to be a degree of selective description of France and French people. It has to be nonetheless a description which is true. The selection of people to portray in *Action!* and the nature of the information given fulfil the more instrumental of Buckby's aims: to equip a child to visit France for a holiday or short exchange visit and to encourage positive attitudes. However these aims are not necessarily compatible with the more general aim of promoting understanding of French people. In *Action!* the image of French people is superficial and so positive that it is scarcely credible; we do not get close enough to understand them and there is almost no basis for understanding, such as might be provided by portraying problems and attitudes and the living of everyday life. The superficial portrayal of the people leads to a less than realist image.

However, turning from people to places, the textbook does provide a realist view of two French cities: Paris and Boulogne. The geography is real, the places exist. Photographs of places and items reinforce this. The question of choice of location highlights the issue of places having to be perceived as real and this being at least as important as their actual reality. Paris and Boulogne are probably the two places children are most likely to have heard of and to visit (and of course this can now create an influence in the opposite direction with teachers choosing to visit places that the textbooks present). On the other hand, it is highly debatable whether Paris and Boulogne can be said to represent France as a whole. Thus although there is topographical realism and the use of photographs of actual places and people lends credibility, the selection is unrepresentative, lacking the orientation towards balance and comprehensiveness.

In summary the view of France and its people Buckby has selected is consistent with his approach to language and cultural studies. Judged according to criteria of realism, places and situations are realistic but not representative. The portrayal of people and social interaction is however inadequate. French people in *Action!* are unreal and the opportunity for understanding and a development of pupils' social experience does not exist.

The Case Studies

Having discussed the features common to all the teaching observed — in the background and the textbook — we turn now to individual teachers. As explained above, all the teachers in both schools were observed and interviewed, and their work and views taken into account in this report. Four teachers and four 3rd year classes were then selected for observation as case studies. There follows here a description at the etic level of the four teachers and classes. This will then form the basis of a typology at the emic level described in this chapter and developed in Chapter 6.

Mrs Johnson and class 3 (Hillside School)

Mrs Johnson, unlike the other three teachers in the study, did not train as a languages teacher but as an art teacher. Her move to language teaching resulted from her ability and interest in French being called upon in a previous school when there was an unfilled vacancy for a teacher of French. At Hillside, Mrs Johnson taught only French, most at the lower age and ability levels. She had been at Hillside for six years but prior to this had been teaching the new 'communicative' approach to French in another school. Her own experience of studying the language extended to 'A' level, her experience of France being drawn from numerous holidays — starting already while still at school — and visits to friends' homes in France. Her own active interest in France was evident in the school where she organised school visits to France and at the time of the research was hoping to set up an exchange scheme.

Class 3 were the fourth out of six sets and could be described as a middle to low achievement group. There were slightly more girls than boys in the class (for details see Table 3.7). The group was observed to be on the whole rather sullen and uncooperative with a couple of enthusiastic exceptions. This characteristic would manifest itself in a general reluctance to respond to teacher questions and be involved in the lesson. Initially Class 3 were a difficult class to handle and so Mrs Johnson dealt with them more strictly than with a similar 3rd year group she took. There were a couple of 'difficult' girls in the class. Mrs Johnson had to work very hard at gaining the co-operation of the class but in some ways had quite a personal relationship with them which included asking them about their homelife, holidays and so forth.

On the whole it was this lower ability type class that Mrs Johnson preferred to teach as she found them to be more interested in, and she was more able to teach them about, French culture. She preferred, and found more fulfilling herself, being able to teach about French culture rather than feel obliged to concentrate on language all the time. This is an interesting point raised by another of the teachers too. There is often discussion about how to maintain the interest of schoolchildren but it is assumed without further question that teachers will find their work interesting. Mrs Johnson found straight teaching of language 'very dry'.

The class met twice a week each time for 1 hour 10 minutes. Class 3 lessons took place in the upper school and therefore not in Mrs Johnson's own classroom. It was a fairly pleasant room with windows down each side but very little in the way of subject decor, by contrast with her lower school room. Mrs Johnson's classroom in the lower school was always attractively decorated with information about France either prepared by pupils or actually from France. This included posters, signs, stamps and pictures. There were also French magazines lying on a desk at the front of the class. The room was always very pleasant and clearly a French classroom. The third year room on the other hand was a multi-purpose classroom and only from time to time did French decor appear on the walls. The exception to this was a large framed poster of Joan of Arc at the front of the class. Possibly because of its position by the door, or because of its permanence, it was not very noticeable.

Class 3 lessons were characterised by a relatively large amount of information about France and its people, the overall emphasis being upon knowing and appreciating France. In the spirit of the textbook, the language was learned as a resource for a visit to France. Perhaps it is fair to say then that the language teaching was contextualised within cultural information rather than the reverse which is more the case for the other teachers. The information was varied in its presentation and included the use of a variety of materials, anecdotes from her own experience and items brought into the class from France. Although the emphasis in the class was not exclusively upon language learning Mrs Johnson used a relatively large amount of classroom French and on occasion introduced language which was not central to the course — not included in *Action!*.

The most striking feature of Mrs Johnson and Class 3 lessons was their very practical nature: how to survive a visit to France, what to expect as a visitor and how to cope with it. As already outlined this is the approach taken in the textbook and therefore used by all the teachers to some extent. Mrs Johnson, however, extended this approach using anecdotes from her own experience. The situations and the extent to which the information could be perceived as general or purely anecdotal varied. For example she talked about her experience of reserving a place on a campsite in France to explain the use of an international reply form and she explained you can buy them locally. On another occasion she warned the class about the hazards of booking a hotel room in Paris. How important it is to book a room at the back of the hotel where it is much quieter, otherwise they, the pupils, would be 'woken at 3 in the morning with dustbin men coming around . . .' as she was. This type of approach was not only practical but also entertaining. Mrs Johnson believed it is the sort of information pupils want to be given about France, how to go about things, as she said in her interview:

> They are interested in how to go about things, like making a telephone call. There are three ways of making a telephone call in France, explaining the ins and outs of that. How to go about booking in places. How to ask people the way. Things like that.

The survival approach could also be seen in the language teaching. This was illustrated when a pupil on one occasion expressed concern about not being able to give directions in French. Mrs Johnson reassured him it was more important for him to be able to understand than to give directions, the assumption being that he would be more likely to be in a position where he would have to be directed in French than to direct.

Mrs Johnson frequently spoke in French to the class, either to manage the lesson or more generally to expose them to vocabulary. This again had a tendency to take on an instrumental purpose and a clear example of this occurred when introducing the class to Paris. She had just shown the class a video of people booking into a hotel in Paris. In the video all had not gone smoothly and clients had made complaints. After the video Mrs Johnson wrote two phrases on the board 'c'est ennuyeux' and 'c'est incroyable' and told the class 'if you can come up with phrases like that . . . they'll think she understands . . . pull their socks up . . . instead of thinking these British can't be bothered to learn [French]'. She then had the class repeat 'c'est incroyable' and urges them to 'say it as if you really mean it . . .'

This instrumental or 'survival' approach was supported by a wide range of materials — videos, magazines and artefacts from France. From visits to France and correspondence with contacts in France Mrs Johnson had built up a stock of 'authentic' French items. These varied from sweet packets, maps and postcards to tapes of French radio and supermarket announcements. The artefacts, just like the anecdotes were woven into the structure of the lesson which is otherwise formed by the textbook. The anecdotes appeared to be spontaneous, arising from a stimulus in the textbook or pupil interest. The artefacts were often central to the lesson but were used on the whole to illustrate or make tangible something introduced in the textbook. For example on one occasion she showed the class some Michelin guides as well as reading the textbook description of them. Mrs Johnson was the only teacher who — during the period of observation — introduced pupils to items from France.

After this general summary of the main characteristics of Mrs Johnson's approach to teaching culture, the following account of one lesson, expanded from fieldnotes, will give some flavour of the teaching.

Lesson

At the beginning of the lesson Mrs Johnson immediately moves two girls from the back of the class to the front — these are the girls Mrs Johnson finds troublesome. She asks pupils a number of questions in French such as their names, where they live and they reply in French. She asks one boy in French whether he lives in a large or a small house. He says 'in between' — demonstrating that he responds to the content of the question rather than concentrating upon giving an answer in French.

The teacher asks who has visited France and about half the class put up their hands. Most have stayed in a youth hostel in Boulogne on a school trip. She asks how many have stayed in an English youth hostel and none of the pupils have. Mrs Johnson uses a lot of arm movement with her talk.

She directs the class to turn to page 165 of their textbooks to go through their homework. This was to answer questions about 'une fiche de l'auberge de jeunesse' which was printed on the page. The questions were in French but pupils were to answer them in English — they were questions about the person who filled in the form. One of the questions is about the person's address — 'rue Louis Bleriot'. Mrs Johnson asks, 'who is Louis Bleriot?' and a pupil replies 'A famous Frenchman'. Mrs Johnson goes on to remind the class that they came across Louis Bleriot in Book I. A pupil remembers he 'flew across the channel'. Mrs Johnson seeks more information — what made him famous? The pupil replies he was the first person to do so.

Mrs Johnson stresses, in going through the form, that it is important they know what the French words mean in case they go to France and have to fill in such a form.

The class goes on the the next page where Mrs Johnson reads a passage in English about visiting a French youth hostel. The passage says there are always some beds free if you just turn up, but it is a good idea to book ahead. Below the passage are two letters from British people to youth hostels in France. Mrs Johnson tells the class to look for differences between these letters and how they (the pupils) would normally write a letter. She tells them to look at the first letter only and gives them some time. Nobody understands the last sentence. Mrs Johnson explains, '. . . very high faluting way of writing something . . . we use two words . . . Yours faithfully.'

The pupils read and translate the letter. Mrs Johnson asks what is different in how the letter is set out, to how we would set a letter out usually. One pupil suggests it is short. Another that the addresses are at the top and bottom of the page. Mrs Johnson replies 'good' and repeats this. Another pupil says that we don't normally put the other person's address on a letter. Again she repeats this as being correct, 'what else?' she keeps prompting. A pupil says that the date is at the top of the letter and Mrs Johnson asks, 'Where do we normally put the date?' Below the address.

She tells the class to read the second letter in silence and then they translate it in class. She asks who has received a letter from a French person? Two of the pupils say they have. She asks them where they, the French, put their address?

Pupil: on the back of the envelope.
Teacher: Yes . . . back of the envelope.

She says the address doesn't go on the letter but on the back of the envelope and a pupil asks if that is in case it gets lost? She replies 'ehm, yes'.

Mrs Johnson instructs the class to get out their rough books and write a similar letter for 5 people to stay 4 nights in a youth hostel — choose a date. She asks:

Teacher: What do you do on the bit at the top?
Pupil: (inaudible)
Teacher: Hillside and today's date.

The class get on and do this. After a while Mrs Johnson stops them and draws their attention to page 167. She reads the English passage. This is about different people seeing a jumble of pictures in different ways. She tells the class, as in the textbook, to write down the images they see in the jumble of pictures in the order they see them and to do so in French. She gives them 2 minutes to do this. She then calls out the items, and the pupils point to them in the book. When this is complete they move on to the next exercise in the book. 'Les familles des mots'. Again, Mrs Johnson reads the English description of the game.

> Try to make up as many families of three as you can, from the words in blue. Only put into a family words which have something in common.

She gives the class a minute to find one family of words and give a reason why they are a family. This takes them up to near the end of the lesson but to finish she asks pupils in French if they eat in the school canteen and what they ate yesterday.

Interview

After the period of observation, Mrs Johnson agreed to an informal interview in which information about her qualifications, teaching experience, knowledge of France and views on French teaching were gathered. With respect to the importance of talk about France in French lessons, Mrs Johnson stressed the problem pupils have, in her view, in perceiving French people as real — supporting our earlier emphasis on evaluating the realism of the textbook:

I: You bring a lot of information about France into your French lesson, the ones that I have observed. Do you think that is very important?

Mrs. J: Yes, otherwise it is just a non-descript place that they are learning a language for that they don't know very much about. I think it is important to know that French people are human beings just like us. It is amazing, children can learn things as a school subject and not relate it to things that go on outside.

She later made the same point about the country itself, when responding to the interviewer's question as to whether pupils initiate topics by asking questions about France:

Mrs. J: It depends if they have been to France or not but they definitely like hearing about what happens in France. Some they don't know that it happens so they don't ask questions. It's not in their vocabulary, it's

outside their imagination. They don't know anything about it so they
can't ask questions about it.

Later in the interview she emphasised the importance of taking pupils to
France, and unknowingly confirmed our analysis of the significance of the
topographical realism of the textbook:

Mrs. J: School visits? Definitely. We started them off with weekend visits
going to Boulogne. The '*Action!* Book One' is very . . . It's great
actually after they have been to Boulogne and found places on the
photo, same as the photographs. They are actually seeing it. It is
actually France that is in the textbook.

Observation had suggested that much of the cultural information was
introduced into lessons without necessarily being planned in advance. The
spontaneity of this approach might however lead to a lack of coherence. In
pursuing this question, the interview indicated that Mrs Johnson had as a
framework her view that Class 3 did not need an 'academic' approach but
rather a tourist orientation, confirming the interpretation of classroom

I: Would you say that there was certain things that you would specifically
try and teach children about France, like a core of knowledge that you
think they should have about France? What sort of things would you
teach?
Mrs. J: Well all the children that I teach are children that are not going to
use it later or as an academic subject. Not going to go on and study at
university.
I: Are they a low ability that you teach, well middle to low?
Mrs. J: No a lot of them are quite high. But there are not very many of the
children in school who will take a language as an academic subject
when you think about it. They will all probably need it for when they
are going on holiday and I think that is the sort of thing that you should
aim for really. Being able to go into a shop, being able to book into a
youth hostel, hotel or camp site. Things like that.
I: When you are teaching, would you say that you plan a lot of what you
are teaching about France or is a lot of it spur of the moment,
something that comes up?
Mrs. J: It depends on what I can remember.

Despite this emphasis on a distinction between different kinds of class, she also expressed the view that all pupils should have some knowledge of France. Her contrast of 'language' with 'background work' reflects a widely established interpretation that the 'core' of language teaching should be *language* learning.

Mrs. J: You will get an academic class that want to learn the language but I still think an academic class should know something about the ordinary everyday life of France.Even if you just mention it . . . I don't think a language should just be taken on its own.

I: What about what they learn about French culture and geography?

Mrs. J: There is not really a lot, I don't think, in this. It is a shame actually that they haven't got this as part of the new G.C.S.E. It isn't in at all, it's only a language subject. I think if you wanted to do a course which brought in background work, you would have to make your own up.

Her criticism of the newly introduced examination suggests that the contrast between language and culture will continue to dominate many classrooms.

Mr Clarke and class 4 (Hillside School)

Mr Clarke was the head of language at Hillside School. He taught at the grammar school before it combined with the secondary modern school and became a comprehensive. He studied French at university, having been at a grammar school himself, and spent a year as an Assistant in a school in the north of France. He considered this experience as the most significant in contributing to his own knowledge of France and in structuring subsequent visits. He holidays in France and visits friends he made whilst working there. He also teaches German but no other subjects.

Class 4 were the top achievement class at Hillside and had a reputation of being an intelligent class. They were observed to be a fairly subdued class and the girls particularly coy about speaking French. However their attitude seemed positive and they were interested in the work. The relationship between Mr Clarke and the class was an interesting one. Mr Clarke joked with, encouraged, guided and teased various members of the class at the same time distancing himself, for example often referring to the boys by their surnames. Many of the pupils apparently enjoyed the tongue-in-cheek humour and ribaldry. Others were virtually silent. Mr Clarke said he enjoyed teaching Class 4 and he described them as 'as close to an old grammar class as you can get — very keen to learn'.

The class met twice a week, once for 1 hour 10 minute, then for 40 minutes only. The class was taught in multi-purpose rooms, each lesson taking place in a different room. The class was a large one and, by contrast with Class 3, seemed crowded. Pupils sat in pairs of desks which contributed to a more formal atmosphere. There were more girls than boys.

The general atmosphere was a strongly academic one, where a great deal of ground was covered in each lesson, and in contrast to the other three classes there was no drawing or games. There was also only a minimum of classroom French, usually confined to a French greeting at the beginning of the lesson. -

The underlying ethos of Class 4 was a serious approach to French as an examination subject. Mr Clarke said that as a top ability class they were interested in French as an examination subject. Time was therefore spent on grammar and language exercises and there was rapid progression through the textbook. Regular homework was set and checked, and responsibility lay with pupils for handing it in.

Although the emphasis was upon language learning there was still a considerable amount of cultural content which was qualitatively different from that included by the other teachers. Its inclusion appeared spontaneous, particularly when anecdotal, and was combined with textbook information, sometimes read in class or given as homework. The contrast with other classes lay in the divergence from textbook information. On the whole the other teachers stuck fairly closely to the information in the textbook and extra information, even if anecdotal, corresponded to the basic structure and information type. By contrast Mr Clarke offered more divergent information which could be described as less relevant to a visit to France but more relevant to the everyday lives of the French.

Mr Clarke believed that it is this more general information in which upper classes are interested. He said 'You can talk to a top set third year even about things which are not of immediate relevance to them, road signs, the highway code, generalised customs. (. . .) they are intelligent enough to see that one day that sort of knowledge will be of use to them'. Lower ability children are more interested in directly relevant information. Examples of the topics Mr Clark referred to during the period of observation included military service and the police force in France, French car number plates and the regions they refer to, and the system of discipline in French schools.

Because of the different rates of progression through the textbook it is difficult to draw comparisons on specific topics between classes. However both Class 3 and Class 4 studied Paris and this contrast usefully demonstrates two very different approaches. Mrs Johnson showed Class 3 videos of booking into a hotel, told anecdotes of her own experience of Paris and showed them Michelin Guides and hotel brochures. Mr Clarke on the other hand instructed the class to read the 'Paris Touristique' section in the textbook for homework and quizzed them about it in the following lesson asking such questions as how long would you have to spend in the Louvre if you wanted to spend 3 minutes in front of each statue or picture. In general although a wider range of subjects were addressed by Mr Clarke, his classroom style meant he often gave an interpretation, through brief comments, which led to his purveying a sense of 'strangeness' about France. An example of this was his comment on the Tuileries, 'burnt down in one of the countless revolutions they've had'. When talking about a French town hall he described the portakabin-type building with a flag which he said looked 'ridiculous'.

In short, the emphasis in lessons was quite serious and clearly oriented to passing final examinations. Thus most of the lesson content was serious language learning; there were no games, little role play and no drawing. In addition the cultural information could be serious and extended, dealing with issues not included in the textbook. However this was combined with comments which suggest an image of France and the French people as being slightly bizarre, an effect we shall describe as the 'strange' image.

Two lessons described on the basis of fieldnotes will give some insight into the way in which these general characteristics are realised in the classroom.

Lesson 1

This lesson takes place in a room that looks like a careers room. It has large information posters on the walls. One, for example, has hints on job interviews. The class is a very big one and the room feels packed. Pupils sit in pairs at desks.

Class turns to page 72 ('*Action!* 3') and look at the French school timetable. They read and translate it into English. Mr Clarke points out the free period. Next they listen to a French dialogue on tape and try to work out the timetable for Friday and Saturday. Mr Clarke says it's difficult because of the tone of the children's voices. He goes on to say 'everyone knows they have a nice long lunch hour'. He also explains that in France the children get free lessons singly or in blocks. Normally if they're free and it's through the day they are 'put in a room and expected to work'

Next they turn to page 73 and 'le bulletin scolaire' which Mr Clarke describes as 'A report remarkably similar to the ones (you had in) 1st year . . . remarkably strange names sometimes.'

He asks the class what they can say about the report. Pupils reply, biology quite good, talks too much in maths, good at French, good results in English, German pronunciation not good. Mr Clarke says the French have problems pronouncing German. French use marks out of 20 for everything.

Teacher: 'Mme Directrice' . . . what do you think they are?
Pupil: Head of the school.
Teacher: Right, something said by the head of the school.

On page 75 they look at symbols of school subjects but pupils aren't able to say what they stand for — they look back in their books for the answers. Then Mr Clarke reads the French school survey which gives details of what pupils think of their school and how much homework they do. Mr Clarke says that they (the class) probably don't do as much homework as the French. Some of the class look surprised.

He writes the date and title on the board and tells the class they are going to do the exercise in the textbook together. They do a survey of the class asking the same questions as in the French survey. For example their favourite and most useful lessons. Mr Clarke talks for some time about how useful lessons are not necessarily favourite ones and that next year they will be making a choice. He says they may be able to compare their answers with those from the year before.

One of the questions asks whether they are happy to attend school in the country they are in at the moment. Mr Clarke explains that living in France makes it quite possible to go to a school in another country if you live on the border. He says the question is therefore difficult for us to appreciate.

Finally, the class listens to a dialogue on tape. It is an interview of a French boy who goes to school near Paris. The idea is to get the gist of what is being said.

Lesson 2

There is no French introduction to this lesson — the class is sitting when Mr Clarke arrives. He instructs the class to turn to *Action!* page 70

(Book 3). The class reads through the French section 'une semaine de Paris' and answer questions about it in French. Next they read a section in English with Mr Clarke saying that one day they might have to be an interpreter. The following section is a three way conversation between a receptionist in a hotel, a teacher and pupil, except the pupil talk is blank and pupils are to act as interpreter between a French receptionist and English teacher. The first translation is 'tell him I'd like a single room.' Mr Clarke says, '. . . harder for us . . . un and une . . . natural to the French as they do it from birth'. He goes on to explain it's not enough to know the word for room, pupils also have to know whether it's 'un' or 'une'. Further along in the dialogue, the teacher wishes to buy postcards and stamps. The receptionist directs him to 'un tabac'. Mr Clarke asks the class why, and why you can't buy them in Hillside. One of the class replies, they don't have sub-post offices.

In the last few sentences of the conversation the pupil has to thank the receptionist.

'Merci' one pupil suggests.
'A bit more polite'.
'Merci Monsieur'.

Mr Clarke tells the class to write down the translated sentences for their homework.

Interview

Mr Clarke's interview was an opportunity to pursue the difference in ways of teaching higher and lower sets. Like Mrs Johnson he suggested the pupils in lower sets did not need as much knowledge of French language and he too distinguished between language and teaching about France. The latter is thus a contribution to pupils' wider education:

Mr. C: I think with the least able children you are teaching them about France partly because you know they are not going to require much French and you are trying to justify French being on their timetable by giving them some cultural opening up.

I: Justifying to them?

Mr. C: I think you are justifying to yourself. I think in a sense you have to justify it to them but I doubt it justifies it to them. On the other hand I don't know there are many subjects on the timetable that would justify themselves to them but I think to justify it to the education system there ought to be something more than saying 'I'm trying to teach them a language'. So I tend to work on the view that I have to expand their cultural awareness. I mean we are the only subject that is specifically putting them into a position where they are studying a particular group or race or whatever. I know that geography and history and other subjects look at these from another angle but we are saying — look here is a bunch of people who speak a different language, this is what else is different about them. So to them it is more than the language. At the other end and as you go up it becomes more the language and less that, so that by the time you get to the top end you are throwing in the cultural things because you think in general terms the kids will say 'Gosh that is interesting, I would like to go there. It sounds fascinating' hence you get these exchange trips full of the brightest kids who have learned about France and would like to find out what happens over there and also will retain it maybe and will say to themselves when they are twenty-five 'it was interesting ten years ago'. So that it is much more a background thing to them. You are chiefly teaching a language and hoping that as you go along you make it sound interesting and one day maybe in a situation when they have to use it! The less able child you are really doing something which is to do with their cultural awareness and possibly will achieve nothing in relation to France.

Later he contrasted the pursuit of examination success in the grammar school system with current aims. Today, he suggested, there is a broader task: not simply education of the intellect but of the whole person. Again in this extract Mr Clarke emphasises the special role of language teaching, although this time he indicates some affinity with history and geography.

Mr. C: We have got to be able to educate their whole selves to be more receptive as people and in French you have a special advantage in which to do it. I imagine in history and geography as well. You can say to them imagine yourself in this situation. When I have had children they have never said anything but you can see the look on their faces, 'what is he wasting time for?'. I tend to say 'I bet some of you think, why is he wasting some of the lesson talking about . . .' and you can see them nodding. So you tell them because you are trying to open up their minds to other things. You don't say it in those terms but you make them interested in France you make them interested in French people and that it isn't just the language that we learn. I suppose it is in the more able groups that very often think it is a waste of time but judging by the fact that they still opt for it and they have had a lot of cultural stuff in three years and patently it drops off after that for the most able kids — you start thinking I have got to teach them to do that and whilst the French background is still there — it patently must decrease because you become more aware of the need to learn. So if they have had most of the cultural work in three years and they are still picking it, we haven't switched them off by any means it is just there is a little doubt in some of their minds 'Is he teaching me ready for my examinations'. I think it is very easy got rid of because they are able enough to appreciate that what you are doing is worthwhile to them in another way.

In the last words of this extract Mr Clarke expresses a view of children's perceptions which accords with the classroom observations of the 'serious' character of Class 4. It remains however a moot point whether pupils' perceptions determine the teacher's response or whether — as we shall suggest below — the particular combination of teacher and class produces the style of language teaching and learning which is peculiar to the situation.

Finally, the question of whether there is a specific body of information on France to be presented to a class was also raised with Mr Clarke. He too denies that this is so but reveals a guiding framework which in his case is in the form of a desire to overcome prejudice and create tolerance.

Mr. C: I don't know whether there is a specific list of things that I would say I would hope I would have taught over X years. I think it is more of a case whenever you get any signs coming through of these irrational prejudices you try to suggest tolerance to discuss the differences from a Frenchman's point of view if you like. Say if you were a Frenchman this is what you would think about the English. For example they say 'Frenchmen undercook their food' and you say 'Well I've known French people who say that we overcook our food, try looking at it from that point'. Obviously they still think that if you put a knife into a piece of meat and blood oozes out it is not nice but then if you talk to a Frenchman about the way we cook a piece of steak we tend to burn it and I think it is more a generalised tolerance of difference that I try to get across (. . .) I don't think there is anything specific that I want to get across because I would rather get them to the stage where they think 'I would like to go to France' and form their own impressions. I don't want them all to come out as manic francophiles like me I want them to go to France with an open mind and come back and say 'well I still don't like them' — which is acceptable. I mean they can see the country and say 'I don't like France, I don't like French people', or come back and say 'right it's a great place, or come back and say — I can take it or leave it' but I think it ought to be just that we have opened their minds up to taking France for what it is rather than for what somebody has told them it is.

Miss Saunders and class 1 (Newfarm School)

Miss Saunders studied languages at university, specialising in German. She spent a year in teacher training at the local university, did her teaching practice at Newfarm, and secured a job there. She had been at Newfarm for six years at the time of the research. Of the four case-study teachers Miss Saunders had the least experience of France. Her visits included school visits, a youth visit, and three exchanges. However she had spent about a year and a half in Germany as part of her degree. She expressed some regret that she had not spent more time in France. 'Children are very quick to say "that is stupid" but you have got to try to explain to them that a French person may find what we do stupid and it is just a difference and not necessarily an inferiority. I think the more you go to France the more you are in a position to explain that to them. I wish I had been to France more.' She had first specialised in sciences and then changed to languages, staying on an extra year in the sixth form to do so. Miss Saunders was also greatly involved in the dramatic activities of the school.

Class 1 were the top achievement group out of the three 3rd year classes studying languages, and the only group to be studying French and German. They were considered, by both language teachers, to be a very bright and enthusiastic group, a pleasure to teach. The relationship between teacher and class was a very good one. The class appeared diligent and obedient, but at the same time lively and interested. Miss Saunders was able to joke with the class, and she said of the class, 'The overall characteristic of the class is that they just seem keen all the time. They want to know more and they like to achieve, they like to get things right.' Again the class was largely female.

The class met twice a week for French, each time for 1 hour 10 minutes. The lessons took place in Miss Saunders' room which was a light and pleasant room usually well decorated. The class was a large one and

filled all the available seating. Newfarm, being a more recently built school
was equipped with tables rather than desks. Pupils sat in rows of tables,
four to a row, which created a less formal atmosphere.

The achievement level of this group was comparable with that of Class
4 at Hillside but the lessons and teachers' perceptions of the class were very
different. Miss Saunders, although describing the class as very keen, did
not think that examinations have impinged on them yet. The keenness was
competitive within the frame of lessons but not necessarily with examinations as a future goal. The atmosphere of the class was then less serious,
and less restricted in its activities.

Lessons were characterised by the use of lots of drawing and games.
The emphasis was on learning the language, with the culture introduced for
interest. The emphasis was also on enjoyment and creativity and the
classroom decor reflected this. Of all the third year classes observed Class 1
were the only group to be taught French in a highly decorated room. The
walls were usually covered in pupils' drawings and the decor was changed
quite often. Most of the work related to France and included information
signs, pictures of French food and drink and childrens' designs for graded
Franch certificates which on the whole were based on the French flag.
There were also various textbooks on display along the side of the room.
Miss Saunders included drawing quite frequently in her language lessons
with Class 1, often as an exercise. There was a variety of activities,
including grammar instruction and tests, language exercises, games, drawing, role play and dialogues. Many of the activities were of Miss Saunders'
own design rather than taken specifically from the textbook. She said she
did not use the teacher's book too much but read it for a general view of
what it was trying to get over, and worked from there. The range of
methods of teaching included use of a video-recorder to tape and play back
pupils writing and acting out French weather forecasts. This lesson was
very excited and demonstrated Miss Saunders' relaxed style as she joked
with the pupils and encouraged them to invent funny names, her own
example being 'Michel Poisson' for the well-known weather forecaster
Michael Fish!

Her approach was flexible and in informal discussion she expressed
the need to be sensitive to the way the class was feeling. During one lesson
the class read plays in French from a book called *Au Troisième Top* all of
which were to do with meals in France. After the lesson Miss Saunders said
that she had not planned to do that lesson but was tired of 'Food' in
Action!, on which there is so much material, and so decided to do the plays
instead.

Like Mrs Johnson, Miss Saunders introduced the class to vocabulary which is not in the textbook. However she did not contextualise it by reference to a visit to France, but presented it as part of the overall appreciation of language, and as fun. An example came towards the end of one lesson. She wrote, *'prestidigitateur'* on the blackboard, the pupils had then to make as many French words as possible from it.

In her general management of the class she did not use French very much although she often greeted and dismissed the class in French and used certain recurrent French phrases, for example to tell them which page number to turn to in the textbook, a technique which was quite common among all the teachers observed.

The cultural information was not a major part of these lessons but arose spontaneously and often as a joke or point of interest. The information was brief and generally taken from the textbook. It is this naturally occurring type of information which Miss Saunders, in common with Miss Leybourne, believed was most appreciated by pupils. She said, 'They are interested in food. They like the fact that the French drink their coffee from bowls instead of cups in the morning, that sort of thing. Just little snippets of information rather than enormous great chunks. They don't like to go into it in any great depth I find.' This brevity and sense of fun is however inclined to portray what we called earlier a 'strange' image of France.

Again we offer extracts from fieldnotes as an indication of the conduct of lessons.

Lesson

The classroom walls have been stripped bare. Although pupils have their textbooks out Miss Saunders tells them to keep them closed. She goes through some food vocabulary. First *'legumes'*. The class goes through the vegetables. Miss Saunders points out the language similarity that cabbage is *'choux'* in French, and cauliflower *'choufleur'*. Next they turn to fruit: which fruits can pupils name. One of them is a plum. She asks what a dried plum is called?

Turning to cheeses she says there are more than 400 types of cheeses in France and that she will get the poster of cheeses out sometime. The class continues to name sorts of meats, desserts and drinks. Then vocabulary for a little — *'un peu'* and more *'encore'*. Miss Saunders says 'you know, encore! again!' She describes cherry as the colour all the 4th year are wearing at the moment — *'cerise'*.

The class are instructed to look over page 121 and Miss Saunders prepares a tape. The class listen to two conversations, the first about seats taken on transport. The second conversation is about food being offered at the table — how much the person likes or dislikes it. Some of the foods mentioned are: sausages, soup, fruit, apple juice. '*Escargots*' are mentioned and the class say 'ugh!'. Frogs' legs are also mentioned. Miss Saunders asks which foods pupils like. She also mentions le *Croque Monsieur*. The class seem more restless than usual. Miss Saunders describes le *Croque Monsieur* and some pupils groan at the idea.

Next they turn to pages 121 and 120, also page 112. The class are to develop conversations that could take place in a French household at lunchtime using phrases from the textbook. Miss Saunders specifies everyone must say two sentences. She comments to me she is sick of doing food. The pupils act out their plays — most include '*bon appetit*'. Chicken, salad, orange and mineral water are most commonly used. This takes them up to the end of the lesson.

Interview

Miss Saunders' interview indicated she shared the view held by Mr Clarke that pupils should be encouraged to be tolerant:

Miss S: I think it is important to teach them that there are differences between one culture and another, one way of life and another. I think some of the things the children find most interesting is not the oddities of French language so much as the funny things that the French do or the things that they think are funny. I think you have got to put over to them the idea that it may seem strange to us but that does not necessarily mean it is wrong.

In answering the question about whether there is a body of knowledge to be taught, Miss Saunders agreed with the two previous teachers in stressing rather an opportunist approach and she too indicated that she did not plan in advance what might be discussed in class. She implicitly relied on the structure of the textbook and saw lessons as integrated wholes rather than as having separate language and culture components.

Miss S: No, I wouldn't say there is a core of information. I think the most important information is that which appears naturally in the course of what you are doing. I don't think you should really or can really say suddenly — right we are now going to have a lesson on what the French do at Christmas say or what the French family life is like. I think it emerges as you teach. If you are talking about staying in a youth hostel or staying in a hotel in France then the system emerges during the course of the teaching because then they can tie the two together and they can see well yes — that is how the French do it — that is how we do it. This is what the French say at that point and that is why we say it and I think the same applies to family life and travel and schools and anything whatever particular topic you are dealing with in the lesson as a whole. I think the things have to be tied together and you wouldn't just separate them out.

Miss Leyborne and class 2 (Newfarm School)

Miss Leyborne was the head of languages at Newfarm and had been so for eight years. Of all the teachers observed she had the most experience of other countries. Her experience included working in an international school in Belgium and as a secretary in Germany. She has friends in Germany and France to whom she writes and visits. However her experience of France itself is not as extensive as of Germany and it was German she studied at university. Her experience of France is limited to holidays and school visits and although she has a good friend in France, she too is a teacher.

Miss Leyborne believed her different kinds of experience of France and Germany have implications for her teaching:

I don't teach French as well as I teach German because although I have been a lot and actually been in families and not just a visit or in a hotel, there are loads of cultural things that I just don't know . . . whereas in Germany I can safely say I have experienced everything . . . I have experienced school, work and family in Germany.

She also prefered the German way of life to the French way of life. She said of French life:

although I am enthusiastic about certain things, it's not the same. I don't have the same emotional commitment to French culture that I have for the German.

However despite this she was convinced of the importance of culture in language teaching and hoped she was able to teach classes something about France and that her own feelings did not colour the impression she gave.

Class 2's two 70-minute lessons per week were held in Miss Leyborne's own classroom. The classroom was on the ground floor of the school with windows down one side of the room overlooking the school field and the railway. The room was therefore bright and pleasant. Tables in the classroom were organised into rows of four children each, facing the front. At the front there was often an overhead projector which Miss Leyborne used rather than the blackboard. Exercise books were stacked neatly on the shelving also at the front of the classroom and textbooks along the side. Unlike those at Hillside, children at Newfarm shared textbooks between classes and were not able to take them home. There were wall displays from time to time, of pupils' work or information about France, but there was not a great emphasis upon this.

Class 2 was a middle to low achievement class. They were the lowest set to study language at Newfarm but were roughly comparable with Class 3 at Hillside. Third year examination results were disparate showing a range of pupils within the class. Although there were some quiet members, generally the class was, by contrast with Class 1, a lively group with some enthusiastic members. The relationship between teacher and class was a difficult one sometimes appearing antagonistic. Time was spent on controlling the class, telling off certain members and sending pupils out. Miss Leyborne therefore found she was unable to do work which she would have liked to have done or that she felt she could do with a class such as Class 2. Exercises and games were often interrupted in lessons and abandoned in favour of more controllable activities.

Typical lessons began with the class queueing outside the classroom before the lesson. The start of the lesson was often marked with the teacher and class exchanging a rehearsed and familiar greeting in French:

— *Bonjour la classe*
— *Bonjour Madame*
— *Ca va?*
— *Ca va bien merci et vous?*
— *Ca va*

Miss Leyborne stressed at the beginning of the observation period that she thought it was important to teach basic language skills before progressing to other work. Thus there was an emphasis in lessons upon language skills and vocabulary which were frequently tested and retested if pupils performed badly. However, much of the language learning was through games as suggested by the textbook. The textbook was dominant in all these lessons and as the book was used quite extensively this meant the cultural information in the book was covered too and formed the greater proportion of information about France and French culture in Class 2 lessons. The general impression given was thus a neutral one and was presented with very little personal interpretation by the teacher. However information about France was often compared to something in this country. For example '*La Lotterie Nationale*' was compared to the football pools. Thus information was constantly grounded in pupils' own experience, which was something Miss Leyborne saw as most interesting to this class — 'something that is relevant to their lives' — although this would often be in the form of contrasts too.

Observations indicated that talk about France was sometimes initiated by a member of the class asking a question. One boy in particular asked a great number of questions. However, questions were also seen to be irrelevant at times and certain class members made remarks or jokes of them. Miss Leyborne did however believe the class were genuinely interested in France, particularly if information was presented to them in small amounts as the lesson progressed. Like Miss Saunders she found pupils were much more interested in 'snippets' of information rather than extended work. On one occasion she produced a photocopied sheet she had prepared about the different climates in France but the class showed little interest, one member remarking that it was more like a geography lesson than French. In the end, to restore discipline, the class was instructed to copy out the sheet. This illustrated what Miss Leyborne said in an interview:

> I don't prepare any cultural information at all because I think if I went in and said, right, we are going to talk about schools in Germany today or the schools in France I think they would just start talking amongst themselves and maybe catch half of it.

Extracts from fieldnotes will again indicate how lessons usually developed.

Lesson

After settling the class, having the textbooks given out and establishing the page that they are going to work from (page 62, '*Action! 2*') Miss

Leyborne asks a number of questions about the coach map in the textbook such as 'Is there a coach or bus for Calais?' 'The coach leaves at what time?' The information is all on the map for the pupils to respond.

Next they play a game of guessing the length of time the class can be in silence, and then how long they can hold their breath. One pupil suggests 'Miss to make it fair you have to hold your breath'.

Next Miss Leyborne points out a French town in the book and tells the class that it has a twin school with a school in a local town. She then sets up the tape recorder with an *Action!* tape. The class have to listen to the tape and answer a question in the pause. The questions relate to the map in the textbook and are in a dialogue form. At first Miss Leyborne extends the pause. The class look bored and fidgety and Miss Leyborne starts to get annoyed. She repeats the exercise without extending the pause and members of the class complain that it's too fast. One says 'French always speak fast', Miss Leyborne replies 'No, they don't'. She establishes the tape was too difficult and so asks her own questions such as which town is south of Cucq? What does Bagatelle offer?

Pupil: Attractions
Teacher: What attractions?
Pupil 2: Zoo
Pupil 3: Restaurant
Pupil 4: Grillade
Teacher: What is grillade?
Pupil: (inaudible)
Teacher: No
Pupil: Dinner outside
Teacher: Yes, what do we call it?
Pupil: Barbecue

(This information is all displayed for pupils in a small 'authentic' advertisement in the textbook.)

She then goes on to tell them a bit about the picnic area which has no seats but is covered over.

Next Miss Leyborne writes ten 24-hour clock times on the board (in digits) and tells the class to copy them into their books. She then says the times in French and the class eliminate them as she does — this is a game similar to bingo. When they are finished pupils ask if they can do it again and she says perhaps at the end of the lesson. Next she gives the class five minutes to make up as many sentences as they can using the times. Pupils use the textbook and exercise books to construct sentences which they then go through.

Miss Leyborne asks some questions about the coaches and then they go on to look at the timetable on page 63. She asks them a number of questions about the timetable and says to one pupil (s)he'll never get by in France with the wrong pronunciation of *'horaire'*. Miss Leyborne tries hard to get pupils to answer but a lot of the class just aren't listening. For one place she asks:

I: Where would you go when you got there?
P: The fish and chip shop.
I: There aren't any
I: Mairie
P: Post Office
P: Tourist Information
I: In French . . .

Miss Leyborne next writes three questions on the board from her book and underlines the places and times. The questions are asking about arrival and departure times to various places. She explains that by changing the times and places of these sentences they can ask lots of different questions. She then develops this into a game, asks the other a question, the second half replies, and then they change around. This continues until the end of the lesson.

Interview

Miss Leyborne's interview revealed a difference in her view of the notion of a body of information to be taught. At the same time it is evident that she links specific kinds of information with her aims for culture teaching which are similar to those stated by the other teachers: to extend pupils' vision of the world beyond their own town and region:

Miss L: The things I think they should know is that and, I always get it in because I tell them the difference between a French child for instance who has this horrendous long day at school and goes home and has this homework as well. Frankly, I think if you are a conscientous child in France you haven't got time for hobbies in the evening. You've got your Wednesday off but that is about it.

and because of her greater knowledge of Germany she also draws on her work in German lessons:

Miss L: German teenagers because they have more positive interests I think this leads on this shorter schoolday that they are involved in clubs and things more than ours and the closer family ties. They would never know that unless you really pointed it out. Closer family supervision. The fact that families in my opinion, my experience, do more together than they do in England and I think that that is what keeps them out of trouble, out of vandalism. You know you don't see vandalised 'phone boxes and things in Germany. Germans tell me they do but I've never seen them and I think that needs pointing out, the fact that it needn't happen here.

I: So you seem to be saying.

Miss L: Quality of life. I like to point out quality of life because I honestly think that German and French family life is of a higher quality than ours. I tell them that, I tell them straight out.

I: Do you think you tell them so they can improve their quality of life over here, sort of like a model?

Miss L: Yes I tell them to see beyond Newfarm. I always tell them straightaway that there is more to life than Newfarm because they honestly can't see more and that one way out is to travel and see what other possibilities there are and that they will improve as people if they can see how other people are.

Miss Leyborne also comments on the difficulty of creating links between subjects. Like Mr Clarke she suggests that pupils' perceptions separate language and culture, but she goes on to reflect on where responsibility for this lies:

Miss L: I can't remember what we were doing once but it was something where I was talking about the country and it had arisen from what we had been doing and I heard one pupil — it wasn't Class 2 it was a couple of years ago — say I thought this was supposed to be a French lesson — they think that each subject is totally divorced from the next. They don't make the connection in their minds at all. I think it's our fault. I have said before — look you know you can't divorce the language from the country and that means a bit of geography and history about that country as well but I know I have never convinced them. They think French and German are learning French and German and nothing else. I think that is a failure on what we are doing because a pupil who has said that has not seen any relevance of what he is doing to a real country or real people. He ought to because he is bright. He asks questions about French people. I thought it was a strange thing for him to say. Mind you I don't know how seriously you can take his comments because he deliberately sets out to provoke.

Miss Leyborne shares Mrs Johnson's enthusiasm for school visits, contrasting them both with ordinary holidays and also with the learning which takes place in the classroom:

Miss L: I think the exchange changes their minds more than the lessons but the point is it affects so few children. You've just got to talk to the others or get the people who have been on exchanges to convince them. But now we have school holidays often going to Switzerland and Germany, they come back with good reports about the young people they have met and that all helps. I have found it can be broken down.

She points out however that visits are not always successful in reducing prejudice or changing preconceptions. Some evidence for this has already been quoted from pupil interviews in Chapter 4 and Miss Leyborne's discussions with pupils after the event are clearly intended to reduce difficulties and the impact of unfortunate experiences:

Miss L: But you see the point is a lot of them get their prejudices reinforced. They actually get them reinforced when they go. They find what they are looking for. You know they go out looking for these horrible things and of course you find it if you look hard enough. So that they get reinforced. You do get the odd bad experience. When we were in M. they had one evening in a French family and they ate with that family and then the family brought them back to the Centre. I had been telling them about these lovely French meals and how the mother would have spent all day preparing it etc. and some of them came back and said 'all I got was hamburgers and chips'. It's because they thought this is what they would eat. They won't eat the French food and so they had given them this food they thought they were used to instead of giving them the French stuff. Others have come back and said it was French food and it was horrible. Bits floating around and I didn't know what it was and I didn't know what that was. So they all just had all their fears confirmed. But the vast majority enjoyed themselves so there you are. It is just the luck of the draw. I say — it is the luck of the draw and just shows you there is no typical French person and no typical French family and they are all different. I say — look there is not two of you had the same experience so it just shows you each family is an individual family and you can't make sweeping generalisations about anybody and they listen but it is touching too few, that experience because you can't get them all over there.

Finally Miss Leyborne's view of the textbook is interesting in the contrast with Mrs Johnson's opinion on the decision to set the scene in Boulogne, but also in comparison with our own analysis of the realism of the overall image:

Miss L: I suppose it is a start but you see the children who have been there (Boulogne), they don't particularly like it because they have been with their parents. They said — 'oh it's horrible and everybody speaks English anyway'. And it's true. If they went they would speak English because they are so used to having English people there and that tends to be a bad town to pick. But, yes, I suppose they could have dotted on any town and started them off. It's hard to say because you could say Boulogne is as typical as anywhere.

and

I don't find it gives any particular image of France to be honest. I find it very neutral, the *Action!* book, it's up to the teacher. It doesn't leave me with any particular impression about France. When it comes to the shops it explains the shops but so briefly it's up to you to talk about how beautiful it is to look at the character or something. But it's a starting point anyhow, all the textbooks are and it's up to the teacher. No textbook ever does the teacher's job.

Summary

The four cases studied, although very different, have much in common. Most obviously all four classes followed the same course through the textbook. The textbook with its flash cards, audio and video tapes was central to all the French teaching in both schools and in most lessons the textbook was used. This is a frequent feature of language teaching in general and contrasts with some other subjects which adopt a more eclectic approach to materials. As far as cultural information is concerned in all the classes observed, the textbook provided a potential core of information and in fact teachers relied on the textbook for cultural information a great deal. Building on this core of information, teachers variously used their personal experience and other materials, or artefacts from France. However on the whole these were again determined by the textbook. Only the topics included in the textbook were covered, and other information was integrated with the topic currently being studied from the textbook.

Although pupils asked questions and showed interest in cultural information their contributions to it were negligible. In all classes the flow of information was in one direction, from the teacher to the pupils. The personal experience included was that of the teacher, although (s)he sometimes referred to school visits. Pupils had also been on school visits to France but did not volunteer information or comment and were not frequently asked, during the lessons observed. As we saw above however teachers did suggest in interviews that they drew on pupils' experience of visits and exchanges during the periods immediately before and after the event. Observation showed that this was not noticeably extended to lessons at other times.

Although, as we saw from interviews, the teachers shared the view that cultural studies in language teaching is important for a number of reasons, on the whole the emphasis in the lessons was toward language learning. Cultural information was a subsidiary issue and could be described as central to the lessons in only one of the classes, class 3. Three features of this class and teacher are particularly interesting:

(1) The class is a medium to low ability achievement class. The teacher takes the view that pure language teaching is of little relevance to such a group and knowledge about the culture is likely to be of more use.
(2) The teacher was not trained as a foreign language teacher but moved over to language teaching a number of years ago.
(3) The teacher visits France regularly and has a considerable personal interest in and enthusiasm for France which she expressed in interviews.
(4) The teacher finds it more interesting herself to teach lessons of this kind and classes which respond to cultural information.

Perhaps the most important conclusion to draw from the case-studies is that there is much variation in approach or style of teaching, and that this impinges on the kind of cultural knowledge and information to which pupils are exposed. It is to the question of variation in approach that we turn next, and to an attempt to isolate and characterise those aspects of the teaching which are particularly significant in teachers' approach to the cultural studies element of foreign language teaching.

Teaching Styles

In adding to our observations of work in the classroom a number of extracts from interviews with the teachers we have already begun to move from analysis of features of teaching as they appear to the outsider — an etic level analysis — to an interpretation of observations from within the perspective of those involved. In fact interviews suggested that the etic level analysis was significant in emic level terms, that for example the identification of teachers aims and methods implied in their classroom procedures corresponded with their own statements. The distinction between emic and etic levels is a useful analytical procedure, but is essentially two perspectives on the same phenomena. We found from both perspectives both common ground and differences in the practices and aims of the four teachers and their classes. In moving now to another level of significance, in which we attempt to isolate those features which distinguish one teaching approach from another, we can begin the process of developing descriptive models of culture teaching. Such descriptive models will then form the basis of our attempt in Chapter 6 to relate teaching processes and pupil attitudes and knowledge.

Developing the notion of 'style'

Early observations suggested that any attempt to describe ways of teaching culture in terms of individual teacher traits would be based on a false assumption, namely that a teacher's approach to culture teaching would be static and independent of the situation in which he or she fi" him/herself, regardless of the character of the class being taught. In fact teacher style was observed to be highly dependent upon the class with which he/she is dealing and the teacher is particularly influenced by his/her perceptions of the ability of the class. A teacher is also influenced by the behaviour of the class — whether discipline or motivation problems — although problems of behaviour are more acute in classes perceived as low ability and thus the two are ultimately inseparable.

The concept of 'style' had therefore to be extended to cover a teacher interacting with a particular class in a specific situation. 'Styles' can therefore be described in the following way.

Teacher X
        }   Style XA
Class A

Teacher X⎫
                ⎬ Style XB
Class B   ⎭

The first stage of observations covered years 1 to 3 at a variety of achievement levels. It was clear in view of the above argument, and considering recent changes in textbooks and teachers, that past experience of the third year pupils could not be retraced by observing current first and second year classes. It would not be possible to establish what kind of knowledge and information had been available to the third year class in earlier years. Since the cultural content was clearly linked to the language teaching and, in turn, to the particular 'style' of a class and teacher, the current first and second year classes could not be assumed to be sufficiently similar to the third year to be an adequate basis for any speculation on the history of the third year classes. This follows the view taken by interactionist sociologists who regard any social activity, in this case a lesson, as the result of negotiation between those present. The apparent power differentials and a high degree of structure makes this negotiation less obvious in the classroom than in many other situations. None the less the negotiation between a teacher and class at a particular time in their school career is peculiar to that situation and cannot be reconstructed on the basis of other observable phenomena.

Having described the four case studies ethnographically above, we can now re-consider them here from the point of view of 'style' (Table 5.2). The styles can be characterised in terms of a number of factors which appear most salient in contributing to the classroom experience of another culture. Each of the four styles was given a name for convenience and to indicate the overall character of the approach.

— The survival approach (Style ZD)
— The language enjoyment approach (Style XB)
— The language skills approach (Style WA)
— The academic approach (Style YC)

The factors which comprise a style reflect the open-ended definition of culture introduced earlier and are not intended to be all-inclusive. The aim was to identify those factors most salient in differentiating teaching styles with respect to culture teaching; other factors present were not considered significant for differentiation. The eight factors are as follows:

(a) French artefacts
(b) Personal experience/current information
(c) Classroom decor

TABLE 5.2 *Styles in the case studies*

School	Class	Style
Newfarm: Teacher W (Miss L.) (Head of Department)	A. Medium/Low Achievement (Class 2)	WA
Teacher X (Miss S.)	B. High Achievement (Class 1)	XB
Hillside: Teacher Y (Mr C) (Head of Department)	C. High Achievement (Class 4)	YC
Teacher Z (Mrs J)	D. Medium/Low Achievement (Class 3)	ZD

    (d)   Use of classroom French
    (e)   Flexibility of approach
    (f)   Progression through the textbook
    (g)   Culture emphasised
    (h)   Images of France

The eight factors are those which, to an observer, appear to contribute to the classroom experience of French culture. They were the result of observations rather than predetermined. Similarly the rating of the teachers on these factors is based wholly upon observations and not upon reported information, such as the interview data cited above. On the other hand the factors and their descriptions are couched in terms which are intended to be familiar to teachers — and in principle to pupils — because they interpret classroom observations from within the universe of meaning which teacher and class share.

It is important to stress that the factors and the distinctions within them are not intended to be value judgements about the teaching style. The factors are intended to describe the nature of the experience of a given class and teacher in respect of the cultural knowledge expressed in the class. The factors are those which differentiate the styles and above all represent a teacher's management of knowledge in a particular class in the context of his or her perceptions of the needs of that class. Interview data gives an impression of the beliefs underlying their teaching style and the restrictions upon it.

Factors comprising a style

The eight factors which comprise a style will be further refined, for example in terms of degree by 'strong', 'medium' and 'weak/not present' (some of the factors have other distinctions which will be described below). The distinctions within each factor are not based upon a specific count of instances but on qualitative analysis of fieldnotes. The first stage of analysis suggested a binary distinction between a factor being strongly represented or not present (or present in a negligible way). However, observations of several factors suggested that this polarised description would not be adequate, and it was decided that a 'medium' category was justified.

Our descriptions differ from, for example, ratings derived from an observation schedule in two important ways:

—   the main aim of the research is qualitative rather than quantitative and this extends to the ratings within the factors,

—   the ratings are comparable within this research rather than absolute: each of the four styles can only be described by comparison with the other three — and implicitly with others in the two schools insofar as observations of them helped to clarify the concepts; it is not known how they might be compared to other teachers and classes in other schools.

Since, however, our research as a whole is case-study oriented, with pupils being compared with each other within the parameters of the study, it is adequate to characterise styles by internal comparisons. The styles are then linked to the internal comparisons of pupils' test scores and interview analyses. In order to test their generalisability the factors could be used as instruments for observing other French teachers and classes.

We propose next an abstract characterisation of each factor before considering how they combine in particular styles:

(a) French artefacts

This factor differentiates the extent to which the teacher brings things from France into the class. It can mean anything from a French stamp, postcards or bus tickets to tape-recordings of French radio advertisements. This, apart from school visits to France, is the pupils' only contact with 'real' France, by which we refer to objects originating in and imported from France. As Starkey (1986) argues, the possibilities of authentic materials are endless but on the whole teachers tend to remain fairly conservative, generally reproducing more of the same artefacts as are contained in the textbook. In the four case studies, a distinction could be clearly seen between one class who, during the period of observation, were exposed to French artefacts and the other three who were not. Another study, perhaps more widely based, could make distinctions within this factor which might relate to the kind of artefacts used and the sort of discussion which surrounds them.

(b) Personal experience/current information

The core of cultural knowledge expressed in the classroom is contained within the textbook but this second factor recognises the extent to which the teacher introduces his/her own experience or more up-to-date information. In some respects this factor can be regarded as the verbal equivalent to 'French artefacts'. It represents attempts by the teachers to introduce some 'real' France into the class in the form of their own experience — although it is not always presented as such (see below). The factor covers all the experience which teachers relate to pupils, whether it is an anecdote about their last holiday in Paris or some up-dating of information about France, such as the price of stamps. Each case is the teacher's expression of information which (s)he has as the result of her/his experience of France, irespective of whether it is from a number of years ago or a number of days ago. It may also be information reported to the teacher and not the direct result of a personal visit to the country. The important difference between 'anecdote' and 'information' lies in the mode of presentation to the class. The way in which the teacher acquired the two apparently different types of knowledge may be the same but the presentation of the first type as a personal story is coloured by pupils' views of the teacher, the second can be accepted as impersonal 'fact'.

When interviewed, teachers generally emphasised the value of elaborating upon the textbook with their own experience. They believed pupils respond more to such experience than to the textbook alone. Personal experience, or more up-to-date information, are still however determined by the structure of the textbook: any extra information the teacher introduces is always relevant to the topic currently being studied in the textbook. Although this may maintain continuity, it also means certain areas are covered but others neglected, as was evident from pupil interviews too. The introduction of personal experience is usually the direct result of the teacher interacting with the class and the textbook, and is largely unrehearsed.

It is worth considering the possible range of teacher experience at this point. Although the nature of the four teachers' experiences of France was varied in extent and content, on the whole their experience is centred on schooling or holidays. Any employment in France was in the education system. Visits to France are either school visits or holidays. Personal contacts which the teachers have maintained in France are, without exception, with teachers (or *surveillants*, i.e. students employed to supervise pupils in French schools). This accounts for the lack of other work settings or working life in general about which teachers can talk from their own experience, and is compounded by the neglect of the world of work in the textbook.

The distinction between those teachers who are described as including personal experience, and those not, was an easy one to make. It is by coincidence that the personal experience division distinguishes between the two schools. One explanation which is supported from interviews is to be found in teachers' training and professional identities. The teachers at Newfarm are both specialists in German and have less experience of France, with respect both to number of visits and variety of experience. Teachers at Hillside are now specialists in French (although one was not trained as such) and both have visited France regularly for a number of years.

(c) Classroom decor

To some extent this is a 'background factor' since it only seems to contribute to an overall French amosphere of a lesson (see also Classroom French) rather than expressing any new information about France or being the focus of attention in a lesson. It is difficult to determine to what extent pupils notice their surroundings, although it is possible to determine whether or not they contribute to it. Work on the walls at Newfarm, particularly in Miss Saunders' classroom, was largely the work of pupils — not just those in the third year, of course — and therefore tended to be illustrations from the textbook, such as road signs, drawings of food or Christmas cards.This contrasts with Mrs Johnson's classroom in the lower school where a number of French artefacts covered the walls, such as posters and stamps and there were some French magazines on tables at the front of the class.This kind of decor would be more likely to extend the image of France. However Mrs Johnson's classroom in the upper school —

where the case study class was taught — was relatively bare for most of the period of observation. Thus class decor potentially has two functions:

— to inform and influence a pupil's image of France.
— to contribute to a French atmosphere in the lesson.

However in view of the nature of the decor and the fact that the wall displays are not referred to in lessons it is the second of these which is most evident in the classes observed.

It would have been possible to make a number of distinctions when evaluating classrooms according to decor: for example, frequency of decor change, wall coverage, extent of pupil contribution, nature of decor, or range of decor content. In the event, a three way distinction was made:

— frequently changed, pupil created, class decor
— infrequent class decor (small amounts and/or infrequently changed)
— no French decor.

(d) Use of classroom French

Early in classroom observations we noted the distinction between a first and third year class where the first year class was not only more apparently enthusiastic but also had a greater French atmosphere to it. This was largely, we felt, due to the greater French use of French identities/names and classroom French, i.e. using French for managing the lesson. On another occasion a supply teacher took over a third year class and used French almost exclusively, including French pronunciation of children's names. It is also interesting to note in characterising styles, that the teacher who emphasised culture most also used more French language in the classroom than the others.

We suggest then that the extent to which a teacher uses French for interaction with pupils is another background factor, not necessarily contributing new information but 'atmosphere'. 'French atmosphere' is a difficult concept to describe but it refers to a quality in some lessons which surrounds and engrosses the class more fully in French. The problem with this concept arises when deciding whether it is actually an atmosphere to do with France, French as a subject, or something else again. Certainly class decor and classroom French serve to make the classroom experience more complete, and give a fuller, stronger identity to the subject. It may be that 'background' factors develop positive attitudes to French lessons and hence to France, as opposed to providing specific information and developing pupils' images. This remains, however, speculative.

(e) Flexibility of approach

This is a wide ranging variable which refers to the nature of the interaction in the classroom, reflected in the degree of structure the teacher imposes. It describes the extent to which the teacher uses a variety of techniques in an evidently planned way to structure the flow of the lesson, as compared to an apparently more spontaneous approach. By this we refer to a more relaxed style with less use of exercises and traditional methods of teaching. It also reflects the extent to which the textbook is relied upon rather than using other materials. Although these two issues could have been treated separately, the two are in fact difficult to separate. For on the whole there was little use of other materials. Most was taken from the *Action!* course, including supporting materials such as tape-recordings. A wider range of materials potentially exposes pupils to a broader or more varied image of France. When they are from the same course, however, they provide a variety of angles for viewing the same image and therefore reinforce it. When other materials were used they were woven into the structure of the course rather than moving in another direction or taking another view. Thus on the whole the textbook dominates, but more so in the less flexible approaches.

(f) Progression through the textbook

This factor charts the range of topics covered. A class that has proceeded furthest through the textbook can be assumed to have covered the greatest number of topics since all classes cover each topic in the textbook in the given order. The extent of the information covered by the class on each topic, however, cannot be taken for granted. A teacher may progress quickly through the textbook by avoiding pages and sections (s)he does not consider central to language learning, or by avoiding any divergence from the text and concentrating on moving through it quickly.

(g) Culture emphasised

This factor relates to the culture/language orientations of lessons; that is, how much time and interest is devoted to teaching about another culture as opposed to pure language teaching. The distinction is made here between whether learning about France seems central to the lesson or additional to the language. In this respect it could be described as a summary descriptive factor (as can 'Images of France' below).

Only one of the styles can be described as giving major attention to the cultural/background studies aspect of 'French' as a subject. The other three approaches, although all very different, were primarily concerned with

French language. In these cases French culture is peripheral to the main lesson. The factor is not purely a question of time allocated. The point at which culture becomes central to the lesson is not necessarily when it is balanced 50–50 with language teaching. It depends on the stance taken towards cultural studies in language teaching. In the four case studies the division was clear between one class and the other three. We shall describe the 'survival approach' as emphasising culture because:

— time was allocated for teaching about France
— language teaching had a clearly evident orientation to preparation for experience of another culture rather than as an end in itself.

(h) Images of France

This factor summarises how the teacher portrays France and the French people: whether the overall image is a 'positive' one, 'neutral' or whether the French are portrayed in a slighly odd or 'strange' way. It is important to note that these three images are not put forward as the only three possible, a negative image of France is also possible, although it was not encountered among the styles observed. 'Strange' is not a substitute for 'negative' and the images cannot be regarded as a continuum. It refers more to an almost eccentric image, slightly humorous.

The four case study styles

Having enumerated and described the eight factors which contribute to a style, we turn again to the four case studies to illustrate how those factors combine to create specific styles, bearing in mind that a style is a combination of 'teacher A with class X'. First of all, we can characterise the four case studies as general summaries linking our ethnographic descriptions and the style factors.

The survival approach (Mrs Johnson and class 4)

The survival approach contains a relatively large amount of cultural knowledge. The overall emphasis is upon cultural knowledge, including language, to survive a visit to France and thereby encourage pupils to believe they should go. This approach is very much in the spirit of the Action! course in general.

The language enjoyment approach (Miss Saunders and class 1)

The emphasis in these lessons is on an appreciation of language. The emphasis is upon language rather than culture, and upon enjoyment in the lesson. This is most clear when the style is contrasted with the academic approach. The academic approach is less wide-ranging in its use of materials and range of activities and the teacher makes many references to exams, options and the future. Teaching and learning are serious activities, although moments of humour are present too. The enjoyment approach on the other hand is flexible and the overall emphasis in the class is on enjoying a lesson or series of lessons in the present.

The language skills approach (Miss Leyborne and class 2)

The language skills approach places emphasis upon the learning of basic language skills through the use of exercises, names and tests. The textbook is dominant in this approach and most of the cultural information is from this source. Although cultural information could not be described as central to this approach, that which is included in the textbook is covered comprehensively.

The academic approach (Mr Clarke and class 3)

The academic approach is clearly focused upon examination success and language learning to a high standard is central. The cultural information is a combination of textbook information and the teacher's personal experience. Thus on the whole, more of a verbal account than any physical representation (apart from those in the textbook) is given. The nature of the information is different from that in the survival approach as it includes information which is less obviously directed at a visitor to France.

Comparison of the four styles

In the account of the discovery of the eight factors, it was pointed out that they are significant in relative rather than absolute terms. Thus the detailed characterisation of the four styles must be made by comparison between them. The first stage of comparison is made in Figure 5.3 which illustrates four different styles in terms of the eight identified factors and includes teachers' evaluation of classes' ability. Most of the variables are represented by a dark, medium or white shading which distinguishes the amount and variety of cultural information. The dark shading means that by comparison with the other case studies, this particular variable is strongly present, the white that it is absent or very weak. 'Image' is a non-quantifiable characterisation and, like 'emphasis', summarises the other

STYLES OF CULTURAL TEACHING

VARIABLE	Survival Cultural knowledge to survive a visit	Language Enjoyment Enjoyment of language learning	Language Skills Disciplined learning of basic skills	Academic Learning language for future examinations
IMAGE overall image expressed	POSITIVE	STRANGE	NEUTRAL	STRANGE
1. EMPHASIS Whether emphasis is on cultural knowledge				
2. DECOR Range and quality of class decor about France				
3. CLASS FRENCH Use of French for instructions				
4. ARTEFACTS Items used in class with French origin				
5. EXPERIENCE Teacher talk about France inc. personal experience and current affairs				
6. FLEXIBILITY Range of materials/methods; less structured approach to lesson				
7. TEXTBOOK PROGRESSION	2	3	4	1
PERCEIVED ABILITY OF CLASS	M/L	H	M/L	H

FIGURE 5.3

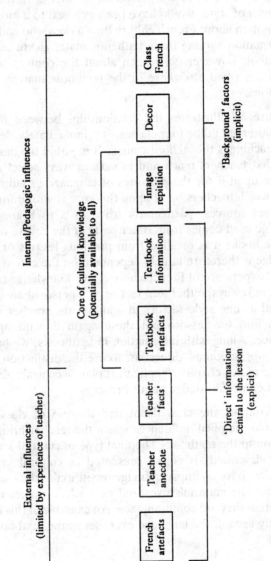

FIGURE 5.4

variables. 'Textbook' is presented as a gradation specifically for comparison of topic coverage. The class who had progressed furthest through the textbook is rated 1. A class exposed to all the factors included in the descriptions of styles would have been exposed to a more extensive range of information about French culture than a class who had not, the nature of the information varying from 'authentic materials' to teacher accounts. A style cannot, however, say much about the content of the information which is described elsewhere in the textbook analysis and ethnographic descriptions.

Figure 5.4 illustrates the relationships between the types of information observed in the four classes. It is immediately clear that the core of all the teaching is the *Action!* course. It is within the basic structure of the course that teachers teach and in various ways select from the text and elaborate upon it for the purposes of language or cultural teaching. The ways in which teachers build upon this core is with information they have from other sources, particularly from visits to France. Sometimes the knowledge used comes from other parts of the course or another place in the same book; it is recalled from previous lessons or years. This extra knowledge is therefore largely dependent on the extent and nature of the teachers' experience of French culture. The knowledge can be presented in two different ways, either as a fact or as a personal anecdote. These were combined as one style factor. In addition the teacher may bring French artefacts into the lessons but these again depend upon the teachers' experience. Along with information in textbooks, we have described this type of information as 'direct' or, to use the distinction introduced at the beginning of this chapter, 'explicit'. It plays a central role in the lesson and is presented as knowledge about France.

By contrast the class decor and the use of classroom French are background, 'implicit' influences which the teacher brings to the situation in addition to the textbook. The final type of cultural knowledge could be similarly described. It is not presented as cultural knowledge but can nevertheless have an impact. 'Image repetition' is the use of certain images throughout the materials over and over which makes them familiar and suggests that they are commonplace. An example of this is the sorts of food repeatedly used in the language exercises in the textbook.

6 Models of Cultural Studies Teaching and Learning

Purpose and Status of the Models

The purpose of this chapter is to bring together the different dimensions of the research, the different aspects of teaching and learning, and to explore the relationships between them. At the centre of our concern are the relationships among styles of teaching, pupils' attitudes and pupils' perceptions in the four classes which became case studies. We shall, however, also draw into the picture other factors in pupils' environment inside and outside school in the two forms in which they were studied: statistical associations, and interview transcripts.

The first stage of our account is descriptive. The models we shall develop are a means of apprehending as a whole the undoubted complexity of cultural studies teaching and learning. We first present in a 'framework model' the various elements we have isolated for investigation and the relationships among them. In the second step, four models are proposed which highlight relationships among those elements which were found to be in some sense 'significant.' In some cases this is a question of statistical significance and in others of observed significance. In this second phase, then, the models comprise significant relationships but they do not pretend to determine causality among the relationships. We are simply saying that in a given model a specific mix of factors is found, that these factors are associated with each other to make precisely that model or picture of teaching and learning rather than the following or preceding one.

The latter point also emphasises that the models are developed from particular case studies within the general case study approach and that these particular cases are analysed and presented relative to each other. Perhaps most evident is the relativity of the descriptions of teaching styles. The characteristics used form the dimensions according to which the styles may be differentiated from each other. Similarly, attitude scores and degrees of ethnocentricity were established within the sample.

Ethnocentricity with respect to the French occupies a position between attitudes to the Germans and the Americans, and the placing of each pupil on a rating of high, medium or low is relative to the sample as a whole. These are not absolute ratings or even ratings related to other samples elsewhere.

In short, these models are interpretative rather than explanatory. Their purpose is to depict in such a way that the essence of the process of teaching and learning about the French way of life is made evident, whilst maintaining an awareness of the incidental procedures and products which sometimes conceal that essence. Pupil perceptions, for example, are often wrapped up in associations with particular learning experiences, as we have seen in earlier chapters. Teaching styles are related to teachers' perceptions of pupils' linguistic achievements and their assessment of the character of a class. The models will tend to highlight the 'essence' because they have a summarising function, but they should be seen as a culmination of previous chapters where the incidental, the associated, the connotated complexity of influences, attitudes and perceptions has been demonstrated at greater length.

The second stage of our account is analytic and evaluative. Each model will be analysed for its implicit theory of cultural studies teaching and learning. Principally we shall discuss for each model the view of the relationship between language and culture, the aims in teaching aspects of culture, the theory of language and culture learning, and the methodology. Where the first stage was intended to depict and interpret the essence of the experience, this analysis aims to make explicit the beliefs and values which appear to determine the general nature of the experience within each model.

The evaluation of the theories underlying each model will be based on criteria from our own view of cultural studies. That view has been introduced elsewhere (Byram, 1989) and will be made briefly explicit here. The purpose of this evaluation is not to produce a negative and destructive criticism of the four models but to suggest how they might be developed and refined in a specified direction. That direction is itself subject to discussion and may be considered by some to be controversial, but at least it will serve as a means of identifying the need for refinement of a range of existing practices within and beyond the scope of the case studies. For it is evident that these models are not in themselves generalisable, even though they may resemble in certain combinations of characteristics the practices in other cases elsewhere. The central value of case studies and their evaluation is similar to that of comparative studies: by offering insight — in the sense of seeing from within — into other people's worlds of experience, case studies suggest that all experience — including the reader's — is contingent, neither arbitrary nor unchangeable, and this offers new perspectives and opportunities for analysing one's own experience and thereby changing it.

The Framework Model

Our research cast a wide net because it was intuitively evident that the teaching and learning processes of the classroom are only a part of pupils' personal and vicarious experience of other cultures. Not all the factors we thought might be significant were found to be so. None the less, we propose first to give an overview of the experience we attempted to catch in our net. In Figure 6.1 we present the factors which were investigated and the interactions which proved significant.

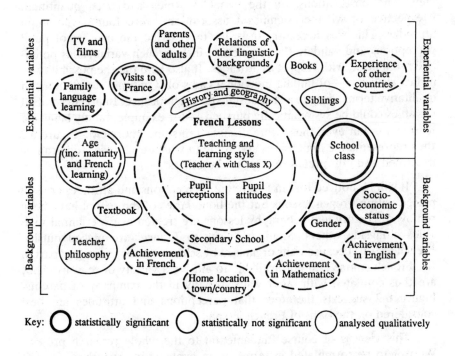

FIGURE 6.1 Framework model of factors and interactions

At the heart of our investigation are pupils' perceptions and attitudes. In Figure 6.1 they are placed within the boundaries of French lessons, and the school as a whole, because it is there that a deliberate effort is made to have an effect upon them. Factors external to the school were analysed in Chapter 3 as 'background' and 'experiential' variables, and this has been reflected in the framework. Two factors which are themselves complex — 'age' and 'school class' — have characteristics of both dimensions and have been placed across the divide. 'School class' involves factors both inside the school — allocation by achievement, teacher-class relations — and outside — social class, gender. We have also attempted to depict the different research techniques and summarise the findings in terms of statistically significant associations and qualitatively analysed observations or interview data.

From Figure 6.1 we go in Figure 6.2 to an enlargement and simultaneously a simplification which represents only those factors which became central to our investigation. Our combination of quantitative and qualitative techniques allowed us in principle to analyse further, in interviews and observations, all the variables which had been quantified, irrespective of whether significant associations were found with pupil attitudes. This was necessary in order to describe the context of pupil perceptions and validate the decision to include such variables as potentially significant with respect to attitudes. It also held out the possibility — in fact realised — of finding individual cases of significant associations in qualitative terms, despite a lack of statistical significance. In practice not all variables could be systematically pursued — for example, family language learning — but even these were discussed in some interviews. Figure 6.2 thus represents the dimensions according to which each case study can be described and interpreted relative to the others.

It will be noticed that in Figure 6.2, perceptions and attitudes are still placed within French lessons but the boundaries of the school have been removed. History and geography lessons are treated as experiential variables alongside others. Similarly 'visits to France' are placed outside French lessons because visits organised by school are not an integral part of the French course and not available to all, for a variety of reasons. They are thus conflated with other visits, usually in the company of parents. Figure 6.2 suggests therefore that perceptions and attitudes are best considered on the basis of French lessons.

This view is of course fundamental to the whole research project. Were it to be formulated in terms of an explanatory hypothesis then it would be that French lessons affect pupils' perceptions and attitudes. Subsequently such a hypothesis would have to be refined to the effect that

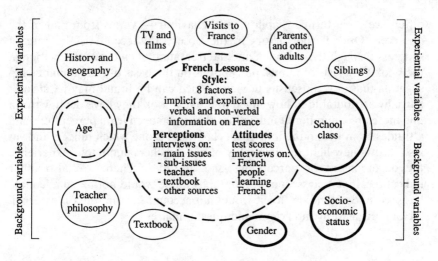

FIGURE 6.2 Model of significant factors and interactions

different kinds of French lessons affect perceptions and attitudes in different ways and that the kind of lesson is a function of the kind of class and teacher involved. Our research is, however, more interpretative than explanatory and within this perspective our intuition that French lessons would be central to any account of how perceptions and attitudes are formed and modified would also have to be re-formulated. For it has become evident that an interpretative account of the genesis of perceptions and attitudes has to include both the experience of French learning as common ground and the differential experience of different school classes. It has become evident too that though this remains fundamental, non-school factors are also very important.

What are the indicators of the importance of French lessons and of different French classes? Consider first the evidence on attitudes based on quantitative data. 'Age' is not significantly associated with attitudes, whereas 'membership of a school class' and 'gender' are. Thus the three years of maturation — which includes the experience of learning French — are not in themselves a significant factor. Yet the 'school class' variable suggests that a combination of age, of gender, of shared experience of French lessons, and of many other variables is significantly related to attitudes. In itself this is rather unsatisfactory because it is not specific. It is however given further support by classroom observations and teacher interviews. Observations suggest that there is a distinctive character to the teaching and learning of each class. Teachers also articulate their feeling that each class is different, although the basis of their explanation for the difference — in terms of ability and behaviour — varies from that of the observer. One of the factors in the observer's account is the rate of progress through the textbook and the treatment of cultural information in the book. Analysis of pupils' perceptions on the basis of class membership suggests that any consensus in views which can be found may be at least partially attributable to how much of the textbook they have dealt with. In fine there are a number of indications that a perspective on perceptions and attitudes from within the individual classroom is one which reflects and yet also throws new light on the reality of how teachers and pupils experience the development of perceptions and attitudes. There are also other indications that a classroom ethnography alone would not be an adequate basis for understanding, for it would not account for the role of 'external' factors revealed by interviews and questionnaires.

Four Models of Culture Teaching and Learning

As we have emphasised throughout, it is a fundamental characteristic of our study that we are proposing interpretative models of teaching and learning which are grounded in observations and described relative to each other. For this reason we shall present and discuss the models in relative terms.

From the 'framework model' of the previous section, we can isolate those factors which are to be found co-existing in French lessons: style, perceptions and attitudes. Whatever the origins and causes of each of these three, the process and product of culture teaching and learning in the classroom are a function of their combination. Yet there is no doubt that culture teaching and learning outside the classroom contribute to the specific nature of the three factors. It remains an unquantified — and perhaps unquantifiable — proportion, but the evidence of our study suggests that while attitudes may be much influenced by external variables, perceptions are much influenced by internal ones. Moreover if the term 'internal' were extended to school-organised visits to the foreign country, perceptions would be even more under internal influence. As long as such trips are not, however, integral to teaching and extended to all pupils, we feel obliged to treat them as an external factor.

Style, perceptions and attitudes have been analysed separately in earlier chapters. In bringing them together, in Table 6.1, we are demon-strating that they co-exist and inter-act. Because the specific terms of the models are relative to each other it is possible to compare the whole

TABLE 6.1 *Four models of culture teaching and learning*

Variable	Model A (Class 1) Miss S	Model B (Class 2) Miss L	Model C (Class 3) Mrs J	Model D (Class 4) Mr D
Style†				
decor	3	2	2	1
class-French	2	2	3	1
artefacts	1	1	3	1
experience	1	1	3	3
flexibility	3	2	3	1
Perceptions††				
food	3	3	3	2
special meal	1	1	1	1
food reputation	3	2	3	3
jobs	3	2	3	3
housing	1	1	1	1
education	1	1	2	3
politics/history	2	1	1	2
geography	3	1	2	3
growing up/religion	1	1	1	1
language	1	1	1	1
people/buildings	2	2	2	3
Attitudes†††				
Rank order:				
French	1st	3rd	7th	2nd
Germans	2nd	1st	9th	6th
Americans (n.s.)	12th	2nd	7th	9th

† 3 = strong presence; 2 = medium presence; 1 = weak/no presence.
  (cf. Figure 5.3, Chapter 5).
†† 3 = more knowledge; 2 = little knowledge; 1 = no knowledge/consensus
  (cf. Table 2.5, Chapter 2).
††† (cf. Table 3.41, Chapter 3).

models with each other, in order to highlight 'characteristics' of a model,
i.e. combinations of variables within it.

372   CULTURAL STUDIES IN LANGUAGE LEARNING

Consider, for example, the comparison of classes by perceived ability — without doubt a dominant feature of schools' principles for organising learning in ability 'sets'. In terms of attitudes and perceptions models A and D, with high achievement classes, are very similar. Only on the variable 'education' is there a difference of 'more' to 'no' class knowledge and on 'people/buildings' from 'more' to 'less'. On other variables in perceptions they are identical, and on attitudes towards French people they are almost equivalent in rank order. But a glance at style reveals only one identical variable, 'artefacts,' which is weak or not present; all other variables are differently rated in the two models. It would be easy to conclude that 'style' has no 'effect' on perceptions and attitudes but this would be misguided. First it must be remembered that style was defined as a combination of teacher and class, not as a definition of teaching alone. Second, and as a refinement of the first point, it must be borne in mind that the models are not explanatory but descriptive. They describe how two different styles co-exist with similar configurations of perceptions and attitudes. Those two different styles were characterised — under the labels 'language enjoyment' and 'academic' — as present-oriented and future-oriented respectively. However, insofar as there is a weight of evidence to suggest that perceptions, if not attitudes, are influenced by classroom teaching and learning, this comparison indicates that both styles are conducive to refinement of perceptions in similar ability groups.

Another dimension of comparison is by attitude ranking. Table 6.1 shows that model C differs noticeably from the other three on this point. The model also differs in style, with a strong presence of all but one variable (decor). In terms of perceptions this model is more similar to A and D than B, even though it is comparable to B in terms of perceived ability. Again the main point is that style C can co-exist with relatively negative attitudes, a conclusion which might be considered counter-intuitive. The greater refinement of perceptions compared to Model B may also indicate that style C has had a greater impact.

Yet another dimension of comparison is by teacher 'identity,' by which we refer to the fact that in both models A and B the teachers were trained as Germanists, had more experience of Germany than France, and expressed some reservations about their own ability to inform pupils about France. In models C and D the teachers were clearly francophile and had a rich experience of French life. It is reasonable to suppose that it was this difference which was reflected in the strong presence of the 'experience' variable in models C and D, the relating of personal experience of France during lessons. Despite this similarity, that 'experience' meets with quite different 'attitudes' in the two models. In models A and B however, attitudes — which it will be recalled were *not* significantly associated with achievement in French in statistical terms — are ranked high and meet with little or no relating of experience by teachers.

Other interpretations and comparisons are possible: for example, the similarity we have noticed before across all four models of no knowledge consensus on issues not dealt with in the text book, or the fact that every style factor except 'experience' is represented in all three degrees of presence. The purpose of such comparisons should however always be to further illuminate the particular configuration of features which comprise each model.

Before moving on to an evaluation of the models, some further clarification of their status is needed. We propose to do this by returning to our first comparison, in which we used the dimension of 'perceived ability,' in order to distinguish between the teacher perspective and the observer perspective. It will be recalled from Chapter 5 that both Miss Leyborne and Mrs Johnson considered their classes to be difficult to handle, as well as being of below average ability. 'Difficult' refers above all to behaviour and motivation. Observations in the classroom, and the models derived from them, did not however take this element into direct consideration. The 'flexibility' variable may appear to be a response to lack of motivation — as a means of retaining pupils' attention — but 'flexibility' was also found with the high ability, motivated class in model A. It should also be recalled that 'class ability' differs from class attitude to the French and that no significant association was found between individuals' achievement in French language — or mathematics or English — and their attitudes. Because of the general dominance of ability rating in teachers' thinking about pupils — institutionalised through the notion of 'setting' — and because of the particular concern of language teachers with measurement of linguistic achievement, the lack of association with attitudes runs counter to professional intuitions. In short, the models, though grounded in investigation of experience in the classroom — through observations and interviews — do not interpret from only the teacher's or pupils' viewpoint, but from the investigators' which aims to incorporate and expand on the other two.

A Critique of the Four Models

The view we take of the purpose of cultural studies within foreign language teaching has been explicated at length elsewhere (Byram, 1989). In brief we argue that the cultural studies element — integral as it is to the whole process of language and culture teaching — can be an extension of learners' social world, a widening of their 'social space' to include cultures and societies other than the nation and ethnie within which they are brought up and socialised. It is however not simply a matter of increasing or adding more of the same kind of experience. To the extent that other societies differ — although similarities are also acknowledged — learners are exposed to qualitatively different experience. Their response can be merely to assimilate the new experience to the culturally-specific ways of thinking they already possess — in which case the process is indeed no more than an increase of existing modes of experience. They can however also — with pedagogical aid — adapt their existing ways of thinking, or adopt new ones, to cope with new experience in a new and more appropriate fashion. We have coined the phrase 'tertiary socialisation' to express this.

In order to identify the process of such change we draw upon schema theory. A schema is, in one definition, 'a data structure . . . for representing generic concepts in memory . . . a schema contains, as part of its specification, the network of interrelationships that is believed to normally hold among the constituents of the concept in question' (Rumelhart, 1980:34). All kinds of concepts are included: those underlying objects, situations, events, sequences of events, actions and sequences of actions. It is our contention that many schemata are culture-specific and that learning a foreign language could and should involve modification of learners' schemata as a consequence of exposure to new kinds of experience. We do not propose to repeat here the theoretical discussion of how such modifications might take place (cf. Byram, 1989: 102–19), but rather to consider in what ways the four different models of teaching established here might be extending learners' experience of their social world. It can be said in advance that none of the models appears to involve the challenge to learners' existing schemata and their existing concept of their own ethnicity which is proposed in our earlier publication.

'Language enjoyment', model A, presents culture in terms of meanings for the new words which are to be learnt. Those meanings indicate that the new words are not merely new encodings of known (English) concepts, but that they introduce new ways of interpreting specific aspects of reality. Simultaneously the learners' knowledge of reality, of the world, is extended by vicarious report. The new words and their meanings are added to existing words and meanings. Reality and the words required for talking about it are extended.

This kind of extension means however that learners acquire knowledge of another culture within the framework of schemata of their existing cultural knowledge. Aspects of the other culture are presented as they arise from the language and are structured in terms of linguistic behaviour for specific situations, rather than in terms of structural relationships with other cultural phenomena. The situations are themselves without specific reference to culturally different schemata of knowledge or expectations of behaviour; they are decontextualised from French culture and recontextualised in terms of the classroom and expectations about classroom activities. By presenting new vicarious information about an extended part of reality, and treating it as part of classroom activity, classroom play, the new information is assimilated to existing 'English' schemata, rather than requiring the formation of new ones.

Similarly the implicit theory of language acquisition appears to be that pupils learn new linguistic behaviour by association with classroom activities *per se* rather than through rehearsal or imitation of activities normally located outside the classroom. Since the linguistic behaviour is thus a repetition or at best an extension of existing competence, pupils have to be encouraged by making the activities enjoyable in themselves rather than opening up new experience. One way of doing this — together with others such as the use of drawings or video-recordings — is to provide 'interesting' information about higherto unknown parts of the world. The 'interest' arises from the selection of information which is slightly 'strange' and different from comparable knowledge of the known world. This information amuses without threatening the security of existing knowledge and expectations of what is 'normal.' It is assumed that pupil motivation is kept alive by providing enjoyment in the here and now, by using cultural information to help maintain that enjoyment. The motivation is present-oriented and cultural information is similarly introduced into the present time and place.

In this model the purpose of foreign language teaching as part of secondary education appears to be to extend pupils' linguistic repertoire and, vicariously, their knowledge of the world. Yet the absence of a planned, structured 'core' of information or experience indicates that there is no intention to challenge learners' existing views. The centre of the world remains the culture-specific normality familiar to pupils and part of their social identity. Any challenge to this ethnocentric view would have to be structured and deliberate, taking into consideration existing schemata and the ways in which they can be modified.

'Language skills', model B, presupposes that language usage and culture can be separated, at least for pedagogical purposes. The teaching can concentrate on the manipulation of the language system independently of contextualised cultural meanings. Meanings attributed to the language under manipulation are without import and may well be supplied from the learners' own culture. Here too there is focus on motivation through present-orientation. Thus cultural meanings introduced into the foreign language may be meanings created within the classroom, within the culture of the classroom. The presentation of unstructured items of information associated with the simulated situations of the classroom is an importation of 'local colour' separated from the cultural structures of the situation which is being imitated.

In this approach the 'neutral' presentation of discrete items of information implies that acquisition of knowledge of the foreign culture is, as in the previous model, an extension of existing competence by providing new words and grammatical structures which are essentially a repetition of existing ways of referring to and expressing existing experience. The separation of language and cultural information leaves the learner without a necessary link between new experience in two different aspects of experience. The comparison of aspects of cultural information with phenomena in pupils' own culture assumes that new information will be assimilated to existing schemata. The separated learning of vocabulary encourages the same process of assimilation and the reduction of new words to being simply codifications of existing words.

The 'neutral' presentation of cultural information and the emphasis on language skills suggests that the purpose of language teaching in this model, as in the 'language enjoyment' model, is to extend competences and knowledge on an existing basis, rather than create a new basis on which to build new experience and competences.

'Survival', model C, with its much stronger emphasis on providing cultural information, assumes that language system and culture are closely related. The exact nature of the implicit view of the relationship is difficult to define. The language is however presented as far as possible in the context of the foreign culture. The introduction of artefacts and other teaching aids supported by accounts of the teacher's personal experience involves an attempt to project the language learner in imagination into the unknown reality of France culture. This contrasts with the emphasis on simulation in the here and now of the two previous models where the attempt to import information about the foreign culture into the classroom, runs the risk of removing its foreignness and encouraging assimilation to the learners' own culture. Thus in the 'survival' model, language is filled with cultural meanings which are different from those of the learners' culture. Yet they are also different from those of the native of the foreign culture and remain essentially ethnocentric to the learners' culture.

This last point is also pertinent to the implicit theory of acquisition of culture and language. The learners are offered experience which is new but it is not presented from the native viewpoint. Learners are encouraged to maintain their own viewpoint, and the distinction between learner and foreigner. The notion of 'survival' ensures this distinction. On the other hand, learners are encouraged to accept the new experience as being something which cannot be simply assimilated to existing schemata of knowledge. New schemata are needed but they are additional to existing ones, do not challenge them and thus do not challenge the ethnocentric viewpoint.

Yet the introduction of personal accounts encourages an imaginative response which, though vicarious, opens up developments of new expectations. The 'positive' image of the 'survival' model is not simply a question of encouraging positive attitudes but also of facilitating an imaginative response. The association of new words and grammatical system with this positive image suggests that the acquisition of language is integral with the acquisition of new culture experience. In contrast to previously described models it does not simply see cultural knowledge and experience as subordinate to language learning in the role of providing interest and motivation.

The purpose of language teaching implicit in this model is that learners should be exposed to new experience, both linguistic and cultural, which will draw upon their imaginative faculties. In short the experience is presented in an ethnocentric way, but the aim is not simply to extend existing language competence and knowledge of the world. It attempts to integrate new language and knowledge competences with an imaginative response.

The 'academic' model D is examination-oriented and, because current examinations assess linguistic competence, this model concentrates on presenting the language. Information about the culture is none the less frequent and based on personal teacher experience, but it is not systematic and not closely linked to the framework of situations and meanings offered by the textbook. Neither is it linked specifically to linguistic phenomena. The 'strange' image implicit in this model helps maintain a distance between learners and foreign culture, which also reinforces the impression that the main issue is language learning independently of cultural information.

The theory of cultural learning implied in this model suggests that pupils' vicarious knowledge of the world is extended by increased awareness of new facts. The facts are assimilated to ethnocentric schemata by suggesting that where they duplicate or can be considered to be imitative of existing knowledge, they are to be regarded as 'strange.' This does not necessarily mean that they are evaluated negatively or that attitudes are influenced negatively, but it does not challenge and therefore it reinforces the ethnocentric framework. Given the separation of cultural information from language learning, the model suggests that the meanings and grammatical structures of language can be acquired on the basis of existing language competence: the foreign language system is an encoding of learners' existing first language system.

The implicit philosophy of secondary school language teaching in this model is that it should equip pupils for the future. The equipment it offers is an examination qualification, some extension of existing linguistic competence, and of existing information about the world. The information is vicarious but provided by a trustworthy source. It is to be added to the existing information base and assimilated, but it contributes to learners' general development by making them more knowledgeable of their widening social context as they mature.

Drawing Conclusions

It will be recalled that the models described above are a means of differentiating between teachers and classes. The models do not explicate the common ground on which each is founded. In this final section we shall return to common issues affecting all the models by suggesting some conclusions drawn from a consideration of all the evidence presented in this and earlier chapters.

The emphasis in our research has been not just on charting what effect language teaching might have on pupils' views but how that effect might be taking place. We have not attempted to describe the process of effect or influence from non-school factors. This is not just a consequence of research funding or potential problems of research design. It is rather because teaching and learning processes inside school are more amenable to change and improvement than those in the outside world. So a description of the processes of the language teaching classroom would serve as a useful and necessary basis for introducing improvement. We have none the less to face the possibility that external processes might be more powerful than those in school, and before we move, in the next chapter, to discussing curriculum development, we shall consider the evidence concerning the differential influences in more detail.

It is in the nature of our research that an analogy with judicial interpretation of evidence springs to mind. We have presented a range of different kinds of data — both quantitative and qualitative — and used methods of analysis associated with both explanatory and interpretative research traditions. On the whole the former have been put to the service of the latter as a means of guiding our interpretations of interviews and observations, although we also presented a standard analysis and discussion of statistical associations between attitudes and a range of environmental variables, in Chapter 3. And again it is important to recall the limitations of generalisations from case study research such as ours. As a consequence of all this it is possible for other interpretations to be put on our data, both quantitative and qualitative, and we have attempted to facilitate that by presenting here, and in the companion volume, a large amount of interview data. We remain none the less conscious of the fact that only full access to all interview transcripts and field-notes would allow an adequate re-assessment.

Having established these various caveats, we can begin to answer our fundamental questions: what effect does language teaching have on pupils' views of other cultures and how does it relate to the effects of other factors in their environment. Our distinction between attitudes and perceptions introduced in Chapter 1 continues to be relevant, for it seems that they are affected differently. To take perceptions first, the weight of evidence, above all from Chapters 2 and 4, is that pupils who have been taught French in secondary school have more, and more differentiated, images of the French way of life than do those in primary school. The accuracy of the images may be in doubt but the amount of information secondary pupils can give about French food — a topic so frequently introduced into French lessons — is a clear indication of an increase. Another powerful source of information is the visit to France, however short or long and whatever the circumstances. This is potentially part of our focus on the teaching process insofar as many but not all pupils participate in such a visit under the auspices of the school and the French teacher. Until, however, it is an integral and obligatory part of French teaching for all pupils, it is a factor which sits uneasily on the margin of the process which might be considered for improvement.

Take now the question of attitudes. Explanatory statistical evidence did not indicate any significant association between learning French and attitude change. Evidence from interviews indicated first that the instrument devised to measure attitudes was satisfactory, and second that there was no clear qualitative indication that attitudes are necessarily affected by learning French. Indeed it is evident from the models described in this chapter that, in model C, a group of pupils taught by an enthusiastic francophile teacher may well remember much of the information the teacher gives them but are none the less as a group less positive in attitudes than other classes, whose fund of information may be less and whose teacher is less enthusiastic. The weight of evidence seems to be that external factors affect pupils' attitudes more than does learning French in school. Again the power of the experience of visiting the other country seems to be significant, yet cannot be considered a fundamental aspect of teaching.

In our view, the effect of language teaching on pupils' views is, in short, disappointing. Despite the fact that teachers and educational policy-makers subscribe to the belief that foreign language teaching should encourage positive attitudes and further pupils' understanding of cultures other than their own, and despite the genuine efforts of teachers in our study to realise these aims, the outcome seems to be no more than an acquisition of separate and largely de-contextualised information which does not amount to an understanding of or insight into another people's way of living and thinking. It is disappointing but scarcely surprising. It is not surprising because, given the overwhelming power of the extra-school environment, only a purposefully structured effort during the few hours of foreign language teaching could hope to counterbalance and modify the influence of the media, of parents, of peers and siblings and so on. Yet observation indicates in our four case study classes that teachers' efforts are usually incidental to their concern with other matters and remain unstructured and haphazard; and we believe that in this respect our case study is representative of many others. One significant illustration of this situation is the treatment of pupils' visits to the foreign country, either with parents or under school auspices. Such visits can have both favourable and unfavourable consequences for attitudes and perceptions, but there is little attempt to prepare and follow-up visits in a structured and integrated way.

It should by now be evident that this and earlier critical comments are not directed at teachers personally, neither those in our study not teachers in general. For it is evident from our study that teachers are not in a position to make changes independently, even though they recognise the problems themselves. Text books, examinations, teacher training are just some of the circumstances which are beyond the control of the individual. Nor are we suggesting that the teaching process cannot possibly have more and better effects on pupils' views. It may be disappointing at present but this does not mean that it cannot ever counteract and modify extra-school factors. This would be unnecessarily pessimistic and a logical *non sequitur*. The way forward is rather to consider how a structured approach can be developed and introduced into language teaching, and it is to this question that we turn in the final chapter.

7 From 'Pure' Research to Curriculum Development

An'Ideal Model' of Culture Teaching

In the review of the context for our study in Chapter 1 we suggested that there are some signs in some countries of a new or renewed interest in teaching culture. Although there are few such signs as yet in British foreign language teaching, they will no doubt soon follow[1] and the opportunity for changing and improving current practices soon arise. In this final chapter we wish to anticipate the opportunity and discuss the relationship between our study, which in a 'pure research' mode has attempted to describe, explain and interpret the phenomenon of culture teaching as it currently exists, and curriculum development, which attempts to intervene and instigate change in a particular direction.

We identified in Chapter 1 four areas of cultural studies which need further theoretical and empirical research and development:

— the value and purpose of cultural studies within general education
— the didactics of cultural studies, founded on an analysis of culture, a theory of culture, a theory of culture learning and the relationship of a curriculum for language and culture teaching to general curriculum theory
— the methodology of language and culture teaching adapted to the circumstances of general education in, usually, secondary schools
— the assessment of pupils' learning and the evaluation of the teaching and learning process.

In principle the development of an adequate approach to cultural studies should deal with each of these in a logical order, from a definition of aims through curriculum and learning theory to methodology and assessment and evaluation. In practice the luxury of working from first principles and constructing cultural studies from fundamentals does not exist. Each of the four areas must be clarified and brought into operation as practical opportunity dictates. For, as our study has shown, cultural studies teaching and learning already exists, and to pretend otherwise would be ill-advised.It would be to pretend that new practices and aims can be imposed without reference to existing ones, and that is a recipe for failure. Success is more likely to come from recognition and modification of current practices and the intuitions on which they are based through co-operation between researchers and teachers. Our decision to produce a companion volume to this one, which we hope will facilitate that co-operation, is a first but important step. The collection of views and experience across national boundaries in another, associated book (Buttjes & Byram, 1990) is another.

Our emphasis on practice does not however signify that there is no place for theory, for there is still a need to have an end clearly in view towards which any modifications are directed. Rather than a theoretical construction from basic principles, however, we would propose an 'ideal model' towards which to direct existing models. Such a model would embody as many as possible of the principles underpinning theoretical discussion of each of the four areas.It would also have to be created with current models in mind lest all contact be lost between the ideal and the current, and with it the possibility of modifying the latter towards the former. Such an ideal model would of course be to some extent contentious, because it would embody specific views and decisions on the four areas in need of review.

We have argued in Chapter 1 of the companion volume that foreign languages should be taught for 'cultural understanding'. This goes a stage beyond the teaching of languages for purposes of reading foreign literatures or, more recently, in order to facilitate tourism. 'Language for cultural understanding' embraces both of these earlier concepts but also helps the learner towards acquiring a capacity for cognitive analysis of a foreign culture, people and artefacts and for affective response to experience of another culture. The analogy is drawn with ethnography, an approach to other cultures which is both analytic and empathetic but which does not require unquestioning acceptance of either the foreign or the native culture.

As a development of this view we propose a model of language learning in which the language learner is an ethnographer, carrying out fieldwork on the foreign culture. Rather than a model of teaching and learning in which information is transmitted from teacher to pupil — as was the case in the models described in Chapter 6 — the ethnographic fieldwork model is oriented towards developing a particular mode of thinking by teaching methods of cultural analysis rather than ready-made accounts of the culture. The processes of ethnographic analysis are to be taught, not the products. It is not a question of replacing teachers' informal information by a more scientific ethnographic monograph on the other culture, but of teaching pupils how to produce an ethnographic monograph for themselves. The objection that this is not feasible for pupils in the early years of secondary education can be met from experience with the well-known material *Man: a Course of Study* (MaCoS, 1968–70, from unpublished material developed at Bristol Polytechnic in which pupils have learnt 'How to Study a Way of Life' (Thorn, 1989) and from our own work described in the companion volume.

It will become apparent below that the model we propose involves the learner in a visit to the culture. Our model is developed with the European language learner in mind, and modern transport makes a visit of some kind quite feasible. Let it be noted in passing that other situations can still benefit from an ethnographic model as is apparent in material developed by Zarate and associates (Arruda *et al.*, 1989). Their purpose is not so much to prepare pupils for a visit to France but for any contact with foreign people and cultures, even within their own country. The emphasis in their view of foreign language lessons is on a re-appraisal of the tourist view of other cultures which so dominates travellers' experience as a result of commercial exploitation.

In order to move now to a more precise description of an 'ideal model', let us consider first some of the general conditions necessary to its success. In our four descriptive models in Chapter 6 we emphasised that teaching style must be related to pupils' perceptions and attitudes: the models stress that teaching cannot be considered separately from other factors in the model. The first general condition we suggest is therefore that a greater awareness and acknowledgement of the significance of pupils' existing perceptions and attitudes — and of the power of extra-school sources — must be developed by teachers (our companion volume offers some material to do just this). This would then lead to recognition of the possibility and indeed the necessity of using pupils' views as an integral part of the ideal model.

The second condition is that there has to be a full integration of visits to the foreign culture with work in the classroom. This implies therefore that all pupils must be able to participate in such visits, irrespective of cost. For it is only in such circumstances that classroom teaching before and after the visit can be developed as a seamless whole with the visit itself. Some practical objections may spring to mind at this point, but the cost of foreign travel in general, the provision for fieldwork as part of other subjects in the secondary curriculum, and the lead already given by some schools, some countries' educational policies and the European Communities are enough to indicate that this condition is not impractical.

Our third condition is focused on examinations, curricula and textbooks. Although it is common to refer in policy and other documents to the social and human aims of foreign language teaching, there is usually very little realisation of them in the detailed curricular documents or syllabuses which schools use. Examinations too bear little evidence that these aims are considered important enough to assess. The lack of adequate assessment procedures is clearly a problem but not an excuse. As a consequence, textbooks are written with the main focus on language learning, as if this could be separated from culture. Any secondary focus is then on supplementing the language teaching with 'useful' information about the culture, without due consideration of the nature or status of the information or the way in which it is to be learnt by pupils and taught by teachers. Before any real progress towards an ideal model can be envisaged, it is evident that more explicit recognition of cultural studies within foreign language teaching has to be introduced into all these influential elements.

In short we are suggesting a shift of emphasis in language teaching as a whole towards a more explicit and equal treatment of cultural studies together with language studies. In the companion volume and in an earlier book (Byram, 1989), we have suggested that language teaching should be considered to consist of four elements: language learning, language awareness, cultural awareness and cultural experience. We do not propose to repeat our account of these and their interrelationships. Suffice it to say that it is in the nature of this proposal that an 'ideal model' should in principle be comprehensive, encompassing all four elements. Here we shall however confine our discussion to 'cultural experience' and 'cultural awareness' whilst bearing in mind their relationships with other elements, as well as with each other.

A first distinction to be made between 'cultural awareness' and 'cultural experience' is that the former has a comparative and generalising purpose whereas the latter is specific. In 'cultural experience' teaching, pupils are presented with aspects of, say, French culture and are to experience and analyse it in a way analogous to the duality of participant-observation (Spradley, 1980). On the one hand they are encouraged to become personally involved in the foreign culture in order to develop an insider's understanding of it. On the other, they must also stand back and observe the foreign culture and their own experience of it. Such observation may lead to a written account or may be simply comment and discussion. In both cases the observation should then be fed into 'cultural awareness' teaching as a component on which to construct a comparative study of cultures including reflection on the native culture. The perspective created by comparative techniques should thus afford critical insight into foreign cultures and also, very importantly, into their own. We are thus suggesting a close link between 'experience' and 'awareness' but also a difference in level similar to that between individual ethnographies and general anthropological reflection. We are not assuming however that this relationship requires a chronological separation, that 'experience' must be complete before 'awareness' can begin, for the two will benefit from mutual enhancement through a dialectical relationship. 'Awareness' teaching will inform 'experience' by indicating which areas of culture should be given the learner-ethnographer's attention, and 'experience' learning can be drawn on for comparative purposes, however limited in the first instance. Furthermore, as earlier chapters have shown, pupils do not begin foreign language classes bereft of knowledge or even personal experience of foreign cultures, and this must, we have argued, be deliberately integrated into the whole process.

In Table 7.1 we provide a schematic overview of our 'ideal model' and the relationship between 'experience' and 'awareness.' We also indicate how some factors in our earlier descriptive models can be related to the model. Our purpose in doing this is to indicate which factors in current practice might be developed and modified in the direction of the ideal. We have also indicated, in parentheses, factors which were investigated in our study — pupil experience of the foreign country and non-school sources or their perceptions — and shown to be important, even though they were not introduced into the classroom process.

The 'experience' part of the model, it will be noted, does not include any precise suggestions for teaching methodology, beyond the implication that pupils should learn the methods of doing ethnography and that the teacher shall be a resource together with others, rather than an authority passing on 'guaranteed' analysis or information. We have above all indicated that classroom sources should be part of a whole which includes the visit. Some classroom sources will be authentic artefacts from the culture in question and, insofar as they have a linguistic component will provide a link with 'language learning'. As a consequence of participating and observing — and learning how to observe, ask questions and analyse — pupils will produce oral or written accounts of parts of the foreign culture.

TABLE 7.1 *An ideal model of cultural studies teaching and learning*

Ideal model	Aspects of descriptive models
Cultural Experience Ethnographic methods oriented:	
— teacher as resource,	experience and flexibility
— classroom (authentic) materials	artefacts, class French and decor
— visit, leading to: pupils' ethnographies	(pupil experience)
Cultural Awareness Comparative anthropological methods oriented:	
— pupils' ethnographies	
— pupils' preconceptions	pupils' perceptions
— other sources	(external sources)
— other ethnographies and	
— pupils' native culture	
— foreign views of native culture	
— ethnographies of native culture	

In the 'awareness' part of the model pupils' ethnographies become part of the resources of which comparative questions may be asked. Other components of this 'resource-base' are, first, pupils' preconceptions which they bring to language lessons from external experience before and simultaneous with their language learning, and second, other sources of non-scientific perceptions and accounts of the culture such as children's comics, television advertisements and so on. Finally, because pupils' own ethnographies are unlikely to be complete or sufficiently thorough, other ethnographies, by anthropologists or journalists for example, should also be included. All this forms one part of the resource base, with its focus on the foreign culture. It is complemented by accounts of pupils' native cultures: their own experience, informal, non-scientific views from foreign people and formal ethnographies, again by anthropologists, journalists and perhaps novelists.

It will be evident that in this second 'awareness' part of the ideal model there are no links with our descriptive models. This is an indication of the lack of existing methods susceptible of modification and of the fact that this part is more innovatory in both content and methodology. On the

388 CULTURAL STUDIES IN LANGUAGE LEARNING

other hand for both parts of the model, language teachers may well find considerable inspiration from humanities or social sciences teachers. As we have already suggested, there have been several experiments in teaching based on anthropology and sociology. We have however also argued that attempts to impose new models of teaching and learning without due regard to existing ones are likely to fail or even be counter-productive. This applies in particular to the issue of teachers' existing teaching skills and experience, focused above all on language. To suggest that they must abandon their training as linguists and language teachers to embrace anthropology and teaching humanities would inevitably lead to a rejection of the shift of emphasis proposed here. Even though many teachers share a perception of the significance of culture teaching as part of the foreign language teaching process, they would not wish to abandon their commitment to foreign language and culture. This is fully justified, for it is the perspective from a foreign culture and the experience of that culture through its language, of living the language, that is the unique contribution of foreign language teaching to young people's general education.

Perspectives and Applications

It would be easy to speculate further on questions of methods and on refinements and details of our ideal model, which is at this point no more than an outline. We shall refrain from doing so because the main purpose of this book has been to present the findings of our research and, more importantly, because speculation on methods is best carried out in the context of practice in the classroom. We have indicated that the emphasis should be on process more than product, on pupils learning ethnographic techniques and anthropological approaches rather than information on selected parts of the foreign culture. We have also suggested that resource-based learning is appropriate. The development of techniques in the classroom and during a visit needs to be guided both by this general orientation and by teachers' professional intuitions concerning the most productive ways of working with pupils.

Another reason for avoiding too much speculation at this point is that our descriptive models are at best illustrative of the basis on which developments must be founded. As case studies they no doubt embody some characteristics of all teaching and, we hope, will be sufficiently recognisable and related to other teachers' practices to stimulate self-reflection and appraisal. To suggest that they are a sufficient base for general speculation would, however, be mis-guided. Thus one direction for development of the work presented in this and the companion volume is towards experimentation with cultural studies teaching in the classroom.

A second broad direction is towards further research, to supplement and enrich our case study with further empirical investigations and theoretical argument. In particular it is necessary to recall that our study was situated in one particular geographical region, with its own social and historical background. It was clear from statements in teacher interviews that they believe that the geographical location is significant. It is important to establish whether this really is the case. Similarly the lack of racial or ethnic mix in the schools and their environments suggests *prima facie* that they cannot be representative of schools with pupils from many ethnic origins. This too should be put to the test. Thirdly, teachers themselves implied that they taught in certain ways as a consequence of the geographical location and its presumed influence on pupils' attitudes and perceptions. Studies of other teaching styles in other locations would throw more light on this and begin to build up a wider basis of knowledge of culture teaching on which to found the curriculum development discussed above.

Such further studies and replications of our research would have the added advantage of refining our research instruments, for example our features of a 'teaching style' or our techniques for analysing interview transcripts. The exploratory nature of our enterprise has been ever present in our minds throughout the project.

A third area for future work is that of assessment and evaluation: the assessment of pupils' learning and the evaluation of the teaching and learning process. The former is important both in itself and because without it the shift of emphasis we have argued for is less likely to take place. The nature of the assessment depends of course on the decisions on aims and aproaches. In our model, where processes are more important than products, assessment of how much factual knowledge has been acquired would be at best only part of the assessment procedure. What would need to be assessed is pupils' ability to ask appropriate questions, to give a participant's account, to analyse cultural phenomena, to carry out meaningful comparisons and to reflect on their own culture and cultural identity. These would be new areas of concern for language teachers, but as with issues of methodology, it would not be necessary to start from nothing. Links would have to be made with curriculum development in other subject areas — particularly humanities — where some experience of these questions already exists. This issue is however a good illustration of the inter-dependence of theoretical research and curriculum development, for it is evident that refinements of our view of the aims of culture teaching

— or alternative arguments — would necessitate changes in assessment. It is also probable that assessment practices and teachers' views will help refine theoretical arguments concerning the nature of culture teaching and its educational purposes.

Evaluation of teaching and learning is another area where research and development are inseparable. If methodology is to take into account the findings of research into existing practice, then formative evaluation of practical methods would need to be a combination of theoretical orientation from a particular perspective and practical refinement according to experience and the dictates of circumstances. The principles of this kind of relationship are well-known ground and need not delay us here. What is important is the need to pursue a number of developments simultaneously and combine the insights and experience of researcher and teacher together.

There is, then, much to be done. We trust that this book will be a useful contribution to the task of educating young people through foreign languages and cultures.

Note

1. At the time of going to press, the publication of 'Initial Advice' to the Secretary of State for Education by a Working Group established to advise on a 'national curriculum' includes a new emphasis on culture and cultural learning.

Appendix 1: Interview Schedule (Secondary Pupils Version)

I Introductory section

As you know from filling in the questionnaires for us, we are just interested in your views and opinions about other countries and languages. there are no right or wrong answers — we really want to know what you think. Like your answers to the questionnaire everything you say will be confidential, private — we will be the only ones to listen to what you say. We are tape-recording the interviews as it takes too long to write anything down. If at the end of the interview you want to change anything that you have said, we can do that.

First I wanted to ask you — (can you remind me?)
Have you ever been abroad?

Which countries?
How often?

Is there any *country/any other* country which *you would like to visit* if you had plenty of money? Which and why?

Have you ever *imagined living abroad?* If you imagine living abroad *as an English person*, where would you *most like it to be?*
Least like it to be?

If you *weren't English which nationality* would you *most like* to be?
Which nationality would you *least like* to be? Would you *really like* to be *another nationality?*

(If France not mentioned)
What *would you think of being French?*
Would you be *as happy to be French as English*, or not?

II Core Questions

Family and Daily Life

If you were *asked by somebody what is the same*, what is *different*, what would you say?

(Interviewer plays role of potential visitor, e.g. after initial open response)

— I'm going to stay with a *French family*, what will it be like?
  (similarities and differences) — I don't want to interrupt their *daily life* and *daily routine*, what will that be like? (similarities, differences)
— The family live *in Paris, what kind of house or flat* will they have?
— There are *two children* (one 12 years old, one 17) what will their *school day* be like?
— Are there any *other things* about family life — do the children have a *different kind of family* life to yours/ours?
— Have you *ever lived/would you like to live* for a few weeks in a French family?

Food

Can we talk about something else now? I believe you learn quite a lot about *food in France*.

Can you *describe a typical French meal*, say dinner. What would they start with, what next . . . What would they drink?

Is this the *kind of meal* people have *every day*?
(If Yes) What about a *meal for a special occasion*, e.g. a birthday?
What about special *meals at Christmas or New Year*?
(If No) When would they eat the kind of meal you have described?
Can you now describe an ordinary meal?

What do people have for *breakfast*?

What *time* do people have — *breakfast*?
                              — the meal in *the middle* of the day?
                              — the *evening* meal?

Do you think *French people think the same or differently about food* to English people?

Do you know that *French food is supposed to be among the best in the world*, that posh English restaurants usually serve French food?

(Yes) — *Why do you think this is so*?

Do you know *what the French think about English food*?

Do you think *French people like food from other countries*?

French people's views of others

How do you think *French people think about*
— *Britain as a country?*
— *the English people?*

Do you know that the *French think that the English are unfriendly and that England* is cold and wet?

If someone said that to you, *what would you say and what would you feel?*

Do you think *French people prefer some foreigners to others?*

Do you think the fact that we are in the *Common Market makes a difference to the way we think about the French* and *they think about us* (or about other nations)?

Have you ever *felt like a foreigner?*

Work and economic structure

Can you describe the jobs of the people in your textbook?

— the men

— the women — do they work?

What other jobs do people do?

Are there jobs in France which don't exist in England?

Do the French have unions/strikes/serious attitudes to work?

Are they better paid, have easier working life?

Clothes and appearance

(Various pictures of individuals or groups)

I'd like to talk about *how people dress* and what they *look* like.

Do you think some of these *people look French* and *others English?*

— which ones?

— why — Is there *something special* about the way they *dress?*

If you saw a group of *boys and girls in your town, would you notice they were French*, without hearing them speak?

If you saw a group of *adults in your town,* would you *notice they were French*, without hearing them speak?

Are there other *nationalities you would easily recognise?*

Do you think it is possible to *describe a 'typical' Frenchman?*

Do you think it is possible to *describe a 'typical' French teenager?*

Do you think it is possible to *describe a 'typical' French woman?*

Are there *differences between French people from different parts of France* (e.g. North and South)?

Do you know that French clothes, *Parisian fashion* is very *famous?* (Yes) What do you *imagine it to be like?*

III Sub-issues

Housing

What *kind of home* do you think *your family* would have if you lived in France, if your *father had the same job?*

What *kind of home* do you think *a teacher* would live in?
What *kind of home* do you think a *factory worker* would live in?
What *kind of home* do you think a *doctor* would live in?

Can you describe *inside somebody's home in France?*

What about *differences amongst houses from one region to another, from* town/city *to countryside?*

Do homes have gardens?

Do you think of the French as *having better houses* and flats *than other Europeans* or not?

Who do you think of as having *the best standard* of living in *Europe?*

Who do you think of as having the *best standard of living in the world?*

Education system

Can you try to imagine going to a French school and describe what it is like.

(Possible stimulus questions)

What are the *teachers* like?

What *time* to you go to school?

How much *free time* do you get?

Do you get *homework?*

How much *holiday* do you get?

Are there *subjects* you don't do in your school?

How many *days* do you go to school each week? Which?

Would you *prefer* to go to a *French school*?

Can you tell me anything about other schools:

Primary schools

Universities

What young people do when they *leave* the secondary *school*

Do they get some kind of *training for work*?

What *qualifications* can young people get?

Political structure and world role

Have you ever seen anything about French politics, (the President, the elections, demonstrations, Green Peace . . . on television or anywhere else? e.g. any names you know.

Politics
Would you be able to *tell somebody about French elections, parliament* or how the system works?
Why does France have a President?

What do you know about the *Channel Tunnel?*
What *differences* do you think it will make to have a Channel Tunnel?
— to us
— to the French
What do you know about the *Common Market?*
Does it make a *difference*?
— to us
— to the French

History

What do you know about the history of France?

(Stimulus questions)

What happened in the *2nd War?*
What happened in the *1st War?*

Are there any *famous French people* you could name, why are they famous?

Do you know if France has any *connections with other countries* like we do with Commonwealth countries?

Does France have connections with other countries today, *are they friendly to some more than others?*

Do you think that France has an *important part/role* to *play in the world?*

How do you think the *French see their position in* (a) Europe; (b) the world? What do you think the French think of *England's position?*

Growing up, religious and military institutions

I'd like to ask you about what you *imagine it is like to grow up in France?*

If you try to describe a child growing up from birth . . .

> Tell it as if it were *the story of the life of a French boy/girl.*
> Do they have any *religious festivals* to do with growing up — like being christened?

(Photo of priest/church) Is there anything else you can tell me about *church and religion in France?*

When *young people get older* — your age and older — does their life differ from yours, e.g. do they have to become soldiers, do *national service?*

If you imagine what it is like being your age in France, how would you describe it?

> Is it *different for girls/boys?*
> Would you *prefer to grow up in France or England?*
> Would you prefer to live in England or France *as an adult?*
> Do you think it's *the same for men/women* (start according to sex of interviewee) in France as in England?

Language and Art (and Science)

When French children learn English in schools, *what kind of English do you think they learn?*

What *kind of French do you think you learn?*

Do you know anything about *any differences in the way people speak?* (dialects, accents and Breton, Occitan, etc.)

Do you know of any *words* which French has taken *from English* (recently)?

Do you think all the *French people approve* of this?

Have you *read any French books* in English — or in French?

Have you seen any *French films on TV* or at the cinema?

Are there are any *books, paintings* or *music from France that are famous*?

Does *music* play an important part in French life?

Are there *famous buildings* you have heard of or seen?

Any *famous scientists* you know of?

Leisure, media

Let's talk about what people do in their *spare time*.

Imagine again *you are talking to someone* your *own age* who is *going to France* for the first time and they ask you *how they can spend their spare time*.

(Do you know about *colonie de vacances, classes de neige*?)

Imagine again you are talking to *an adult* who is going to France for the first time and they ask you how they can *spend their spare time*.

What advice would you give them, what do French people do?

(Stimulus questions)

— At the *weekend*
— In the *evening*
— In the *summer holidays* (and winter holidays)

When do working people go on summer holidays, *how long* for — how long are *school holidays*?
— Is it *different in the towns and country*?
— Is it *different in the North, South* or any other region?

Are there are *sports* which an English person could learn and would find interesting?

Which *sports* do you think are *most important* to the French?

Do you know anything about *French TV (or radio)*?

Do you know anything about *French newspapers*?

Have you ever *seen one, or a picture of one*? What can you remember about it?

Have you heard any French *pop music*?
How does it compare with English/American?

(Discuss *sources of information* mentioned on individual questionnaires)

Can you tell me anything about:

— *French TV* and/or *radio*?
— *French films*
— What do you *learn about France* from them?
— French *newspapers*
— French *music*
— Other sources of information.

Geographical knowledge

Which parts of France do you think would be *most interesting to visit*? or which *to live in*?

Have you visited France, what do you remember?

If little/no knowledge of major regional differences ask them to compare: *north v south* 'South of France/Riviera'; *Britanny v rest* of the north etc.; *Paris v the rest*.

(*Outline map as stimulus*)

Have you ever heard anything about the *people living* in *these regions*?

Do you live in a village, in the country or a town in England?

Do you think it would *feel similar living in a village/country town in France*?

Ask them to say what information they would add to the map (e.g. names of places, rivers, position of industries, mountains etc.)

IV Sources

How much is *France in the news* (compare other countries)?

How much do they learn about *France in other lessons*?

How much did they learn in *primary school* about France?

V Additional questions vis à vis Learning French, and the French

Some of:
1. Do you *enjoy learning French?* Are you going to continue next year?

   Have you always liked/disliked . . . why? (gender differences).

   Is that *the same for other languages*, if learnt?

2. Other languages.
   Would you like to learn another language (compare with French)?
   Why would you like to learn another?
   Do you think people should learn French or another language?
   Why do you think they should/shouldn't?

   Are there any other languages which you think are more important to learn?

3. What do you think *your parents thought of you learning French?*

   What would they say *if they heard you speaking French?*

   What *would your friends think?*

   What do you think your parents think of French people? (and other nationalities)

4. Do you think you have learnt a lot about *France and French people in French lessons?*

   How do French people seem to you — very different/similar to the English.

   If you saw a French boy/girl at a party would you speak to him/her, or wait for him/her to speak to you first?

5. If you were staying with a French family and you *didn't understand something someone said, what would you do? How would you feel?*

6. *What does it feel like to be foreign?*

Appendix 2: The Ethnocentricity Measure

The ethnocentricity measure consisted of eight booklets and one practice booklet. The booklets are identical except for the concept in question:

Practice booklet: 'James Bond'

Booklet 1: 'myself'
Booklet 2: 'my friends'
Booklet 3: 'people who live near me'
Booklet 4: 'people who live in Newcastle'
Booklet 5: 'English people'
Booklet 6: 'French people'
Booklet 7: 'Germans'
Booklet 8: 'Americans'

Each booklet contains twelve polarities with a seven part continuum on which pupils were asked to mark their response to the concept in question. One page from one booklet is illustrated here.

How to use this booklet

This booklet is like the one you practised with. First you are given the name of something (like James Bond). Then, on each page there is a pair of words, one at each end of a line. There are spaces on the line in which you can put a cross to show *how* closely one of the words describes how *you* feel about the thing named. Is it very, fairly, just a bit or neither one nor the other? For example, if you thought James Bond was just a bit bad you might put your cross like this:

JAMES BOND

good   :   :   :   :   ✗ :   :   :   bad

     very   fairly   a bit   neither   a bit   fairly   very

If you thought neither good nor bad, or both good and bad. you would put your cross in the middle:

good   :   :   :   ✗ :   :   :   :   bad

     very   fairly   a bit   neither   a bit   fairly   very

There are no right or wrong answers, so don't worry. We are interested in what *you* think, not anyone else. Remember some of the words won't seem to fit, but think of the feeling the word gives you. We will work through the booklet as quickly as possible. Don't look back at your earlier answers.

FRENCH PEOPLE

weak   :   :   :   :   :   :   strong

     very   fairly   a bit   neither   a bit   fairly   very

References

ACTON, W.R. and WALKER DE FELIX, J. 1986, Acculturation and mind. In J.M. VALDES (ed.), *Culture Bound*. Cambridge: Cambridge University Press.

ADORNO, T.W., FRENKEL-BRUNSWIKE, E., LEVINSON, D.J. and STANFORD, R.N. 1950, *The Authoritarian Personality*. New York: Harper & Row.

ALLPORT, G.W. 1954, *The Nature of Prejudice*. Cambridge, Massachusetts: Addison-Wesley

— 1988, *Observation in the Language Classroom*. London: Longman.

ALLWRIGHT, D. 1983, Classroom-centred research on language teaching and learning. *TESOL Quarterly* 17(2), 191–204.

A P U 1985, *Foreign Language Performance in Schools*. London: DES.

ARRUDA, M., ZARATE, G. and ZUNDERT, D.V. 1989, *Evaluer le regard touristique*. Paris: BELC.

BERELSON, B. 1971, *Content Analysis in Communication Research*. New York: Free Press.

BOGARDUS, E.S. 1925, Measuring social distance. *Journal of Applied Psychology* 9, 299–308.

BRIERLEY, D.W. 1967, The use of personality constructs by children of three different ages. Unpublished Ph.D. thesis. University of London.

BROWN, R. (ed.) 1976, *Children and Television*. London: Collier Macmillan.

BUCKBY, M. 1980, *Action! Graded French* Book 1 and Teachers Book 1. London: Nelson.

— 1981, *Action! Graded French* Book 2 and Teachers Book 2. London: Nelson.

— 1983, *Action! Graded French* Book 3 London: Nelson.

BUCKBY, M. *et al.* 1981, *Graded Objectives and Tests for Modern Languages*. London: Schools Council.

BURGESS, R.G. 1985, *Strategies of Educational Research: Qualitative Methods*. Brighton: Falmer.

BURSTALL, C. *et al.* 1974, *Primary French in the Balance*. London: NFER.

BUTTJES, D. (ed.) 1981, *Landeskundliches Lernen im Englischunterricht*. Paderborn: Schoningh.

— 1988, Landeskunde-Didaktik und landeskundliches Curriculum. In K–R Bausch *et al.* (eds), *Handbuch Fremdsprachenunterricht*. Tübingen: Franke.

BUTTJES, D. and BYRAM, M. (eds) 1990, *Mediating Languages and Cultures*. Clevedon: Multilingual Matters.

BYRAM, M.S. 1986, Cultural studies in foreign language teaching, *Language Teaching* 19, 322–36.

— 1989, *Cultural Studies in Foreign Language Education*. Clevedon: Multilingual Matters.

BYRNE, D. 1971, *The Attraction Paradigm*. New York: Academic Press.

CAIN, A. 1988, Enseignement et apprentissage de la civilisation au cours de langue dans le second cycle. In A. CAIN (ed.), *L'enseignement de la civilisation*. Paris: INRP.

CANAVAN, S. *et al.* n.d., *Graded Objectives in French: Attitudes in N. Ireland Schools*. Belfast: Queen's University School of Education.

EDWARDS, A.D. and WESTGATE, D.P.G. 1987, *Investigating Classroom Talk*. London: Falmer Press.

FURNHAM, A. and BOCHNER, S. 1986, *Culture Shock*. London: Methuen.

FURTH, M. 1980, *The World of Grown-ups*. New York: Elsevier.

GARDNER, R.C. and LAMBERT, W.E. 1972, *Attitudes and Motivation in Second Language Learning*. Rowley, Mass: Newbury House.

HARE, G. 1987, Preparing to teach contemporary French society at A-level. *Modern Languages* 68, 1, 5–12.

HARRISON, B. 1990, *Culture and the Language Classroom*. London: British Council.

HARVEY, O.J., HUNT, D.E. and SCHRODER, H.M. 1961, *Conceptual Systems and Personality Organization*. New York: Wiley.

HAWKINS, E.W. 1987, *Modern Languages in the Curriculum* 2nd edn. Cambridge: Cambridge University Press.

HMI (Her Majesty's Inspectorate) 1987, *Modern Foreign Languages to 16*. London: HMSO.

HOLSTI, O.R. 1969, *Content Analysis for the Social Sciences and Humanities*. New York: Addison Wesley.

HOWATT, A.P.R. 1984, *A History of English Language Teaching*. Oxford: Oxford University Press.

JAHODA, G. 1962, Development of Scottish children's ideas and attitudes about other countries, *Journal of Social Psychology* 58, 91–108.

JOHNSON, N.B., MIDDLETON, M.R. and TAJFEL, M. 1970, The relationship between children's preferences for and knowledge about other nations. *British Journal of Psychology* 9, 282–40.

KATZ, P.A. 1983, Developmental foundations of gender and racial attitudes. In R.L. LEAHY (ed.), *The Child's Construction of Inequality*. New York: Academic Press.

KELLER, G. 1990, Stereotypes in intercultural communication: effects of German-British pupil exchanges. In D. BUTTJES & M. BYRAM (eds), *Mediating Language and Culture*. Clevedon: Multilingual Matters.

KELLY, L.G. 1976, *25 Centuries of Language Teaching*. Rowley, Mass: Newbury House.

KIM, Y.Y. 1988, *Communication and Cross-Cultural Adaptation*. Clevedon: Multilingual Matters.

KIRSCHNER, B.F. 1972, Introducing students to women's place in society. *American Journal of Sociology* 78, 1051–1054.

LAMBERT, W.E. 1974, An alternative to the foreign language teaching profession. In H.B. ALTMAN & V.E. HANZELI (eds), *Essays on the Teaching of Culture*. Detroit: Advancement of America Press.

LAMBERT, W.E. & KLINEBERG, O. 1967, *Children's Views of Foreign Peoples*. New York: Appleton-Century-Crofts.

LITTLEWOOD, W. 1981, *Communicative Language Teaching*. Cambridge: Cambridge University Press.

MACOS, 1968–70, *Man: A Course of Study*. Cambridge, Mass: Education Development Center.

MALTZ, H.E. 1969, Ontogenetic change in the meaning of concepts as measured by the semantic differential. In J. SNIDER and C.E. OSGOOD, *The Semantic Differential: A Sourcebook.* Chicago: Aldine Press.

MEHAN, H. 1979, *Learning Lessons.* Harvard University Press.

MITCHELL, R. 1985, Process research in second language classrooms. *Language Teaching* 18, 330–52.

— 1988, *Communicative Language Teaching in Practice.* London: CILT.

NOSTRAND, H.L. 1979, The 'Emergent Model' applied to contemporary France. *Contemporary French Civilisation* 2, 277–93.

— 1985, Horizontal coordination: foreign languages and social studies. *Modern Language Journal* 69, 1, 41–45.

OSGOOD, C.E., SUCI, G.T. and TANNENBAUM, P.H. 1957, *The Measurement of Meaning.* Urbana Ill.: University of Illinois Press.

PEEVERS, B.H. and SECORD, P.F. 1973, Development changes in attribution of descriptive concepts to persons, *Journal of Personality and Social Psychology* 27, 120–28.

PHILLIPS, D. (ed.) 1988, *Languages in Schools: From Complacency to Conviction.* London: CILT.

PIAGET, J. 1975, *The Development of Thought: Equilibration of Cognitive Structures.* New York: Viking.

POWELL, R. 1986, *Boys, Girls and Languages in School.* London: CILT.

RAASCH, A. *et al.* (eds) 1983, *Beiträge zur Landeskunde im Fremdsprachenunterricht.* Frankfurt a.M.: Diesterweg.

RAY, J.J. and LOVEJOY, F.M. 1986, The generality of racial prejudice, *Journal of Social Psychology* 126, 4, 563–64.

RISAGER, K. 1986, Cultural studies and foreign language teaching in Denmark. Paper given at the Durham Symposium - revised in D. BUTTJES and M. BYRAM (eds), *Mediating Languages and Cultures.* Clevedon: Multiligual Matters.

ROBINSON, G. 1985, *Crosscultural Understanding.* Oxford: Pergamon.

ROBINSON, J.P. and SHAVER, P.R. 1973, *Measures of Social Psychological Attitudes.* Ann Arbor: Institute of Social Research.

RUMELHART, D.E. 1980, Schemata: the building blocks of cognition. In R.J. SPIRO *et al.* (eds), *Theoretical Issues in Reading Comprehension.* Hillsdale, N.J.: Lawrence Erlbaum Associates.

SANDERSON, D. 1982, *Modern Language Teachers in Action — A Report on Classroom Practice.* York: University of York/Nuffield Foundation.

Schools Council (1981) *Graded Objectives and Tests for Modern Languages: An Evaluation.* London: Schools Council.

SEDLACEK, H.N., BROOKES, G.C. and CHAPEL, E.A. 1971, Problems in measuring racial attitudes: An experimental approach. Report submitted to the Cultural Center for the University of Maryland. (ERIC Document Reproduction Service ED 058 330).

SEELYE, H.N. 1984, *Teaching Culture.* Lincolnwood, Ill: National Textbook Co.

SHERMAN, R. and WEBB, R.B. (eds) 1988, *Qualitative Research in Education: Focus and Methods.* Brighton: Falmer.

SNIDER, J. and OSGOOD, C.E. 1968, *The Semantic Differential: A Sourcebook.* Chicago: Aldine Press.

SPRADLEY, J.P. 1980, *Participant Observation.* New York: Holt, Rinehart, Winston.

STAGER, R. and OSGOOD, C.E. 1964, Impact of war on a nationalistic frame of reference. A change in general approval and qualitative patterning of certain stereotypes. *Journal of Social Psychology* 24, 187–215.

STARKEY, H. 1990, World studies and foreign language teaching: converging approaches in textbook writing. In D. BUTTJES & M. BYRAM (eds), *Mediating Languages and Cultures*. Clevedon: Multilingual Matters.

STARKEY, H. 1986, The global learner and foreign languages. paper given at the Durham Symposium - revised in D. BUTTJES and M. BYRAM (eds), *Mediating Languages and Cultures*. Clevedon: Multilingual Matters.

STERN, H.H. 1983, *Fundamental Concepts of Language Teaching*. Oxford: Oxford University Press.

STILLWELL, R. and SPENCER, C.P. 1974, Children's early preferences for other nations, *European Journal of Social Psychology* 3, 3, 345–49.

TAJFEL, H. 1973, The roots of prejudice: cognitive aspects. In P. WATSON (ed.), *Psychology and Race*. Chicago: Aldine Press.

THORN, R. 1989, Recording contemporary culture. Seminar paper, University of Durham, February 1989.

VALDES, J.M. (ed.) 1986, *Culture Bound*. Cambridge: Cambridge University Press.

WARR, P.B., FAUST, J. and HARRISON, G.J. 1967, A British ethnocentrism scale. *British Journal of Social and Clinical Psychology* 6, 267–77.

WESTGATE, D., BATEY, J., BROWNLEE, J. and BUTLER, M. 1985, Some characteristics of interaction in foreign language classrooms, *British Educational Research Journal* 11, 271–81.

ZARATE, G. 1986, *Enseigner une culture étrangère*. Paris: Hachette.

— (ed.) 1988, Observer et décrire les faits culturels. *Etudes de Linguistique Appliquée* 69.

ZIRKEL, P. and GREENE, J.F. 1976, Cultural attitude scales: A step towards determining whether programmes are bicultural as well as bilingual. In A. SIMOES (ed.) *The Bilingual Child: Research and Analysis of Existing Educational Themes*. London: Academic Press.

Index

Note: Page references in italics indicate Tables and Figures